AUTOMOBILE CLUB · SOUTHERN CALIFORNIA

WE'RE ALWAYS WITH YOU.SM

1900 · 2000

MEXICO

Baja California

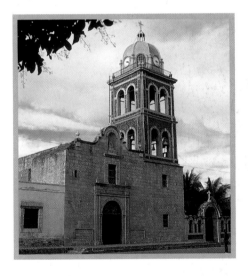

Baja California ‡ Baja California Sur

WE'RE ALWAYS WITH YOU.℠

—— 1900·2000 ——

Cover:
Beachside at Cabo Pulmo on Baja's East Cape

Page 2:
Sunset over Baja's central desert

Page 3:
Mission Nuestra Señora de Loreto

Page 5:
Cactus in "The Rock Garden" near Cataviña

Page 6:
Sunset at Playas de Tijuana

Page 7:
Kayaks on the shore, Bahía de la Concepción

Although information presented in this publication has been carefully researched and was as accurate as possible at press time, the Automobile Club of Southern California is not responsible for any changes or errors that may occur. Readers should keep in mind that travel conditions in Baja California change rapidly. The Automobile Club is not responsible for the performance of any agency or service mentioned in this publication. It is wise to verify information immediately before your visit.

Only attractions or establishments that are approved by an Automobile Club of Southern California field representative may advertise. The purchase of advertising, however, has no effect on inspections and evaluations. Advertisements provide the reader with additional information that may be useful in selecting what to see and where to stay.

Additional advertisements (excluding attractions and establishments) for travel-related services may also be included in ACSC publications. Acceptance of these advertisements does not imply endorsement by ACSC.

ISBN: 1-56413-446-6
Printed in the United States of America
Copyright © 1998 by Automobile Club of Southern California
Member Information and Communication Services
3333 Fairview Road, Costa Mesa, California 92626

Table of Contents

Baja California

To many people, its very name carries an exotic connotation of ruggedness and adventure. Despite the long-standing popularity of its border towns and the fly-in fishing resorts near its southern tip, this 800-mile-long arid peninsula remained virtually unknown until recently. Geographically separated from the Mexican mainland and an insurmountable barrier to all but the hardiest overland travelers, the interior of Baja California resisted the large-scale intrusions of man for centuries.

But the peninsula's days of isolation are over. The completion of the paved Transpeninsular Highway (Mexico Highway 1) in late 1973 marked the beginning of a new era for Baja California. Once-remote regions are now being drawn into the mainstream of Mexico's rapid economic development, and the population is increasing steadily. A ferry network and a microwave telephone system, along with the paved highway extending the entire length of the peninsula, have established new and effective lines of communication. Increasing numbers of tourists have discovered the distinctive charms of Baja: rugged desert and mountain landscapes, the deep blue waters of the Pacific and the Gulf of California, unique vegetation, Spanish missions, winter sunshine, lush palm oases, unspoiled beaches, excellent sportfishing and friendly people.

Above, a young couple performs the traditional ranchera-style dance; left, a pelican enjoys the sunshine at Bahía de los Angeles.

Detailed descriptions of Baja California's major highways are covered in several chapters in this book. Two chapters cover the length of **Mexico Highway 1**, a paved route extending from the U.S. border at Tijuana more than 1000 miles south to Cabo San Lucas at the tip of the peninsula. Next comes **Mexico Highway 19**, an off-shoot of Highway 1 south of La Paz, which skirts the Pacific coast and saves about an hour's driving time to Cabo San Lucas. Another chapter describes

Mexico Highway 2, which runs an east-west course just below the Mexico-U.S. border from Tijuana to the state of Sonora. **Mexico Highway 3**, which runs a zigzagged path from Tecate to Ensenada and across the peninsula to Highway 5, is the subject an additional chapter. Yet another chapter focuses on **Mexico Highway 5**, which runs southward from Mexicali to Puertecitos, hugging the Gulf of California coastline much of the way.

These route descriptions are divided into convenient sections. Each begins with an introduction outlining the terrain, the route and general driving conditions, followed by a detailed mileage log that lists important landmarks and junctions, roadside facilities and points of interest. Driving times were computed under average driving conditions and are rounded off to the nearest quarter hour. Mileages were compiled with highly accurate survey odometers, but instruments can vary and the mileages may not agree exactly with those contained in the logs. *Towns that contain stores and facilities useful to the traveler are shown in bold italic print.* Also featured are maps and special sections on Baja California's major cities and towns.

Above, colorful arts and crafts for sale in Cabo San Lucas; below, sunset over tranquil Bahía de La Paz.

With the completion of Mexico Highway 1, the establishment of regular airline service, and the accompanying proliferation of new hotels, trailer parks and other tourist facilities, Baja California has become an accessible vacation destination for the average traveling family. At the same time, most of the peninsula has retained its essentially wild character, making it a continuing challenge for the avid off-road adventurer.

For quick reference, key places and roads connecting them are shown on the maps on pages 10 and 11. Heavy lines indicate Mexico highways 1, 2, 3, 5 and 19; lighter lines denote side routes. A detailed index of all place names begins on page 324.

INTRODUCTION

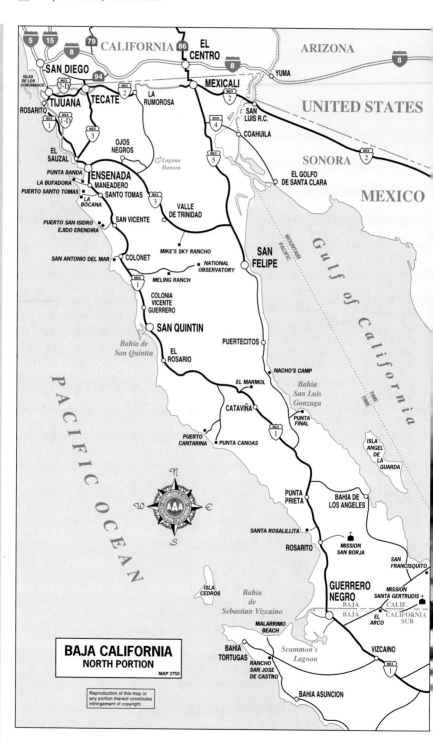

BAJA CALIFORNIA
NORTH PORTION

MAP 2750

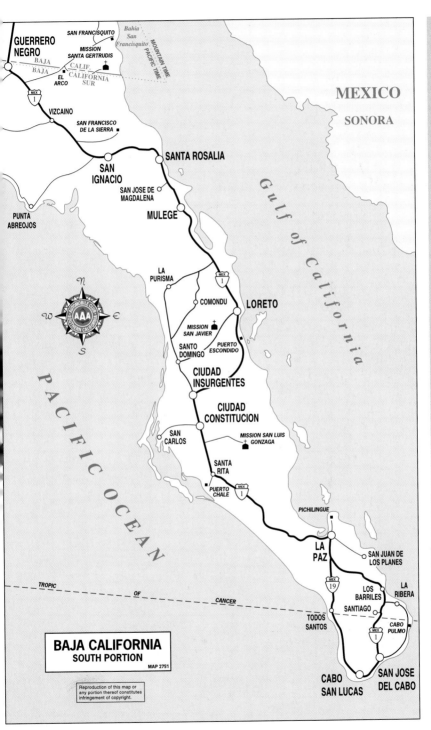

BAJA CALIFORNIA
SOUTH PORTION

MAP 2751

Reproduction of this map or
any portion thereof constitutes
infringement of copyright.

Showing The Way

The key to an enjoyable, rewarding Baja California vacation is careful preparation. The *Baja California* book is a comprehensive guidebook designed to acquaint you with the peninsula's many attractions, as well as its major highways and interesting side routes. It includes important information on travel conditions and regulations for tourists, where to stay and eat, and a variety of other pertinent subjects. You will find it to be both a valuable trip-planning aid and a helpful day-to-day companion during your visit to Baja California. In addition, the Automobile Club of Southern California publishes a companion publication—the large, colorful *Baja California* map. Both should be used by those planning to visit the peninsula.

Geography

Baja California is a very elongated, irregularly shaped peninsula that extends about 800 miles southeastward from the U.S. border. (Traveling Mexico Highway 1, which traverses the rugged peninsula, is a trip of about 1000 miles.) Varying in width from 30 to 145 miles, it is separated from the Mexican mainland to the east by the Colorado River and the Gulf of California (also known as the Sea of Cortez), while on the west it is bounded by the Pacific Ocean. Both coastlines are indented by numerous bays and coves, and many barren islands lie offshore. The backbone of the peninsula comprises a series of mountain ranges—notably the Sierra de Juárez, just below the U.S. border; the Sierra San Pedro Mártir, farther south; the Sierra de la Giganta, along the southern gulf coast; and the Sierra de la Laguna, in the extreme south. The highest point is 10,154-foot Picacho del Diablo, located in the rugged Sierra San Pedro Mártir between the Meling Ranch and San Felipe.

The topography of northern Baja California is similar to that of nearby Southern California. Most of Baja is classified as desert, but sharp regional differences exist. Chaparral-covered hills rise abruptly from the seashore and are dissected by numerous canyons and valleys. The northern mountains resemble California's Sierra Nevada in that they have gradual progressions of foothills on the west and steep eastern escarpments. The Mexicali Valley is part of a great rift that is a continuation of the Imperial Valley. South of the Colorado River Delta, this depression is submerged beneath the Gulf of California.

East of the mountains is an arid desert with scant plant life; some areas are almost devoid of vegetation. In contrast is the Mexicali Valley, where irrigated farmlands flourish on the rich alluvial soil deposited over the centuries by the Colorado River. Central Baja California, which extends from El Rosario to La Paz, is a true desert. The topography of the central desert is characterized by barren mountains separated by rocky valleys and sandy

"The Rock Garden," with its unusual geologic formations, is near Cataviña.

INTRODUCTION

plains. Abrupt slopes rise from the shore of the Gulf of California, while the Pacific side of the peninsula is less rugged. Two major lowlands, both near the Pacific coast, contrast with the sharply contoured landscape of much of the central desert. The Vizcaíno Desert near Guerrero Negro is a vast, sandy plain with little natural vegetation except saltbrush and scattered yucca válida. The Santo Domingo Valley (Magdalena Plain), farther south, is an important agricultural region, of which Ciudad Constitución is the center. Beginning near San Ignacio and spreading southward for more than 100 miles are extensive lava flows. Las Tres Vírgenes, three impressive volcanoes, sit side by side along Highway 1 southeast of San Ignacio, and the Sierra de la Giganta, a jagged mountain range also of volcanic origin, extends from Santa Rosalía almost to La Paz.

The southern reaches of the peninsula, from La Paz to Cabo San Lucas, are part desert and part semiarid. The Tropic of Cancer cuts a path across the region, just south of Todos Santos on the Pacific coast over mountains and through the town of Santiago along Highway 1, heading out to sea near Cabo Pulmo along the East Cape. The region south of La Paz is dominated by the Sierra de la Laguna mountains, which slope downward from their 7000-foot crest toward the coasts.

Climate

The climate of northern Baja California is similar to Southern California. The semiarid coastal zone, from Tijuana to San Quintín, is mild, with summer highs in the 70s and 80s (Fahrenheit); temperatures rise a short distance inland. Winter temperatures are in the 60s during the day and the 40s at night. Fog is common during late spring and early summer. Most rainfall occurs during the winter and the total rainfall varies greatly from year to year. The average winter has more sunny days than cloudy ones.

Depending on their elevation and the direction they face, the inland hills and mountains receive sporadically heavy rains and occasional snow. In the rain shadow east of the mountains including the Mexicali Valley and the Gulf of California coast, is an arid landscape, often called the Sonoran Desert. It is characterized by mild, sunny winters and intensely hot summers, whose high temperatures may reach 110 to 120 degrees. Average rainfall is scant, about 3 inches a year.

The Central Desert of Baja California extends from about El Rosario in the north to Ciudad Constitución in the south; it merges with the Sonoran Desert along the gulf. Rainfall is very irregular, as violent thunderstorms may bring several inches, or a year may pass with hardly a drop of moisture. Winter temperatures are mild and pleasant; the air is clear and the sunshine is brilliant. The Pacific coast section remains mild in summer as far south as the Vizcaíno Peninsula, but the rest of the Central Desert has oppressive summer heat. The hot, dry air of interior places like San Ignacio is easier to bear than the often-humid air of coastal locations such as Loreto.

The southern portion of the peninsula, from Bahía Magdalena to Cabo San Lucas, lies within the tropical climatic zone. It is part tropical desert and part tropical semiarid, but it receives occasionally heavy rainfall as a result of tropical storms between August and early November. Every several years, southern Baja California is ravaged by

BAJA CALIFORNIA CLIMATE CHART

	January Temp.*	Rainfall	February Temp.	Rainfall	March Temp.	Rainfall	April Temp.	Rainfall	May Temp.	Rainfall	June Temp.	Rainfall	July Temp.	Rainfall	August Temp.	Rainfall	September Temp.	Rainfall	October Temp.	Rainfall	November Temp.	Rainfall	December Temp.	Rainfall	Total Annual Rainfall
Cabo San Lucas . . .	64	–	66	–	68	–	70	–	73	–	79	–	81	0.4	82	1.6	81	2.5	79	1.2	72	1.2	68	0.8	7.7
Ciudad Constitución.	59	0.5	61	0.1	63	–	66	–	70	–	73	–	80	0.5	82	1.4	80	1.2	75	0.3	70	0.2	63	0.6	4.8
Colonia Guerrero . .	54	1.5	55	1.6	57	2.0	58	0.5	59	0.2	63	–	66	–	68	0.4	68	0.4	63	0.8	57	1.2	55	1.4	10.0
El Rosario	57	1.0	61	1.0	63	0.8	63	0.2	64	–	70	–	75	–	75	1.0	73	0.2	70	0.8	64	0.8	61	1.1	6.1
Ensenada	54	2.3	55	2.3	59	1.9	59	0.6	63	0.2	64	–	68	–	70	–	68	–	63	0.2	61	0.6	57	2.1	10.2
La Paz	63	0.4	63	–	64	–	70	–	73	–	81	–	82	0.2	84	1.2	82	2.4	77	0.8	70	0.8	63	0.4	6.2
Loreto	61	0.4	63	–	66	–	68	–	73	–	81	–	86	0.4	88	1.6	84	2.4	81	0.4	70	–	63	0.4	5.6
Mexicali	54	0.4	59	0.4	63	0.4	68	0.2	75	–	86	–	91	–	90	0.3	81	0.3	73	0.5	61	0.2	54	0.4	3.1
San Felipe	55	0.4	57	–	61	–	66	–	73	0.4	79	–	81	–	82	0.4	79	0.6	70	0.6	63	–	57	0.4	2.8
San Ignacio	57	0.4	61	0.4	63	0.4	64	–	72	–	75	0.4	81	0.4	82	0.4	79	0.8	64	0.1	64	0.4	57	0.4	4.4
San Vicente	54	2.4	55	2.4	55	1.9	57	0.2	63	–	68	–	72	–	73	–	70	0.1	64	0.1	59	0.7	54	2.1	9.9
Tecate	50	2.4	52	2	53	2	55	0.4	59	0.3	66	–	72	–	72	–	70	–	64	0.2	57	1	52	1.9	10.2
Tijuana	55	2	57	2.4	59	2	61	0.4	66	–	68	–	73	–	73	–	72	–	66	0.4	63	1.2	57	1.8	10.2

*Temperatures are expressed in degrees Fahrenheit • Rainfall in inches. Figures represent official monthly averages.

Vegetation

The unusual vegetation types of Baja California are directly related to its climates. The semi-arid northwest corner, including the Pacific Coast, has wild grasses, chaparral brush and scattered oaks, as in neighboring Southern California. In the towns, palms and other subtropical trees have been planted. Wildflowers are visible along the rural roads in the springtime. Unlike most of the peninsula, the northern mountains have forests of pine and fir blanketing the upper slopes. In sharp contrast is the very arid Sonoran Desert east of the mountains. The natural vegetation generally consists of various low shrubs, along with smatterings of cardón cacti, ocotillo and mesquite; some areas are almost devoid of vegetation. A different landscape is found in the Mexicali Valley, where irrigated farmlands of cotton and grains flourish on the rich alluvial soil deposited by the Colorado River.

Foul weather is not a total stranger to Baja California, as evidenced by this rainy winter's day at the beach near San Quintín.

a hurricane. (On rare occasions hurricanes reach up to the northern coast of the gulf.) Occurring more frequently are severe squalls, called *chubascos.* Rainfall in La Paz averages 6 inches per year, San Antonio 16 inches. The most pleasant weather occurs from November to May, with highs in the 80s and lows in the 50s. Rain is rare during these months. Summers are quite hot, with highs from 100 to 110 degrees, except on the Pacific coast, which is a little cooler.

The Central Desert of Baja California has unique vegetation well adapted for survival in its harsh environment. Because of its geographical isolation, the Central Desert is home to many plant varieties that grow naturally nowhere else on earth. They include the giant cardón cactus, which resembles the saguaro of Arizona and Sonora; the yucca válida, a smaller cousin of California's Joshua tree; and the strange cirio, a tall, columnar botanical oddity which grows only in Baja California and Sonora. Other species, such as agave,

Above, cardón cactus;
below, blue palm

Above, cholla cactus;
below, cirio trees

INTRODUCTION

cholla and barrel cacti, fan palm, ocotillo, palo verde, pitahaya (organ pipe) cactus and elephant tree, with its short, fat trunk, also have relatives in the southwestern United States. Date palms are found in scattered cases, but they are not native to the peninsula; most were planted by Jesuit missionaries during Baja California's colonial era. Along both coasts are dense thickets of mangrove—a common plant of the tropics.

Two major lowlands of the central desert, both near the Pacific coast, offer contrasting vegetation. The Vizcaíno Desert near Guerrero Negro is a vast, sandy plain with little natural vegetation except saltbrush and scattered yucca válida. The Santo Domingo Valley, farther south, is an important agricultural region, growing wheat, garbanzo and sorghum.

The vegetation of the southern portion of the peninsula reflects somewhat higher rainfall. Botanists classify the natural vegetation here as tropical desert and tropical thorn forest, consisting of thick stands of cardón, pitahaya, cholla and other cacti, along with numerous small trees and thorny shrubs. Higher elevations in the Sierra de la Laguna contain some subtropical forest. Cultivated plants include various tropical fruit trees, stately palms and bougainvillea with brilliant blooms of red, purple and orange.

Most of Baja's desert lands produce a rich variety of flora, considering the low precipitation. This is due to good soils, lack of frost and the occurrence of rainfall at different seasons of the year. Plants bloom at irregular times, following the occasional rains. Typically, though, wildflowers in the northern desert appear in the spring, and in the southern desert in the autumn.

Fauna

Baja California's wildlife is as diverse as the terrain. Each animal seeks out its preferred environment, be it chaparral,

Wild burros supervise a vehicle repair along the East Cape.

desert, mountain, canyon, valley, seashore, or any combination of these. The land mammals include mountain lions, big-horn sheep, deer, wild boar (peccary), wild burros and many other smaller animals. Also seen on the Baja penin-sula are a wide assortment of birds and reptiles. These include eagles, hawks, vultures and colorful songbirds in the air, plus a variety of snakes and lizards on the ground.

A Guadalupe fur seal suns itself on a rock near Land's End.

Many of the world's larger marine mammals may also be seen visiting the coastline of Baja California. These in-clude harbor seals, sea lions, porpoises, and Minke, humpback and gray whales. In order to bear their young in the warm waters of the region, gray whales make a yearly migration from northern waters, south along the North American coastline to a series of lagoons along the peninsula. The whales can be viewed from late December through March, most promi-nently in the area around Guerrero Negro, on the border between Baja California and Baja California Sur.

Economy

For many years Baja California's eco-nomic base reflected its population centers, which were in the extreme northern and the southern sections of the peninsula.

Due largely to their proximity to the United States, the cities of Tijuana,

Ensenada and Mexicali are the hubs of economic development in northern Baja California. Tijuana produces a variety of goods, including electronic components, clothing and auto parts. The fourth-largest city in Mexico, it's a leading center of *maquiladora* plants, where foreign-produced components are assembled into finished consumer goods for reshipment abroad. These plants have helped fuel dramatic growth, with the population increas-ing by 6 percent annually in recent years. Mexicali is in the peninsula's most important agricultural region and also has light manufacturing. Ensenada is a busy seaport known for its fish canneries. Tecate, a smaller community along the northern fron-tier, is known for the production of the beer by the same name. In the south, La Paz processes and ships farm products, and Ciudad Constitución has become a farm processing center. The most important industry of cen-tral Baja California is the salt-produc-ing operation at Guerrero Negro. Tourism, however, remains Baja Cali-fornia's leading moneymaker. Millions of tourists each year flock to the border towns and coastal resorts. While the Pacific coast is the focus of resort activity and tourism in the far north, the Gulf of California coast touts the most popular travel destinations south of Ensenada. La Paz and Los Cabos boast the plushest, best-known resorts, but San Felipe, Bahía de los Angeles, Mulegé and Loreto also draw thousands of visitors every year. Fishing is the number one lure in these locales, but beautiful beaches and year-round sunshine are also responsible for attracting tourists to the shores of the gulf.

Most of the central desert was sparsely inhabited until the 1960s, when agricultural development and tourism started to bring rapid growth to parts of this area.

Mexico's economic fluctuations have had relatively little impact on Baja California's economy, which has grown steadily over the past couple of decades. Tijuana has for years had the country's lowest unemployment rate; in 1998 the figure stood around 1 percent.

Shopping

All of Baja is a duty-free zone, so shopping is popular with tourists. Stores offer substantial savings compared to U.S. prices on such imported merchandise as perfumes, jewelry, art objects, cosmetics and textiles. Careful shoppers can also find good buys on Mexican-made articles. Besides the inexpensive souvenirs manufactured locally for the tourist trade, shops offer high-quality pottery, ceramics, guitars,

The street tianguis, or marketplace, in La Paz offers items of all types for sale.

*Above, ceramic cartoon characters wait for a buyer at Puerto Nuevo;
below, colorful rugs are among the finds in Cabo San Lucas.*

blown glass, wrought iron furniture, baskets, silver and leather goods, sweaters, blankets, jewelry and works of Mexican art. Cities most oriented to foreign shoppers include Cabo San Lucas, Ensenada, La Paz, Loreto, Mexicali, Rosarito, San José del Cabo and Tijuana. Shops in other communities cater primarily to the local population.

U.S. residents may bring back, duty free, articles not exceeding $400 in retail value, provided they are for personal use and accompany the individual. For more information, refer to the *Tourist Regulations and Travel Tips* chapter, U.S. Customs Regulations section. U.S. Customs offices at border crossings have a number of pamphlets detailing regulations regarding the import of items purchased in Mexico.

Tourist Regulations & Travel Tips

A safe and enjoyable journey through Baja California will be greatly enhanced by knowing some of the basics of Mexican law and by understanding the day-to-day culture of Mexico. This knowledge will make it easier to interact with the Mexican people and authorities, as well as help to plan a trip to Baja California. The information in this chapter is designed to help make the reader a veteran Baja traveler.

Motorists can enter or leave Mexico at any of six points along the California-Baja California border. There are two ports of entry at Tijuana. The one opposite San Ysidro, California, is open 24 hours. The other Tijuana crossing is at Otay Mesa, 5½ miles to the east, and is open 6 a.m. to 10 p.m. Tecate is open daily from 6 a.m. to midnight. The main crossing at Mexicali is open 24 hours, while a new crossing six miles to the east is open from 6 a.m. to 10 p.m. Algodónes is open daily from 6 a.m. to 8 p.m.

Tourist Regulations

Entering Mexico

Note: Mexican travel regulations are subject to change. Travelers to Baja California should always check with the Mexican consulate or other official agencies to verify current requirements.

U.S. and Canadian citizens who visit the border towns of Tijuana, Tecate, Mexicali, or any other location in Baja California provided the length of stay does not exceed 72 hours, can do so without having to obtain a tourist card. It is advisable to carry proof of citizenship even when traveling where tourist cards are not required. United States passports or birth certificates certified and issued by the federal, state, county or city government where the person was born are accepted. Naturalized U.S. citizens should carry a valid passport, a Certificate of Naturalization, or a Certificate of Citizenship issued by the U.S. Immigration and Naturalization Service; wallet-sized naturalization cards (form I-179) or other documents are not accepted. Citizens of Canada should have a valid passport or birth certificate.

For travel into the Baja California peninsula exceeding a 72-hour stay and mainland Mexico, two types of tourist cards (tourist entry forms) are issued; both are free. The single-entry card is valid for up to 180 days; the exact length of its term is determined by the Mexican immigration official

Auto Club trucks negotiating the road to La Purísima during the 1949 research expedition.

who validates the card. The second kind of tourist card, the multiple-entry card, permits unlimited entry into Mexico for a 180-day period; two front-view photographs are required. If a tourist card is not used within 90 days of its issue date, it becomes void. A tourist who overstays the time limit is subject to a fine.

Note: It is important to have tourist cards validated at the point of entry into Mexico.

Tourist cards can be obtained in the United States from Mexican consulates or the Mexican Government Tourism Office. In California, Mexican consulates are located in Calexico, Fresno, Los Angeles, Oxnard, Sacramento, San Bernardino, San Diego, San Francisco, San Jose and Santa Ana. The Mexican Government Tourism Office is in the Mexican Consulate building in Los Angeles; phone (213) 351-2069. Sometimes, offices of the Automobile Club of Southern California and the California State Automobile Association receive supplies of tourist cards from the Mexican government (these offices also distribute a detailed brochure about tourist cards). Airlines and travel agencies often provide tourist cards for their clients as well. They can also be obtained at the border from Mexican immigration authorities, but it is recommended that travelers acquire their tourist cards before leaving the United States.

Travelers obtaining a tourist card must fill in the necessary information and possess either a valid (current) passport or a birth certificate. Birth certificates must be certified and issued by the federal, state, county or city government where the person was born. Naturalized U.S. citizens must present a valid passport, a Certificate of Naturalization, or a Certificate of Citizenship issued by the U.S. Immigration and Naturalization Service; wallet-sized naturalization cards (form I-179) or other documents cannot be accepted. Citizens of Canada are required to have a valid passport or birth certificate. U.S. residents who are citizens of other nations must have a resident alien card and a passport. The original document presented as proof of citizenship must be carried into Mexico with the tourist card. Photocopies are not acceptable. The tourist card must be certified by a Mexican immigration/customs official at the port of entry. The official can be found at the Immigration Office that bears the sign Servicios Migratorios.

Minors—Any minor (under 18 years) who plans to enter Mexico without both parents must also have a completed and notarized copy of a form granting permission for the minor to enter Mexico. These forms are available at any notary public or at the Mexican Government Tourist Office. A birth certificate, passport or other proof of citizenship is also required. A photocopy of a parent's identification, such as a drivers license, is recommended as well. These documents should be presented when applying for a tourist card. If a child's parents are divorced or separated, the signed letter must be accompanied by the divorce or separation papers. If one parent is deceased, the death certificate must accompany the form in lieu of the deceased's signature; the surviving parent must still sign the form. If a child is under legal guardianship, the guardian(s) must sign the form and provide guardianship papers and, when applicable, death certificates for both parents.

Business Trips—U.S. citizens who desire to transact business of any kind in Mexico must obtain a business form by applying personally at a Mexican consulate. A 30-day form is free. For a two-month to one-year form the business traveler needs to show a passport and pay a fee that ranges from $71 to $116. Individuals must also bring two photos, a letter from the company stating the business to be conducted in Mexico, and proof of the company's validity. Any person traveling on business without this form is subject to a fine.

Automobile Requirements

Information is available at the Mexican Government Tourism Office in Los Angeles, located on the fifth floor of the Mexican Consulate building at 2401 West Sixth Street, 90057; phone (213) 351-2069.

It is illegal for a foreign citizen to sell a motor vehicle in Mexico.

Car Permits—Car permits, or Temporary Vehicle Import Permits, are not required in Baja California **except** for vehicles being shipped to mainland Mexico aboard Baja California ferries. Motorists must, however, carry acceptable proof of vehicle ownership and a valid driver's license. In mainland Mexico a car permit and tourist card are required for the principal driver; passengers and alternate drivers need only the standard tourist card. (In Sonora, these documents are not necessary in San Luis and El Golfo de Santa Clara; they are needed when traveling on Mexico Highway 2 beyond Sonoíta.)

Car permits are issued at all points of entry into mainland Mexico. Both tourist cards and car permits are available in the same building or in nearby buildings. (Because of congestion at the Tijuana crossing, it is easier to obtain these documents at another point of entry.) The permits are free and valid for up to 180 days. Information sheets and application forms for car permits are available at any office of the Automobile Club of Southern California or the California State Automobile Association.

To acquire a car permit, motorists are required to have proof of U.S. citizenship (see the Entering Mexico section for acceptable documents), as well as the **original** current registration or a notarized bill of sale for each vehicle, including motorcycles. Although it is not officially recognized as proof of ownership, the vehicle's ownership certificate (also called vehicle title or, in California, pink slip) should be carried. Motorists whose vehicles are being purchased under finance contracts must obtain written notarized permission from the lien holder (bank, finance company, credit union, etc.) authorizing the applicant to take the vehicle into Mexico. No person may drive a vehicle owned by another person into mainland Mexico **unless the owner is present**. Individuals driving a vehicle registered in the name of the company for which they work must carry a **notarized affidavit of authorization**. Offenders are subject to confiscation of the vehicle or a heavy fine. The original and two photocopies of the driver's license and vehicle registration must be presented.

Only one car permit can be issued per person. For example, one person may not enter mainland Mexico or board a ferry in Baja California with both a motorhome and a motorcycle, even if he or she owns both vehicles. One of the vehicles must be registered to another person in the party, or a second person could obtain a car permit for the extra vehicle by using a notarized affidavit of permission from the owner. Under no circumstances can more permits be obtained than there are qualified drivers (18 years or older) in the party.

Crossing into the Mainland—A recent Mexican regulation, established in order to prevent theft or smuggling, calls for an additional procedure for visiting motorists who enter the mainland of Mexico or cross by ferry from Baja California to the mainland. The visitor must present a credit card—American Express, Diners Club, MasterCard, or VISA—along with a nonrefundable fee of $11. The fee is paid to Banco del Ejercito, which has offices at all border crossings (at the Mexicali crossing, customs and the bank offices are open 24 hours). The motorist signs a declaration promising to return the vehicle to the United States. Failure to pay the fee with a credit card necessitates posting a bond (fianza), a more costly procedure with much paperwork.

Upon returning to the border the motorist gives back all documents to Mexican Customs. It is imperative to surrender all Mexican Government travel documents. Motorists failing to do so must return with them to the border. Otherwise, a large fine will be charged upon the next entry into Mexico.

Insurance—Mexican authorities recognize only insurance policies issued by companies licensed to transact insurance in the Republic of Mexico. Accordingly, motorists preparing to enter Mexico are strongly advised to purchase a separate policy issued through a Mexican-licensed company. Mexican law differs from that in the United States. Persons involved in traffic accidents who cannot produce an acceptable policy may be held by the authorities regardless of the seriousness or type of accident, pending investigation. *Therefore, to be adequately protected, travelers must buy Mexican automobile insurance before crossing the border into Mexico.* **Note:** *In the event of an accident, a report should be filed with the Mexican insurance company before returning to the United States.*

AAA members may obtain this coverage at any office of the Automobile Club of Southern California. Policies are written by the day, with a discount for more than 30 days' coverage, and are issued immediately upon application. The member should call a touring representative in an Automobile Club district office to determine what specifications (vehicle ID number, accessories included on the vehicle, etc.) are needed so that the insurance policy may be accurately written. Low-cost automobile insurance providing one-day coverage within the city limits of Tijuana or Mexicali may be offered for sale in these border cities. Because such policies do not provide coverage for medical payments or for the driver's person and property, the Auto Club recommends that motorists purchase Mexican automobile insurance which provides more comprehensive protection.

The Auto Club also provides information on other travel insurance. A comprehensive travel plan is available which affords medical coverage, includes nonrefundable travel expenses in the event of delay or cancellation, and insures baggage and personal possessions. Also included is air passenger insurance, which covers scheduled or charter flights.

TOURIST REGULATIONS & TRAVEL TIPS

Other Requirements

When taking a lot of expensive foreign-made items such as cameras, binoculars, etc., into Mexico, it is wise to register these articles with U.S. Customs before crossing the border, unless the original purchase receipts are in possession. This will avoid any question that they were purchased in Mexico, in which case duties would be assessed. Only articles having manufacturers' serial numbers may be registered.

Baggage—Baggage is subject to inspection in Baja California at police or military roadblocks (see Highway Travel section in this chapter).

Cameras—Tourists may take one still camera and one motion picture camera (8 mm or 16 mm) or video recording camera and a total of 12 rolls of film or videocassettes. Photography must not, however, be for commercial purposes. Tripods are allowed in most areas, but a special permit is required for their use in historic sites.

Cell phones—Cellular phones have arrived in Baja California, but travelers should not expect full coverage or to rely on their phones in case of an emergency. Coverage is expanding, but remains limited to the cities of the northern border region, with localized coverage in San Felipe and San Quintín, and the far south, between La Paz and Cabo San Lucas, along with Ciudad Constitución. Even in these areas, reception can be erratic, given the peninsula's rugged terrain.

Travelers should consult their cellular provider before taking their phone south of the border, since many companies do not allow roaming outside the United States. Those who plan to spend more than a few days in Baja

California in a given year may consider opening an account with Baja Cellular, the peninsula's cellular service provider. Baja Cellular has offices in all major cities of Baja.

Citizens Band Radios—Mexico has legalized the use of citizens band radios by tourists, and three channels—9, 10 and 11—have been designated for visitors' use. Channel 9 is for emergencies; Channel 10 can be used for communications among tourists; Channel 11 is reserved for localization (directions and information). Permits are no longer required for CB radios. Any linear amplifier or other device that increases the transmission power to more than five watts is prohibited.

Firearms—Guns are not permitted in Mexico except when brought into the country during hunting season for the express purpose of hunting and when accompanied by the appropriate documents (see Hunting in *Recreation*).

Pets—It is advisable to leave dogs and other pets at home because of special inspections, health certificates and the possible refusal of hotel operators to allow pets in their establishments. If an animal is taken into Mexico, it must have both a veterinarian's vaccination certificate for rabies and the Official Interstate and International Health Certificate for Dogs and Cats (form 77-043). If the pet is out of the United States for over 30 days, its owner must present the rabies certificate when returning to the United States.

Trailers—A trailer measuring more than eight feet in width and 40 feet in length requires a special permit, obtainable in Tijuana and Mexicali at the Federal Highway Police Road Office. Permits cost $13 and are issued at the discretion of the officials, since oad conditions in much of Baja California make trailer travel prohibitive.

Returning to the United States

roof of citizenship should always be arried along on trips to Mexico. It nay be necessary to show this document to U.S. officials upon reentering he United States.

U.S. Customs Regulations

ach returning U.S. resident may bring back, duty-free, articles not exceeding 400 in retail value, providing they are or personal use and accompany the ndividual. This $400 exemption may be used only once in a 30-day period. ourists returning from Mexico need ot be absent from the United States or any minimum time to qualify for his exemption. U.S. Customs offices at border crossings have a number of pamphlets detailing these regulations. hey also have information for the business traveler and persons returning with specialized products.

While away, tourists may send gifts not exceeding $50 in fair retail value to persons in the United States without payment of duty and taxes. As many gifts may be sent as desired, provided he total value of gift packages or shipments received by one person in one day does not exceed $50. The words "Unsolicited Gifts" and the value in arge letters should be written on the outside of the package. Alcoholic beverages and tobacco products are not ncluded in the privilege, nor are perfumes valued at more than $5. These bona fide gifts need not be included on he customs declaration nor within the customs exemption of returning travelers. Gifts accompanying a resident at he time of his or her return must be

declared and included within an exemption.

Bringing certain agricultural products across the border is prohibited, including many fresh fruits and vegetables, eggs, and some meat and poultry items. Failure to declare all agricultural items can result in delays and fines of up to $1000. Meats, produce and birds taken from the United States to Mexico may not be allowed to reenter. One liter of liquor per adult (21 years and older) is allowed.

An increasing number of Americans are purchasing medications in Mexico for personal use. They may be brought in legally if the following regulations are observed. The medications must be declared to the U.S. Customs agent at the border. They have to be approved by the Food and Drug Administration for use in the United States. A written prescription from the physician must accompany the medication. The quantity is limited to a three-month personal supply.

Travel Tips

Currency

In 1993, Mexico adopted a new system of currency, sometimes known as nuevos pesos. The former currency, due to years of inflation, had denominations that numbered 1000 times the present coins and bills. Astronomical prices resulted. Under the new system, 100 centavos equal 1 peso. Coins come in denominations of 10, 20 and 50 centavos and 1, 2, 5, 10 and 20 pesos. Bills also come in 10 pesos and run in denominations of 20, 50, 100, 200 pesos, etc.

At the time of publication the exchange rate between Mexican and American

For Seafood Lovers, It's a Gastronomic

By David J. Brackney

Louisiana serves up its fiery Cajun, New England its chowders, Milwaukee its knackwurst. Like her neighbor to the north, Mexico offers a bevy of regional foods, and that certainly includes Baja California.

One thing in a word sets Baja cuisine apart, and that's seafood. Oh sure, you can order a shrimp cocktail at any Mexico City neighborhood market, or stab your fork into a grilled filet of fish at a thousand and one Guadalajara diners, but in the kitchens of Baja, it goes far beyond such conventions.

Cachanillas, as Baja natives are known, partake in more seafood and prepare it in a greater variety of ways than do their countrymen just about anywhere on the Mexican mainland. In a region where nobody lives more than a couple of hours' drive from the water, the catch of the day is a

Puerto Nuevo lobster dinners typify the Baja California seafood experience.

currency was about 9.7 pesos to the dollar, with an individual peso worth about 10.3¢. The exact value of the peso can fluctuate from week to week, however. In any case, travelers should expect rates to deviate depending on the time and place of a transaction. *Mexico uses the same symbol ($) to denote pesos as the United States uses for dollars.*

Although most Mexican Government agencies and many business establishments quote prices in pesos, U.S. dollars are readily accepted in tourist areas of Baja California. **Prices contained in this publication are listed in dollar equivalents as they were quoted at press time.**

Members traveling beyond the immediate border zone are strongly urged to convert at least some of their funds into Mexican pesos. While U.S. dollars have become commonly used at tourist-oriented businesses and in resort areas, they are frequently not accepted in locations distant from the border or away from major tourist destinations. Since travelers usually lose

Paradise

fixture on the menu as surely as *carne asada* or chicken tacos.

What is the catch? What is it not along this 800 mile-long peninsula, from the chilly Pacific off Tijuana and Ensenada to the tepid waters of the lower Sea of Cortez. Seabass, albacore, yellowtail, mahi mahi, wahoo and cabrilla are just a few of the most common entrees from the deep. Oysters, shrimp, scallops, clams and (at a hefty price) abalone are the leading cast from the shellfish side of the menu.

Often in restaurants, the menu will be no more specific than to say *pescado*, Spanish for fish. In the end, preparation may matter more, with some of the more common methods including *a la parilla* (grilled); *mojo al ajo* (seasoned with garlic); and *empanizado* (breaded). Of course the number of house recipes, specific to one luxury resort or hut on the beach, could fill many a shelf full of cookbooks.

Fish tacos, seldom seen away from the coast, are another staple throughout Baja. This is usually a soft tortilla wrapped around filets of fish, breaded shrimp or lobster (that's right, lobster). Speaking of the red crustacean, it's one of the main culinary draws to the region. On a good weekend, you may join more than 1000 visitors in downing a full-course dinner at Lobster Village in Puerto Nuevo, or maybe you'll try the lobster burritos at Mama Espinosa's in El Rosario, if not a lobster omelet for Sunday brunch in Ensenada.

Sportfishing, meanwhile, has an extra attraction for anglers here. Take some of the day's catch to the restaurant of your choice, and odds are the kitchen staff will happily fix it to your specifications for dinner. It's only fitting in a land where the tag line for one eatery proclaims, "Our fish slept in the ocean last night."

money each time they exchange currencies, a good rule to follow is this: if you pay in pesos, try to receive change in pesos; if you pay in dollars, attempt to receive your change in dollars.

With exchange rates in flux it is especially important to obtain a clear understanding about prices, whether in dollars or pesos, before making a purchase or agreeing to a service. Sales tax in Baja California (both states) is 10 percent. Usually included in the base price of goods and services, it occasionally appears added to the bill. In Mex-

ico, U.S. currency can be converted into pesos at some banks, which usually give the best exchange rates. Certain currency exchange firms on both sides of the border also offer good rates. All large towns in Baja California have banks, but business hours are slightly different from those of their U.S. counterparts: Monday through Friday most open at about 9 a.m., close between noon and 2 p.m. and reopen from 4 to 6 p.m.; they are closed on all Mexican holidays. Some banks will send and accept wired funds. Arrangements should be made through the bank and the local telegraph office.

Traveler's checks are accepted at most hotels and large tourist restaurants, and can be cashed at Mexican banks; they are not accepted at gasoline stations and most stores and restaurants. U.S. credit cards—American Express, MasterCard, VISA and occasionally Diners Club—are accepted at many tourist establishments in Tijuana, Ensenada, Mexicali, La Paz and Los Cabos. Outside these areas, though, travelers should be prepared to pay cash for most transactions. Since business establishments in Baja California's more remote areas frequently keep very little cash on hand, smaller denomination traveler's checks and currency are more readily accepted. It is wise to have enough cash to cover several days' needs.

Facilities and Services

While it is generally advisable for travelers to bring everything they need into Mexico from the United States, Baja California does have facilities for those who need to obtain or replenish supplies. Most communities have small **markets or general stores** offering a limited selection of merchandise. Only in major cities and towns can travelers expect to find such items as clothing, pharmaceuticals, sporting goods, hardware and fuel for camp stoves. U.S.-style supermarkets are located in Tijuana, Rosarito, Mexicali, Tecate, Ensenada, Loreto, Ciudad Constitución, La Paz and Cabo San Lucas; prices average about the same as those in the United States.

Although the large cities and popular resorts in Baja California offer fine **accommodations** and many **tourist facilities**, smaller Mexican communities are distinctly different from their U.S. counterparts. Some have very few retail businesses and lack accommodations, restaurants, public restrooms, telephones and auto repair facilities. In emergencies, however, townspeople are usually pleased to help travelers in any way they can.

Postal service extends throughout Baja California, but letters can take two or three weeks in transit—even when mailed from a town with scheduled air service. For those sending letters to Baja California from the United States, we recommend registered mail or using a courier service to ensure their safe arrival. Telephone and telegraph terminals are now located in most towns on the peninsula. In cases of emergency, travelers can send messages via government radio, which has terminals in most of the peninsula's communities.

Telephone numbers printed in this book include the international code 01152, the city code of two or three digits (shown in parentheses), and the local number of five or six digits. For local calls in Baja California you need to use only the five or six digits; these shortened numbers appear in all local advertisements and telephone directories. For example, the state tourism office in Ensenada has the local number 72-30-00, which you use in that vicinity. To call from the United States, dial 01152 (61) 72-30-00 (do not dial "1" before 01152).

Public telephones in Mexico, though commonplace, have long been infamous for their lack of reliability. That situation is changing, spurred in large part by the influx of foreign capital into the country's phone system. As a result, coin-operated phones have all but disappeared, replaced by phones that accept pre-paid calling cards. These cards are for sale at businesses through-out Baja California and allow the user to make local or long-distance calls.

Another new trend in tourist zones is the emergence of public telephones designed for making only international phone calls. These phones, complete with signage and instructions in English, allow the user to make collect calls to another country or charge those calls to a credit card. Though generally reliable, these phones are notorious for their steep per-minute charges and can only be recommended for use in emergency situations.

Time Zones

The northern state of Baja California observes Pacific Time, the same time as the state of California. Baja California Sur, the southern state, observes Mountain Time. Its clocks are one hour ahead of California's throughout the year. Both Mexican states are on daylight-saving time from the first Sunday in April until the last Sunday in October.

Holidays

A number of major holidays are observed in Mexico. In addition, smaller communities may observe some religious feast days.

January 1	New Year's Day
February 24	Flag Day
March 21	Benito Juárez's Birthday
March-April	Palm Sunday Easter Sunday
May 1	Labor Day
May 5	Cinco de Mayo
September 15-16	Independence Day
October 12	Columbus Day (Día de la Raza)
November 1	Day of the Dead
November 20	Revolution Day
December 1	Presidential State of the Nation Address
December 12	Feast of the Virgin of Guadalupe
December 25	Christmas

Language

Many Baja Californians speak at least some English—especially in the areas most frequented by tourists. Outside these areas, however, the number of bilingual residents decreases significantly. Very few gasoline stations beyond Ensenada have English-speaking employees; neither do most shops, stores, cafes, or even some hotels, trailer parks and government agencies. Some knowledge of Spanish is certainly helpful to the traveler. The tourist armed with a good English-Spanish dictionary, a basic Spanish phrase book and a little patience will do quite well in Baja California. Included in this guidebook's *Appendix* chapter is a section entitled Speaking Spanish, which contains useful Spanish words, phrases and sentences, as well as a simple pronunciation guide. Don't be bashful about trying out your Spanish—the Mexican people are usually very patient and helpful with visitors who make an attempt to speak their language.

The Metric System

Mexico uses the metric system of weights and measurements. Speed limits are posted in kilometers and gasoline is sold by the liter. Knowledge of

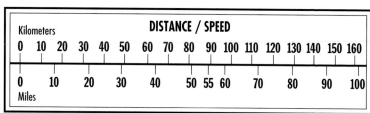

METRIC CONVERSION

CUSTOMARY		METRIC
One inch	=	2.54 centimeters
One foot	=	0.30 meters
One mile	=	1.61 kilometers
One quart	=	0.95 liters
One gallon	=	3.79 liters
One pound	=	0.45 kilometers
One psi*	=	6.89 kilopascals

METRIC		CUSTOMARY
One centimeter	=	0.39 inches
One meter	=	3.28 feet
One kilometer	=	0.62 miles
One liter	=	1.06 quarts
One kilogram	=	2.21 pounds
One kilopascal	=	0.145 psi*

*Pounds of force per square inch.

TEMPERATURE

To convert Fahrenheit to Celsius, subtract 32 from the Fahrenheit temperature, multiply by 5 and divide by 9; to convert Celsius to Fahrenheit, multiply by 9, divide by 5 and add 32.

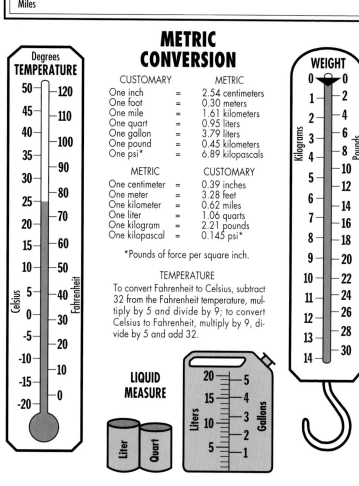

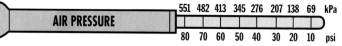

simple conversion factors for kilome-ers/miles and liters/gallons is essential, and may help prevent getting a speed-ng ticket or being overcharged at the gas pump.

Health Conditions and Medical Emergencies

Health conditions in Baja California are good, but tourists anywhere may react unfavorably to any change in their environment—particularly in their drinking water. Probably the best way to avoid the intestinal disturbance known as the *turistas* or "Montezuma's revenge" is to avoid overindulgence in food, beverages and exercise, and to get plenty of rest. Travelers should avoid tap water; fresh bottled water and good beer, soft drinks and juices are readily available. Choose carefully when selecting dairy products and fresh fruits and vegetables. It is inter-esting to note that Mexicans often con-tract a malady similar to the *turistas* when they visit the United States. Smallpox and other vaccinations are no longer necessary for entry into Mex-ico or reentry into the United States.

Baja California has good physicians and dentists, along with well-equipped hos-pitals, clinics and pharmacies, but they are found only in the largest cities and towns. Small towns may have clinics with limited facilities. The local Red Cross (*Cruz Roja*) can also be helpful. Since medical facilities are scarce else-where on the peninsula, travelers should carry first-aid kits and know how to use them. In case of emergency, help can be summoned via a govern-ment radio network, which is available for public use in most communities.

Travelers having emergencies any-where in Baja California may contact the Binational Emergency Medical Committee, located in Chula Vista, at (619) 425-5080 (available 24 hours). This voluntary organization works with both Mexican and American authorities to help travelers stranded due to accident, illness, legal difficulty or lack of money.

In addition, emergency critical-care air transport service operates throughout Baja California with in-flight physicians and nurses. The following companies offer 24-hour emergency air service. Air-Evac International, located in San Diego, can be reached at (619) 278-3822, or toll-free within Mexico at 95 (800) 010-0986. Critical Air Medicine, also in San Diego, may be contacted at (619) 571-0482, or toll-free within Mex-ico at 95 (800) 247-8326. Transmedic, in Ensenada, has phone numbers 01152 (61) 78-14-00 and 78-28-91. Its street address in Ensenada is Avenida Ruiz 842, Interior 3, Zona Centro.

Highway Travel

Baja California's paved highways are generally well signed and well main-tained, although they are quite narrow by U.S. standards; the widths of High-ways 1, 2, 3, 5 and 19 range from about 19 to 25 feet in most places. Shoulders are nonexistent along many stretches, and turnouts are rare. In some areas the pavement has a rounded crown and rests on a raised roadbed; this makes careful steering important, because vehicles tend to drift to the right. High winds can also create driving difficulties, especially for operators of recreational vehicles, trucks and vehicles pulling trailers. Large, oncoming trucks and buses pose a real danger on hills and curves, because some drivers like to straddle the center line. Safe speeds for all vehi-cles are less than on most US highways:

TOURIST REGULATIONS & TRAVEL TIPS

Road conditions in Mexico are not always excellent, as shown in these photos taken along Mexico Highway I, and the road between San Felipe and Puertecitos.

40 to 50 m.p.h. on level terrain, 20 to 30 m.p.h. in hilly or mountainous areas. Driving at night should be strictly avoided. Cattle and other livestock commonly wander onto the asphalt at night for warmth, and have caused many serious accidents as a result. If night driving is unavoidable, motorists should reduce their speeds drastically.

Travelers should be alert for occasional roadblocks of armed police or military personnel at which vehicles are searched for arms or drugs. Most inspections amount to a few questions and a wave-through. Sometimes, however, officials will make a more thorough inspection of a vehicle and luggage. Tourists should cooperate fully with the police, and those who do so will normally be treated with courtesy and respect in return. Those who feel

they have received unfair treatment should contact the U.S. Consulate in Tijuana and the tourist assistance offices located in several cities. Visitors who encounter trouble or require emergency services while in Mexico should immediately contact the office of the State Tourism Department or, if there is no office nearby, notify local police. In Tijuana, Rosarito, Ensenada, Tecate, Mexicali and San Felipe, the following three-digit telephone numbers are operating: police 134, fire 136, Red Cross (medical) 132. Outside major cities, Mexican government authority rests with the *delegado*, an elected official who oversees all emergencies and civil or legal disputes; he can be found at the *delegación municipal* or *subdelegación*. In more isolated places, authority is usually vested in an appointed citizen who reports to the nearest *delegado*.

Road Signs

Mexico has officially adopted a uniform traffic sign system in which many signs are pictorially self-explanatory. Some of the most common appear below with Spanish-English definitions.

STOP

ESCUELA
School

PUENTE ANGOSTO
Narrow Bridge

GANADO
Cattle

CRUCE F.C.
Railroad Crossing

Yield Right of Way

CURVA PELIGROSA
Dangerous Curve

CAMINO SINUOSO
Winding Road

HOMBRES TRABAJANDO
Men Working

VADO
Dip
(across arroyo)

VADO
Dip
(across arroyo)

ZONA DE DERRUMBES
Slide Area

TOURIST REGULATIONS & TRAVEL TIPS

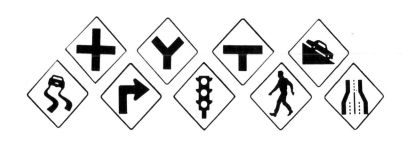

One Way

Two Way

Left Turn Only

Speed Limit

Keep to the Right

No Passing

NO VOLTEAR EN U
No U Turn

No Parking
8 a.m. to 9 p.m.

PROHIBIDO ESTACIONARSE
No Parking

One Hour Parking

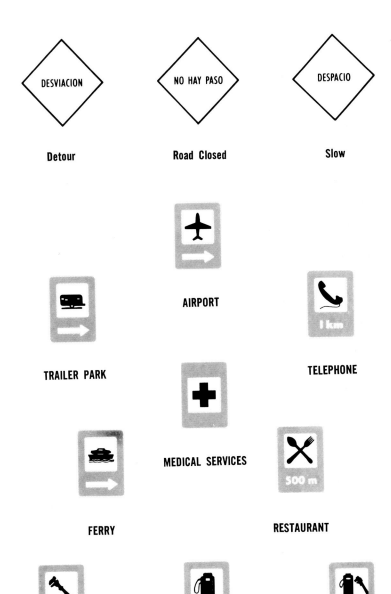

DESVIACION

Detour

NO HAY PASO

Road Closed

DESPACIO

Slow

AIRPORT

TRAILER PARK

TELEPHONE

MEDICAL SERVICES

FERRY

RESTAURANT

GAS & MECHANICAL SERVICE

TOURIST REGULATIONS & TRAVEL TIPS

Most gasoline stations (PEMEX stations) can be located by their colorful signage, but in some rural locales, they may be less prominent, like this portable station in Ojos Negros, right.

Though not the Wild West by any means, Baja California is not immune to crime, especially in tourist centers. However, travelers who use common sense and follow these precautions can greatly reduce their chances of falling prey:

1. Lock the car at all times.

2. Avoid night driving whenever possible. When driving after dark, park only in well-lighted areas.

3. Carry as much cash as necessary, but use travelers checks whenever possible.

4. Money should not be carried all in one wallet or purse.

5. Keep a list of all travelers checks and credit card numbers.

6. Never leave valuables in the car or hotel room.

Gasoline

Gasoline is usually available along Baja California's major highways, but because local shortages sometimes occur, travelers are advised to keep their fuel tanks at least half full. This is especially important during long holiday weekends, when resort areas sometimes experience shortages. All gasoline sold in Mexico is distributed by *Pemex (Petróleos Mexicanos)*—the government-controlled oil monopoly. Pemex stations can be found in most cities and towns on the peninsula, but some long stretches of paved highway without stations do exist, most notably the 200-mile section of Highway 1 between El Rosario and Villa Jesus Maria. Freelance vendors sometimes sell gas along this route, dispensing fuel straight out of cans with markups far above established pump prices. Prudent motorists will top off their tanks before setting out on this long stretch

of highway. The next longest gasless stretch is the 84 miles on Highway 1 from Mulegé to Loreto.

Most Pemex stations are easily identified by their vivid red, white and green signage, clearly visible along major highways and city streets, but there are exceptions. In some locales, especially small towns, the "station" may be nothing more than a single pump sitting in front of a general store, or a tanker truck with a hose attached parked in the driveway of someone's house.

The method used to establish octane ratings in Mexico differs from that used in the U.S. Consequently, higher ratings may appear on Pemex pumps. Premium grade unleaded fuel, called *premium*, has an octane rating of 93. Widely available from the border south to Ensenada and San Felipe and in the vicinity of La Paz and Los Cabos, it is rather scarce in the central part of the peninsula. Regular grade fuel, called *magna*, is sold at all gasoline stations. It has an octane rating of 87. Leaded fuel, known as *nova*, has all but disappeared from the nation's filling stations. Diesel fuel is sold from pumps plainly marked "diesel," and is available at most stations that carry premium. The *Baja California* map published by the Auto Club indicates where gasoline and diesel are available at towns throughout the peninsula.

Some vehicles do not run well on Mexican gasoline, especially older ones that require high-octane leaded fuel. The use of low octane fuel commonly causes pinging and preignition, conditions that can result in engine damage. If pinging or loss of power should occur, a gasoline additive may alleviate the problem. Mexican gasoline may occasionally contain water or other impurities. To prevent clogged fuel lines and carburetor jets, motorists should be prepared to clean or replace their in-line fuel filters if necessary while in Baja California. When gasoline is obtained in out-of-the-way locations (especially when it's pumped from drums), travelers occasionally filter the fuel through a chamois cloth.

At press time, fuel prices in pesos per liter were 3.58 for *magna*, 3.97 for premium and 2.82 for diesel. Converted into dollars and gallons, these figures equal about $1.40 for *magna*, $1.55 for *magna sin* and $1.10 for diesel. Some stations have been known to overcharge. It is a good idea to have a calculator handy to check the price charged. Be sure that the pump registers zeros when the attendant starts filling the tank. Most Pemex stations accept dollars, but often at an exchange rate unfavorable to dollar-paying customers. Motorists will almost always come out ahead by paying in pesos.

The service provided at Pemex stations varies from one facility to the next. Generally, however, travelers should be prepared to check their vehicle's oil, water and air. Pemex attendants do not usually clean windshields, but if they do a small tip is expected. Motorists will find it convenient to carry paper towels and glass-cleaning fluid, as these products are not usually provided.

Emergency Road Service and Auto Repairs

The Green Angels, a government-sponsored group whose sole purpose is to provide free emergency assistance to tourists, regularly patrol Baja California's major highways, supposedly passing any given point at least twice a day. Their staff are mechanics (some bilingual) who carry limited spare parts and gasoline (provided at cost) and who can radio for assistance.

Before traveling in Mexico, the vehicle should be in top mechanical condition. Tires, including spares, should be inspected for tread wear and proper inflation, and all fluid levels should be checked. Brakes, batteries, shock absorbers, filters, pumps and radiators all warrant special attention. The wise traveler will carry extra belts and hoses, as well as the tools needed to install them.

*The state-sponsored Green Angels patrol the highways and
provide assistance to stranded motorists.*

There are automobile dealerships in Tijuana, Mexicali, Ensenada, Ciudad Constitución and La Paz, and skilled mechanics can be found in most larger towns on the peninsula. But although competent mechanical help is relatively easy to find in Baja California, parts are not. Most vehicles on the road in Baja are products of Ford, General Motors, Chrysler, Volkswagen and Nissan—parts for other makes are extremely scarce. Even in major cities, a breakdown can sometimes result in a considerable wait for parts. And in rural areas, while local mechanics are wizards at salvaging parts from junk cars and are adept at repairing vehicles of less than recent vintage, many are bewildered by the complexities of fuel injection, air conditioning, anti-smog devices and electronic ignition.

Backcountry Travel

When the paved Transpeninsular Highway was completed in 1973, Baja California became an accessible destination for virtually anyone with a car. Many off-road "purists" bemoaned the loss of what they regarded as their special domain. Their worries were unwarranted, however, because the "old" Baja California still exists, as any traveler who leaves the security of the pavement soon discovers. Despite the peninsula's rapid growth and development, most of its territory remains a wild, rugged frontier—a timeless land of vast, empty spaces, unspoiled beaches, lonely ranchos and roads that by and large are little better than mule trails. Baja California's backcountry is difficult to traverse and is definitely not for those seeking comfort and amenities. But for travelers with the proper vehicles and equipment, it offers beauty, solitude and adventure. To enter this fascinating realm is to leave the jet age behind and experience a region little touched by "civilization."

*Traversing backcountry roads is best accomplished
using sturdy, high-clearance vehicles.*

Baja's roads can take their toll on even the sturdiest of vehicles.

A journey into the remote reaches of the peninsula requires careful planning and preparation. Before leaving the pavement, travelers should let someone know where they are going and what is the planned return time. Tourists might consider traveling under the buddy system—with two or more vehicles in a caravan—and plan to be as self-sufficient as possible as facilities are extremely scarce. Enough extra gasoline to extend the vehicle's range by at least 50 miles should be taken, and if possible stored outside the vehicle. Five gallons of water per person should be carried, along with ample nonperishable food for two weeks' sustenance. A good first-aid kit is essential. A supply of plastic bags will protect cameras and other valuable items from the ever-present Baja California dust. For a complete list of recommended equipment, see the Suggested Supply Lists section in the *Appendix*.

Although some of Baja's dirt roads are occasionally maintained and regularly traveled, others are seldom-used tracks that are downright grueling. Even the "good" roads have bad stretches, and any unpaved route is only as good as its worst spot. Along many of the peninsula's back roads, the traveler can expect to encounter jarring, washboard sections, deep sand, hazardous arroyo crossings, precarious curves, rocks jutting upward from the surface and grades reminiscent of roller coasters. These roads can damage any vehicle. As a result, backcountry travel in Baja California calls for a specially prepared heavy-duty rig, preferably one with four-wheel drive. It should be equipped for high clearance, with oversize tires, extra low gears, and protective steel pans beneath the engine, transmission and gasoline tank. Dual rear tires are not advisable because they do not easily fall into existing road tracks. As important as the proper vehicle is the driver who proceeds slowly and cautiously; to attempt to go too fast is to invite disaster.

There are few road signs in Baja California's backcountry—probably because local residents assume that anyone driving the back roads knows where to go. As a result, numerous unsigned junctions confront the motorist. In many cases, however, both branches leaving a fork soon rejoin one another. If an unsigned junction is reached, a good rule to follow is to choose the most heavily traveled fork; it will either be the correct route or will often lead to a ranch where directions can be obtained. Be sure to take along the Automobile Club of Southern California's *Baja California* map and check all junctions against those indicated. Remember, however, that odometers vary, and the mileages may disagree with those on the map.

Extensive off-pavement travel in Baja California involves camping out. When selecting camping equipment, keep in mind that high winds often whistle across the desert, and temperatures can be quite cool at night. Camping is allowed almost anywhere, but the bottoms of arroyos should be avoided, where flash floods sometimes occur. All trash that cannot be burned should be packed out. Wood for campfires is not abundant in the desert, but cactus skeletons make suitable fuel.

The prospective off-pavement explorer has a wide variety of routes and destinations from which to choose. Some of the most rewarding are described under the designation *Side Route* within the highway chapters. Travelers who are inexperienced in traveling the backcountry of Baja California should begin with one of the trips outlined in this book.

Tourist Assistance

Tourist Assistance/Protección al Turista provides assistance to visitors who experience legal difficulties with local businessmen or police. Offices throughout the peninsula are listed below. Tourist Assistance recommends the following steps to tourists who believe they have received inappropriate treatment by Mexican police: (1) Observe or ask for as many of the following as possible—the officer's name (most police wear nameplates), badge number, department (municipal, state, federal) and car number. (2) If there is a fine, go to the nearest police station to pay it and ask for a receipt. Traffic tickets received in Tijuana may be paid by mail from the United States. (3) Write out the complaint and mail it to the attorney general.

Ensenada *State Tourism Office, on Blvd. Costero (Lázaro Cárdenas) at Calle las Rocas, next to the other state government buildings; phone 01152 (61) 72-30-00 or 72-30-22.*

La Paz *State Tourism Office, on the Tourist Wharf at Paseo Alvaro Obregón at 16 de Septiembre; phone 01152 (112) 4-01-00 or 4-01-03.*

Mexicali *State Tourism Office, on Calle Calafia at Calzada Independencia in the Centro Cívico, Pasaje Tuxpan 1089; phone 01152 (65) 55-49-50 or 55-49-51.*

Rosarito *Blvd. Juárez and Calle Acacias next to the police station; phone 01152 (661) 2-02-00.*

San Felipe *State Tourism building, at Avenida Mar de Cortez and Calle Manzanillo; phone 01152 (657) 7-11-55 or 7-18-65.*

San Quintín *State Tourism building, on west side of Hwy. 1 at Kilometer 178.3,*

Colonia Vicente Guerrero; phone 01152 (616) 6-27-28.

Tecate *State Tourism Office, on the south side of the plaza; phone 01152 (665) 4-10-95.*

Tijuana *State Tourism Office, on the fourth floor of Edificio Nacional Financiera, corner of Paseo de los Héroes and José María Velazco, Zona Río; phone 01152 (66) 34-63-30 or 34-68-73. Second office on Calle 1 at Avenida Revolución; phone 01152 (66) 88-05-55.*

The U.S. Consulate, in Tijuana on Calle Tapachula near the Caliente Racetrack, offers assistance to U.S. citizens traveling in northern Baja California. Travelers should report to the consulate any inappropriate treatment they receive by Mexican police. Questionnaires concerning police mistreatment are available at the consulate. The consulate is open Monday through Friday, 8 a.m. to 4:30 p.m.; call 01152 (66) 81-74-00 during these hours. For after-hour emergencies call (619) 692-2650, or write to P.O. Box 439039, San Ysidro, CA 92143 U.S. In Baja California Sur, U.S. citizens can obtain help in Cabo San Lucas from the U.S. consular agent, located at Boulevard Marina y Pedregal No. 3. The phone is 01152 (114) 3-35-66.

TOURIST REGULATIONS & TRAVEL TIPS

History

Before the arrival of the Europeans, Baja California was inhabited by numerous tribes of Indians. The main linguistic groups from north to south were the Yumans, Guaicura, Huchiti and the Pericu. While most of the tribes are now extinct, archeological evidence and the written histories of the early Europeans have shown that these Indians were hunter-gatherers. Their most enduring legacy has been the fantastic cave paintings and rock art that can be found along the length of the peninsula.

Following the conquest of central Mexico, rumors of great wealth to the west attracted the conquistador Hernán Cortés, who in 1535 sailed from the west coast of Mexico into present-day Bahía de La Paz. There he established a small colony, naming the bay and land Santa Cruz (modern-day La Paz). Due to supply shortages, the colony was abandoned in 1537.

Exploration of the peninsula's coastline was continued in 1539 by Francisco de Ulloa and in 1542 by Juan Rodríguez Cabrillo. In 1596 Sebastián Vizcaíno reestablished a colony at the site of Cortés' settlement and renamed the bay La Paz. This colony also failed due to a shortage of supplies. In 1602, Vizcaíno explored the Pacific Coast of the Californias, produced the first detailed maps of the area and established place names, most of which are still in use.

Continued rumors of great wealth in pearls attracted more Spaniards to the Gulf of California in the 17th century, although their efforts were rewarded with only moderate quantities of the semiprecious gems. Francisco de Ortega in 1628, Alonzo Gonzales in 1644, and Bernardo Bernal de Pinadero in 1663 were among those who came to the Gulf of California, but they added little in exploration and knowledge of Baja California.

In 1683, Isidro de Atondo y Antillón attempted to set up a colony at La Paz, but conflict with the Indians forced him to relocate to the site of modern San Bruno. An 18-month drought exhausted the provisions and he disbanded the colony in 1685. Along with him on this journey was Padre Eusebio Kino, whose urging resulted in renewed efforts 12 years later under the Jesuit religious order to convert the Indians to the Roman church.

On October 15, 1697, Padre Juan María Salvatierra landed on the east coast of the peninsula with six soldiers. He founded a mission at Loreto, which became the first permanent Spanish

Mission Nuestra Señora de Loreto marks the site of the first permanent Spanish settlement in Baja California.

Abandoned adobe ruins have been a part of Baja's landscape since the Spanish era.

settlement in California, and for the next 70 years the Jesuits controlled Lower California. The Jesuits financed their own venture, with the Spanish government supplying only the soldiers.

The padres were brave, undiscouraged by the wild surroundings. They charted and explored the east and west coasts of the peninsula, and developed pioneer agricultural settlements. The mission fathers taught the Indians to cultivate the land. Grapes were grown and wine pressed to be exchanged for goods from Mexico. They founded 23 missions, 14 of which were successful; they instructed the Indians in religious matters and taught them useful arts; they made a network of trails connect-

ing the missions, took scientific and geographical notes, and prepared ethnological reports on the native peoples.

But they were unable to conquer disease, and epidemics plagued the population. With thousands of Indians dying and many killed in revolts, the elaborate political and economic structure established by the Jesuits began to weaken. Then, just as the priests were preparing to move north, enemies of the Jesuit order spread tales in Spain that the mission fathers were accumulating great wealth and power. Acting with dispatch, the Spanish government expelled the Jesuits from California in 1768.

Baja California Pictographs

Scattered throughout the mountains and canyons of Baja California are thousands of figures (human, animal and unknown symbols) painted onto the rock walls. When the Spaniards arrived in the peninsula and saw these pictographs, they inquired as to the meaning of these mysterious drawings. The native inhabitants could only respond that they did not know the meaning of the figures, but that they had been left behind by a long-departed race of giants. Most of the pictographs (meaning painted figures) are found in the central section of the Baja peninsula, although there are many sites in the northern part of the peninsula as well.

Archaeological evidence from the pictograph sites, which include grinding stones, arrowheads, scrapers and carved bone, place the creators of the magnificent artworks between 5000 and 10,000 years ago. Some of the pictographs are done in only one color (red), while others are done in combinations of red and black.

While the exact meaning and purpose can only be conjectured, they are generally believed to be related to hunting rituals.

Today these sites are protected by the Mexican government and it is illegal for anyone to visit them without being accompanied by an officially authorized guide. A list of authorized guides can be acquired from local civil authorities or sometimes from the front lobby at better hotels. These guides charge a fee for their services. Most of these sites are located in remote areas in rugged terrain. Some are so far off the beaten path that they require overnight pack trips with horse or burro to get there.

The uniqueness and mystery of these fascinating symbols more than offset the difficulty encountered in getting to them. One can't help but wonder if the native Indians who created these drawings had any idea that hundreds of years later the sketches would remain, intriguing visitors from other lands and cultures.

Rock carvings offer proof of early tribal Indian habitation on the peninsula.

Later that same year, 13 padres of the Franciscan Brotherhood, under the leadership of the small, energetic Padre Junípero Serra, landed at Loreto. A quick appraisal convinced them that their work lay in Alta (Upper) California near what is now San Diego, although they founded one mission on their way northward. In 1773 the Franciscans were succeeded on the peninsula by the Dominicans, who successfully carried on the establishment of the missions until the system was attacked by the Mexican government. In 1832 the Mexican government ordered the secularization of all missions and their conversion to parish churches. The Dominican missions in the north, however, were considered the only vestiges of civilization there and were retained until 1846. Some of the mission churches are still in use, while the ruins of others can be seen along the back roads of Baja California. A government-sponsored program of mission restoration is currently in progress.

Far from the seat of government in Mexico City, Baja California soon became the forgotten peninsula—a haven for criminals, smugglers and soldiers of fortune. Lower California was a land torn by internal strife and poverty.

The Mexican-American War (1846-48)—which finally separated the Californias—created further turbulence, and there were hard feelings toward the new neighbor to the north. Moreover, investment of American capital in land and mines kept Mexico suspicious of U.S. intentions. The notorious filibuster William Walker only confirmed these suspicions when he invaded Lower California in a surprise attack and proclaimed himself president. Though he was soon relieved of

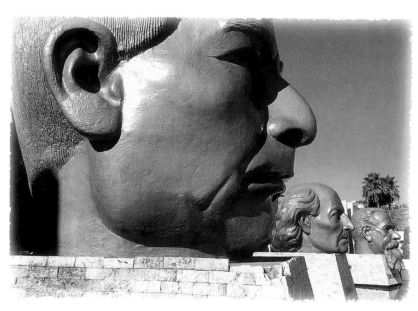

Juárez, Hidalgo and Carranza, major political figures in Mexico's history, are memorialized in bronze in Ensenada's Plaza Cívica.

In the 1930s, visitors had to travel ill-defined dirt roads across inhospitable terrain.

his position, other rebels were quick to step into the gap. In 1911, in activity peripheral to the Mexican Revolution, Mexican Ricardo Flores Magón led the rebellion known as the Tijuana Revolution. Tijuana was successfully taken by the rebels, but Flores' inability to implement his theories caused the rebellion to fail. Thereafter, a succession of politically appointed governors maintained precarious rule over this troubled area.

Prohibition in the United States brought uncertain prosperity to the border towns. Americans entered Mexico in droves, seeking the pleasures of a more liberal rule. It was not until 1938 that Mexican President Lázaro Cárdenas declared a "deep preoccupation" with the future of Lower California. Gamblers and undesirables were routed, and intense agrarian and educational reforms were instituted. In 1952, under the leadership of President Miguel Alemán, the northern part of Baja California officially became a state of Mexico, with an elected government in the state capital, Mexicali. The official name of this northern state is Baja California, although it is often referred to as Baja California Norte. In 1974 the southern half of the peninsula (below the 28th parallel) officially became Mexico's 31st state, Baja California Sur, with La Paz as its capital.

Road signs posted by the Automobile Club of Southern California survived weathering and abuse to serve Baja travelers in bygone decades.

Hillside developments such as these condominiums near Rosarito reflect the rapid growth of modern-day Baja California.

Each state is divided into *municipios* (municipalities), roughly equivalent to American counties. The state of Baja California, population about 2,300,000, is divided into *municipios* bearing the same names as its cities: Tijuana, Ensenada, Rosarito, Tecate and Mexicali. Baja California Sur, with a population of about 400,000, contains the *municipios* of Mulegé, Loreto, Comondú, La Paz and Los Cabos. These population figures are estimates based on the 1995 census.

The last 25 years have seen great progress for Baja California, with population and economic gains that have outpaced the rest of the country. In spite of its isolation, rugged terrain and arid climate, the peninsula is gradually yielding to man's efforts to make it a productive land. Indeed, those very aspects have played a key role in its economic development. The waters that isolate Baja also harbor a bounty of sea life, giving rise to lucrative commercial and sport fishing industries. Many tourists are drawn to the region by the remoteness and year-round sunshine of the desert, factors that have hindered other types of development. Through government assistance, farming cooperatives have sprouted, while foreign investment has fueled a dramatic increase in *maquiladora* assembly plants along the northern frontier. And with the completion of Mexico Highway 1, Baja California entered the modern era, growing and prospering as a mechanized land and a prime tourist objective.

Mexico Highway 1—
Tijuana to Guerrero Negro

Until 1973, the only way to reach the tip of Baja California by passenger car involved driving to Topolobampo or Mazatlán on the Mexican mainland, then crossing the Gulf of California by ferry to La Paz. Paved roads probed into the interior from the border and from La Paz, but they were separated by a vast, sparsely populated desert traversed by a rough, meandering track that could break even the sturdiest of off-road vehicles.

In late 1973, however, road crews working north and south at a feverish pace met near Rancho Santa Inés, completing the paving of a modern highway extending the entire length of the peninsula. Mexico Highway 1, Baja California's new lifeline, was named La Carretera Transpeninsular Benito Juárez (Benito Juárez Transpeninsular Highway) after one of Mexico's most revered heroes. The official dedication was made in December by then-President Luis Echeverría Alvarez in ceremonies held at the 28th parallel, near Guerrero Negro.

Designed to promote the peninsula's economic development, the paved highway allows for the movement of Baja California's internal commerce, and it has been an important stimulus for the peninsula's recent growth. It is no coincidence that in October 1974, less than a year after the completion of Highway 1, the territory of Baja California Sur became a full-fledged Mexican state.

To the tourist, the Transpeninsular Highway brings within reach the mountains and valleys of the north, the fascinating central desert and the beaches of southern Baja California. Convenient overland access to fine hunting and some of the world's best sportfishing is now available. Tourism has been further encouraged by the completion of government-financed hotels and gasoline stations along the highway. Automobile touring in Baja California, once a dream, is now a reality.

Because it is more than 1000 road miles from Tijuana to Cabo San Lucas, this book takes two chapters to fully describe Highway 1. This chapter covers the highway and the cities along it from Tijuana south to the 28th parallel, the border between the states of Baja California and Baja California Sur.

A huge fountain of spray shoots skyward at La Bufadora, near Ensenada.

Crossing The Border

The San Ysidro-Tijuana border crossing, open 24 hours, is the world's busiest international gateway. While Mexico-bound tourists are normally waved through the border station without formality, travelers returning to the United States must stop for inspection. This can result in congestion, especially on weekends and holidays, when delays of more than two hours can occur. On weekdays, carpool lanes (for four or more persons) are open into San Ysidro.

Interstates 5 and 805 lead from San Diego directly to the international border. When approaching or returning from the border, particularly after dark, drivers should be alert for persons (undocumented immigrants) crossing the freeways. Before driving into Mexico, drivers are encouraged to read the *Tourist Regulations and Travel Tips* chapter, and purchase Mexico automobile insurance.

Border sea wall near Tijuana

Tourists wishing to drive to the border and cross into Tijuana on foot can find a number of parking lots on the U.S. side in San Ysidro. They are located near the border on Camiones Way (west of I-5) and at the end of San Ysidro Boulevard (east of I-5). Parking rates run $2 for a half-hour, but only $6-8 for 24 hours. Some lots provide security, others do not; inquire before parking. On the Mexico side, taxis and buses are available, or the visitor may continue walking a half mile to downtown Tijuana via a pedestrian bridge over the Río Tijuana.

The Otay Mesa crossing is located just east of the Tijuana International Airport and just south of SR 905/Otay Mesa Road. It is open daily from 6 a.m. to 10 p.m. This border crossing is particularly useful for travelers returning from Mexico on weekends. Delays are not nearly as long as at San Ysidro, but on weekends and holidays motorists may have to wait an hour in line. From San Diego, the Otay Mesa crossing can be reached by taking SR 905 east from either I-5 or I-805 to Otay Mesa Road. Continue east for about four miles, following signs to the border.

From the south, the crossing is reached via a bypass which loops around southern and eastern Tijuana to Otay Mesa (both sides of the border are called "Otay Mesa"). Motorists approaching Tijuana from the south via Highway 1-D (the toll road) should exit onto Highway 1 at the Rosarito Norte interchange, then follow the highway, which is four-lane divided, 7½ miles to the bypass, named Libramiento. The motorist should watch for "La Mesa-Tecate-Mexicali" signs, then bear right onto the bypass and follow signs marked "Aeropuerto."

Although the bypass route is continuous in nature, it changes names several times between Highway 1-D and the Otay Mesa crossing. As the airport area is approached, signs in Spanish indicate the Otay Mesa border crossing (*Garita de Otay*) and separate lanes for heavy vehicles (*Vehículos Pesados*) and for light vehicles (*Vehículos Ligeros*), which include automobiles and recreational vehicles.

Tijuana

(See also *Lodging & Restaurants*.)

Pacific coast gateway to Baja California, Tijuana is the largest city in the Baja peninsula and the fourth largest city in Mexico. Estimates of the city's population vary widely, although most tallies put the current number at somewhere around 1,500,000. The city is also the seat of government for the *municipio* (county) of Tijuana. The name Tijuana is believed to be derived from the Yuman Indian word *Ticuan* which means "near the sea." Originally centered in the river valley, the city has since expanded into the surrounding hills and canyons. The central commercial district lies just south of the San Ysidro border crossing, but due to the rapidly growing population and increased commercial investment, the city now parallels the United States border from Otay Mesa in the east to the Pacific Ocean on the west. The intermittent-flowing Río Tijuana (Tijuana River) traverses the central business district, crosses the international border, flows in a northwesterly direction and finally empties into the Pacific Ocean. Tijuana's climate brings mild summers (highs in the 80s Fahrenheit) and cool winters (highs in the 60s Fahrenheit). Night and morning fog occurs in the late spring and early summer.

Before the arrival of the Europeans, the area was inhabited by members of the Yuman-speaking Indian group. By the mid-19th century the region was home to a few isolated cattle ranches, and in the 1870s the Mexican government built a customs house along the U.S.-

One of several traffic circles, called **glorietas**, *along the* **Paseo de los Heroes** *in Tijuana at dusk.*

Mexico border. Then in 1888 a short-lived gold rush in northwestern Baja California created an economic boom, and by 1889 the town of Tijuana was established. At the start of the Mexican Revolution in 1910, revolutionary leader Ricardo Flores Magón and his followers (Magonistas) occupied Tijuana, but on June 22, 1911, Mexican federal troops defeated the Magonistas and retook the city. From 1920-1933 Prohibition, which prohibited the sale, manufacture and consumption of alcoholic beverages within the United States, provided an almost instant economy for Tijuana. Hollywood celebrities were among the flood of "thirsty" Americans seeking out the proliferating number of cantinas, casinos and bordellos. With the repeal of Prohibition in the United States and the outlawing of gambling in Mexico, Tijuana experienced an economic depression. The Mexican government responded by declaring all of Baja California as an economic duty-free zone. Americans have since been crossing the border in search of retail bargains in ever-increasing numbers, filling the void of tourist revenues.

Tijuana has become a world-class city, known as well today as a center for international and domestic trade, manufacturing and commerce as it is for tourism. While there are still large areas of abject poverty, as there are in most major cities, Tijuana now boasts modern office buildings, new industrial and manufacturing complexes, an international airport, several universities, museums, libraries, shopping centers, sporting events, recreational facilities and much more. One of the sources of economic growth is the *maquiladoras*, manufacturing plants built with investment capital from businesses in foreign countries such as

the United States, Japan and South Korea, among others. Tijuana produces a wide variety of manufactured goods, including electronic components, automobile parts and clothing.

Improved roadways and an updated transportation network within the city have helped facilitate the transition to a modern city. At the same time, vast numbers of workers and their families

This colorful water tower soars over the Río District of Tijuana.

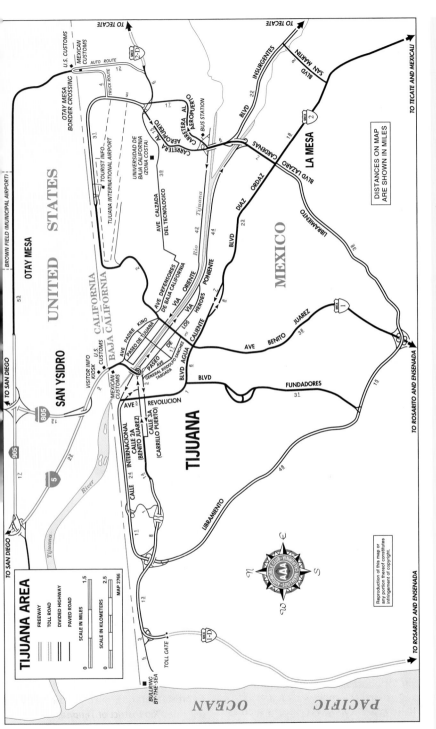

DISTANCES ON MAP
ARE SHOWN IN MILES

Reproduction of this map or
any portion thereof constitutes
infringement of copyright.

TIJUANA AREA

FREEWAY
TOLL ROAD
DIVIDED HIGHWAY
PAVED ROAD

SCALE IN MILES
0   1.5   2.5
SCALE IN KILOMETERS
0   MAP 2766

TO TECATE

TO TECATE

TO TECATE AND MEXICALI

TO ROSARITO AND ENSENADA

TO ROSARITO AND ENSENADA

TO SAN DIEGO

TO SAN DIEGO

UNITED STATES

MEXICO

OTAY MESA

SAN YSIDRO

BAJA CALIFORNIA
CALIFORNIA

TIJUANA

LA MESA

PACIFIC OCEAN

BULLRING
BY-THE-SEA

TOLL GATE

BROWN FIELD (MUNICIPAL AIRPORT)

U.S. CUSTOMS
MEXICAN CUSTOMS
AUTO ROUTE
TRUCK ROUTE

OTAY MESA
BORDER CROSSING

TOURIST INFO

TIJUANA INTERNATIONAL AIRPORT

UNIVERSIDAD DE
BAJA CALIFORNIA
(ZONA COSTA)

CARRETERA AL AEROPUERTO

CARRETERA AL AEROPUERTO

BUS STATION

BLVD INSURGENTES

BLVD SAN MARTIN

BLVD CARDENAS

BLVD LAZARO CARDENAS

LIBRAMIENTO

AVE CALZADA DEL TECNOLOGICO

Rio Tijuana

BLVD DIAZ ORDAZ

VIA ORIENTE

VIA PONIENTE

LOS HEROES

AVE DEFENSORES DE BAJA CALIFORNIA

AVE PADRE KINO

PASEO DE TIJUANA

PASEO DE TIJUANA

AVE

GENERAL RODOLFO SANCHEZ TABOADA

BLVD AGUA CALIENTE

BLVD FUNDADORES

AVE BENITO JUAREZ

LIBRAMIENTO

VISITOR INFO KIOSK
U.S. CUSTOMS
MEXICAN CUSTOMS

AVE REVOLUCION

CALLE INTERNACIONAL
CALLE 2A (BENITO JUAREZ)
CALLE 3A (CARRILLO PUERTO)

CALLE

River

Tijuana River

have relocated from the Mexican mainland—lured by the top minimum wage and one of the highest standards of living in Mexico, and proximity to the United States. All of these factors have combined to make Tijuana one of the fastest-growing cities on the North American continent. This has also provided the city with a large, educated, middle-class economic base.

Tourism remains one of the major industries for Tijuana, and Mexicans attempt to cater to a wide range of interests. Tourists can find museums, historical sites, architectural monuments, bullfights, dog racing, *charreadas* (Mexican rodeos), shopping districts, restaurants and nightclubs. In general, the city exudes a warm welcome to visitors, with friendly and helpful people always willing to provide assistance.

Shopping

Probably the most popular tourist objective in Tijuana is shopping, partially due to the town's status as a duty-free port. U.S. dollars are accepted almost everywhere and some stores even accept U.S. credit cards. While English is spoken at most shops in the downtown area and at principal shopping centers, some knowledge of Spanish is helpful in other parts of the city. Mexican-made goods include tile, ceramics, wrought iron, leather goods, rugs, blankets, basketry, hand-made lace and an assortment of liquors.

The best-known shopping area is the downtown district (Centro) on **Avenida Revolución**, home to all types of retailers, from a Sanborn's department store to smaller shops and vendor booths that line the sidewalks and occupy the numerous arcades. Virtually every type of merchandise sold

in Tijuana can be found along this street. **Avenida Constitución**, one block west of Avenida Revolución, has a good selection of shoe stores. These shops are popular with the local residents.

The **Mercado de Artesanías (Crafts Market)**, on Calle 2 between avenidas Negrete and Ocampo, contains a large number of booths selling a variety of crafts and clothing. The primary crafts are pottery and clayware.

Tijuana is well known for automotive work. In the downtown area is a district that specializes in **automobile services**; it is bordered by Calle 3, avenidas Ocampo and Pío Pico, and Calle 8. Shoppers here will find bargains on seat covers, painting and body work. Most auto shops have an English-speaking manager.

Plaza Río Tijuana, located on Paseo de los Héroes in the Río Tijuana district, is the city's largest shopping mall. It contains large department stores such as Dorian's, Sears and Comercial Mexicana, along with specialty shops, several restaurants, bakeries and a movie theater. Across the way is the **Plaza del Zapato (Plaza of Shoes)**, a mall that specializes exclusively in shoes and boots. Next door is the attractive **Plaza Fiesta**, built in the traditional colonial style; it features an assortment of eating and drinking establishments.

The colorful **Mercado Miguel Hidalgo**, at Paseo de los Héroes and Avenida Independencia across from the cultural center, is known primarily for fresh produce and other grocery items. There are also some arts and crafts stalls at this market.

Additional shopping can be found at the **Pueblo Amigo** on Vía Oriente a

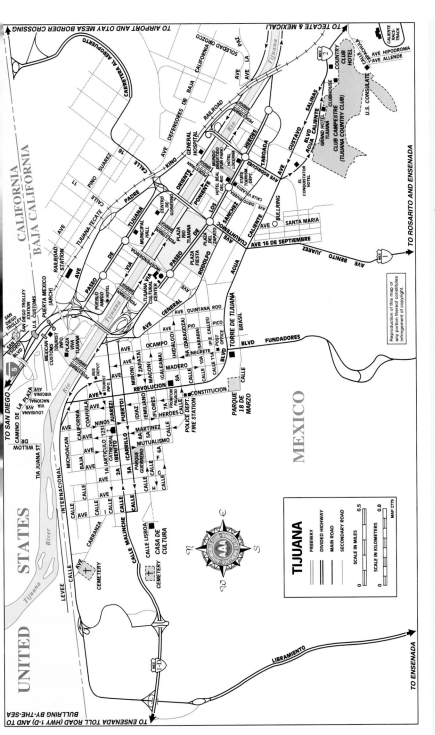

half-mile southeast of the border crossing, the **Plaza Patria** on Boulevard Díaz Ordaz in the La Mesa district, and along **Boulevard Agua Caliente**.

Dining

With a long and varied list of eating places, Tijuana has fare to please all tastes. Mexican food is the top draw, but there's much more to choose from: steaks, seafood, ethnic cuisine (Chinese, French, Italian, etc.), U.S.-style coffee shops and a growing legion of well-known fast-food franchises.

The following are some of the better-known restaurants throughout the city. Some of the restaurants listed here are AAA approved; more information about these can be found in the *Lodging & Restaurants* chapter. Non-AAA-approved restaurants are also listed here as a service to visitors.

In the Downtown (Centro) district: **El Viejo Tijuana** (Mexican), on Avenida Revolución between calles 4 and 5; **El Torito Pub** (Mexican), on Avenida Revolución between calles 2 and 3; **Iguanas-Ranas** (Mexican cuisine and steak) at Avenida Revolución and Calle 3; **Sanborn's** (varied menu), at Avenida Revolución and Calle 8; **Tia Juana Tilly's** (varied menu), on Avenida Revolución at Calle 7a; and **La Costa Perdin's** (seafood), on Calle 7 between Avenida Revolución and Avenida Constitución.

In the Río Tijuana district: **California Restaurant** (varied menu), in Plaza Río Tijuana shopping center; **Guadalajara Grill** (Mexican cuisine, steaks and seafood), Paseo de los Héroes and Avenida Diego Rivera; **La Fogata** (steak, carne asada), on Paseo de los Héroes 114; **La Taberna de Infante** (Mediterranean cuisine), on Avenida

Diego Rivera between Paseo de los Héroes and Via Poniente; **El Acueducto** (international), in the Hotel Lucerna on Paseo de los Héroes; **Ochoa's Restaurant** (varied menu), on Paseo de los Héroes 61, three blocks west of Hotel Lucerna; and **Buenos Aires Restaurante Argentino** (Argentine cuisine), at the corner of Avenida Sánchez Taboada and Calle 9.

In the Agua Caliente district: **Bocaccio's** (continental cuisine), near the Tijuana Country Club on Boulevard Agua Caliente 2500; **Matteotti's Restaurant & Bar** (international cuisine), at Boulevard Agua Caliente 8871; **Restaurante Shangri-La** (Chinese), on Boulevard Agua Caliente near the Grand Hotel Tijuana. The Grand Hotel Tijuana, on Boulevard Agua Caliente just east of Avenida Rodríguez has three good restaurants–**Plaza Café** (breakfast buffet, Mexican), **Hacienda Las Torres** (Mexican) and **Grand Bistro** (continental cuisine).

The restaurants named here are just a few of those in the main tourist zones; hundreds more options await adventurous diners who seek them out in this booming border metropolis.

Nightclubs

Tijuana offers more nightlife, and in more forms, than any other city in all of Baja California. Next to shopping, it's the biggest draw for the thousands of border-crossers who head this way each weekend. As with other tourist activities, Avenida Revolución is ground zero for Tijuana night life, packed with bars and clubs that vibrate till the pre-dawn hours. Younger revelers are especially prevalent, including many high school and college students and military personnel from nearby San Diego.

MEXICO HIGHWAY 1 - TIJUANA TO GUERRERO NEGRO

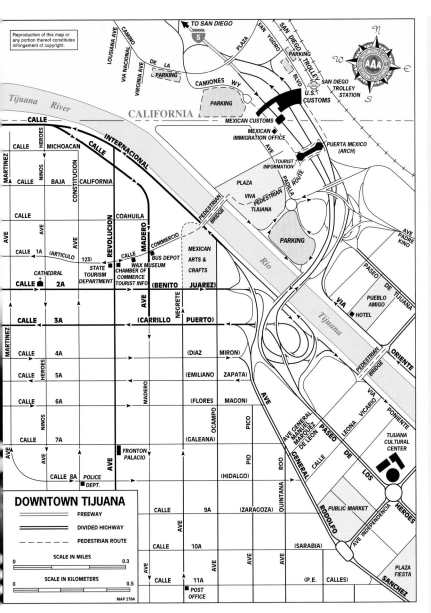

There's something for all likings here: raucous stage shows, rowdy dance clubs with deafening music, sports bars with banks of TV monitors, and upscale discotheques with cover fees and strictly enforced dress codes.

On Avenida Revolución, some of the popular spots are **The Caves**, between calles 5a and 6a; **Las Pulgas**, across from the Frontón Palacio; **Tia Juana Tilly's**, next to the Frontón Palacio at Calle 7a; **Iguanas-Ranas**, corner of

MEXICO HIGHWAY 1 - TIJUANA TO GUERRERO NEGRO

✓ *Quick Guide to Tijuana*

Tourist Information Assistance

Secretaría de Turisma or SECTUR (State Tourism Office) *Main facility on the fourth floor of Edificio Nacional Financiera, corner of Paseo de los Héroes and José María Velazco, Zona Río (see* Tijuana *map). Open Mon.-Fri. 8 a.m.-3 and 5-7 p.m., Sat. 9 a.m.-1 p.m. Phone 01152 (66) 34-63-30 or 34-68-73; FAX 34-71-57. SECTUR Second office on Calle 1 at Avenida Revolución. Open Mon.-Sat. 9 a.m.-7 p.m., Sun. 10 a.m.- 5 p.m. Phone 01152 (66) 88-05-55.* SECTUR is an excellent source of tourist information with a very helpful staff. They also offer *Protección al Turista* (Tourist Assistance), which provides legal help for tourists who encounter problems while in Tijuana.

Camara Nacional de Comercio, Servicios y Turismo or CANACO (National Chamber of Commerce) *Calle 1 and Avenida Revolución, across the street from the SECTUR office. Open Mon.-Fri., 9 a.m.-7 p.m.; phone 01152 (66) 85-84-72.* Tourist information is provided, as well as information on accommodations, restaurants and retail outlets.

Comité de Turismo y Convenciónes de Tijuana (Tijuana Tourism and Convention Bureau) *On Paseo de los Héroes at Calle Mina. Open Mon.-Fri. 9 a.m.-6 p.m. Phone 01152 (66) 84-05-37.* General tourist information is available here.

United States Consulate *Calle Tapachula 96, Colonia Hipodromo, near the Caliente Racetrack. Open Mon.-Fri., 8 a.m.-4:30 p.m., except U.S. and Mexican holidays. Phone 01152 (66) 81-74-00. In case of an* emergency *involving a U.S. citizen, pertinent information may be left with the message service at (619) 692-2650.* Legal assistance, information on obtaining a visa and national disaster information is offered.

Newspapers

Several English-language tourist newspapers, including the *Baja Shopper, Baja Visitor* and the *Baja California Sun*, are distributed at tourist information centers, hotels and certain stores. In addition to advertisements, they contain information about tourist attractions in Tijuana and other parts of Baja California. The *San Diego Union-Tribune* and the *Los Angeles Times* are sold at some newsstands and hotels. Tijuana has several Spanish-language dailies, including *El Heraldo, Baja California, El Mexicano* and *Zeta*. Newspapers from Mexico City are also available in Tijuana. One of the best sources for newspapers, magazines and other reading materials is **Sanborn's**, with locations at the corner of Avenida Revolución and Calle 8a, and in Plaza Río Tijuana.

Radio and Television Stations

Due to its proximity to the United States, many California television and radio stations are received in Tijuana and northern Baja California. Tijuana also has several television stations of its own, as well as receiving television transmissions from Mexico City. Mexican radio stations feature a variety of music, including ranchera, mariachi, la banda and rock 'n' roll.

Driving in Tijuana

Many visitors find their car to be the most convenient means of transportation, but the traffic in Tijuana can be a bit daunting. (Be sure to have Mexican auto insurance before driving across the border—see Automobile Requirements in the *Tourist Regulations and Travel Tips* chapter.) Many wide, through streets facilitate traffic flow, but outside of the main business districts the side streets are often unpaved and contain ruts and potholes. Speed bumps are common. The old downtown, referred to as Centro, including avenidas Revolución and Constitución and calles 2 and 3, can be very congested. Watch for the many one-way street signs. Traffic circles *(glorietas)*, such as those found along Paseo de los Héroes and Paseo de Tijuana, often pose a challenge for visitors. When entering a traffic circle, bear right, then follow the flow of traffic counterclockwise. Patience and persistence will prevail. Some traffic lights in Tijuana resemble the old-fashioned American signals of the 1940s and 1950s and are not readily visible. Most parts of the city have street parking and most shopping malls have adequate parking. The more congested parts of town, such as Centro, have a number of pay parking lots; parking meters are becoming increasingly common in this section. Some visitors prefer to park on the San Ysidro (California) side of the border and then rent a car in Mexico. Several major American auto rental agencies have facilities in Tijuana.

Local Transportation

A typical taxi ride within town or from the border area costs anywhere from $4-8 on average, although sometimes bargaining can lower the fare. From the border to Avenida Revolución, the asking price is $5, but bargaining can sometimes bring it down. For all trips, a price should be agreed upon before getting into the cab. There are also *taxis de ruta* (route taxis), operating along preset routes, that will pick up and drop off passengers anywhere along the line. These taxis are color-coordinated according to their route and have an average fare of 50¢.

City bus lines provide service to all parts of Tijuana, running frequently in the downtown area and on major thoroughfares. Like the route taxis, the city buses are color-coordinated according to their designated route. The basic fare is only about 25¢. (For bus travel between Tijuana and other parts of Baja California, see Bus Service in the Transportation section of the *Appendix*.)

MEXICO HIGHWAY 1 - TIJUANA TO GUERRERO NEGRO

The futuristic Tijuana Cultural Center houses a museum, a performing arts stage and the spherical Omnitheater.

Calle 3a; **People's Sports 'N' Rock**, corner of Calle 2a; **Mike's Disco**, corner of Calle 5a; and **Hard Rock Cafe**, at Calle 2a.

Several more clubs can be found on in the Río Tijuana District, including **Baby Rock**, **Guadalajara Grill**, and **El Zaguah**, all at the corner of Paseo de los Héroes and Avenida Diego Rivera. Just to the east of that corner on Paseo de los Héroes is **Ochoa's Cocktail Lounge**, an upscale piano bar.

Several hotels feature lobby bar entertainment as well, among them the **Hotel Lucerna**, at Paseo de los Héroes 10902; the **Grand Hotel Tijuana** at Boulevard Agua Caliente 4500; and the **Hotel Plaza las Glorias**, Agua Caliente 11553.

Points of Interest

CENTRO CULTURAL TIJUANA (TIJUANA CULTURAL CENTER) *Paseo de los Héroes and Avenida Independencia. 01152 (66) 84-11-11 or 84-11-32. Open daily 10 a.m-8 p.m. Museum free. Omnitheater shows: adults $2.50, children ages 3-10, $1.25.* This ultramodern complex is one of the finest of its kind in all of Mexico, boasting an anthropology museum, a 1000-seat performing arts stage, the Omnitheater, an art gallery, gift shops and a restaurant. The museum contains archaeological, historical and handicraft displays. The performing arts hall offers a variety of musical and dramatic programs. **Omnitheater**, a spherical theater located in the Cultural Center, presents large-format, three-dimensional films n various subjects. Gift shops offer books and handcrafted goods for sale. The Tijuana Cultural Center was designed by the noted Mexican architect Pedro Ramírez Vásquez.

MONUMENTO DE LA FRONTERA (BORDER MONUMENT) *Near the Pacific Ocean in Playas de Tijuana, north of the bullring.* At the fence separating Tijuana from Imperial Beach, California, sits the monument marking the western terminus of the Mexico-United States boundary. Bilingual plaques give the history of the border region.

MUSEO DE CERA (WAX MUSEUM) *Calle 1 near Avenida Revolución. Open Mon.-Fri. 10 a.m.-7 p.m., Sat.-Sun. 10 a.m.-8 p.m. Adults $1; children ages 5 and under, free.* Visitors are greeted by life-like figures from history, cinema and music, both Mexican and foreign. A few examples include Emiliano Zapata, Pedro Infante, Mahatma Gandhi, Bill Clinton, and the comedy team of Laurel and Hardy.

NUESTRA SEÑORA DE GUADALUPE CATHEDRAL *Calle 2 and Avenida Niños Héroes. Open dawn-dusk.* The twin towers of this classic example of Mexican cathedral architecture rise majestically above the old downtown district. This is

an active cathedral with daily worship services.

PARQUE TENIENTE VICENTE GUERRERO *Calle 3 at Avenida F.* This pleasant park is named in honor of Lt. Vicente Guerrero, who successfully led the federal troops against the revolutionary forces of Ricardo Flores Magón in 1911. The Héroes of 1911 Monumento is dedicated to the defenders of Tijuana during the revolution.

Spectator Sports

BULLFIGHTS *The season runs from May through Sep. with Jul., Aug. and Sep. being the busiest months; held on selected Sun. at 4 p.m. Ticket prices range from $17 to $35 (the shaded side of the arena is always more expensive). Tickets can be obtained from Five Star Tours, phone (619) 232-5049, and at the bullrings.* Some of the world's top matadors perform in Tijuana, with bullfights alter-

The Border Monument straddles the international frontier at Playas de Tijuana.

nating between El Toreo and Plaza Monumental (Bullring-by-the-Sea).

El Toreo *2 miles east of downtown Tijuana on Blvd. Agua Caliente. 01152 (66) 86-15-10.*

Tijuana's two bullrings—Bullring-by-the-Sea, above, and El Toreo.

Plaza Monumental (Bullring-by-the-Sea) *6 miles west of downtown Tijuana via Hwy. 1-D. 01152 (66) 80-18-08.*

CHARREADAS (MEXICAN RODEOS) *Most weekends from May through Sep. Events alternate among several charro grounds in the Tijuana area. Most charreadas are free. For more information call the Mexican Government Tourism Office at 01152 (66) 81-94-92.* These colorful equestrian events feature ornate costumes and festive music.

DOG RACING *Greyhounds race around an oblong track in pursuit of a mechanized prey in this fast-paced spectator sport.*

Caliente Racetrack *3 miles east of downtown Tijuana off Blvd. Agua Caliente. (619) 231-1910. Greyhounds run nightly at 7:45 p.m. and on Sat. and Sun. at 2 p.m. General admission free. Turf Club Restaurant open Wed.-Fri. 7-11 p.m.* Wagering on U.S. horse racing and professional sports teams can be made at the sports book windows.

JAI ALAI *Jai alai is a fast-moving court game using a ball and a long curved*

Caliente racetrack

wicker basket strapped to the wrist. Wagering is legal and popular with spectators. At present, though, the sport is in a state of limbo in Tijuana, following the closure of the Frontón Palacio in late 1997. The situation may change and interested parties should call (619) 231-1910 or 01152 (66) 85-25-24 for further information. The Frontón is located at the corner of Avenida Revolución and Calle 7.

◤⁄◿ Travelogue

Tijuana to Rosarito via Old Highway 1
(15 mi., 24 km.; 0:45 hrs.)

Highway 1—the old road—is a toll-free highway leading from the international border at Tijuana to Ensenada. The route passes through a modern maze of interchanges, southeast along Paseo de los Héroes, then south at the Cuauhtémoc monument (follow signs marked "Ensenada" or "Rosarito"). The 11 miles between Libramiento and Rosarito are four-lane divided highway. After curving through commercial areas, then low hills and farmland, Highway 1 crosses the toll road just north of Rosarito.

00.0 **Tijuana (U.S. border crossing).**

01.9 **Boulevard Agua Caliente (see *Mexico Highway 2*). Ahead to the left are the downtown bullring and the Caliente Racetrack.**

05.7 **Interchange with Libramiento, a bypass that skirts the southern part of Tijuana.**

07.2 **La Gloria (San Antonio de los Buenos), a village with a Pemex station and a few stores.**

15.4 **Rosarito, town center.**

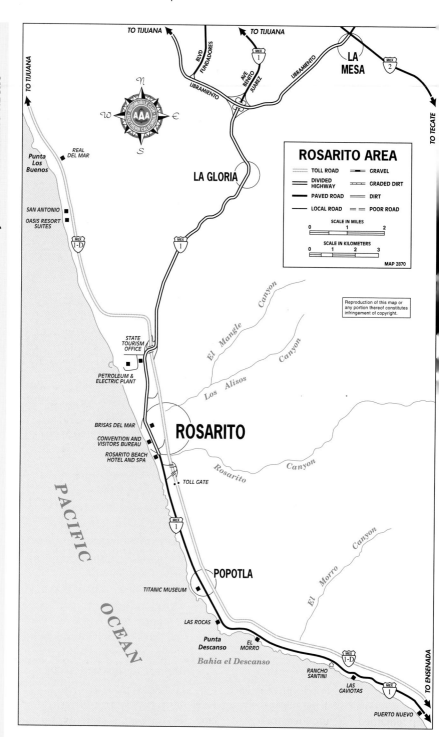

Rosarito

(See also *Lodging & Restaurants* and *Campgrounds & Trailer Parks*.)

On a favored Pacific Ocean site fronting several miles of white sandy beach, Rosarito enjoys a mild semiarid climate similar to that of coastal San Diego County. Also known as Rosarito Beach/Playas de Rosarito, the town is situated at the junction of divided Mexico highways 1 and 1-D, both of which are four lanes from Tijuana. With its pleasant environment and proximity to Southern California, the town is one of the fastest growing in Baja California.

Rosarito's reputation as a vacation spot began in 1927 with the opening of the Rosarito Beach Hotel, the focus of recreational activities for many decades. The village became a destination for fly-in celebrities from the United States who sought seclusion. With the paving of the highway in 1930, a small stream of tourists started to travel the 15 miles south from the border to Rosarito's shores. Still a village in 1960, it has become a bigger boom town with each succeeding decade. As if to acknowledge that growth, the city formally incorporated in 1996, becoming the fifth *municipio* in the state of Baja California. About 100,000 reside in the new *municipio,* which stretches from the hamlet of San Antonio, near Playas de Tijuana, southward to La Misión. About a quarter of that total live in the core urban area.

The city's name and economy got another boost from the Oscar-winning 1997 film "Titanic." Rosarito was headquarters for production of the movie, and a 90-percent scale model of the ship remained a fixture there for months. Local businesses have scrambled to cash in, with restaurants and shops naming themselves for the ill-fated ocean liner. A Titanic museum has opened as well, featuring photos, memorabilia and a short video on the making of the $200 million movie. Future movies may emerge from the city as 20th Century Fox has built a permanent studio south of town, and Mexican officials have formed a commission to attract more movie-makers to the area.

Meanwhile, a growing number of hotels and motels serve tourists, and luxurious condominiums keep rising along the water's edge. A large oil-fueled power plant north of town supplies electricity to Tijuana and Rosarito. Favorite pastimes are swimming and surfing in the ocean, and horseback riding along the beach or inland; bicycle and motorcycle races start and finish here. (The Rosarito-Ensenada 50-Mile Fun Bike Ride takes place every April and September, attracting throngs of visitors.)

With these activities and ongoing growth, local leaders must grapple with trying to preserve Rosarito's relaxed atmosphere and remaining open space—the very virtues that have drawn so many people to vacation and live here.

Shopping

As a booming tourist town, Rosarito boasts hundreds of shops that sell the full gamut of Mexican specialties. Paintings, leatherwear, blankets, handicraft items and other keepsakes are all in plentiful supply. Furniture and pottery are local specialties among the handmade goods. Like other tourist towns, liquor and pharmaceutical goods are mainstays as well. The newest trend involves items from the locally made movie "Titanic." T-shirts, caps and other "Titanic" souvenirs are for sale in shops and from freelance vendors selling them from makeshift stands and car trunks.

Ceramics and goods of other types for sale south of Rosarito.

Boulevard Benito Juárez, the town's main thoroughfare, is the primary shopping drag as well. Stand-alone shops, open-air bazaars and minimalls crowd the length of this north-south artery, sharing frontage with hotels, restaurants, dance clubs and other tourist magnets. Most of the larger hotels have gift shops as well. **Quinta Plaza**, in the northern part of town, has a **Comercial Mexicana** discount store, restaurants, shops and a convention center. This tourist strip starts near the Rosarito Norte exit off Highway 1 and runs south through town to the Rosarito Beach Hotel, near the Rosarito Sur exit.

Dining

More than 100 restaurants await visitors to Rosarito, ranging from walk-up taco stands to sit-down dining rooms with gourmet menus and imported wines. Seafood is the number one fare, gracing the menus of virtually every restaurant in this beachside town, with fish tacos and lobster being the local specialties. Chinese, French, Spanish and other ethnic foods can be found too, along with quail (another local specialty), steak and plenty of Mexican food.

The following are some of the better-known restaurants throughout the city. Some of the restaurants listed here are AAA approved; more information about these can be found in the *Lodging & Restaurants* chapter. Non-AAA-approved restaurants are also listed here as a service to visitors.

Many of the best-known restaurants are in the tourist zone, on or near Boulevard Benito Juárez. Among them are **El Nido Steakhouse** (steak, seafood), Boulevard Juárez 67; **Chabert's Restaurant** (French, international cuisine), in the Rosarito Beach Hotel at the south end of town; **Ortega's Oceana Restaurant & Bar** (varied menu), 1001 Boulevard Juárez; **Los Pelícanos** (steak, quail, seafood), on the beach at Calle Ebano 113; **La Casa de Mole** (Mexican), Boulevard Juárez between calles Rene Ortiz and Acacias; and **El Molino** (varied menu), Boulevard Juárez 82.

Several more popular restaurants lie south of town on the free road (Highway 1) to Ensenada. The best-known of these include **La Fonda** (seafood, Mexican), on a seaside bluff at kilometer 59; **La Casa de la Langosta** (seafood), at kilometer 45; and two restaurants at **Calafia Ocean Resort** (varied menu), at kilometer 35.5. Then there's Puerto Nuevo, seven miles south of Rosarito on the free road and home of **Lobster Village**, where close to 40 restaurants serve thousands of lobster dinners on busy weekends. Most have informal atmospheres and many enjoy fine views up and down the coastline. Strolling mariachis serenade visitors and curio shops hawk a wide range of wares, helping complete the south-of-the-border atmosphere.

Besides those listed here, there are many more fine restaurants in Rosarito and environs. Some are little known to tourists, and beckon those with the time and inclination to seek them out.

Nightclubs

With its growing number of night spots, Rosarito is attracting more and more cross-border revelers, although it's still quieter after dark than Tijuana or Ensenada. Numerous restaurants and hotels have dancing, live music and other nighttime entertainment. Nearby the Festival Plaza on Avenida Mar Adriatico is the popular discotheque **Papas & Beer**. South of town there are discotheques at the **Oasis Beach Resort**, kilometer 25 on the free road to Ensenada, and the **Calafia Ocean Resort**, at kilometer 35.5. For live music on the weekends there's **Las Rocas Hotel & Suites**, at kilometer 38.5 on the free road, and **New Port Beach Hotel**, at kilometer 45.

Point of Interest

TITANIC MUSEUM *On Old Highway 1, 4 miles south of town center. No phone.*

MEXICO HIGHWAY 1 - TIJUANA TO GUERRERO NEGRO

Open Sat. 2-6 p.m. when film production not taking place, Sun. 10 a.m.-6 p.m. Admission $5. The museum is located on the 20th Century Fox studio lot, where most of the film "Titanic" was shot during late 1996 and 1997. Partial sets and numerous props from the movie are on display, ranging from children's toys and an unfinished card game to life boats and an empty first-class hallway. A 25-minute video on the movie's making is also presented.

◤◢ Travelogue
Rosarito to Ensenada via Old Highway 1
(50 mi., 82 km.; 1:15 hrs.)

South of Rosarito, Mexico highways 1 and 1-D run parallel to one another for 24 miles along the rocky Pacific shore-

✓ Quick Guide to Rosarito

Tourist Information and Assistance

Rosarito Convention and Visitors Bureau *In Oceana Plaza on Blvd. Juárez in the southern part of town. Open Mon.-Fri. 8 a.m.-5 p.m., Sat. 10 a.m.-1 p.m. 01152 (661) 2-03-96; (800) 962-2252.*

Secretaría de Turismo or SECTUR (Mexican Government Tourism Office) *Blvd. Juárez and Calle Acacias next to the police station. Open Mon.-Fri. 9 a.m.-7 p.m., Sat. and Sun. 10 a.m.-4 p.m. 01152 (661) 2-02-00.* They also offer Protección al Turista, which provides legal assistance to tourists in need.

Newspapers

The English-lanugage *Baja Sun* (published in nearby Ensenada), contains information and useful advertisements on all of Baja California, including Rosarito. The *Los Angeles Times* and *San Diego Union-Tribune* are sold for a markup at a few venues in town. Spanish-language newspapers from Tijuana are widely available.

Radio and TV

Given its proximity to the border, Rosarito receives strong signals from numerous U.S. radio stations, and even more come in after dark. Tijuana's many radio stations are available as well. In addition, nearly all hotels have satellite dish antennas to receive both U.S. and Mexican TV channels.

Driving in Rosarito

Most visitors will do the majority of their driving along the Boulevard Benito Juárez, which runs parallel to the coastline. The boulevard is paved along its length, with potholes and inconspicuous stop signs being the main hazards for unsuspecting motorists. Most of the streets between Juárez and the ocean are also paved. Going inland, though, the pavement quickly ends, and dusty streets can turn to mud after rain storms.

line. At La Misión the old highway turns inland, climbs onto a level plateau, then curves gradually down to the coast at San Miguel, where it joins the divided highway leading into Ensenada. Caution: Speed berms on Boulevard Teniente Azueta just west of downtown Ensenada can damage vehicles if taken too fast.

00.0	**Rosarito, town center.**
01.7	**Popotla, a scattered seaside settlement with a large trailer park for permanent residents.**
05.7	**Calafia Resort, built on terraces overlooking the sea, has dining, a disco, a museum and a mobile home park with overnight accommodations.**
06.6	**Las Gaviotas, a residential subdivision overlooking the ocean.**
13.0	**Cantamar, an oceanside resort complex with a Pemex station, and Puerto Nuevo, a community with more than 30 restaurants specializing in lobster.**
23.8	**La Misión is a quiet village located in a steeply walled valley. On the south side of the valley are the ruins of Mission San Miguel, founded in 1787. The highway climbs out of the valley past abrupt volcanic bluffs via a series of narrow switchback curves.**
43.0	**San Miguel Village, a beach camp at the junction of highways 1 and 1-D. The rocky beach here is popular with surfers.**
44.4	**Junction with Highway 3, which leads northward to Guadalupe and Tecate (see** *Mexico Highway 3***). Just past the interchange is El Sauzal, a**

sprawling community with a large fish cannery.

48.0	**Junction. Although Highway 1 swings inland here, the preferred route into downtown Ensenada (signed Centro) follows the coastline to the right.**
50.4	**Ensenada, at the intersection of boulevards Teniente Azueta and Costero.**

▶◢ Travelogue
Tijuana to Ensenada via Toll Highway 1-D
(68 mi., 109 km.; 1:30 hrs.)

The toll highway—a divided, fully access-controlled expressway—provides the fastest and safest route to Ensenada. Stopping along the highway is prohibited except in emergencies; call boxes are spaced along the expressway for travelers in distress. Many ramps offer access to seaside resorts and various points of interest. From the international border, follow the prominent "Ensenada Toll Road" (Ensenada Cuota) signs along Calle Internacional to Mexico Highway 1-D. This route parallels the border fence and bypasses much of Tijuana's congestion. Detours are common, however, and traffic is sometimes routed through downtown streets. Highway 1-D runs west to the first toll station at Playas de Tijuana, then turns south, following the scenic shoreline most of the way to Ensenada. Caution: Speed berms on Boulevard Teniente Azueta just west of downtown Ensenada can damage vehicles if taken too fast.

Tolls used to vary widely depending on vehicle size, but in February 1998 were fixed at 48 pesos (about $4.90) for all vehicles. The fares are collected in one-third increments at each of three toll gates. The state tourism office operates tourist information booths at the Playas de Tijuana and San Miguel toll gates on summer weekends and during U.S. holiday periods.

00.0	Tijuana (U.S. border crossing).
04.4	Exit for Playas de Tijuana and Bullring-by-the-Sea. No toll is charged to this point.
04.8	Toll station, Playas de Tijuana.
12.0	Real del Mar, a resort complex with a hotel, tennis courts and a golf course.
13.0	Exit for San Antonio.
17.4	Rosarito Norte interchange; junction with Highway 1 to Rosarito. (Although most tourists take this highway to Rosarito, the town is described previously in the log for Old Highway 1, which passes directly through Rosarito.)
20.8	Rosarito Sur interchange; junction with Highway 1. To the east rises the impressive Mesa de Rosarito.
21.1	Toll station, Rosarito.
32.1	Exit for Cantamar and Puerto Nuevo; junction with Highway 1. Puerto Nuevo (Newport) is a fast-growing community with a hotel and Lobster Village, described above under restaurants in Rosarito.
40.0	Exit for La Fonda, site of a popular restaurant, and the village of La Misión, which is 2.9 miles beyond.

44.4	Exit for La Salina (see *Campgrounds & Trailer Parks*).
47.4	Exit for Bajamar, a resort development with houses, condominiums, a hotel, tennis and a golf course, the Bajamar Country Club.
51.1	El Mirador, a rest stop with a gift shop and restaurant. An overlook high above the water provides a sweeping coastal panorama. At this point, Highway 1-D makes a sharp turn, which requires a reduction in driving speed. The next several miles are subject to slides.
57.7	Exit for Playa Saldamando campground.
60.4	Toll station, San Miguel.
60.9	Exit for San Miguel Village; junction with Highway 1. The last eight miles to Ensenada are on a toll-free divided highway.
62.3	Junction with Highway 3, which leads northward to Guadalupe and Tecate (see *Mexico Highway 3*). Just past the interchange is El Sauzal, a sprawling community with a large fish cannery. Many hotels, motels and trailer parks are located along the beach between here and Ensenada.
68.3	Ensenada, at the junction of boulevards Teniente Azueta and Costero.

MEXICO HIGHWAY 1
Distance Table

This table give distances between major points in Baja California both in miles and in kilometers; the italicized (upper) figures indicate miles, while the figures in regular type (lower) denote kilometers. All figures have been rounded off to the nearest whole mile or kilometer. To find the distance between two points, first find the northern point and read down the column below the name. Second, find the southern point and read across the column to the left of the name. The intersection of the two columns shows the distance. Note: Figures are based on the use of Mexico Highway 1-D (Toll Road) between Tijuana and Ensenada.

From \ To	Ensenada	Colonet	San Quintín	El Rosario	Cataviña	Bahía de los Angeles Jct.	Guerrero Negro	San Ignacio	Santa Rosalía	Mulegé	Loreto	Ciudad Constitución	La Paz	Cabo San Lucas
Tijuana	68 / 109	144 / 232	187 / 301	223 / 359	299 / 481	364 / 586	444 / 714	532 / 856	577 / 928	615 / 990	699 / 1125	788 / 1268	922 / 1483	1059 / 1704
Ensenada		76 / 123	119 / 191	155 / 249	231 / 372	296 / 476	376 / 605	464 / 747	509 / 819	547 / 880	631 / 1015	720 / 1158	854 / 1374	991 / 1594
Colonet			43 / 69	79 / 127	155 / 249	220 / 354	300 / 483	388 / 624	433 / 697	471 / 758	555 / 893	644 / 1036	778 / 1252	915 / 1472
San Quintín				36 / 58	112 / 180	177 / 285	257 / 414	345 / 555	390 / 628	428 / 689	512 / 824	601 / 967	735 / 1183	872 / 1403
El Rosario					76 / 122	141 / 227	221 / 356	309 / 497	354 / 570	392 / 631	476 / 766	565 / 909	699 / 1125	836 / 1345
Cataviña						65 / 105	145 / 234	233 / 376	278 / 449	316 / 510	400 / 646	489 / 789	623 / 1005	760 / 1226
Bahía de los Angeles Jct.							80 / 129	168 / 271	213 / 344	251 / 405	335 / 541	424 / 684	558 / 900	695 / 1121
Guerrero Negro								88 / 142	133 / 215	171 / 276	255 / 412	344 / 555	478 / 771	615 / 992
San Ignacio									45 / 73	83 / 134	167 / 270	256 / 413	390 / 629	527 / 850
Santa Rosalía										38 / 61	122 / 197	211 / 340	345 / 556	482 / 777
Mulegé											84 / 136	173 / 279	307 / 495	444 / 716
Loreto												89 / 143	223 / 359	360 / 580
Ciudad Constitución													134 / 216	271 / 437
La Paz														137* / 221*

*Distance via Mexico Highway 19 is only 96 miles, 154 km.

Mexico's Silent Testaments to Fatal

MEXICO HIGHWAY 1 - TIJUANA TO GUERRERO NEGRO

By David J. Brackney

Mexicans are renown for preserving the memories of their dead. That much is apparent to anyone who has walked among the magnificent gravestones of their cemeteries, been in Mexico for November 1 "Day of the Dead" observances...or driven along the nation's highways.

So it goes in Baja California, where shrines of all size and description line the roadways, marking the spots where traffic accidents claimed the lives of drivers and passengers. Usually placed by the loved ones of the deceased, these shrines can range from a simple cross to elaborate, gated structures the size of a small mausoleum. Most typically, they resemble a doghouse in size and form, replete with the angled roof.

Inside or out, an inscription will bear the victim's name, dates of birth and death, and perhaps a short epitaph. Religious icons are typical—a crucifix, cross or image of the Virgin of Guadalupe, Mexico's patron saint. Old or new, shrines are usually well maintained, and few show evidence of serious disrepair. Often they are bedecked with fresh-cut flowers, photos of the deceased or accompanied by votive lights that burn in silent remembrance.

Along straight, flat expanses of road (such as Highway 1 near Ciudad Constitución), one may drive for a number of miles without seeing a shrine. On more dangerous stretches—narrow, winding passages with sheer drop-offs—several may appear within a short distance, frequently in clusters. In some cases, the guardrail may remain torn away where a vehicle plunged off the road, its crumpled, rusting carcass lying hundreds of feet below the pavement.

By no means are these markers limited to highways, but can be found wherever someone met his or her fate. In his 1941 classic "The Log From The Sea Of Cortez," Steinbeck wrote of a humble memorial placed where a fisherman had emerged sick and weak from his boat and died before making his way home. A little cross and a flickering candle inside a kerosene can marked the spot, and the author waxed philosophically on its significance:

"It seems good to mark and to remember for a little while the place where a man died. This is his one whole lonely act in all his life. In every other thing, even in his birth, he is bound close to others, but the moment of his dying is his own."

Whatever inspires those who place them, these roadside memorials bear poignant testimony to the perils of careless driving—tangible and more blunt than any classroom lecture or a legion of more conventional highway signs.

Accident Victims

How Mexicans remember fatal crash victims: Two simple crosses on the road
to San Javier, a more typical shrine north of San José del Cabo,
and a stately monument near Ciudad Constitución.

Ensenada

(See also Lodging & Restaurants.)

The third largest city in Baja California, Ensenada, meaning cove or small bay, occupies a lowland that slopes gradually downward from scrub-covered hills to the shore of lovely Bahía de Todos Santos. Thanks to its scenic setting, beautiful beaches, numerous duty-free shops, excellent sportfishing, abundance of fine accommodations and proximity to the United States, Ensenada is the peninsula's foremost summer resort. Hundreds of thousands of vacationers and weekend tourists flock to the city every year. The climate is very similar to that of San Diego, with mild, pleasant winters and sunny summers kept cool by refreshing sea breezes. Rainfall averages about 10 inches per year, most of which occurs from December through March.

With its protected harbor and modern dock facilities, Ensenada is also Baja California's leading seaport. It has become a major port of call for cruise ships, which drop hundreds of tourists and their dollars into the town each week. Some of the agricultural wealth of the Mexicali Valley is brought to Ensenada by truck, loaded onto ocean-going freighters and shipped to mainland Mexico and the Orient. Commercial fishing and seafood processing are other important contributors to the local economy; just west of the city is the largest fish cannery on Mexico's Pacific coast. Also in Ensenada is Bodegas de Santo Tomás—one of the nation's biggest wineries.

In 1602, 60 years after Juan Rodríguez Cabrillo's voyage of discovery along the Pacific coast, Sebastián Vizcaíno sailed into the bay and was so enthralled by its beauty that he named it after all the saints—Ensenada de

Ensenada enjoys a beautiful bayside setting.

Todos los Santos. Lack of fresh water precluded the establishment of a permanent settlement for more than two centuries, but the bay was a frequent port of call for the treasure-laden Manila galleons and for the privateers who preyed on them, as well as for whaling ships and fur traders. In the early 19th century, ranchers moved into the area, and Ensenada became a supply point for the missionaries and pioneers trying to secure a foothold in Mexico's northern frontier. In 1870 gold was discovered at nearby Real de Castillo, and Ensenada boomed, soon becoming an important supply depot for the miners. In 1882 it was made the capital of the territory, and two years later it became headquarters for a land company organized to colonize a huge land grant covering much of the peninsula. Shortly after the turn of the century, however, the mines gave out, the land company folded, the capital was moved to Mexicali, and Ensenada dwindled into a sleepy fishing village.

The Port of Ensenada plays host to numerous cruise ships.

In the mid-1930s, two important factors combined to bring about a resurgence for Ensenada. First, agricultural reform and development in the Mexicali Valley created the need for a seaport to handle the export of farm products. And second, the completion of the paved highway from Tijuana permitted large numbers of American tourists to discover the area's rich recreational potential. Ensenada prospered and continues to grow; the city's population is about 230,000. Today it is the seat of government of the *municipio* of Ensenada, which extends south to the 28th Parallel and includes shoreline on both the east and west coasts of the state of Baja California.

Probably because of its dual position as both an important commercial center and a popular resort, Ensenada has two separate business districts. The downtown area, containing stores, banks, restaurants, cantinas and offices patronized primarily by local residents, is along avenidas Ruiz and Juárez. Tourist activity, on the other hand, centers on Avenida López Mateos and Boulevard Costero (Lázaro Cárdenas), which are lined with motels, restaurants, nightclubs, sport-fishing firms and dozens of shops catering to visitors.

Summer and U.S. holidays are the busiest times for tourism in Ensenada, but a number of events bring in the crowds throughout the year. These include Carnaval (Mardi Gras), which typically takes place in February; the Newport-Ensenada Regatta, which brings thousands of sailboats south

MEXICO HIGHWAY 1 - TIJUANA TO GUERRERO NEGRO

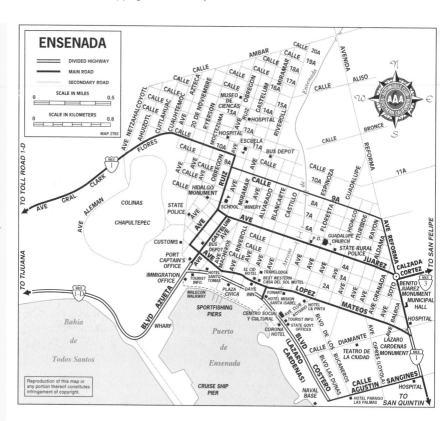

from Newport Beach, California, each April; the semiannual Rosarito-Ensenada 50-mile Fun Bike Ride in April and September; and the Baja 500 and Baja 1000 off-road races, held in June and November respectively.

Shopping

The city's easygoing, low-pressure atmosphere makes shopping in Ensenada an enjoyable experience for most tourists. In addition to the great savings on duty-free imported goods, Mexican-made items are also good buys. These include pottery, jewelry, baskets, ceramics, leather goods (jackets, sandals and purses), wrought iron furniture and embroidered clothing. Most shops have fixed prices, although

discounts can often be had for shoppers buying several items. The chief shopping strip is **Avenida López Mateos**, between Avenida Castillo in the east and Avenida Ruiz in the west, with a concentration of shops rivaled only by Avenida Revolución in all of northern Baja. There are many pharmacies here as well. Nearby is **Centro Artesenal/Mexican Hand Crafts Center**, a large group of arts and crafts stores on Boulevard Costero (Lázaro Cárdenas) at Avenida Castillo.

Consumer goods are in abundant supply, too, including food, auto parts and camping supplies. Avenidas Ruiz, Juárez and Reforma and the streets around them boast many shops that sell such products. The city also has many attractive supermarkets and discount stores.

Dining

Ensenada boasts hundreds of restaurants of all descriptions—from sidewalk cafes and open-air seafood stalls on up to fancy steak-and-seafood establishments. Some of the restaurants listed here are AAA approved; more information about these can be found in the *Lodging & Restaurants* chapter of this book. Non-AAA-approved restaurants are also mentioned here as a courtesy to our readers.

As the main tourist strip, Avenida López Mateos is crowded with restaurants of all types. Among the restaurants found on or near this street are **La Tortuga** (steak, seafood), at the corner of Avenida Riveroll; **El Palmar** (seafood), at Avenida Ryerson; **El Charro** (broiled chicken, Mexican), at López Mateos 475; **Mariscos de Bahía de Ensenada** (seafood), just east on Avenida Riveroll; **El Cid** (varied menu),

A rainbow adds to the beauty of the Plaza Cívica in Ensenada, below, and this towering flagpole stands guard over the plaza and malecón.

inside the El Cid Motor Hotel; and **Viva Mexico Taquería** (tacos, steaks and carne asada), at Avenida Granada. Another notable establishment on López Mateos is **El Rey Sol**, at the corner of Avenida Blancarte, the oldest French restaurant in Mexico.

One block south on Boulevard Costero (Lázaro Cárdenas), are several more popular restaurants, including **Casamar** (seafood), at Costero 987; **El Campanario** (varied menu), in Hotel Misión Santa Isabel; and **Cosmo's Restaurant** (varied menu), at Avenida Macheros.

Farther out but worth the drive are **La Cueva de los Tigres** (seafood, steaks and Mexican cuisine), on the beach three miles south of town via Highway 1 and gravel road; and the **Restaurant at Punta Morro** (seafood and varied international cuisine), three miles north of town on Highway 1 in the hotel of the same name.

Seafood lovers seeking a true Mexican atmosphere will enjoy **Plaza del Marisco**, a series of outdoor restaurants on a narrow street between Boulevard Costero and the waterfront, just east of the Tourism and Convention Bureau. Fish tacos, soups and combination plates are the primary attractions here, where fervid barkers urge would-be patrons to try *their* stand for the best seafood in town. Sidewalk vendors and strolling musicians work the plaza to complete the ambiance.

Many more good restaurants abound in and around Ensenada, from fancy dinner houses to small cafes, along with an increasing number of U.S.-style fast-food franchises.

Nightclubs

Ensenada serves up plenty of action when the sun goes down, mostly in the tourist zone centered along Avenida López Mateos. Two of the best-known night spots are on Avenida Ruiz, just north of López Mateos. There visitors will find **Papas & Beer**, the popular discoteque that rocks till the pre-dawn hours, especially on weekends. Across the street is the legendary **Hussong's Cantina**, a local fixture for more than 100 years. A well-worn bar with old photos on the wall and sawdust on the floor, Hussong's is packed on weekends and holidays, with crowds that spill onto the sidewalk outside. Both Hussong's and Papas & Beer have their own gift shops on López Mateos.

Other night spots nearby include **Rincón del Sol**, on López Mateos near Avenida Castillo, **Sam's Disco Bar**, López Mateos 925, and **El Langostín**, on Avenida Riveroll between López Mateos and Boulevard Costero. Elsewhere, **Casamar Restaurant Bar**, at Costero 987, offers live music most nights of the week, while El Ancla Lobby Bar, at the corner of Costero and Avenida Medusas, is home to **La Marea** discotheque. In addition, the hotels **Bahía**, **Villa Marina**, **El Cid**, **La Pinta**, **Las Rosas** and **San Nicolás** offer live entertainment and dancing.

Points of Interest

BODEGAS DE SANTO TOMÁS *Avenida Miramar at Calle 7. 01152 (61) 78-25-09. Wine tasting and tours daily at 11 a.m., 1 and 3 p.m. Tour charge $2.* One of the largest wineries in Mexico, Santo Tomás has several aging rooms at this location. English-speaking guides conduct tours, which last about one hour,

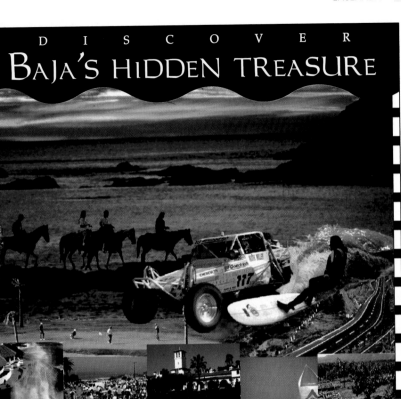

MEXICO HIGHWAY 1 - TIJUANA TO GUERRERO NEGRO

Quick Guide to Ensenada

Tourist Information and Assistance

Secretaría de Turismo or SECTUR (State Government Tourism Office) *On Blvd. Costero (Lázaro Cárdenas) and Calle Las Rocas, next to the other state government buildings. Open Mon.-Fri. 9 a.m.-7 p.m., Sat. 10 a.m.-3 p.m., Sun. 10 a.m.-2 p.m. 01152 (61) 72-30-22 or 72-30-00.* Protección al Turista (tourist assistance) provides tourist information and legal assistance to tourists.

Tourist and Convention Bureau *A booth is located on Blvd. Lázaro Cárdenas near the western entrance to the city. Open Mon.-Fri. 9 a.m.-7 p.m., Sat. 9 a.m.-2 p.m. and Sun. 10 a.m.-2 p.m. Phone 01152 (61) 78-24-11 or 78-36-75.*

Newspapers

The English-language *Baja Sun* contains travel information, articles about Ensenada and other parts of Baja California, and numerous useful advertisements. The *Los Angeles Times* and *San Diego Union-Tribune* are available in a few locations. The Spanish-language *El Mexicano* gives news of Ensenada and the state.

Radio and TV

Several American radio stations come in during the day, and more can be heard at night. Ensenada, of course, has its own radio stations. Radio Bahía Ensenada, 1590 AM, has an English/Spanish program on Saturday, 4 to 6 p.m. Most important hotels have satellite dish antennas to receive several American television stations, in addition to the Mexican channels.

Driving in Ensenada

Away from the heavily traveled arterial streets—those marked on the map with heavy black lines—Ensenada is not a difficult city for finding one's way; much of it is flat and laid out in a grid pattern. It is important, however, to watch for traffic lights and street signs; lights are often small and hard to see from a distance, and some streets are one way. In most of the city there is little problem parking on the street or in the local shopping centers, although in the business districts street parking is scarce and parking meters require Mexican coins.

Local Transportation

Taxi service is readily available downtown and at hotels. In Mexico the ubiquitous taxi driver soliciting customers is sometimes an annoyance to the tourist, but once hired, he is usually friendly and courteous. Be sure to agree on the fare before getting in. Local bus service is offered at low prices for those who wish to ride to the outlying districts and who enjoy mixing with residents. Intercity buses follow both highways 1 and 1-D (the expressway) to Tijuana. Long-distance buses head south toward La Paz (see Bus Service in the Transportation section of the *Appendix*).

followed by tasting. The winery is building a new cultural center on the site and owns a book store, market and restaurants across the street.

CENTRO CÍVICO, SOCIAL Y CULTURAL *Blvd. Costero at Avenida Club Rotario. Grounds open daily 8 a.m.-7 p.m., to 9 p.m. in summer.* Also known as Riviera del Pacífico, this building once served as a glamorous resort and casino renowned for its impressive Mediterranean architecture. It remains one of the most attractive buildings in Baja California. Now it is a cultural center with an art gallery, a museum and attractive gardens containing historic monuments and plaques. It is also a site for many local civic and social events.

Museo de Historia *01152 (61) 77-05-94. Open daily 9 a.m.-2 p.m. and 3-5 p.m. Admission: adults $1; ages 7-12, students 50¢.* This museum presents artifacts and exhibits related to the Indians and missionaries of the region. Guided tours are available in English and Spanish.

CHAPULTEPEC HILLS *Via Avenida Alemán.* This attractive residential section overlooks the city and is an excellent vantage point for photographers. Another scenic viewpoint is the hill at Avenida Moctezuma and Calle 12.

MALECÓN *Along the water between Blvd. Azueta and Arroyo de Ensenada.* Opened in mid-1997, this harborside promenade makes for a pleasant stroll by daytime or night. Midway along the new walkway is a towering flag pole more than 300 feet in height, from which a massive Mexican flag flies during fair weather. Along its route, the walkway also passes the

Well-manicured gardens and Spanish architecture make the Centro Cívico one of the most attractive retreats in Ensenada.

Plaza Cívica, sportfishing piers and the state's largest fish market.

MUSEO DE CIENCIAS DE ENSENADA
Avenida Obregón between calles 14 and 15. 01152 (61) 78-71-92. Open Tue.-Fri. 9 a.m.-5 p.m., Sat.-Sun. noon-5 p.m. Admission: adults $1.25, ages 3-12, $1. This science museum features astronomy, oceanography and marine life exhibits for the region. A special exhibit stresses endangered animal species.

NUESTRA SEÑORA DE GUADALUPE
Calle 6 and Avenida Floresta. Built in the Spanish Colonial style, this church's impressive twin towers make it one of the most prominent structures in Ensenada.

PLAZA CÍVICA *Blvd. Costero (Lázaro Cárdenas) at Avenida Riveroll.* This landscaped court contains 12-foot-high busts of Mexican heroes Juárez, Carranza and Hidalgo. Horse-drawn carriages for sightseeing depart from here.

TEATRO DE LA CIUDAD *Calle Diamante between avenidas Reforma and Loyola. 01152 (61) 77-03-92.* Musicals, dancing and theatrical productions reflecting Mexico's culture are presented here on a regular basis.

▰◢ Travelogue
Ensenada to Colonet
(76 mi., 123 km.; 1:45 hrs.)

Leaving Ensenada, Highway 1 is an undivided four-lane road as far as Maneadero. It passes through commercial districts, then enters a coastal lowland where olives, vegetables and chili peppers are the principal crops. Beyond Maneadero, open countryside gives way to chaparral-clad slopes. The highway is quite narrow, and careful driving is essential. Thirty miles south of Ensenada, Highway 1 crosses the wide, beautiful Santo Tomás Valley, passing the vineyards of the valley's namesake winery. It then winds among steep hills and grassy valleys to San Vicente, where dairy and beef cattle graze. From here to Colonet, the landscape gradually becomes drier and less rugged.

00.0	**Ensenada, at the intersection of boulevards Teniente Azueta and Costero (Lázaro Cárdenas). Follow Costero south to its end at the new naval base entrance, then turn left.**
01.9	**Junction with Highway 1, turn right.**
04.9	**El Ciprés, site of Ensenada Airport and a large military camp.**
06.9	**Turnoff to Estero Beach. The paved side road leads past several curio shops to a popular beach resort area. The sandy beaches and quiet waters of Bahía de Todos Santos are ideal for water sports.**
09.4	**Junction with road to Baja Country Club.**
10.6	**Maneadero, a community of about 55,000 people, at the junction with the paved road to Punta Banda (see Side Route to Punta Banda). This fast-growing agricultural market center has two Pemex stations, several small restaurants and many markets and other stores, including auto parts shops. Drivers should watch for unmarked speed bumps.**
21.6	**Ejido Uruápan, which offers camping, hunting and hot springs.**
26.5	**Junction with the gravel road to La Bocana and Puerto Santo Tomás (see Side Route to Puerto Santa Tomás).**

28.9   Santo Tomás (see *Campgrounds & Trailer Parks*), a village that has become well-known because of the domestic wine of the same name. A Pemex station and general store are located here. Ruins of Mission Santo Tomás are located just west of the trailer park.

45.6   Junction with the paved road to Ejido Eréndira (see Side Route to Ejido Eréndira).

51.9   A rough dirt road leads to the ruins of Mission San Vicente Ferrer, 0.6 mile to the west.

52.6   San Vicente, a busy farming center with a population of 6000. Facilities include two Pemex stations, several stores, cafes, a motel, tire shops and an auto supply house.

75.6   Colonet, at the junction to San Antonio del Mar (see Side Route to San Antonio del Mar). Colonet, a center for farmers and ranchers in the area, offers a selection of goods and services.

🚐 Side Route

Maneadero to Punta Banda and La Bufadora

(14 mi., 23 km.; 0:30 hr.)

(See also *Campgrounds & Trailer Parks*.)

This short side trip is an ideal excursion for visitors to the Ensenada area and is a popular family outing for local residents. The route offers spectacular views of the Pacific and Bahía de Todos Santos en route to the main attraction, La Bufadora—a natural sea spout that shoots spray high into the air.

From its junction with Highway 1, BCN 23 winds through olive orchards and cultivated fields for a few miles, then leads onto Punta Banda, the rocky peninsula that forms the southern end of Bahía de Todos Santos. Seven miles west of Maneadero is the turnoff to Baja Beach and Tennis Club, a private resort. Another mile west is a group of trailer parks and campgrounds on the shore of the bay; La Jolla Beach Camp and Villarino Camp offer extensive camping facilities. A growing number of vacation homes, shops, restaurants and other buildings are being built

Punta Banda provides a spectacular view of the Todos Santos Islands.

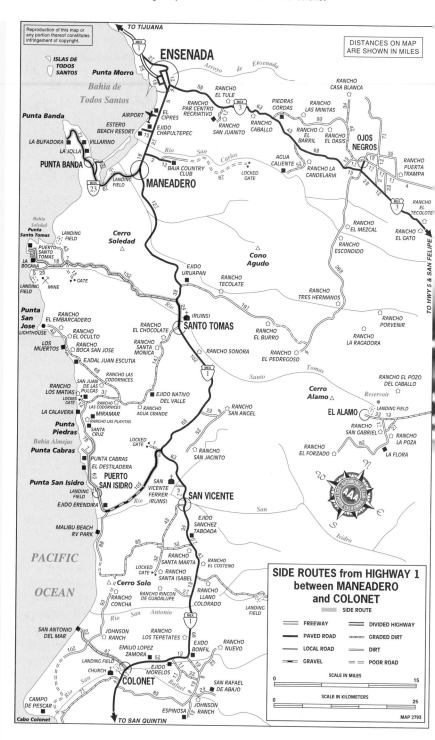

SIDE ROUTES from HIGHWAY 1
between MANEADERO
and COLONET

MAP 2793

Rows of curio shops and a new paved parking lot await visitors at La Bufadora.

in this area, although most of the land remains undeveloped.

Beyond the trailer parks and camp-grounds, the road twists and climbs toward the summit of the peninsula and drops to the edge of a small rocky cove that is popular with skin and scuba divers. Located here are three small restaurants and a shop offering diving supplies. Near the western tip of Punta Banda, the road ends at a parking lot (fee), where steps lead to La Bufadora. La Bufadora's most dra-matic activity occurs during incoming tides, when the tallest salt-water columns are launched out of this blowhole. This area has undergone a major upgrade recently, with newly paved parking areas and walkways, and permanent structures to house the large number of food and curio stands.

🚐 Side Route
Santo Tomás to La Bocana and Puerto Santo Tomás
(15 mi., 24 km.; 1 hr.)

Visitors are attracted to this route by the scenic, rocky Pacific coastline. The graded road, suitable for sturdy passen-ger cars, follows the Santo Tomás Val-ley west to La Bocana, then winds along the coast northwest to Puerto Santo Tomás.

The road branches off Highway 1 at Ejido Ajusco, just north of Santo Tomás. After passing vineyards, fenced pastures and grain fields it follows the contours of the northern wall of the valley; an old route can be seen mean-dering along the sandy streambed below.

The road reaches a junction at 15.7 miles. The fork to the left goes to a

The coastline along the Pacific at La Bocana is rugged and beautiful.

tion with Highway 1 the road follows the east wall of a narrow, attractive tree-lined canyon, past chaparral-clad slopes similar to those of many parts of Southern California. About 6.4 miles from the main highway the road crosses a bridge as the canyon empties into a larger wider arroyo, which the road follows for 4.3 miles to a junction.

campground and a cement plant. The right fork leads to the tourist village of La Bocana de Santo Tomás, which offers rustic cabins with gas stoves and electricity, a small store, boats for rent and a small freshwater lagoon; a minimal charge is made for camping. The drive north from La Bocana offers good views of sharply eroded cliffs, offshore rocks and the rugged coastline. A number of attractive American vacation houses face the sea. The road has some rough spots as it approaches Puerto Santo Tomás, a small fishing village with rustic houses and campsites for rent. Trails suitable for motorcycles and four-wheel-drive vehicles crisscross the area.

🚙 Side Route
Highway 1 to Ejido Eréndira, Puerto San Isidro and Points North
(13 mi., 21 km.; 0:45 hr.)

The signed junction with the paved road to Ejido Eréndira is 6.9 miles north of San Vicente. From its junc-

To the right is Ejido Eréndira, a farming community located just inland from the ocean. Facilities include two cafes, some stores and a Pemex station. Cabins, RV spaces and fishing boats are available for rent. Two miles beyond Ejido Eréndira the road reaches the beach, changes to a rough dirt surface, then turns northward and soon arrives in Puerto San Isidro, site of a government-operated oyster and abalone hatchery and a small cluster of dwellings overlooking the coast. The road continues northward along the rocky coastline for five miles to Punta Cabras, a collection of rustic beach homes and an electric plant under construction. There is little sandy beach along this stretch, but explorers will enjoy the cliffs, the rock shelves jutting into the water and the many seawater spouts. North of Punta Cabras is a long sandy beach on crescent-shaped Bahía Almejas.

🚐 Side Route

Colonet to
San Antonio del Mar
(8 mi., 12 km.; 0:30 hr.)

This partly graded dirt road, which leaves Highway 1 at a signed junction on the northern outskirts of Colonet, is in fairly good condition all the way to the coast and can be traveled in dry weather by all types of vehicles. It follows sparsely vegetated, gently rolling terrain for 4.3 miles. At this point there is a sweeping view of the coast before the road makes a brief, steep descent to the coastal lowland. At 4.7 miles is a junction with a dirt road to Johnson Ranch, 0.6 mile to the right. Proceed straight ahead for San Antonio del Mar. A number of beach houses and permanent trailers are located here and primitive campsites are available for a small fee. The beach area, backed by high dunes, is beautiful and affords good clamming and surf fishing.

◢◿ Travelogue

Colonet to Valle de San Quintín
(44.5 mi., 72.8 km.; 1 hr.)

South of Colonet the highway widens slightly as it crosses a level plateau dotted with occasional cultivated fields. After descending a steep hill into Camalú, Highway 1 reaches a flat, nearly featureless coastal plain. Approaching Colonia Guerrero, the motorist can glimpse the high Sierra San Pedro Mártir to the east; visible ahead are the ocean and the volcanic cones across Bahía de San Quintín. In this same area there is a narrow, reconstructed bridge over the Río Santo Domingo. Beyond Colonia Vicente Guerrero (see *Campgrounds & Trailer Parks*), the road runs in a straight line across level farmland to San Quintín.

00.0	Colonet, at the junction to San Antonio del Mar.
01.7	Junction with a good dirt road that leads to Cabo Colonet, site of a small fishing cooperative eight miles away.
07.8	San Telmo de Abajo, at the junction with an improved dirt road to San Telmo, Meling Ranch, the National Observatory and Mike's Sky Rancho (see Side Route to Meling Ranch).
18.4	Camalú, which has a Pemex station, clinic and a variety of supplies and services.
27.1	Colonia Vicente Guerrero (see *Campgrounds & Trailer Parks*) is a busy, fast-growing agricultural center. Facilities include a motel, a hospital, Pemex station, telegraph and post office, stores and cafes.
27.5	Turnoff to Posada Don Diego and Mesón de Don Pepe trailer parks (tourist information is available at the latter).
41.5	San Quintín, a center for farmers and ranchers in the area, offers a variety of goods and services.
44.5	Lázaro Cárdenas, at the military camp.

🚐 Side Route

Highway 1 to Meling Ranch
(31 mi., 50 km.; 1:45 hrs.)

Wide and graded most of the way to Meling Ranch, this road can be driven in a passenger car during dry weather. From the village of San Telmo de Abajo on Highway 1, about eight miles south of Colonet, the road winds between low, scrub-covered hills for 5.8 miles to the small village of San Telmo, which is picturesquely nestled in a small

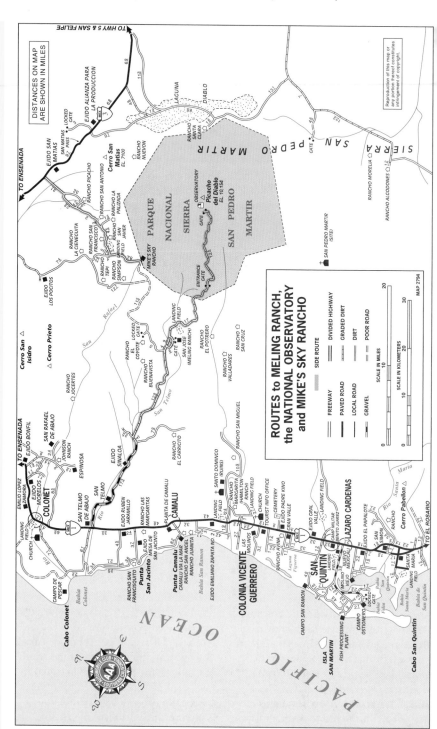

MEXICO HIGHWAY 1 - TIJUANA TO GUERRERO NEGRO

ROUTES to MELING RANCH,
the NATIONAL OBSERVATORY
and MIKE'S SKY RANCHO

bowl-shaped valley. Beyond San Telmo the road passes Ejido Sinaloa and enters hilly country. At mileage 17.3 is the junction with a road on the left leading to Rancho Buenavista. The route to Meling Ranch now ascends a rocky arroyo, emerges onto a high ridge and winds through low hills to a junction at mileage 31.1. The turnoff for Meling Ranch is 0.4 mile ahead; the main road continues to the National Observatory.

Meling Ranch, also known as San José, is the product of a marriage uniting two pioneering families—the Melings and the Johnsons. Both families settled in northern Baja California in the early 1900s. The ranch house, rebuilt after the ranch itself was destroyed during the 1911 revolution, is a model example of the structures of that era. Today's 10,000-acre cattle ranch offers its guests comfortable accommodations, family-style meals, a swimming pool and horseback riding; pack trips into Sierra San Pedro Mártir National Park can be arranged by reservation. A 3500-foot graded airstrip is just east of the ranch. The daily rate for two persons—room and meals—is $110. For information and reservations call (760) 758-2719 or write Apartado Postal 1326, Ensenada, Baja California, Mexico.

▣ Side Route
Meling Ranch to the National Observatory
(30 mi., 48 km.; 1:15 hrs.)

The remarkably clear air atop the high Sierra San Pedro Mártir prompted the Mexican government to build a modern astronomical observatory on a rounded summit 9000 feet in elevation, across from Picacho del Diablo,

highest point on the peninsula. Thanks to the graded road built to aid construction of the observatory, visitors now have a chance to explore Sierra San Pedro Mártir National Park—a magnificent region of rocky peaks, forests of pine and fir, freshwater streams and mountain meadows. The graded road to the observatory is somewhat rough and steep, requiring high-clearance vehicles. Snow is a regular occurrence in winter, and the road can be impassable after heavy storms.

From the turnoff to Meling Ranch the road curves through rolling fields, then climbs steadily into the mountains. At beautiful forest-rimmed Corona de Abajo Meadow the road enters Sierra San Pedro Mártir National Park. No hunting is permitted in the park, but fishing, camping, hiking and backpacking are allowed. An entrance fee is sometimes charged at the gate for day use and overnight stays. Beyond the entrance station the road continues for 12.4 miles to a highway work station; from here visitors must walk the last mile to the observatory. The observatory is not open to the public, but near it is a viewpoint with a breathtaking panorama of Picacho del Diablo, the barren desert far below and the Gulf of California on the distant horizon. The return descent toward the west allows a view of broad ranges of hills extending to the Pacific Coast.

Valle de San Quintín
(See also *Lodging & Restaurants* and *Campgrounds & Trailer Parks*.)

The attraction of Bahía de San Quintín dates back to the late 19th century, when an English land company was authorized by the Mexican govern-

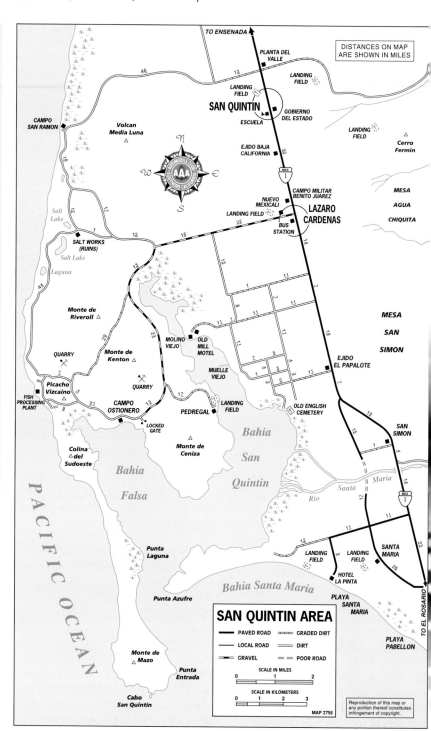

DISTANCES ON MAP
ARE SHOWN IN MILES

TO ENSENADA

PLANTA DEL VALLE

LANDING FIELD

LANDING FIELD

CAMPO SAN RAMON

Volcan Media Luna

SAN QUINTIN

ESCUELA

GOBIERNO DEL ESTADO

LANDING FIELD

Cerro Fermín

EJIDO BAJA CALIFORNIA

MEX 1

MESA

AGUA

CHIQUITA

Salt Lake

CAMPO MILITAR BENITO JUAREZ

NUEVO MEXICALI

LANDING FIELD

LAZARO CARDENAS

BUS STATION

Salt Lake

SALT WORKS (RUINS)

Laguna

Monte de Riveroll

QUARRY

Monte de Kenton

MOLINO VIEJO

OLD MILL MOTEL

MESA

SAN

SIMON

MUELLE VIEJO

Picacho Vizcaino

QUARRY

EJIDO EL PAPALOTE

FISH PROCESSING PLANT

CAMPO OSTIONERO

PEDREGAL

LANDING FIELD

OLD ENGLISH CEMETERY

SAN SIMON

LOCKED GATE

Colina del Sudoeste

Monte de Ceniza

Bahia San Quintin

Bahia Falsa

Rio

Santa

Maria

MEX 1

PACIFIC OCEAN

Punta Laguna

LANDING FIELD

LANDING FIELD

SANTA MARIA

Punta Azufre

HOTEL LA PINTA

Bahia Santa Maria

PLAYA SANTA MARIA

TO EL ROSARIO

Monte de Mazo

Punta Entrada

PLAYA PABELLON

Cabo San Quintin

SAN QUINTIN AREA

▬▬ PAVED ROAD	▦▦ GRADED DIRT
— LOCAL ROAD	═ DIRT
▬▬ GRAVEL	═ ═ POOR ROAD

SCALE IN MILES

0   1   2

SCALE IN KILOMETERS

0   1   2   3

MAP 2756

Quick Guide to San Quintín

Tourist Information and Assistance

Secretaría de Turisma or SECTUR (State Government Tourism Office) *On west side of Hwy. 1 at Kilometer 178.3, Colonia Vicente Guerrero. Open daily 8 a.m.-3 p.m. 01152 (616) 6-27-28.* Bilingual staff at this roadside office offer tourist information and can provide legal assistance to tourists.

ment to colonize the eastern shore of the bay. Crops were planted, and the colonists built a grist mill, a customs house and a pier. The enterprise was dependent on dry farming, however, and a prolonged drought caused the colony to fail. Evidence of the past can be seen at the Old Mill Motel, which contains some of the original mill machin-

Tranquillity settles over Bahía de San Quintín.

ery, and farther south along the bay where pier pilings march into the water. A re-creation of a pioneer farm, with buildings and equipment reminiscent of the early 20th century, is located a short distance east of the Old Mill Motel. Another reminder is a collection of wooden English crosses in the lonely, windswept cemetery.

Today, San Quintín has two faces. One, the San Quintín Valley, has a population of about 22,000 in an urbanized area strung out haphazardly for several miles along the highway. The valley's two commercial zones, San Quintín and Lázaro Cárdenas, serve as market centers for a developing agricultural region. The many businesses here cater primarily to local residents, but services are available to travelers as well. Facilities include

long-distance telephones, a movie theater, a large new church, numerous shops, motels, restaurants, banks, two clinics, two Pemex stations, mechanics and auto parts houses. The surrounding farmland produces large quantities of barley, tomatoes, strawberries, potatoes, peppers and other vegetables.

The other face of San Quintín is the nearby bay—one of the most popular tourist destinations between Ensenada and Mulegé. The sheltered waters of the U-shaped inner bay separate the cultivated fields of Valle de San Quintín from a row of volcanic cones to the west. Across a narrow sandspit to the south is the outer bay, which is more open to the winds and heavy surf of the Pacific Ocean. Bahía de San Quintín is a seasonal paradise for sports

The rugged beauty of the central desert is evident along Highway 1 south of El Rosario.

men. Black brant (a type of goose) migrate to the area each winter and are popular game. Good surf fishing and clam digging enhance the appeal of the beaches along the shore of the outer bay. Fishing from boats is excellent in both parts of the bay (see Fishing under Water Recreation in the *Recreation* chapter). The quiet waters of the inner bay provide a fine, protected anchorage for small boats. Explorers with heavy-duty vehicles can make the adventurous trek to the western shore of the inner bay and the Pacific beaches beyond, where good primitive campsites can be found.

▀⁄⁄ Travelogue
Valle de San Quintín to El Rosario
(33 mi., 53.2 km.; 1 hr.)

Highway 1 narrows south of San Quintín. The road passes a group of roadside communities and a series of cultivated fields, then crosses a bridge spanning the bed of the intermittently flowing Río Santa María. Due to flooding, this and several other bridges in the region were reconstructed and may be narrow. Thirty miles beyond San Quintín the road turns sharply inland, soon reaching a summit from which there are expansive views of the ocean and the countryside to the northeast. From the mesa, the highway drops into a wide valley and enters El Rosario.

00.0   **Lázaro Cárdenas, at the military camp.**

01.4   **First turnoff to Bahía de San Quintín. This dirt road leads 3.6 miles to the shore. A better road follows.**

03.2   **Junction with the dirt road to Muelle Viejo, the ruins of a pier constructed by an unsuccessful English colony, and to the Old Mill Motel.**

07.9   Junction with the paved road to the Hotel La Pinta.

09.0   Turnoff on a dirt road to El Pabellón RV Park.

16.1   Junction with the unmarked short dirt road to El Socorrito, a seaside village that offers sportfishing and scuba diving.

35.8   Rosario de Arriba, the primary settlement of El Rosario. The much smaller Rosario de Abajo, which contains the ruins of Mission Nuestra Señora del Rosario, lies about a mile west via a dirt road. The total population for both communities is about 4000. Before the completion of the Transpeninsular Highway and the peninsula's microwave telephone system, El Rosario was considered the last outpost of civilization in northern Baja California. It is now a quiet agricultural community and highway stop, with gasoline, auto parts, restaurants (see *Lodging & Restaurants*), two motels and groceries. A museum containing a nice variety of items from northern Baja California is located here. For entrance to the museum, inquire at Mamá Espinoza's Restaurant on the bend of the highway.

▶◢ Travelogue

El Rosario to Cataviña
(76 mi., 122 km.; 2 hrs.)

Leaving El Rosario, Highway 1 turns east and follows the wide, cultivated Arroyo del Rosario for a few miles, then crosses the valley and climbs into a region of low, deeply eroded hills. Soon the terrain begins to conform to the armchair traveler's notion of Baja, with cirio trees and giant cardón cacti appearing alongside the highway. With its blue skies, expansive views and abundance of unique vegetation, the Central Desert of Baja California is one of North America's most fascinating desert regions. After continuing southeast through ranges of hills and wide valleys, the highway enters a spectacular landscape of large boulder formations interspersed with dense thickets of cirio, cardón and other varieties of desert vegetation. The landscape will remind some motorists of Joshua Tree National Park in the California desert. In return, this stretch of Highway 1 requires very careful driving. Many sections from El Rosario to south of Cataviña are rough and marred by potholes, which seem to reappear as fast as road crews can fill them in. Moreover, the road crosses several deep arroyos that are subject to flash flooding. In the heart of this "rock-garden" zone are Cataviña and Rancho Santa Inés.

Heading south, El Rosario marks the last Pemex station before Villa Jesús María, a distance of 200 miles. Gasoline is sometimes sold at the Hotel La Pinta in Cataviña or by roadside vendors toting 5-gallon cans and charging steep markups. These supplies are unreliable, however, and motorists should make sure they have enough gas to cross this long stretch.

00.0   El Rosario.

04.8   A bridge carries Highway 1 across Arroyo del Rosario.

08.1   Cirio trees begin to appear, their weird forms reaching skyward in a profusion of shapes. Aside from a small stand in Sonora on the Mexican mainland, these plants

MEXICO HIGHWAY 1 - TIJUANA TO GUERRERO NEGRO

The boulder-strewn desert of central Baja, also known as the "rock garden," is home to the exotic cirio tree (on the left) as well as cardón cacti and other plantlife.

grow nowhere else in the world.

14.5   Junction with a good dirt road leading 39 miles to Punta San Carlos and a network of roads which provide access to several fishing camps.

31.3   Junction with a rough dirt road to Rancho El Cartabón.

38.3   Signed junction with an unpaved road to the adobe ruins of Mission San Fernando Velicatá, founded in 1769 by Father Junípero Serra, who went on to estab-

lish Alta California's chain of missions. Passenger cars can make this trip in dry weather.

39.8   El Progreso, which has a cafe. Once a busy construction camp, El Progreso is now all but abandoned.

46.8   Junction with the road to Santa Catarina and Punta Canoas (see Side Route to Puerto Catarina).

55.2   San Agustín, which consists of an abandoned government-built trailer park and a highway maintenance camp. From behind the camp a sandy road leads to Rancho San Agustín.

57.1   Junction with a good dirt road leading to El Mármol (see Side Route to El Mármol). Near the junction are two cafes.

63.0   Highway 1 now enters a region of impressive, boulder-strewn countryside. The Mexican government has created a park here, and the natural environment is protected by federal law.

74.1   Arroyo de Cataviñacito, a deep arroyo with tall blue fan palms and occasional pools of water. The first elephant trees are seen near here, their short, fat trunks seemingly squatting among the boulders.

76.3   Cataviña (see *Lodging & Restaurants* and *Campgrounds & Trailer Parks*), set in the midst of "rock garden" scenery. A market, two cafes and a mechanic's shop are on the left; on the right is a government-built trailer park and the Hotel La Pinta, which sometimes sells gasoline.

Hikes over beautiful desert landscape may be taken in any direction from the village.

🚗 Side Route

Highway 1 to Punta Canoas and Puerto Catarina
(46 mi., 74 km.; 2:30 hrs.)

This trek, which descends through scenic desert to unspoiled Pacific shores, actually has two destinations. The branch to Punta Canoas is used to measure the mileage and time given above. This is a trip for seasoned, well-prepared adventurers in high-clearance, heavy-duty vehicles; four-wheel drive is desirable. There are no facilities so travelers should carry plenty of

food, water and gasoline, and be prepared to camp out. Sites and experiences include rich displays of ocotillos, cardónes and elephant trees; remote Pacific beaches offer opportunities for clam digging, shell collecting, tidepool exploring and solitude. Surfers occasionally visit, lured more by lack of other surfers than by quality waves.

From its junction with the highway 5.6 miles southeast of Rancho Santa Cecilia (or 29 miles northwest of Cataviña), the road is graded and in good condition for the first seven miles. Although its quality gradually deteriorates, a few sandy stretches present the only obstacles to passenger vehicles as far as Rancho Santa Catarina. This friendly settlement houses

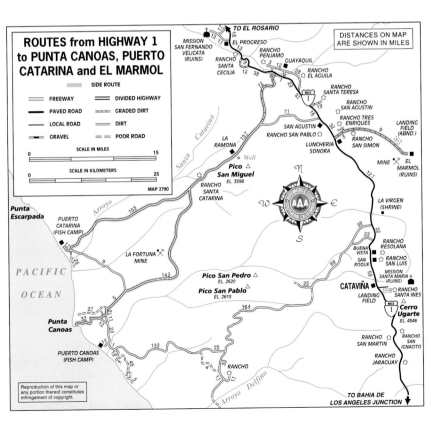

families who raise cattle and a few crops. Fresh water is available for washing and for radiators. After leaving the ranch the road climbs to a plateau. At mileage 20.9 is a junction. To the right, via 16.6 miles of rough road, is Puerto Catarina, once the shipping port for onyx from El Mármol. Bear left for Punta Canoas. The road becomes narrow and rough as it crosses the coastal hills. At mileage 40.2 is another junction; bear left. At mileage 41.9 is a fork. To the right the road leads 3.3 miles to Punta Canoas, site of a seasonally occupied fish camp. Campsites on a shelf high above the rugged coastline are plentiful.

◨◪ Side Route
Highway 1 to El Mármol
(10 mi., 16 km.; 0:30 hr.)

The signed junction with the road to El Mármol is 2.2 miles southeast of San Agustín on Highway 1. The road is smooth, graded and easily passable during dry weather in any type of vehicle. After leaving the main highway, the road runs 0.4 mile to a junction with a remnant of the old peninsular road; on the right is a wooden corral and small gravel quarry. At mileage 0.9 the road passes a windmill and another corral, then veers to the right. After crossing open countryside that is sparsely covered with cacti and brush, the road flanks an abandoned airstrip, then enters El Mármol, 9.6 miles from Highway 1.

El Mármol was once an active onyx-mining concern, but a drop in the demand for onyx caused the camp to be abandoned in 1958. In 1993 limited mining began again. Blocks and chips of onyx lie strewn across the barren landscape alongside the quarry. A walk

through the remains of the camp reveals the ruins of adobe buildings, a schoolhouse made of unpolished onyx, the carcasses of long-abandoned trucks and an interesting cemetery. Caution: several deep, uncovered wells present hazards; use care when walking here.

◤◿ Travelogue
Cataviña to Bahía de los Angeles Junction
(65 mi., 105 km.; 1:30 hrs.)

From Cataviña, the highway continues to lead southeast through interesting rock-strewn country. After crossing a narrow arroyo, the road climbs to a 2700-foot summit, then descends quickly to the edge of a dry lake. Beyond here the landscape becomes more barren as Highway 1 meanders through low hills, ascends a 2200-foot saddle and drops onto the basin of Laguna Chapala. This vast, desolate dry lake becomes a sea of mud following heavy rains. After crossing another range of low barren hills, the highway traverses a sandy plain to the junction with the road to Bahía de los Angeles. This region is a showcase for the typical vegetation of Baja California's central desert: cirio, cardón, cholla cactus, ocotillo, elephant trees and yucca válida.

00.0   Cataviña.
00.7   **Junction with the 0.8-mile paved road to Rancho Santa Inés, which offers a clinic, motel, campground, cafe, a paved airstrip and information for off-road explorers.**
07.4   **Rancho San Ignacito. In late 1973, road crews working north and south met here as they completed the paving of Highway 1. A small monu-**

ment on the west side of the highway marks the spot.

18.6 El Pedregoso, a mountain composed entirely of jumbled boulders. Before the completion of the paved highway, this was an important landmark for peninsula travelers.

33.7 Laguna Chapala Junction. Here a graded dirt road, signed Calamajué, provides access to Bahía San Luis Gonzaga and other points along the northeastern shore of the peninsula. At the junction is a cafe.

34.5 Rancho Chapala. Stretching away to the east is the broad expanse of Laguna Chapala, with its bed of cracked clay.

50.8 Junction with a rough road to Campo Calamajué, a fish camp.

65.3 Junction with the paved road to Bahía de los Angeles (see Side Route to Bahía de Los Angeles). A highway patrol station is located here. The junction is sometimes called Punta Prieta, although the original settlement bearing this name is eight miles to the south.

 Side Route
Highway 1 to Bahía de los Angeles
(42 mi., 68 km.; 1 hr.)

(See also *Campgrounds & Trailer Parks.*)

This scenic seaside town is reached via a rough paved highway, starting at the above-described junction, 8.4 miles north of Punta Prieta. From this point it heads east across a sandy plain where the typical vegetation of Baja California's central desert is particularly abundant; it includes cardón, cholla and garambullo cacti, as well as cirio, ocotillo and yucca válida. Brightly colored wildflowers carpet the floor of the desert in early spring. Barren mountains are on the horizon. After about 10 miles, the road veers slightly to the right, passes through a gap in the mountains, then descends to the edge of a large dry lake. At mileage 28 is the signed junction with a rough dirt road to Mission San Borja; the road to the mission from Rosarito on Highway 1 is better and easier to drive. After a gentle downhill run through a canyon, the highway drops quickly to the shore of the Gulf of California.

With high, barren mountains as a dramatic backdrop to the west and several offshore islands jutting up from the deep blue waters of the gulf, Bahía de los Angeles is one of the beauty

Cataviña provides the only accommodations for many miles in either direction along Mexico Highway 1.

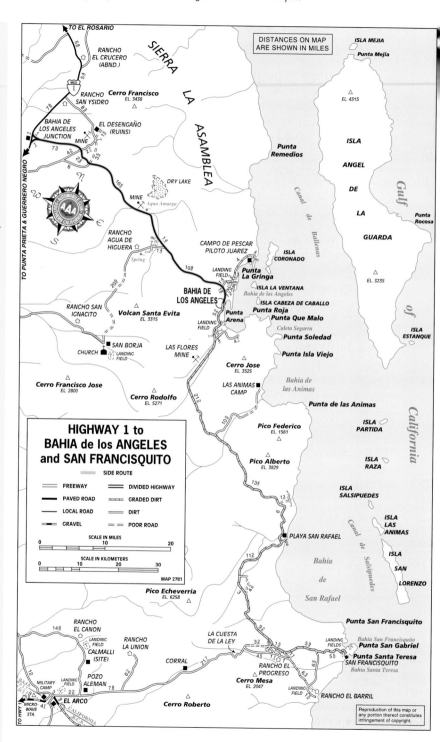

MEXICO HIGHWAY 1 - TIJUANA TO GUERRERO NEGRO

TO PUNTA PRIETA & GUERRERO NEGRO

DISTANCES ON MAP
ARE SHOWN IN MILES

TO EL ROSARIO

RANCHO
EL CRUCERO
(ABND.)

SIERRA LA ASAMBLEA

ISLA MEJIA
Punta Mejia

RANCHO
SAN YSIDRO

Cerro Francisco
EL 3438

BAHIA DE
LOS ANGELES
JUNCTION
MINE

EL DESENGAÑO
(RUINS)

MINE

DRY LAKE

Aqua Amarga

EL 4315

ISLA
ANGEL
DE
LA
GUARDA

Canal de Ballenas

Punta
Remedios

Punta
Rocosa

EL 3235

RANCHO
AGUA DE
HIGUERA

Spring

CAMPO DE PESCAR
PILOTO JUAREZ

LANDING
FIELD

Punta
La Gringa

ISLA
CORONADO

RANCHO SAN
IGNACITO

Volcan Santa Evita
EL 3315

BAHIA DE
LOS ANGELES

LANDING
FIELD

Punta
Arena

ISLA LA VENTANA
Bahia de los Angeles

ISLA CABEZA DE CABALLO
Punta Roja
Punta Que Malo
Caleta Segarra
Punta Soledad

ISLA
ESTANQUE

SAN BORJA
CHURCH
LANDING
FIELD

LAS FLORES
MINE

Cerro Jose
EL 3525

Punta Isla Viejo

Cerro Francisco Jose
EL 2800

Cerro Rodolfo
EL 5271

LAS ANIMAS
CAMP

Bahia de
las Animas

Punta de las Animas

Pico Federico
EL 1561

ISLA
PARTIDA

Pico Alberto
EL 3829

ISLA
RAZA

ISLA
SALSIPUEDES

PLAYA SAN RAFAEL

ISLA
LAS
ANIMAS

ISLA
SAN
LORENZO

Bahia
de
San Rafael

Canal de Salsipuedes

Gulf

of

California

California

HIGHWAY 1 to
BAHIA de los ANGELES
and SAN FRANCISQUITO

SIDE ROUTE

FREEWAY   DIVIDED HIGHWAY
PAVED ROAD   GRADED DIRT
LOCAL ROAD   DIRT
GRAVEL   POOR ROAD

SCALE IN MILES
0   10   20

SCALE IN KILOMETERS
0   10   20   30

MAP 2781

Pico Echeverria
EL 6258

RANCHO
EL CANON

LANDING
FIELD
CALMALLI
(SITE)

RANCHO
LA UNION

LA CUESTA
DE LA LEY

CORRAL

RANCHO EL
PROGRESO

Cerro Mesa
EL 2047

LANDING
FIELDS
Punta San Francisquito
Bahia San Francisquito
Punta San Gabriel
Punta Santa Teresa
SAN FRANCISQUITO
Bahia Santa Teresa

Punta San Francisquito

POZO
ALEMAN

MILITARY
CAMP
LANDING
FIELD

MICRO-
WAVE
STA.

EL ARCO

TO HWY 1

BAJA
CALIFORNIA
SUR

Cerro Roberto

LANDING
FIELD
RANCHO EL BARRIL

Bahía de los Angeles offers some of the most beautiful scenery along the Gulf of California.

spots of Baja California. Known to regular visitors as "L.A. Bay," it is protected by 45-mile-long Isla Angel de la Guarda, which provides a fine sheltered anchorage for boats. Sportfishing is excellent. Fishing trips can be arranged, and there are several launch ramps for private boats. Facilities include a paved airstrip, stores, restaurants, a bakery, three trailer parks, three motels and an inn. In the center of town are a plaza park, town hall, and a museum that displays sea life and artifacts relating to the mining and history of the region. Isla Raza, a reserve for migratory waterfowl, is a bird-watcher's paradise. Dirt roads run both north and south of the town past vacation homes to remote beaches where good campsites can be found. In addition, a graded road winds southeastward from Bahía de los Angeles to remote San Francisquito. Gasoline is sometimes available here, dispensed from 55-gallon drums. Motorists can expect to pay a steep premium, however, and supplies are by no means certain.

Point of Interest

MUSEO DE HISTORIA NATURAL Y CULTURA *West side of plaza park in Bahía de los Angeles. No phone. Open daily 9 a.m.-noon; also 2-4 p.m. except in summer. Donation.* This small museum features excellent displays on sea life in the Gulf of California and Baja California fauna. Indian artifacts are also on display, as is a vintage Auto Club map of Baja California from the pre-Highway 1 days. Books on the region in English and Spanish are sold as well.

🚐 Side Route

Bahía de los Angeles to San Francisquito

(81 mi., 130 km.; 3:45 hrs.)

A journey through scenic desert hills and valleys to a secluded bay on the Gulf of California (Sea of Cortez) is

Two tourists greet the day under a **palapa** *at Bahía de los Angeles.*

graded all the way. Because it is isolated, a motorist can travel great distances without seeing another automobile, so a fully equipped, sturdy high-clearance vehicle is a must. The road travels inland most of the way due to the rugged coastline. Numerous subtropical desert plants grow along this route, especially cardón, elephant tree, ocotillo, cholla and sagebrush.

In the southern part of the village of Bahía de los Angeles the road turns right, then soon bears left. For several miles the bayshore, lined with houses and a trailer camp, is visible. Heading south between two mountain ranges, the road later climbs through hills. At 27 miles a side road goes north to Las Animas Camp, used by fishermen. Follow the large sign that points southeast toward Punta San Francisquito. The road now climbs through hills, then drops almost to Bahía San Rafael. Visible in the gulf are several small islands,

and in the distance is the large Isla Tiburón. The road once more heads inland, climbs a steep grade, then gradually descends in an easterly direction toward the coast. At 68 miles is a junction; to the right is a road to El Arco. Turn left and drive 13 miles to San Francisquito. On the way two roads branch southeast to El Barril, a large cattle ranch that includes many Mexican ranchers and several American vacation homes. Keep left at each junction; the direction to the coast is mostly northeast.

On Bahía Santa Teresa, a small, attractive bay with a long sandy beach, is the rustic fishing resort named Punta San Francisquito. It has cabañas, a restaurant and bar, electricity during the evening hours, fishing boats and an airstrip. Most guests arrive by airplane. About a mile north of the resort, on Bahía San Francisquito, is a beautiful cove sheltered by rugged headlands. Here is found a fish camp with a mechanic's shop. Camping is permitted for a small fee, and fishing is good.

◤◢ Travelogue

Bahía de los Angeles Junction to Guerrero Negro
(80 mi., 129 km.; 1:45 hrs.)

For the first 15 miles after leaving the Bahía de los Angeles junction, Highway 1 continues to cross a level, sandy plain. It then climbs into hilly country sparsely vegetated with cirio and elephant trees. Extra caution is required in this section, which is characterized by steep dropoffs, sharp curves and a narrow roadway. Near Rosarito, several flat-topped buttes dot the horizon to the east. Turning almost due south, the highway descends gradually onto the windy Vizcaíno Desert, one of the most desolate portions of the entire peninsula. Only hearty yucca válida and scattered clumps of saltbrush interrupt the uniformity of the sandy landscape.

00.0 Junction to Bahía de los Angeles.

08.4 Junction with the short paved road to the village of Punta Prieta. A bustling construction camp during the paving of Highway 1, Punta Prieta is now a sleepy little hamlet. Facilities include a store, a cafe, a small military camp and a highway maintenance station. On the east side of the highway is a paved airstrip.

18.3 Brief view of the Pacific Ocean from a low summit.

24.0 Junction with a gravel road to Santa Rosalillita (see Side Route to Santa Rosalillita).

32.3 Rosarito, a village with a store, a cafe and a shrine. Rosarito also marks the junc-

tion with the dirt road to Mission San Borja (see Side Route to Mission San Borja).

39.2 Junction with a dirt road leading north along isolated beaches for 18 miles to Santa Rosalillita. This area is popular with surfers.

42.7 Junction with a rough dirt road to El Tomatal.

49.4 Turnoff to Rancho San Angel.

59.0 Villa Jesús María, a farming village with a Pemex station, two cafes and a small store. A paved road leads west to Ejido Morelos, a government-sponsored cattle-raising project, and Laguna Manuela, a lagoon with a fish camp and a sandy beach.

78.4 The 28th parallel separates the states of Baja California and Baja California Sur. Erected on the latitude line is a 140-foot-high steel monument in the form of a stylized eagle, commemorating completion of Highway 1 and the uniting of northern and southern Baja California—a major milestone in the peninsula's history. On the west side of the monument are Hotel La Pinta and a trailer park. The 28th parallel also marks the boundary of the Pacific and Mountain time zones.

80.3 Junction with the paved road to the town of Guerrero Negro, two miles to the west.

◰ Side Route

Highway 1 to Santa Rosalillita
(10 mi., 16 km.; 1 hr.)

A wide gravel road, negotiable in a passenger vehicle, now leads to the Pacific coast and the settlement of Santa Ros-

Pacific Lagoons: Givers of Life for The

By David J. Brackney

Scattered squall lines maraud across the horizon and a hint of a rainbow spans the western sky as a late February day breaks over Scammon's Lagoon. A flotilla of small motor launches bounce their way across the choppy green waters as the coastal sand dunes fade astern. Although more than 400 miles south of San Diego, the wind carries a skin-piercing chill as the boats' occupants don bright yellow rain gear and huddle for warmth. Spirits run high nonetheless as they eagerly scan the waters ahead.

The search is on for the California gray whale, thousands of which descend upon this and other lagoons of Baja California Sur each winter. From Estero de San José at the 28th parallel southward to Bahía Magdalena near Ciudad Constitución, these Pacific coast inlets mark the journey's end for the whales' annual southern migration. Traveling non-stop from the icy waters off Siberia and Alaska, the gray whales begin arriving in late December and reach their peak numbers in January and February. By early April the final stragglers are headed north again.

The whales' cycle of life begins in these lagoons as adults enter courtship and mate, while pregnant cows bear their young after a 13-month gestation period. Sharp-eyed visitors by land and sea will likely see numerous pairs of mothers and newborn calves swimming together before commencing their long trek north.

It's hard to believe that these same waters became massive killing fields twice within 50 years as whalers reduced the grays to near extinction. The carnage began in the late 1850s after the discovery of the breeding grounds by Charles Scammon (for whom the lagoon was named), captain of the U.S. whaling ship *Boston*. Word of the grounds soon spread and the killing peaked during the 1860s; by 1880 the whales were so depleted in number that it was no longer cost-effective to hunt them.

Enough of the whales did survive and reproduce that they eventually rebounded, only to face a new wave of hunting. It began in 1914 when the first Norwegian factory ship appeared off Bahía Magdalena, joined thereafter by vessels from Soviet, Japanese and American interests. This second round of killing peaked in the 1920s, driving the whales once more toward demise.

Not until 1946 did international laws provide full protection for the gray whales, though by then few of the species remained. Even so, the whales have come back impressively in the ensuing decades, and today some 21,000 ply the eastern Pacific waters—close to their original numbers. Limited whaling is allowed to continue off eastern Siberia, intended to feed the region's Eskimo population.

Meanwhile, the whales have once again become a big business, not for their blubber and flesh, but for tourism in towns like Guerrero Negro, San Ignacio and other staging

Gray Whale

Thar she blows! Visitors greet a pair of friendly gray whales.

points for whale-watching expeditions. Each year these communities host thousands of visitors as they embark on outings to the nearby lagoons. Scammon's Lagoon near Guerrero Negro is the whales' number one destination, with more than half of all calves born there, although Laguna San Ignacio attracts the most whale-watchers.

As the gray whales have rebounded, they have extended their range as well, appearing regularly off Cabo San Lucas, with sightings in the Gulf of California as far north as Bahía de los Angeles. Evidence of their comeback is most dramatic during the peak breeding months in the Pacific lagoons. On a fortuitous cruise, lucky observers may spot dozens of whales—surfacing to exhale, hoisting their tales for a dive, performing "spyhops" as they crane their heads above the surface, or breaching clear from the water and crashing back with a thunderous splash.

Time has apparently helped heal any lingering fears or animosity toward humans. Mexican law prohibits vessels from approaching within 100 meters of whales, but in the lagoons the gentle giants will often take the initiative and swim to within a few feet of a boat. On occasion mothers and calves will surface right along side a craft to enjoy a few friendly pats on the head, sending a wave of primal laughter and cheers—and even a few tears—over their one-time predators.

alillita. Leaving the highway 15.6 miles south of Punta Prieta, the new road follows the shoulder of a wide arroyo, above the old road in the sandy wash below. At mileage 8.2 is a junction with a gravel road leading north that connects with the rugged road following the Pacific coast. The road crosses a dirt airstrip at mileage 8.4 and then loops down onto the beach and into Santa Rosalillita, 9.9 miles from Highway 1. Here a government-assisted fishing cooperative harvests abalone and other varieties of shellfish. There are no tourist facilities, but the nearby beaches offer excellent opportunities for shell collecting.

An alternate return route, which is not suitable for standard automobiles, leads south from Santa Rosalillita to several beautiful, isolated beaches. For 15 miles the road meanders along the coastline past beaches covered with small, smooth stones, volcanic rocks and pearly white turban shells. Surfing is good near the rocky points. At Playa Altamira, a good open camping spot, the road turns inland and runs about three miles to meet Highway 1 at a point 6.5 miles south of Rosarito.

🚙 Side Route

Rosarito to Mission San Borja
(22 mi., 35 km.; 2 hrs.)

This, the best route to Mission San Borja, is totally unsuited to travel in a passenger car. There are no steep grades, but the single-track road has a high crown and numerous rough and rocky spots, calling for a sturdy high-clearance vehicle. For those with the proper equipment the trip to this magnificent mission is well worth the time and effort. The road to San Borja begins in Rosarito, a village in the southern part of the state of Baja California.

Rosarito has a store and a cafe, and it should not be confused with the booming tourist town of Rosarito in the

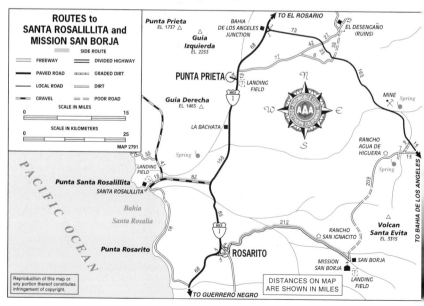

northern part of the state. The route bears right just past a small weather station and leads northeast through open desert past several flat-topped buttes. At mileage 13.6 is a junction; bear left. About two miles beyond the junction is Rancho San Ignacito, a large cattle ranch with a stone-walled corral and a deep well. Beyond the ranch the road makes a rough climb out of a small arroyo, then descends gradually to Mission San Borja, located in a broad valley at the base of high barren mountains.

A visit to remote Mission San Borja, above and below, is a worthwhile trek for the properly equipped explorer.

Mission San Francisco de Borja was founded by the Jesuits in 1759, shortly before the order's expulsion from the New World. The stone church at San Borja was completed by the Dominicans in 1801. At one time the mission served more than 3000 Indians, but the diseases of the white man decimated the native population and the mission was abandoned in 1818. The mission is largely intact and has been restored by the Mexican government. Behind the church are several adobe ruins, including the remains of an irrigation system built by the mission friars. A few families live and farm nearby.

Another road leads north from the mission for 23 miles to a junction with the paved road connecting Highway 1 with Bahía de los Angeles. This road is even rougher than the one described previously; it is steep and narrow, with numerous rocky arroyo crossings.

Mexico Highway 1 —
Guerrero Negro to Cabo San Lucas

For motorists arriving from the north, the 28th parallel marks the gateway to Baja California Sur, but well over half the length of Mexico Highway 1 is still ahead. It's 444 miles from Tijuana to Guerrero Negro, but another 615 remain to the pavement's end in Cabo San Lucas.

Set amid a featureless coastal plain, Guerrero Negro enjoys a stark beauty in its own right, yet belies the wonders that lie ahead— lush palm oases, rugged desert peaks and some of the most spectacular coastline on the continent.

Small towns, trailer parks and beach resorts break up the drive, as do the capital city La Paz and the bustling Los Cabos corridor. By and large, though, beyond the highway shoulders the land remains untamed in this, the least populated state in the Mexican Republic.

Guerrero Negro

(See also *Lodging & Restaurants* and *Campgrounds & Trailer Parks*.)

Located in the midst of the vast Vizcaíno Desert, this hospitable community of about 11,000 has two chief claims to fame. For one, it is the world's largest producer of salt, according to the firm Exportadora de Sal, the town's chief employer. South of town are thousands of evaporating ponds, each about 100 yards square and from three to four feet deep when flooded with sea water. The desert sun evapo-

rates the water quickly, leaving a residue of pure white, hard salt, which is scooped up by dredges and taken by trucks to a nearby wharf. Once dried out, the salt is loaded by conveyor belt onto barges and carried to Cedros Island, where it is transferred into ocean-going freighters. Salt from Guerrero Negro is used in Mexico, the United States and other nations of the Pacific Rim. The spectacle of these vast salt fields—backed by low-slung sand dunes with a few windblown shrubs— conjures up images of frozen tundra of some far-off polar wasteland.

In addition, Guerrero Negro sits at the edge of Scammon's Lagoon (Laguna Ojo de Liebre), the largest breeding ground for the California gray whale. The lagoon, and others like it on the Pacific coast of Baja, is the journey's end for the whales on their annual migration south from the waters off Alaska. The fabled mammals were coming here long before the salt operation arrived, but only in recent years have they gained the outside world's notice on a large scale. Hunted to near-extinction in the 19th century, the whales have recovered strongly and attracted a growing following of human visitors to

This huge steel monument in the shape of a stylized eagle straddles the 28th parallel, dividing the states of Baja California and Baja California Sur.

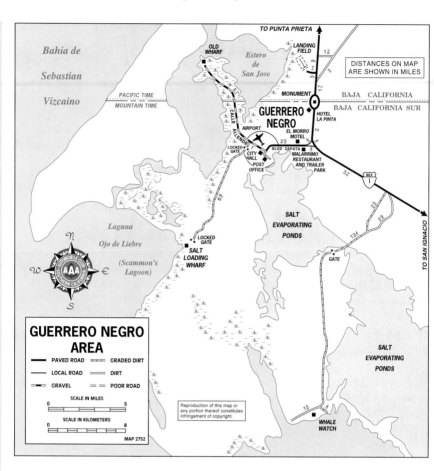

the area. In turn they have helped create a thriving seasonal tourism industry. (See Fauna in *Introduction*).

During most of the year, Guerrero Negro offers little in the way of recreation, although good surf fishing can be found along the remote beaches to the north. The arrival of the whales changes that, however, and from late December through the end of March the town bustles from the influx of outsiders. Several tour companies shuttle visitors from the town to the lagoon, where they board rafts and small motor launches to view (and sometimes touch) the gentle giants.

Hotels fill to capacity during this period and reservations are sometimes necessary weeks in advance.

Gray whales are now protected by the Mexican and American governments, and only authorized tour boats are allowed in the lagoon while the whales are present. Good spots from which to see the whales from land are the old salt wharf, located seven miles west of Guerrero Negro via a dirt road, and the shore of Scammon's Lagoon, which has been designated a natural park by the Mexican government (see Side Route to Scammon's Lagoon).

The name "Guerrero Negro" is the Spanish translation of *Black Warrior*, an American whaling ship that was wrecked at the entrance to the lagoon in the late 19th century. Though not a large town, Guerrero Negro offers a wide variety of services and facilities. There are several motels and trailer parks, restaurants, stores, two Pemex stations, several auto parts houses, mechanics, markets, a hospital, banks and an airport.

Most of the tourist services and facilities can be found in the eastern part of town, which drivers first enter off of Highway 1. Farther west is the company town, where Exportadora de Sal has its headquarters and where most of the workers live. Row upon row of tidy homes with fresh white paint and crisply manicured lawns comprise most of this district. The streets are paved, clean and pothole-free, in sharp contrast with much of the rest of town.

Isla Cedros

Isla Cedros is a barren, rugged island situated about 55 miles west of the Guerrero Negro coastal area. Its inhabitants are supported mostly by a fish-packing plant. It also plays the role of transshipment point for the salt mined at Guerrero Negro, which has no deep water harbor. Ocean-going ships load the salt for export at the port of Cedros (also called El Pueblo), where most of the population of about 6000 live.

Virtually untouched by tourism, Cedros has the character of a typical older Mexican coastal town. Facilities include restaurants, a bank, church, taxis and a couple of inexpensive inns. Visitors are able to find beaches, hire fishing boats and hike over trails to observe the unspoiled natural environment of most of the island. Cedros is

accessible by a local airline, with flights leaving from both Ensenada and Guerrero Negro a couple of times a week.

▶⃫ Travelogue
Guerrero Negro to San Ignacio
(89 mi., 142 km.; 1:45 hrs.)

From the junction to Guerrero Negro, Highway 1 turns inland, heading southeast across the barren Vizcaíno Desert. Near the town of Vizcaíno, however, yucca válida, cardón cacti and dense thickets of low shrubs begin to appear alongside the highway. About 20 miles from San Ignacio, the road passes a group of flat-topped volcanic cones; the dark reddish-brown rocks in this region give further evidence of past volcanic activity. Finally, after winding through low, cactus-covered hills, the highway brings the traveler to the junction with the paved road to San Ignacio. Much of this section of Highway 1 is rough or narrow; drive with care.

00.0   Junction to Guerrero Negro.
05.6   Junction with the graded road to the shore of Scammon's Lagoon, signed Laguna Ojo de Liebre (see Side Route to Scammon's Lagoon).
17.1   Junction with the gravel highway to El Arco (see Side Route to El Arco).
45.4   Vizcaíno (sometimes called Fundolegal), with about 2400 inhabitants, has a Pemex station, three motels, an RV park, cafes, a market, a pharmacy and auto parts. A paved side road leads five miles to Ejido Díaz Ordaz (sometimes called Vizcaíno). This *ejido* is a major government-assisted farming cooperative. Water from deep wells has turned a

Trekking across the frozen north? It only appears that way, driving over one of the vast beds of dried salt along the road to Laguna Ojo de Liebre.

section of forbidding desert into productive fields and orchards; principal crops include spices, strawberries, tomatoes, figs, grapes and oranges. The *ejido* has a clinic, a market and a variety of small stores. Pavement on the side road ends after 16 more miles. From this point, the road is graded earth and leads onto the remote Vizcaíno Peninsula (see Side Route Loop Trip From Highway 1 Around the Vizcaíno Peninsula); this side trip is only for adventurous, well-prepared travelers with the proper vehicles and equipment.

52.4 A paved road leads to Ejido Emiliano Zapata, a large dairy-farming *ejido* or collective agricultural settlement.

57.4 Estación Microóndas Los Angeles, the first of 23 microwave relay stations along Highway 1 in Baja California Sur. The stations are closed to the public.

61.3 Junction with graded dirt road to San Francisco de la Sierra (see Side Route to San Francisco de la Sierra).

73.6 Junction with a graded dirt road to Punta Abreojos (see Side Route to Punta Abreojos). A cafe is located at the junction.

85.8 Junction with a 0.6-mile paved road to a good paved airstrip.

88.6 Junction with the 0.9-mile paved road to San Lino and Paredones, two villages on the outskirts of San Ignacio.

88.9 Junction with the 1.1-mile-long paved road to San Igna-

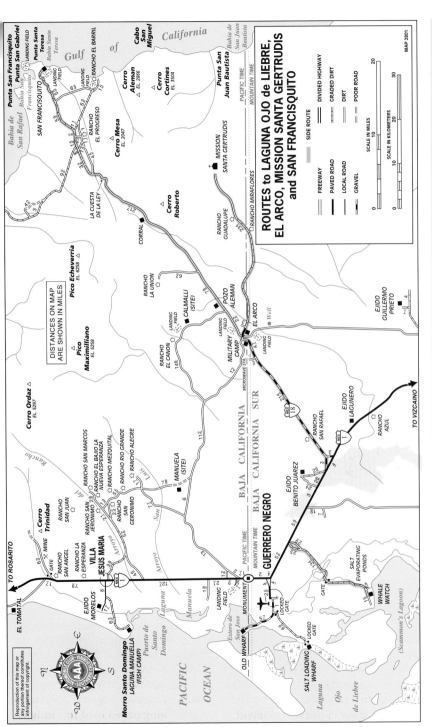

ROUTES to LAGUNA OJO de LIEBRE, EL ARCO, MISSION SANTA GERTRUDIS and SAN FRANCISQUITO

MEXICO HIGHWAY 1 - GUERRERO NEGRO TO CABO SAN LUCAS

cio. Opposite the junction is a Pemex station.

🚐 Side Route

Highway 1 to Scammon's Lagoon (Laguna Ojo de Liebre)
(15 mi., 24 km.; 0:45 hr.)

From late December through March this side trip offers travelers an opportunity to see California gray whales, which make a 6000-mile annual migration from the Bering Sea to bear their young in the shallow waters of Scammon's Lagoon. This route also reveals a wealth of bird life, such as cormorants, herons and pelicans. The second part of the route, about nine miles through salt company property, is open to the public from late December through the end of March. (Exact dates vary from year to year.) The dirt road to the southeastern arm of the lagoon branches off Highway 1 at a point 5.6 miles south of the turnoff to Guerrero Negro; the junction bears the signs "Laguna Ojo de Liebre" and "Parque Natural de la Ballena Gris/Gray Whale Natural Park." While it is wide and graded its entire length, the road is at times sandy for the first couple of miles. During dry weather, however, a passenger car can make the trip if it is driven at a slow, even pace. After leaving Highway 1 the road passes several junctions, at some of which are signs with a picture of a whale and an arrow pointing the way. The side roads in this area belong to Guerrero Negro's salt company and are closed to public use. A salt company checkpoint is 3.9 miles west; after this the road to Scammon's Lagoon crosses a levee between two evaporating ponds, where large salt dredges can occasionally be seen at work harvesting the salt. After another 10 miles the road comes to a small shack, which bears the sign "Parque

Natural de la Ballena Gris/Gray Whale Natural Park." Sometimes admission of about $3 is collected. Just beyond the shack is a fork; the road to the left leads to the best beach from which to observe the massive marine mammals. Binoculars help, since the whales are usually some distance offshore. Tours in small boats are available during whale season for about $20 per trip. Bird-watching tours are also available here. Overnight camping is permitted here, although no facilities have been installed.

🚐 Side Route

Highway 1 to El Arco
(26 mi., 43 km.; 1 hr.)

The road to El Arco, designated Mexico Highway 18, leaves Highway 1 at a well-signed junction located 17.1 miles southeast of Guerrero Negro. The highway is elevated, with a surface of gravel and broken pavement. There are no meals or lodging on this route nor those that follow it out of El Arco. Leading northeast from the junction the road runs through flat, barren terrain until mileage 6.6, when dense desert vegetation suddenly appears; cardónes, yucca válidas, elephant trees, cholla cacti and several brushy shrubs all grow in this "living desert." After continuing gently uphill for several miles, the road rounds a small range of steep, barren hills, then drops into El Arco.

El Arco is a small, scattered settlement situated about a mile north of the 28th parallel—the imaginary line dividing the states of Baja California and Baja California Sur. El Arco began as a gold-mining camp, and for many years was a way-stop on old Highway 1. Now it is a peaceful if worn-looking community that serves as a center for the surrounding ranches. Within the village are a military camp, gasoline pumped from drums, and a church. A little copper mining is done in the vicinity. A landing field is located just south of town. From El Arco, dirt roads lead to numerous points of interest.

Side Route

El Arco to Mission Santa Gertrudis
(23 mi., 37 km.; 1:30 hrs.)

Although this road is wide and graded for the first 17 miles and is in reasonably good condition for its entire length, an ordinary passenger car could have trouble clearing the high center crown and several rough spots. For the properly equipped explorer, however, this is a worthwhile side trip. The road to the mission begins where the paved road through El Arco makes a hard right turn and the pavement ends. Just beyond is a metal sign that at one time indicated the direction to the mission; veer right at this point. From El Arco the road traverses barren desert, passes two large cattle ranches, then meanders through an arroyo to Mission Santa Gertrudis.

Located in a narrow canyon, Mission Santa Gertrudis was founded by the Jesuits in 1752 and was an important supply center during the mission era. After the Jesuits were expelled from Baja California in 1768, the Dominicans arrived here and built the small stone church in 1796. Almost from the beginning, Santa Gertrudis was plagued by insufficient fresh water, and the local Indian population suffered greatly from diseases; the mission was finally abandoned in 1822. In addition to the chapel, which is still in

use, the site contains several other stone ruins, including the remains of an irrigation system dating from the 18th century and a restored adobe belfry. A few ranchers now occupy the area.

Side Route

El Arco to San Francisquito
(48 mi., 77 km.; 2:30 hrs.)

The road to Bahía San Francisquito is generally good by off-road standards and is suitable for high-clearance vehicles. Until recently, however, four-wheel drive was necessary to make the trip because of the infamous grade known as La Cuesta de la Ley. This harrowing plunge, which dropped 400 feet in only 0.4 mile, has been regraded to accommodate most high-clearance vehicles. To locate the route, proceed northeast at the junction by the town hall in El Arco. After 2.3 miles, during which the road negotiates a steep narrow arroyo, the route passes through Pozo Alemán, which many years ago was an important gold-mining center but now looks like a ghost town. Beyond Pozo Alemán, the road traverses a flat plain, then enters a region of rocky arroyos dotted with huge cardón cacti. At mileage 7.9 a road leads left to Rancho La Unión; bear right. The road to the gulf now runs through a series of steep-sided valleys, then ascends a plateau. At mileage 29 La Cuesta de la Ley begins its descent. A major fork is located at mileage 34.9; to the right is Rancho El Barril, a privately owned cattle ranch, while the left branch leads to San Francisquito.

Punta San Francisquito is a rustic fishing resort located on Bahía Santa Teresa (San Francisquito). For details about this community, see Side Route to San Francisquito.

🚐 Side Route
Loop Trip From Highway 1 Around the Vizcaíno Peninsula

Because of the great distances involved and the remote nature of the territory, this trip is unique among Baja California's side routes. The trek onto the Vizcaíno Peninsula should be attempted only by serious off-road adventurers who are equipped to handle the worst that Baja California has to offer—isolation, poor roads, scarcity of fresh water, lack of facilities, frequent dust storms, desert heat and heavy coastal fog.

For the most part, the main routes are well signed, periodically maintained and fairly good by Baja California off-pavement standards. The main highway from Vizcaíno to Bahía Tortugas via Rancho San José de Castro may be traveled by well-supplied, light front-wheel-drive vehicles, but a sturdy high-clearance vehicle is recommended. The other roads on the peninsula contain bad spots that can trap or damage a passenger car or low-clearance vehicle. It is advisable to use the "buddy" system, with a caravan of two or more vehicles traveling together. Plenty of extra water, food and gasoline should be carried, and equipment should be checked against the Suggested Supply Lists in the *Appendix*.

For those prepared for the rigors of this journey, the sheer isolation of this huge, hook-shaped peninsula is the primary attraction. Most of the Vizcaíno Peninsula has seen relatively little human intrusion. The desert scenery, though barren, is unusual and striking. Along the coast are attractive bays and coves, rugged headlands and

miles of wide, beautiful beaches. Fishing and beachcombing are excellent.

The peninsula is not devoid of habitation. There are four fair-sized cannery towns, along with numerous small ranches and fish camps. But none of these settlements is prepared to cater to tourists, although the inhabitants are friendly and helpful. Meals, refreshments and limited supplies can be purchased in Punta Abreojos, La Bocana, Bahía Asunción and Bahía Tortugas. Gasoline, sometimes siphoned from drums, is relatively expensive here. Overnight accommodations, where they exist, are extremely modest, but fine primitive campsites can be found throughout the peninsula (wood, however, is scarce).

From Highway 1, the traveler can enter the Vizcaíno Peninsula at Vizcaíno Junction (44.8 miles southeast of the Guerrero Negro turnoff) or at an unsigned junction 15 miles west of San Ignacio. The following route descriptions are organized as a loop beginning at Vizcaíno (Fundolegal); each segment of the loop is outlined in a separate subsection. Most of the mileages, driving times and route descriptions are based on an expedition made by an Auto Club research team; readers should keep in mind that conditions can change.

🚐 Side Route
Vizcaíno to Rancho San José de Castro
(72 mi., 116 km.; 5 hrs.)

This route onto the Vizcaíno Peninsula has a raised surface most of the way. It is a durable graded route, but is rather rough. Signs appear at most important junctions. Rancho San José de Castro is used here as a convenient route divid-

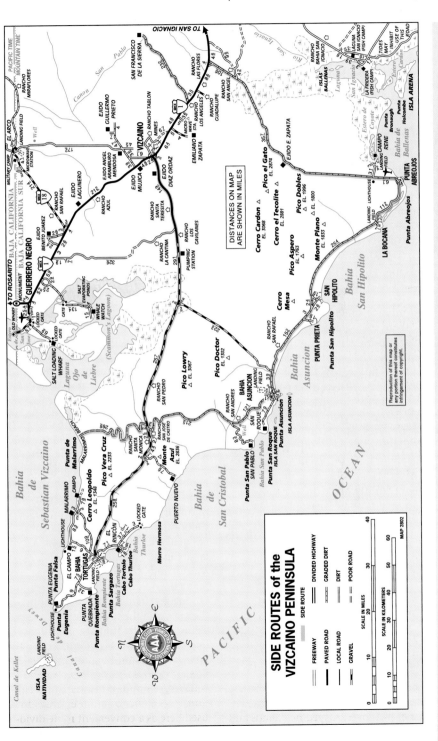

MEXICO HIGHWAY 1 - GUERRERO NEGRO TO CABO SAN LUCAS

SIDE ROUTES of the
VIZCAINO PENINSULA

═══	FREEWAY
━━━	PAVED ROAD
━━	LOCAL ROAD
═ ═	GRAVEL
━━━	DIVIDED HIGHWAY
╍╍╍	GRADED DIRT
═ ═	DIRT
╌ ╌	POOR ROAD
━━	SIDE ROUTE

DISTANCES ON MAP
ARE SHOWN IN MILES

Reproduction of this map or
any portion thereof constitutes
infringement of copyright.

MAP 2802

SCALE IN MILES
0   10   20   30   40

SCALE IN KILOMETERS
0   10   20   30   40   50   60

ing point. The highway continues westward to Bahía Tortugas and is the lifeline between Highway 1 and that port. (The Bahía Tortugas description follows.) After Vizcaíno there is no fuel available until Bahía Tortugas, 103 miles away; Ejido Díaz Ordaz is the last chance for food or supplies of any kind.

Begin by taking the Vizcaíno turnoff from Highway 1 and following the paved road past the irrigated fields, orchards and vineyards of Ejido Díaz Ordaz. The pavement ends after 20 miles, and the graded road continues west across scrub-covered desert. After passing a group of small ranches the road goes through an area of salt flats.

At mileage 44.9 is a junction (signed) with another graded dirt road that heads southwest to join the coastal road 6.4 miles south of Bahía Asunción. At mileage 39.4 a dirt road, which belongs to the salt company and is frequently closed, leads northeast to Scammon's Lagoon and Guerrero Negro. West of this junction the new road begins to climb into low foothills. Elephant trees and cacti grow here, and the bay is occasionally visible to the right. Shortly, the road ascends into mountains, sometimes slicing abruptly through ridges, other times following natural gaps in the hills.

At mileage 70.6, the road reaches the hard-to-find Malarrimo Beach turnoff; it is on the right-hand side about .5 mile east of the San José de Castro sign. After another .5 mile, a dirt road on the left leads 1.3 miles south to Rancho San José de Castro, and connects to the older dirt road leading south to Bahía Asunción.

Rancho San José de Castro, a cattle ranch with a large spring, is also a resi-

dence for magnesite miners. There are no facilities for tourists, but cold drinks are sold and the friendly ranchers provide information and directions.

Side Route
Rancho San José de Castro to Bahía Tortugas
(31 mi., 50 km.; 2 hrs.)

West of the junction of the road to San José de Castro, the new road—bumpy in places—passes Rancho San Miguel, where cold refreshments are sold. At mileage 6.8 a dirt road veers off to the left 8.2 miles to Puerto Nuevo, a small fishing village.

At this point the new road heads through the mountains, sometimes cutting through them, other times following ridge contours. The scenery is fairly desolate on this stretch. At mileage 31.3 the new road drops out of the mountains and enters Bahía Tortugas.

With a population of more than 3000, Bahía Tortugas is the metropolis of the Vizcaíno Peninsula. The town, with its rows of pastel-colored dwellings, sits beneath barren hills on the north side of an almost circular bay, which is one of the finest natural harbors on Baja California's Pacific coast. Bahía Tortugas makes its living from the sea. A large cannery processes abalone, shrimp and other marine products, many of which are trucked or flown to Ensenada. There is no fresh water in the area, and the town's supply must be brought in by ship or truck, or distilled from sea water in a small de-salinization plant. Facilities include numerous stores and cafes, telegraph and radio communications, a medical center, an attractive church, rustic accommodations, a paved airstrip and a gasoline station. Prices are relatively high as all supplies must be hauled in over long distances. The town has an orderly, progressive appearance and is a welcome stop for travelers. From Bahía Tortugas a dirt road runs 16.5 miles to Punta Eugenia at the western tip of the Vizcaíno Peninsula.

Side Route
Rancho San José de Castro to Malarrimo Beach
(27 mi., 44 km.; 2:30 hrs.)

The rough road to Malarrimo Beach takes off northward from the Vizcaíno Junction-Bahía Tortugas route, about .5 mile east of the Rancho San José de Castro sign. After winding through narrow steep-walled arroyos for several miles, it climbs onto barren but colorful mesas, then makes a steep rugged descent into a wide canyon, which it follows to the shore of the Pacific Ocean. This road is subject to periodic closures because of rock slides, washouts and other hazards.

Because of its position on the north-facing side of the Vizcaíno Peninsula, Malarrimo Beach is struck head-on by the prevailing currents of the North Pacific. As a result, it has been the dumping place for flotsam and jetsam from thousands of miles away, including giant redwood logs, World War II food tins, Japanese fishing floats, timbers from sunken vessels and trash thrown overboard from ships. Stories of cases of Scotch and other valuable items being found here are probably true, but Malarrimo has been pretty thoroughly picked over. Still, the careful beachcomber can make some interesting discoveries. The beach itself is very windy, and the best campsites are just inland near the mouth of the

canyon. Driftwood for fires is abundant. Motorists should be cautious of quicksand in some areas along the beach.

Side Route
Rancho San José de Castro to Bahía Asunción
(35 mi., 56 km.; 1:45 hrs.)

The graded road to Bahía Asunción branches south from the Vizcaíno Junction-Bahía Tortugas route .5 mile west of the Malarrimo Beach turnoff; follow the signed road to the left 1.3 miles to San José de Castro, bear left, go 4.3 miles, then turn right (south) onto the dirt road to Bahía Asunción. The road climbs into a range of dark brown mountains, vegetated with cholla, pitahaya and garambullo cacti, along with agave, spiny shrubs and elephant trees. After crossing a saddle, the road descends onto a wide, sloping plain; the ocean is visible in the distance to the west. The road enters a shallow arroyo and follows the sandy bottom for 1.5 miles, then winds upward to a gap between a flat-topped volcanic butte and a range of barren hills. Later the road traverses low, chalk-colored hills, then runs southeast along the base of a volcanic mesa. It rounds the south end of the mesa and emerges onto a sparsely vegetated coastal plain. After dropping into a sandy arroyo, the road turns south and reaches Bahía Asunción at mileage 37.5.

Bahía Asunción is a windblown town of 1500 situated on a low peninsula opposite rocky Isla Asunción. Like Bahía Tortugas, Bahía Asunción is supported by the abalone and lobster trade and has a cannery that ships its products by truck to Ensenada and other towns. Facilities include rustic accommodations, gasoline, cafes, a pharmacy, small stores, a health center, a tiny movie theater, telephone and radio communications, a military camp and an airstrip. A graded road leaves town from behind the health center and runs 7.9 miles northwest along the coast to San Roque, a fishing village.

Side Route
Bahía Asunción to Punta Abreojos
(59 mi., 93 km.; 2 hrs.)

This is one of the easier legs of the loop trip around the Vizcaíno Peninsula. Although the road has a few sandy stretches, there are no steep grades and the surface is regularly graded. After leaving Bahía Asunción, the road parallels the curve of the shoreline along the edge of an arid coastal lowland, running about .5 mile inland from the beach most of the way. Several dirt roads provide access to the shore, which is littered with a variety of shells. Primitive campsites can be found all along the beach, but the wind is constant and wood is scarce. Shore fishing is excellent. At mileage 3.9 is a junction with the graded road that leads north to the Vizcaíno Junction-Rancho San José de Castro road. Eighteen miles from Bahía Asunción the road passes a small shrine, then reaches the junction with a dirt road to Punta Prieta, a fishing village. At mileage 21.7, a road branches right to San Hipólito, another fishing village.

To the north is Cerro Mesa, with its unusual magenta and green rock strata. The road continues to follow the coastline to La Bocana, reached by a turnoff at mileage 47.7. This cannery town of

800 has stores, cafes, a clinic, gasoline and mechanical assistance. Beyond La Bocana the road veers inland and skirts a shallow inlet. The surface from here to Punta Abreojos is smooth hard-packed dirt, which permits speeds of up to 50 mph and is a natural airstrip. South of La Bocana, at mileage 10.9, the road enters Punta Abreojos.

Punta Abreojos has another fishing cooperative with a cannery that sends abalone and lobster to the markets of the north. It sits on a sandy spit between the ocean and a salt marsh. Facilities in this village of 700 include a store, a cafe, gasoline drums, a telegraph office, radio communications and two lighthouses. Just north of Punta Abreojos is an airstrip.

Side Route
Punta Abreojos to Highway 1
(53 mi., 85 km.; 2 hrs.)

This is a long drive over barren, empty land on a wide, graded road. A carefully driven passenger car can make the trip without difficulty, but because some of the road has a jarring washboard surface, travel can be uncomfortable. Leaving Punta Abreojos, the route passes an airstrip, then swings north across level, barren desert. At mileage 6.1 is a signed junction with a road leading 3.1 miles to Campo René, where rustic cabañas and windy campsites can be found on the beach. After skirting the southern flank of flat-topped Cabo Santa Clara Mesa, the road bears northeast across rolling, cactus-covered terrain. Visible to the west is a group of volcanic peaks rising from the desert. Approaching Highway 1 the road enters a "forest" of cardón cacti. To the south, some distance away, Laguna San Ignacio is visible. Highway

1 is reached at mileage 53, 15 miles west of San Ignacio.

🚐 Side Route
Highway 1 to
San Francisco de la Sierra
(23 mi., 37 km.; 1:30 hrs.)

High mesas and deep canyons, a settlement inhabited by traditional ranchers, and trails that lead to Indian cave paintings are features of this isolated route. The road, partly graded with some rough sections, is suitable only for sturdy high-clearance vehicles.

At 27.6 miles northwest of San Ignacio, the route turns off Highway 1. After heading northeast over six miles of level desert displaying cardón, yucca válida and ocotillo, the road makes a sharp, winding ascent onto a mesa. Southeast of the mesa, a vast lonesome canyon may be viewed. Climbing more mesas and passing occasional ranches, the road comes to an abrupt descent at about 22 miles. The village of San Francisco is visible across the canyon. Winding down, then upward, the road reaches the village after 1.5 miles. The high country has barrel cactus, agave, occasional cirios and closely spaced brush. Temperatures are cooler; the climate has more rainfall and is classified as semiarid.

San Francisco de la Sierra (elevation 4500 feet) and vicinity are inhabited by Californios, descendants of Spanish ranchers who settled the interior highlands in the 1700s. Raising mules, horses and goats, they have to the present remained rather isolated from the mainstream of Mexican culture. The village has a school, church and small store; meals are available upon request. Mule trails lead from the village to cave paintings made by Indians several hundred years ago. The drawings are protected by the federal government and visitors must be accompanied by ranchers who are authorized guides. Pack trips to the paintings require three or four days. One small cave is located near the village, but even it requires a guide and a small fee is charged.

San Ignacio

(See also *Lodging & Restaurants* and *Campgrounds & Trailer Parks*.)

For the traveler who has motored through mile after mile of inhospitable terrain, the first view of San Ignacio is one of Baja California's great delights. A forest of date palms and one of the most charming towns on the peninsula are set in the bottom of a wide arroyo surrounded by arid desert. Northernmost of Baja California's major oasis

A skeleton of a gray whale lets travelers know they've reached San Ignacio.

communities, San Ignacio is an attractive, tranquil settlement of about 2000 inhabitants. Its thatched-roof dwellings and pastel-colored business structures are clustered around an imposing stone mission and a tree-shaded plaza.

A skeleton of a California gray whale is on display near the corner of Highway 1 and the paved road leading into town. This road into town passes over a small dam that impounds an underground river that emerges to the earth's surface here. Its waters give life to the city's thousands of palm trees that grow along its banks and provide sustenance for an economy based on agriculture. Dates are the chief crop, but figs, oranges and grapes are also grown commercially. San Ignacio also serves as the market center for the iso-lated cattle ranches to the north and south. To the visitor, it offers hotels and trailer parks, cafes, gasoline, mechanical assistance, telephone service, supplies and an airstrip.

Before the arrival of European explorers, this was the site of a large Indian settlement. Seeing a fertile field for their work, the Jesuits founded a mission here in 1728 and planted the date palms that now cover the floor of the arroyo. After the expulsion of the Jesuits from Mexico, the Dominicans came to San Ignacio and built the present church, which was completed in 1786. Thanks to lava-block walls four feet thick, it remains in an excellent state of preservation and still serves as a parish church. The mission has a small museum, open Monday through

San Ignacio, with its magnificent 18th-century mission,
occupies a palm-lined arroyo surrounded by harsh desert terrain.

The majestic Las Tres Virgenes volcanoes rise above the surrounding desert.

Saturday from 8 a.m. to 3 p.m. Admission is free.

In the rugged, remote mountains both north and south of San Ignacio are hundreds of mysterious cave paintings drawn by prehistoric Indians. Large figures of humans and animals in a variety of colors appear on high ledges and on the ceilings and walls of shallow caves. The origin, age and meaning of this rock art are unknown. One good road leads to the area, and arrangements for mule trips to many of these sites can be made at the hotels in San Ignacio.

South of San Ignacio a dirt road leads 30 miles to Laguna San Ignacio, a site for whale watching. Information on whale-watching outings is available in town. From there a long, graded dirt road travels 100 miles south along the Pacific coast to the agricultural oases of San José de Gracia and Ejido Cadeje, and the large fishing village of San Juanico. Bahía San Juanico has beach campsites and good surfing. From here the road continues to Ciudad Insurgentes in the Santo Domingo Valley.

◤◢ Travelogue
San Ignacio to Santa Rosalía
(45 mi., 73 km.; 1:15 hrs.)

Leaving the palm groves of San Ignacio behind, Highway 1 reenters arid countryside, winding through low hills toward Las Tres Vírgenes, a large mountain mass with three volcanic cones rising majestically above the surrounding desert. After skirting the base of the volcanoes, the road drops onto a cactus-covered plateau. At the end of the plateau looms the first Highway 1 sighting of the Gulf of California. Here too is the steepest grade on the entire length of the highway, dropping seven miles via a series of steep switchbacks to the shores of the gulf. Drivers should exercise caution, watching particularly for trucks rounding the curves. Numerous memorials line the shoulders here, poignant testimony to those who failed to negotiate this section of roadway. At the bottom of the grade, the highway turns south and follows the coastline for 4.7 miles to the junction with the main street of Santa Rosalía.

MEXICO HIGHWAY 1 - GUERRERO NEGRO TO CABO SAN LUCAS

00.0	Junction with the paved road into San Ignacio.
08.8	Junction with a rough dirt road to Rancho Santa Marta, a departure point for mule trips to ancient Indian cave paintings in the rugged mountains north of San Ignacio.
24.0	Excellent viewpoint for Las Tres Vírgenes.
34.1	First view of the Gulf of California.
34.4	Beginning of a series of steep grades and tight curves, as the highway plunges 1000 feet to the shore of the gulf.
40.6	The shore of the Gulf of California.
45.2	Junction with the main street of Santa Rosalía.

Santa Rosalía

(See also *Lodging & Restaurants* and *Campgrounds & Trailer Parks*.)

Santa Rosalía, with a population of 11,000, is a bustling city with narrow, congested streets and a businesslike atmosphere. It used to be a mining town, having been established in the 1880s by the French-owned El Boleo Copper Company. After discovering rich copper deposits here, the mining company imported Indian labor from Sonora, built a pipeline to bring water to the city and constructed a port to handle shipments of processed ore. Mining operations were very prosperous for several decades, but ore deterioration and low demand forced the closure of the mines in 1954. A few efforts have been made since then to revive the industry.

With its row upon row of uniform frame buildings and its large smelters, Santa Rosalía looks like a company-owned mining town, quite different from any other town in Baja California. Even the church of Santa Bárbara seems incongruous, constructed of flat galvanized iron shipped in sections from France. The town consists of three sections, with two plateaus separated by a flat-bottomed arroyo. The

Santa Rosalía was developed by a French copper-mining company.

northern plateau, with its many French-colonial buildings and its panoramic view of the smelter, is especially interesting. (The church alone is worth a brief stop.) Commercial fishing boats are based in the small harbor, which also serves as the terminus for ferry service to Guaymas across the gulf (see *Appendix*, Transportation).

Santa Rosalía is the seat of government for the *municipio* of Mulegé, which also contains Guerrero Negro, San Ignacio and Mulegé. Although Santa Rosalía is not a tourist town, it does offer a variety of facilities, including overnight accommodations, many stores and restaurants, an excellent bakery, a Pemex station, auto parts, mechanical service, banks, telephone and telegraph. Biblioteca

The prefabricated iron church, designed by A.G. Eiffel for the 1898 Paris World's Fair, was shipped in sections around Cape Horn to Santa Rosalía.

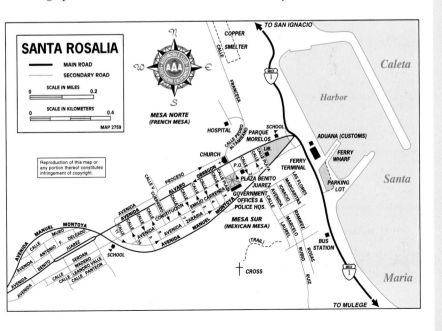

Mahatma Gandhi, the public library at Calle Playa and Avenida Constitución, displays historical account ledgers from the mining company and photographs of past mining and shipping.

▰◢ Travelogue
Santa Rosalía to Mulegé
(38 mi., 61 km.; 1 hr.)

From Santa Rosalía, Highway 1 heads south along the gulf shore for about four miles, offering excellent views of Isla San Marcos, where gypsum is mined and shipped to the United States. After swinging inland, the highway soon returns to the gulf, then turns inland again, passing through barren countryside before rapidly descending to Mulegé.

00.0   Junction with the main street of Santa Rosalía.

05.2   Junction with the 7.5-mile dirt road to Santa Agueda, a quaint farming village that produces papayas, mangos and dates, and has a spring that is the source of Santa Rosalía's water. Although graded its entire length, the road has a rough, washboard surface and a couple of bad spots that could damage a passenger car.

09.0   San Lucas, a fishing village situated on an attractive, palm-lined cove. Good camping beaches can be found both north and south of the village. A signed turnoff leads to San Lucas RV Park.

14.3   San Bruno, a village with an airstrip that has grown up around a fishing cooperative on the gulf shore, 0.8 mile from Highway 1.

17.5   Junction with the dirt road to San José de Magdalena (see

Punta Chivato boasts a seafront resort hotel.

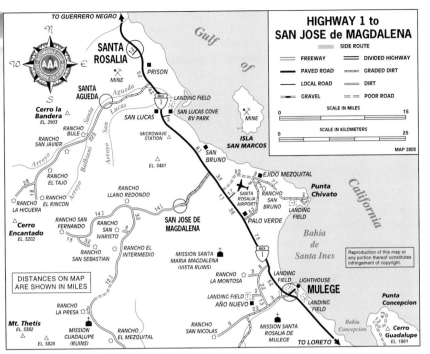

Side Route to San José de Magdalena).

22.0 **Entrance to the Santa Rosalía Airport.**

25.6 **A gravel road leading to Punta Chivato, site of a seafront hotel (see *Campgrounds & Trailer Parks*). Nearby are a good dirt airstrip, a cluster of vacation homes and a camping area on a sandy beach.**

38.5 **Mulegé. Turn left to enter the main part of town.**

🚐 Side Route

Highway 1 to San José de Magdalena
(9 mi., 15 km.; 0:30 hr.)

The short side trip to the picturesque old village of San José de Magdalena can be made in a standard passenger car. The road becomes rough past the village, however, and is only suitable for vehicles with high ground clearance. From a well-marked junction 17.5 miles south of Santa Rosalía on Highway 1, the graded dirt road branches west and traverses a sparsely vegetated plain for 3.5 miles. It then enters a range of barren foothills and negotiates a series of short, steep grades before dropping into a palm-lined canyon. After following the edge of the canyon past several ranches and an interesting cemetery, the road crosses a streambed and arrives in San José de Magdalena. This is an attractive oasis village with groves of stately palms, many colorful flower gardens and thatched-palm dwellings interspersed with concrete-block houses. Farming sustains the local economy; crops include dates, citrus fruits and several varieties of vegetables. San José de Magdalena dates back to Baja California's Spanish colonial days, when it was a visiting station of the Mulegé mission. Evidence of the village's history can be seen in the old stone walls running along the valley floor and in the ruins of a chapel built by the Dominicans in 1774. The Mission Guadalupe ruins can be reached by horseback from Rancho San Isidro, 10 miles southeast of San José de Magdalena.

Mulegé

(See also *Lodging & Restaurants* and *Campgrounds & Trailer Parks*.)

The oasis community of Mulegé is located near the bottom of a lushly vegetated river valley surrounded by barren hills. Its name is a contraction of Yuman Indian words meaning "large creek of the white mouth." The town, which has a population of about 5000, sits on the north bank of the Río Mulegé (Santa Rosalía) about two miles upstream from the Gulf of California. One of the oldest towns in southern Baja California, it began as a mission settlement in 1705. With its air of tranquillity, thousands of date palms and many old-style houses, Mulegé exudes the atmosphere of a quiet, traditional town. Dates are the principal crop, but figs, oranges, bananas and olives are also grown here.

Since the completion of the paved Transpeninsular Highway, Mulegé has become a popular tourist destination, and many visitors have become seasonal or full-time residents. Each winter large numbers of Americans and Canadians, mostly retirees, settle in vacation homes near the river banks or in seaside campgrounds outside town. Fishing, kayaking, snorkeling, scuba diving and sailboarding are all popular with outdoor recreators. Information on these and other activities are available at some hotels and at El Candil restaurant on Calle Zaragoza.

Mulegé's extensive facilities include hotels, trailer parks, restaurants, banks, markets, gift shops, a coin laundry, two Pemex stations, an auto supply store, mechanical assistance and a clinic. The downtown streets, although in good condition, are narrow and restricted to one-way traffic. Most visitors will find it easier to get around by walking.

The palm-lined banks of the Río Mulegé give the appearance of a tropical idyll.

Mulegé basks in an peaceful setting amid a palm oasis near the sea.

Shopping

Food, auto parts and other supplies are readily available in Mulegé. So too are souvenirs of the region, including such staples as ceramics, glassware, wood carvings, clothing and leather goods. Aside from hotels, the majority of the curio shops are found along **Calle Zaragoza** and **Avenida Gral. Martínez Francisco I. Madero**.

Dining

Though not a large town, Mulegé has many restaurants from which to choose, not surprising given its location on Highway 1 and the large number of seasonal residents. There's little in the way of formal dining, but there is a good variety of seafood and Mexican cuisine. The list below is by no means exhaustive, and visitors will

find many more choices, both in town and nearby. Pizza, hamburgers, fish tacos and Chinese food are among the other options to be found.

Some of the restaurants listed here are AAA approved; more information about these can be found in the *Lodging & Restaurants* chapter. Non-AAA-approved restaurants are also listed here as a service to visitors.

Some of the more popular choices are **La Almeja** (seafood), east of town on Playa El Farito; **El Candil** (Mexican), in town on Calle Zaragoza; **Jungle Jim's** (varied menu), east of town on the south bank of Río Mulegé; **Las Casitas** (Mexican), mid-town in the hotel of the same name; and **Los Equipales** (varied menu), north of the main square on Avenida Moctezuma. In addition, the restaurant at the **Hotel Serenidad**, two miles east on Highway 1, is famous for

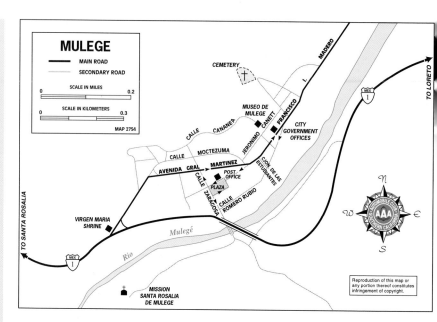

its Wednesday night "fiesta" dinners and Saturday night pig roast.

Points of Interest

MISIÓN SANTA ROSALÍA DE MULEGÉ *Just upstream from the bridge that carries Hwy. 1 across the river.* Founded in 1705 and completed in 1766, the mission has been restored with the help of the government and now functions as a church. Nearby, rocky steps lead up a hill that affords a commanding view of the oasis. To

Misión Santa Rosalía de Mulegé, founded by the Jesuits in 1705, has been extensively restored.

reach the mission from town, go south on Calle Zaragoza (the longest north-south street in Mulegé), cross the river on a small bridge under the elevated highway bridge, turn sharply back to the right and follow a dirt road, first through palm groves then up a barren grade to the mission.

MUSEO DE MULEGÉ *On a hilltop over-looking the town. Open Mon.-Sat. 9 a.m.-1 p.m. Admission $1.20.* A classic building that was formerly a federal prison now houses displays of the history of Mulegé and other places in Baja California Sur. It contains fine artifacts of Cochimí Indians and Mexican settlers, religious objects and paintings by local artists.

SANTUARIO DE LA VIRGEN MARÍA *At the west end of town.* The shrine includes a panoramic painting of Mulegé.

▰◢ Travelogue
Mulegé to Loreto
(84 mi., 136 km.; 2 hrs.)

Beyond the junction with Mulegé's main street, Highway 1 crosses the river and veers eastward toward the Gulf of California, then heads south through barren coastal hills. A dozen miles past Mulegé, the highway reaches the shore of beautiful Bahía de la Concepción, one of the scenic highlights of Baja California. For the next 25 miles, the road parallels the shore of the bay, providing a series of breath-taking panoramas of sparkling blue-green waters, volcanic islands and inviting campsites. From the head of the bay, Highway 1 climbs a low saddle, then emerges onto a long, sandy plain. The rugged backbone of the Sierra de la Giganta is visible to the west. Finally, after winding through scrub-covered hills, the highway drops to a coastal plain near the junction to Loreto. There is no gasoline available on this long stretch of highway.

00.0   **Junction to Mulegé.**
00.7   **Junction with a road leading to Mission Santa Rosalía de Mulegé.**
01.7   **Junction with the entrance road to the Villa María Isabel RV/Trailer Park.**

Beautiful Bahía de la Concepción is famous for its fine camping beaches, excellent fishing and spectacular scenery.

MEXICO HIGHWAY 1 - GUERRERO NEGRO TO CABO SAN LUCAS

13.3	Playa Santispac, a developed public beach on an attractive cove.
14.6	Posada Concepción, a campground on the shore of Bahía Tordillo.
17.1	Rancho El Coyote, opposite a pair of lovely coves with enticing public beaches.
27.0	El Requesón, a small island connected to the shore by a sandspit. The narrow spit is a *playa pública*.
36.3	Junction with a lonesome dirt road that loops around the southern end of Bahía Concepción (see *Campgrounds & Trailer Parks*), then goes north along the eastern side of the bay for 36 miles to Punta Concepción. The road passes a few fish camps and much pristine desert. The last few miles are very rough.
45.7	Rancho Rosarito, a ranch in a small oasis.
46.8	Junction with a road across the Sierra de la Giganta to San Isidro, La Purísima, San Jose de Comondú and San Miguel de Comondú (see Side Route to La Purísima).
54.1	Junction with a scenic dirt road to San Juanico and Bahía San Basilio.
65.2	Junction with a dirt road to Rancho San Juan Londo, 0.2 miles from the highway in a palm grove. This is the site of a Jesuit *visita*, or visiting station, dating from 1705.
84.1	Junction with the paved road to Loreto.

🚐 Side Route

Highway 1 to Ciudad Insurgentes via La Purísima

(118 mi., 190 km.; 5 hrs.)

Because of their isolation, the Purísima and Comondú oases preserve a sense of an earlier era. A graded dirt road across the ruggedly scenic Sierra de la Giganta now leads from Highway 1 to the oasis villages of San Isidro and La Purísima. Wide and well-graded most of the way, the road is suitable for high-clearance vehicles.

The junction with the new road is 47 miles south of Mulegé (or 37 miles north of Loreto) on Highway 1. The road winds through a series of narrow canyons, walled by steep volcanic bluffs. Vegetation is thick and consists of cardón, pitahaya, three varieties of cholla, palo adán, mesquite and dense underbrush. At mileage 11.3 is a junction: to the left is the road to San José de Comondú and San Miguel de Comondú; to the right is a seldom-used portion of the old La Purísima/San Isidro road. Proceed straight ahead. A mile beyond the junction, the road tops a low ridge via a rocky grade, then descends into a long, winding valley. The route meanders in and out of the valley, occasionally crossing sparsely vegetated hills of volcanic boulders, until at mileage 30.7 it reaches the rim of the La Purísima Valley. After dropping 700 feet to the valley floor via a series of steep switchbacks, the road becomes a palm-lined avenue with a stone aqueduct alongside. It passes orchards and cultivated fields before arriving in San Isidro at mileage 35.2. San Isidro, a community of 600 inhabitants, has a cafe, limited supplies, a telegraph, a clinic and a rustic motel.

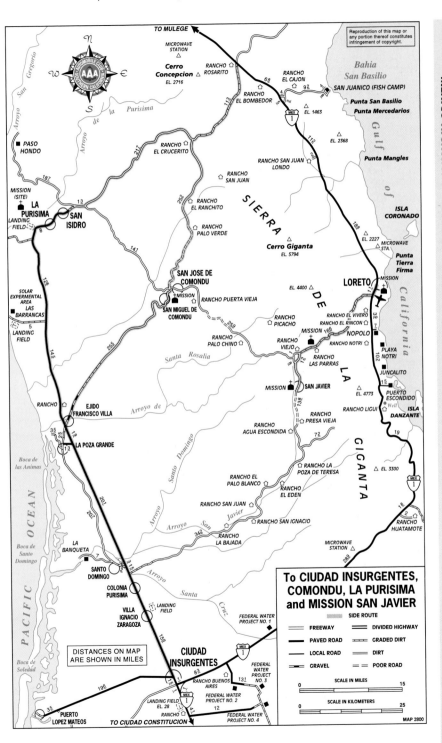

MEXICO HIGHWAY 1 - GUERRERO NEGRO TO CABO SAN LUCAS

To CIUDAD INSURGENTES, COMONDU, LA PURISIMA and MISSION SAN JAVIER

SIDE ROUTE

FREEWAY — DIVIDED HIGHWAY
PAVED ROAD — GRADED DIRT
LOCAL ROAD — DIRT
GRAVEL — POOR ROAD

SCALE IN MILES
0 — 15

SCALE IN KILOMETERS
0 — 25

MAP 2800

DISTANCES ON MAP ARE SHOWN IN MILES

Three miles farther down the valley is La Purísima.

The oasis village of La Purísima sits amid groves of palms in the bottom of a deep valley that is walled in by high cliffs and surrounded by rugged, barren desert. Thanks to an irrigation system fed by spring water, the valley is intensively farmed and yields a variety of crops, including dates, mangos, grapes, citrus fruits, corn, beans and tomatoes. The town itself, with a population of about 700, has a well-worn look. La Purísima began in 1730, when a Jesuit mission was moved here from a site several miles away. The native Indian population was decimated by disease, and the mission was abandoned in 1822; only stone ruins remain. The present village dates from the late 19th century, when the fertile valley was resettled by Mexican farmers—ancestors of today's friendly residents of La Purísima. Modest accommodations can be found here, along with gasoline, meals, limited supplies, a post office and a municipal office. Leaving La Purísima the road continues down the valley for another 3.5 miles to a junction. The right fork is a graded road running northward for 120 miles to San Ignacio; the route to Ciudad Insurgentes bears left here and climbs out of the valley onto a high mesa. Paved most of the way, it then heads southward, winding among barren rounded hills. Thirteen miles from the junction is a signed road to the fishing village of Las Barrancas, site of a joint German/Mexican solar energy project. At mileage 76.8 from Highway 1 (or 34.8 miles from La Purísima), the road arrives at Ejido Francisco Villa—a dusty, windblown farming cooperative. Here the Comondú road angles in from the left, and a road to Poza Grande, another

After traversing many miles of rough road, the oasis of the Valle de la Purísima comes into view.

The municipal hall of the little town of La Purísima faces the town square.

farming community, veers off to the right; proceed straight ahead for Ciudad Insurgentes. The road continues to run in a straight line through open desert punctuated by irrigated fields. Here on the Santo Domingo (Magdalena) Plain, farmers utilize water drawn from deep wells to transform a sandy desert into productive fields of wheat and other crops. About 22 miles past Ejido Francisco Villa is the junction with a 1.5-mile side road to Santo Domingo, a farming community with a store, a cafe and gasoline. Two miles farther is the junction with the road coming in from Loreto and Mission San Javier. Southward 15 miles farther lies the large farm market town of Ciudad Insurgentes. From Insurgentes a paved road leads 24 miles west to the fishing port of Puerto López Mateos.

Loreto

(See also *Lodging & Restaurants* and *Campgrounds & Trailer Parks*.)

Loreto enjoys a scenic setting in a grove of palms and other subtropical trees on the shore of the Gulf of California. The jagged peaks of the Sierra de la Giganta rise abruptly from the coastal plain, forming a dramatic backdrop to the west. Directly offshore is Isla del Carmen, site of a salt works that has operated since the Spaniards first settled. A branch road leads from Highway 1 to the center of Loreto, which is built around a picturesque central plaza and a graceful stone mission. On the shore of the gulf, Calle de la Playa and the *malecón* (sea wall) walkway have recently been refurbished and paved. A stroll along the *malecón* reveals impressive sights:

*The **malecón** in Loreto is an ideal place to relax.*

crashing surf, pelicans and other birds diving for fish, and a vista of azure waters and the rugged island beyond.

Despite its impressive mission church, Loreto gives little indication of the key role it has played in the history of Baja California. Loreto is the oldest permanent settlement in the Californias. It dates back to October 25, 1697, when the Jesuit padre Juan María Salvatierra arrived and founded Mission Nuestra

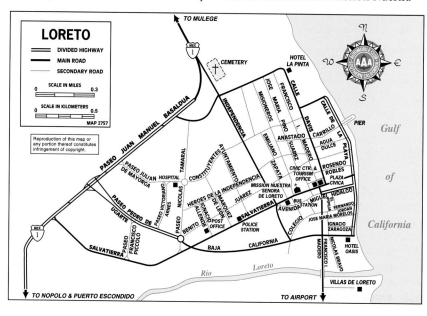

Quick Guide to Loreto

Tourist Information and Assistance

Municipal Tourism Office *On the Plaza Cívica in the municipal hall. Open Mon.-Fri. 8 a.m.-5 p.m. 01152 (113) 5-04-11.* Information and brochures about the region are available.

Señora de Loreto. (The town celebrated its 300th anniversary with a series of events in October of 1997.) For the next 132 years, Loreto served as the capital of Baja California, as well as the commercial and military hub of the peninsula. It was the base from which Junípero Serra began the exploration and colonization of what is now California in 1769; on his journey northward he founded the chain of missions in Alta California. In 1829, after Loreto was devastated by a hurricane, the capital was moved to La Paz.

After more than a century of peaceful slumber, Loreto has rebounded—thanks to its location on Highway 1 and the discovery by sportsmen that fishing off Loreto was good even by Gulf of California standards. Since the completion of the paved highway in 1973, the warm waters of the area have attracted increasing numbers of anglers and tourists each year. Loreto Airport receives regular commercial flights from Los Angeles. FONATUR, a government-managed development group, has also targeted the Loreto area for a major tourist development, patterned after similar projects in Mexico at Cancún and Ixtapa. To date, FONATUR has assisted in developments in the town of Loreto and in resort facilities at Nopaló, five miles to the south. In addition a marina is being developed at Puerto Escondido (Puerto Loreto), 15 miles south of Loreto.

For the time being, however, this town of about 9000 maintains its quiet, small-town ambiance. Fishing and tourism are the bulwarks of the local economy, with tourism playing an ever-increasing role. Facilities include a variety of hotels, trailer parks, numerous shops, two supermarkets, restaurants, a hospital, a bank, a coin laundry, two Pemex stations, mechanical service and auto parts. Typical Mexican articles for sale include shawls, women's clothing, pottery and leather crafts. In 1992 the city became the seat of government for the new *municipio* of Loreto.

Dining

Travelers will find several good restaurants serving a wide range of dishes. Sea food is served almost everywhere, as one would expect in a town where fishing is a major industry.

Some of the restaurants listed here are AAA approved; more information about these can be found in the *Lodging & Restaurants* chapter. Non-AAA-approved restaurants are also listed here as a service to visitors.

Among the well-known restaurants are **El Embarcadero** (seafood, Mexican); **Café Ole** (Mexican), downtown on Avenida Madero; **La Terraza** (steak, seafood), next door to Café Ole; **El Nido** (steaks, seafood), on Calle Salvatierra; **Carmen's** (Mexican, American), at the south end of the *malecón*;

MEXICO HIGHWAY 1 - GUERRERO NEGRO TO CABO SAN LUCAS

Loreto's historic municipal hall faces the Plaza Civíca.

and **La Fuente** (seafood, Mexican), also on Calle Salvatierra. Another good bet is the restaurant at **Hotel Oasis** (seafood, Mexican), just beyond the south end of the *malecón*.

Points of Interest

MISION NUESTRA SEÑORA DE LORETO *Center of town.* The current building was completed in 1752. It has withstood numerous hurricanes, floods and earthquakes, and is still an active church after extensive restoration and remodeling.

Museum *Next door to the mission. Open Wed.-Mon. 9 a.m.-6 p.m. Admission $1.* Fascinating displays about missions, and horse and wagon equipment are presented in this museum. English-speaking docents are usually available to provide tours and information.

PLAZA CÍVICA *Avenidas Salvatierra and Francisco Madero, just east of the*

mission. Laid out in traditional Mexican style, it faces the municipal hall, the tourism office and several stores.

◤◢ Travelogue
Loreto to Ciudad Constitución
(89 mi., 143 km.; 2 hrs.)

South of Loreto, the Sierra de la Giganta rises abruptly from the deep-blue waters of the gulf. For several miles, Highway 1 runs along the base of the reddish-brown mountains, following the dramatic coastline past fine beaches and offshore islands. Then the highway turns inland and climbs rapidly via sharp switchbacks. On approaching the summit, a series of unusual, hat-shaped mountain peaks are visible nearby. After the summit, the road begins a gradual descent along the edge of a deep canyon. Continuing southwest, the highway levels out onto the broad, gently sloped Santo Domingo (Magdalena) Valley.

Though extremely arid, this sandy, cactus-covered lowland has developed into a major agricultural center— thanks to water from deep wells. Highway 1 passes several large farms and a pair of federal water projects before arriving in Ciudad Insurgentes, where it turns south and runs in a straight line along irrigated fields to Ciudad Constitución. Slow-moving vehicles are a common hazard in this final stretch; pass with care.

01.1 Junction with a rough dirt road to Mission San Javier (see *Side Route to Mission San Javier*). This road should only be attempted by sturdy, high-clearance vehicles.

01.7 Junction with the paved road to Loreto's airport. Aero California flies here from Los Angeles. (See *Appendix*, Transportation section.)

05.2 Nopoló, site of a government-sponsored FONATUR resort complex, which is now being developed. Currently in operation are the Eden Loreto Resort, an all-inclusive destination that touts tennis courts, an 18-hole golf course, restaurants, entertainment and more. It's open only to adults 18 years of age and older.

10.0 A dirt road to Playa Notrí, a sandy beach.

14.0 Junction with the short dirt road to Juncalito, a fishing village, where boats for sportfishing are available. The road continues beyond the village to a *playa pública*.

14.6 Posada Concepción, a campground on the shore of Bahía Tordillo.

15.2 Junction with the 1.5-mile paved road to Puerto Escondido (Puerto Loreto), a deep water port once used for shipping products. This beautiful, nearly landlocked bay has been earmarked for development by FONATUR. Many buildings stand half-completed and some infrastructure is in place, but major developments remain far from completion. Tourist facilities that do exist include the Tripui Resort RV Park (see *Campgrounds & Trailer Parks*) and a marina with a boat ramp.

17.1 Rancho El Coyote, opposite a pair of lovely coves with enticing public beaches.

27.0 El Requesón, a small island connected to the shore by a sandspit. The narrow spit is a *playa pública*.

34.0 A steep, scenic dirt road leads southeast to Agua Verde, a fishing village on the Gulf of California. Campsites are available on nearby beaches.

44.6 Turnout overlooking a rugged canyon.

63.0 Entrance to Ley Federal de Aguas #1, a government-sponsored water project that provides fresh water for nearby farms. It has a large Pemex station.

67.5 Buenos Aires and Ley Federal de Aguas #2, a collection of prosperous-looking farms.

73.3 A red, white and green monument marks the junction with Ciudad Insurgentes, an agricultural settlement of about 12,000 with stores, cafes, two Pemex stations, banks, an auto parts store and mechani-

The Spanish Missions

In 1697, Father Juan María de Salvatierra founded the first Spanish mission on the Baja California peninsula at Loreto. Father Salvatierra represented the Jesuit Order of the Roman Catholic Church, which had received permission from the Spanish Crown for the pacification of the native inhabitants and their conversion to the Roman Catholic faith. The Jesuits followed up this first mission with 19 more built during the period 1697-1767.

During this era of Jesuit control there were numerous Indian revolts. The most dangerous revolt occurred between 1734 and 1736, when the Pericu Indians of the Cape region succeeded in killing two of the missionaries and in burning four of the missions (Santiago, San José del Cabo, La Paz and Loreto). A military force was dispatched from the Mexican mainland to quell the rebellion, which it did with brutal efficiency. In addition to this, epidemics of measles and small pox, brought to Baja by the Europeans, further decimated the native inhabitants, who had no natural immune system against these diseases. By 1767, when the Jesuit Order was expelled from all of Spain's colonies for abuse of authority, the Indian population was a mere fraction of its original numbers.

The Baja California mission system was given over to the care of the Franciscan Order in 1768. They created only one mission in the Baja peninsula, San Fernando Velicatá, in 1769. After that they turned their attention north to the more economically promising region of Alta California—the modern U.S. territory of California.

The Franciscans ceded administration of the Baja peninsula missions to the Dominican Order in 1773. Over the next 60 years, the Dominicans established nine more missions in Baja California, but the native population had become so small that the missions were no longer economically profitable. In 1832 all but the nine missions established by the Dominicans were secularized, and shortly afterward these nine missions followed suit. By 1846 the mission era was over.

Mission San Javier, a beautifully preserved example of the Jesuit missions, still serves as a parish for local residents.

cal assistance. The center of town is to the right. The main street continues north as a paved road for 66 miles, then as a graded dirt road following the coast for 139 more miles to San Ignacio; branches lead to San Javier, Comondú, La Purísima (see Side Route to La Purísima) and San Juanico, a very popular surfing area.

88.3 Entrance to the Ciudad Constitución airport. Ciudad Constitución, at the junction with the paved road (Mexico Highway 22) to San Carlos (see Side Route to San Carlos).

Side Route

Loreto to Mission San Javier

(23 mi., 37 km.; 1:30 hrs.)

The trip from Loreto to Mission San Javier is one of Baja California's most rewarding side routes. In addition to one of North America's most beautiful Spanish missions, it offers superlative mountain and canyon scenery. Sturdy, high-clearance vehicles are best for this road, although passenger cars can make the journey with careful driving. The mission can also be reached from the Pacific side of the peninsula, but this approach is considerably longer and has many rocky arroyo crossings.

From a signed junction 1.1 miles south of the Loreto turnoff, the road leads westward from Highway 1 through low rounded hills for about six miles. It then begins a gradual winding climb into the rugged Sierra de la Giganta, following the steep wall of a deep arroyo. At mileage 9.5 there is a rocky section. The old road is visible meandering along the palm-studded floor of the canyon. A mile farther the road swings to the left, offering

Breathtaking views like this await travelers on the road to Mission San Javier.

travelers an excellent view of the gaping canyon below and the blue Gulf of California in the distance. Rancho Las Parras, 12.2 miles from Highway 1, has a small stone chapel and groves of citrus and olive trees. Six miles beyond the rancho is a junction with a rough road to Comondú, 25.8 miles to the north. The road then gently winds for 4.4 miles through a narrow canyon to San Javier. The vegetation changes from desert to steppe (semiarid) because of the increased elevation. Local agriculture involves raising goats and cattle, and growing olives, oranges and mangos.

Mission San Javier sits in the bottom of a deep valley beneath towering walls of dark gray stone. Surrounding the mission is the village of San Javier, which has a small store, cafe, telephone and a divided parkway instead of the usual plaza. The impressive mission is of a Moorish style that is dramatic in its simplicity; its stonework and ornamentation are considered outstanding. This was the second of Baja California's Jesuit missions, founded in 1699 but not completed until 1758. That a church of this size could be built in such a rugged, remote region and survive in such a fine state of preservation to the present day is truly remarkable.

Beyond the mission, the road continues to head southwest down the canyon, fording several arroyos and passing several small ranches. The canyon gradually widens into a broad valley, and irrigated farms appear along the road. Finally, 43.8 miles beyond San Javier, the road reaches the junction with the La Purísima/ Ciudad Insurgentes route. This section takes almost three hours to traverse. From this point it is 15.5 miles to the junction with Highway 1 in Ciudad Insurgentes.

▭ Side Route

Highway 1 to
Ciudad Insurgentes via Comondú
(103 mi., 165 km.; 5 hrs.)

For the first 11.3 miles the route to Comondú is shared with the San Isidro/La Purísima road. Except for these first few miles, which are wide and graded, the road is narrow and winding with numerous steep, rocky grades. The trip to Comondú can be made with sturdy, high-clearance vehicles; however, the southern approach from Ciudad Insurgentes offers a much better road.

The unmarked junction with Highway 1 is 47 miles south of Mulegé and 37

miles north of Loreto. From the junction the road cuts a straight westward swath across open desert for five miles, then begins a gradual ascent through a steep-walled canyon. At mileage 11.3 is an unsigned, four-way intersection. Straight ahead is San Isidro and La Purísima; to the right is an abandoned road. For Comondú, turn left. The road now winds upward over grades of up to 15 percent to the summit of the Sierra de la Giganta; this section is passable by only the sturdiest of four-wheel-drive vehicles driven by experienced drivers. It then crosses a plateau, climbs another summit and descends through a rocky arroyo. After traversing low hills for several miles, the road comes to the edge of a deep canyon. Nestled far below in a forest of date palms is Comondú. Just ahead is a junction near a roadside cemetery. Straight on lies a new graded road to San Isidro and La Purísima. To the left the road drops sharply via a series of steep switchbacks to the valley floor, reaching San José de Comondú at mileage 36.

Comondú is really two villages: San José de Comondú and, two miles farther west, San Miguel de Comondú. The combined population of these twin oasis villages is about 600. Although the surrounding volcanic mesas are nearly devoid of vegetation, the floor of the valley is a seven-mile-long strip of green. Sufficient water from nearby springs nourishes crops of figs, grapes, dates, sugarcane and vegetables. In San José de Comondú, just left of the point where the road enters the village, is the site of a Jesuit mission moved here in 1737; one stone building still stands. The original bells, which date from 1708, hang from a standard alongside the church. San

José also has a grocery store and a clinic. San Miguel has a worn look with many deserted buildings, but possesses an aura of historic charm. It has a general store that also sells gasoline. Meals may be ordered at a private home. Leaving Comondú, a graded road winds down the canyon, which gradually opens up onto a wide, sparsely vegetated coastal plain. The road is wide, well-graded and easy to follow. About 25 miles beyond Comondú (or 61 miles from Highway 1) the road arrives at Ejido Francisco Villa, where it joins the La Purísima/ Ciudad Insurgentes route.

🚗 Side Route
Ciudad Constitución to San Carlos
(36 mi., 58 km.; 0:45 hr.)

The paved route to San Carlos (Mexico Highway 22) leaves Highway 1 in the northern part of Ciudad Constitución. After running alongside irrigated fields for seven miles it traverses gently undulating desert terrain, which is heavily vegetated with cardón, cholla, pitahaya and dense brush. After reaching the mangrove-edged shore of Bahía Magdalena, Highway 22 crosses a bridge and enters San Carlos, located on an irregular peninsula in the bay.

San Carlos (also known as Puerto San Carlos) is a port built to handle shipments of wheat, garbanzo and cotton grown in the Santo Domingo Valley. The port also has a commercial fishing fleet and packing plant (tuna and sardines). With a population of about 6000, it has developed some limited facilities for tourists, including several restaurants and cafes, three motels, a rustic campground, a public beach, several markets, a clinic and a Pemex

Corn is one of the many crops grown in the agriculturally rich Santo Domingo Valley.

station. Visitors find recreation in fishing, boating and whale watching.

At a junction six miles west of Highway 1 on the San Carlos road is a paved road to Villa Benito Juárez. From there a dirt road leads northwest for 28 miles to Puerto López Mateos. In this port, population 4000, whale-watching trips are offered in the winter. By taking this road and then traveling eastward from Puerto López Mateos to Ciudad Insurgentes, the motorist can make a loop trip through this interesting desert area.

Ciudad Constitución
(See *Campgrounds & Trailer Parks*.)

In the 1960s the Santo Domingo Valley (sometimes called Magdalena Plain) was opened to rapid agricultural devel-

Ciudad Constitución serves as a distribution center for the agricultural products of the Santo Domingo Valley.

opment, and within two decades Ciudad Constitución grew from a village into a booming modern city. With a current population of about 48,000, it is the third largest population center in the state of Baja California Sur and the seat of government for the *municipio* of Comondú, which also includes Ciudad Insurgentes. The region is extremely arid, but water trapped for centuries far beneath the earth's surface has been tapped by deep wells, transforming the desert into a checkerboard of attractive farms. The leading crops are wheat and garbanzo; also important are cotton, sorghum, alfalfa, corn and citrus fruits. Some farms also raise livestock. The agricultural products are shipped to the mainland from San Carlos, 36 miles to the west.

Ciudad Constitución is not oriented toward tourism, but offers extensive facilities including hotels, a trailer park, supermarkets, a large public market, large and varied stores, hospitals, banks, an ice house, coin laundries, automobile dealerships, Pemex stations, auto supply stores and auto

repair shops. Among a large number of restaurants and cafes, Restaurant Sancho Panza in the Hotel Maribel offers a variety of fine Mexican dishes. Prices in Ciudad Constitución are lower than in the tourist towns.

►⁄ Travelogue
Ciudad Constitución to La Paz
(134 mi., 216 km.; 2:45 hrs.)

After leaving Ciudad Constitución, Highway 1 runs absolutely straight for more than 30 miles across virtually flat terrain. It then turns southeast and traverses a region of seemingly endless chalk-colored hills and mesas and deeply eroded gullies; numerous sharp curves present driving hazards in this section. Finally, at a high bluff marked by a tepee-shaped shrine, the Gulf of California and Bahía de La Paz come into view, with the city a cluster of white buildings spread along the far side of the bay. Descending rapidly, the highway soon reaches a wide, heavily vegetated coastal plain. After passing through the small bayside set-

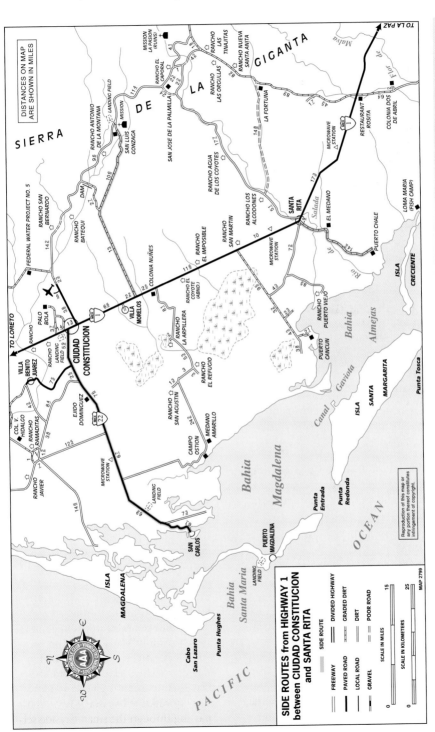

Between Ciudad Constitución and La Paz, Mexico Highway 1 crosses open desert punctuated with chalk-colored mesas and buttes.

tlement of El Centenario, Highway 1 follows the curve of the bay into La Paz, capital of Baja California Sur.

00.0   Ciudad Constitución, at the junction with the highway to San Carlos.

01.5   Junction with the dirt road to Campestre La Pila, a large farm that contains a trailer park and a swimming pool.

07.9   Villa Morelos, a tiny farming community with a cafe.

10.1   Junction with the dirt road to El Ihuagil Dam and Mission San Luís Gonzaga (see Side Route to Mission San Luis Gonzaga).

14.0   Colonia Nuñes, another agricultural settlement. Highway 1 now leaves the region of irrigated farms and enters open desert.

35.6   Santa Rita, a village with a store, cafe and a church. At the north end of the village a dirt road branches west to Puerto Chale (see Side Route to Puerto Chale).

53.9   Junction with a mostly graded dirt road to a cattle and goat-raising region that includes the villages of San Pedro de la Presa, Las Animas and El Bosque. Winding along streams through the scenic Sierra de la Giganta, the road descends to San Evaristo on the gulf coast, 68 miles to the northeast.

61.8   Las Pocitas, a village with a picturesque church, a clinic and a cafe. A graded road leads northeast to La Soledad and San Evaristo.

71.3   El Cien, a settlement with a Pemex station, highway department camp and a cafe.

83.9   Junction with the 12-mile dirt road to El Conejo, a wind-blown Pacific beach that is popular with surfers. Any high-clearance vehicle can make the trip.

99.8   A good graded dirt road to Conquista Agraria and the Pacific coast.

113.3 A summit with a sweeping panorama of Bahía de La Paz and the mountains beyond; a turnout leads to a tepee-shaped shrine. Highway 1 now begins a sharp descent.

123.9 Junction with a scenic paved road leading 24.7 miles north along the shore of Bahía de La

Paz to the mining settlement of San Juan de la Costa. Phosphorus mined here is shipped by freighter to processing plants elsewhere in Mexico for use in the production of fertilizer. The town has gasoline and groceries. A graded dirt road follows the coast 45 miles farther north to the village of San Evaristo; its economy is based on fishing and salt evaporation and it has a protected cove. From there a road winds southwest through the Sierra de la Giganta and connects with Highway 1.

124.4 El Centenario, a small town of about 2000 inhabitants on the shore of the bay, has a Pemex station. The skyline of La Paz is visible across the water.

129.2 Chametla, a settlement at the junction with the 2.1-mile paved road to La Paz International Airport. Aero California, Aeromexico and Mexicana Airlines fly here from Los Angeles and Tijuana (see Air Service in *Appendix*, Transportation).

130.2 At the "Dove of Peace" monument, Camino a las Garzas veers to the right, providing a convenient bypass of central La Paz for motorists bound for the Los Cabos region.

133.5 La Paz, at the intersection of calzadas Abasolo and 5 de Febrero. Turn right here for Highway 1 south to Cabo San Lucas; straight ahead, the road along the bay's shore leads to downtown La Paz and to Pichilingue, the terminal for the Mazatlán and

Topolobampo ferries (see *Appendix*, Transportation).

🚐 Side Route
Highway 1 to Mission San Luis Gonzaga
(26 mi., 42 km.; 2 hrs.)

This route is in generally good condition; however, a sturdy, high-clearance vehicle is needed. From Highway 1, at a point 2.2 miles south of Villa Morelos (10 miles south of Ciudad Constitución), turn east on the road marked Presa Ihuagil. After a mile, cultivated fields give way to native desert covered with cardón and a variety of brush. After 15 miles of flat terrain is the junction with a road leading west to Ciudad Constitución. Just beyond this is a dam, Presa Ihuagil, whose reservoir is only partially filled.

Take the right fork and follow the road along the top of the dam, then curve sharply to the right. The road on the second leg of the trip is rougher than on the first part, as it winds its way southeast over gently rolling land toward San Luis. Abundant vegetation includes cardón and cholla cacti. Several forks off the main road can cause confusion, and the route crosses several streambeds that can be troublesome during or after the occasional rains. For the last five miles ranches and grazing cattle are numerous. At mileage 23.7 is a roadside shrine.

Except for a modern school, the village of San Luis Gonzaga could be a museum piece from the past. The stone mission, founded in 1737, is still in use and has a colorful, well-kept interior. The mission and a companion building formerly used for living quarters face on a large square. Also facing the square are two other stone buildings—

an abandoned store and a former public building that now serves as a kind of dormitory. Adjacent are several farm houses. Cattle ranching and date palms support the inhabitants.

🚐 Side Route
Santa Rita to Puerto Chale
(15 mi., 24 km.; 0:30 hr.)

This route, for the most part, is wide and graded. The road leaves the main highway just north of the village of Santa Rita and descends gently through barren countryside, passes the tiny hamlet of El Médano, then crosses an arroyo. Puerto Chale is a fishing village on mangrove-edged Bahía Almejas. The village has a market and a church. There are no tourist facilities, but fishing is excellent. Snook are said to lurk among the mangroves during winter, scallops are caught and the waters are good for diving.

La Paz

(See also *Lodging & Restaurants* and *Campgrounds & Trailer Parks*.)

Sandwiched between cactus-covered foothills and the arcing shore of the beautiful Bahía de la Paz, La Paz enjoys one of the most picturesque settings of any state capital in Mexico. Offshore is a narrow sandspit known as El Mogote, which separates the main body of the bay from Ensenada de los Aripes, a shallow inlet to the west. Because of its location at the southeastern end of the bay, La Paz's shoreline faces northwest—a fact that becomes readily apparent during one of the city's magnificent sunsets. With its fine beaches, superlative sportfishing, numerous duty-free shops and abundance of tourist facilities, La Paz is quickly becoming one of the top resorts on Mexico's west coast. The ideal time to visit La Paz is November through May, when days are warm and sunny and nights are cool. Summers can be uncomfortably hot, but often a welcome afternoon breeze known as the *coromuel* refreshes the city. Late summer to early fall is the rainy season. Rainfall is scant and varies from year to year; and most of it comes during short, violent tropical storms called *chubascos*.

La Paz has the longest history of any settlement in the Californias—and one of the most turbulent. The bay was discovered by a Spanish expedition in 1533, but the leader and several of his soldiers were killed by Indians shortly after landing. Two years later Hernán Cortés, the conqueror of Mexico, attempted to colonize the site of La Paz; supply problems, however, caused him to fail. The rich oyster beds in nearby gulf waters brought numerous seekers of wealth during the 17th century, and pearls from La Paz found their way into the Spanish royal treasury, but none of the colonies survived more than a short time. The task of colonization fell to the Jesuits, who founded a mission here in 1720. The padres withstood a series of Indian uprisings, but after disease virtually wiped out the Indian population the mission was abandoned in 1749. Today the Cathedral of La Paz stands on its site. Not until 1811 did La Paz become

La Paz enjoys a beautiful location between arid foothills and the city's name-sake bay.

a permanent settlement. In 1829, after Loreto was destroyed by a hurricane, the fledgling village of La Paz became the territorial capital. American troops occupied La Paz during the Mexican War and battles were fought in the streets of the city, but the soldiers returned to the United States after the treaty was signed. The notorious William Walker also attempted a take-over, but he was quickly expelled.

After years of existence as a remote territory, Baja California Sur—one of Mexico's two newest states—has made rapid economic strides, with tremendous gains in population, productivity

The Dove of Peace Monument greets motorists at the entrance to La Paz.

A favorite pastime for both locals and visitors alike is a leisurely stroll along the malecón.

and tourism. As a result, La Paz has evolved from a sleepy little port into a vigorous, modern state capital. It is also the seat of government for the *municipio* of La Paz, which also encompasses the community of Todos Santos. This jolt into the Mexican mainstream has not come without a few growing pains, such as the traffic snarls that occur daily in the narrow downtown streets. The current population numbers about 176,000. Still, there is something of a small-town atmosphere in La Paz, and the city retains touches of colonial grace and charm. Interspersed with contemporary structures and paved streets are colorful gardens, arched doorways and cobblestone sidewalks. Some businesses continue to observe the traditional siesta hour, closing their doors in the early afternoon. And on Sunday evenings, local residents join in the customary promenade along the palm-lined *malecón* (sea wall). The *malecón* also

plays host to the annual Carnaval (Mardi Gras), the largest pre-Lenten celebration on the Baja peninsula.

Shopping

La Paz is a free port and offers the careful shopper good buys on imported merchandise, as well as on Mexican handicrafts. Shops catering to tourists are clustered along **Paseo Alvaro Obregón** opposite the *malecón*. Bargains can also be found in small stores scattered throughout the downtown area just behind the waterfront. Handwoven cotton and woolen articles are made and sold at **Artesanía Cuauhtémoc/The Weaver**; it is located on Abasolo (Highway 1) between calles Jalisco and Nayarít. **Centro de Arte Regional**, on Chiapas at Calle Encinas, is a pottery workshop offering a variety of goods at reasonable prices.

Travelers who wish to replenish their supplies will find several large supermarkets, as well as many small grocery stores, bakeries and fruit markets. At the **Public Market** merchants sell a wide assortment of goods from individual stalls; it is located on Avenida Revolución de 1910 at Degollado. **La Perla**

Offerings from street vendors include tasty snacks.

MEXICO HIGHWAY 1 - GUERRERO NEGRO TO CABO SAN LUCAS

de La Paz is a downtown department store on Mutualismo offering a variety of high-quality merchandise. Other department stores include **Dorian's** downtown and **CCC**, with two stores, near the state capitol and on Colima near Highway 1.

Dining

Being the state capital and largest city in Baja California Sur, La Paz has a wide selection of restaurants to meet all tastes and budgets. Like most towns in Baja, seafood dominates local menus, although many other options are available.

Some of the restaurants listed here are AAA approved; more information can be found in the *Lodging & Restaurants* chapter. Non AAA-approved restaurants are also listed here as a service to travelers.

Well-known establishments include **Trapiche** (Mexican), on the waterfront at Legaspy and Topete; **El Taste** (seafood and steaks), two blocks southwest of Hotel Los Arcos on Paseo Obregón; **Mariscos Mar de Cortes** (seafood), at 5 de Febrero and Guillermo Prieto; **La Pazta** (Italian), in the Hotel Mediterrane on Allende;

Quick Guide to La Paz

Tourist Information and Assistance

Secretaría de Turismo or SECTUR (State Tourism Office) *On the Tourist Wharf at Paseo Alvaro Obregón and 16 de Septiembre (see map). Open Mon.-Fri. 8 a.m.-10 p.m., Sat.-Sun. noon-10 p.m. 01152 (112) 4-01-00 or 4-01-03.* The office is staffed by helpful bilingual personnel with information on the city and surroundings. They also offer Protección al Turista (tourist assistance), which provides legal assistance to tourists.

Newspapers

The *Baja Sun* is an English-language newspaper with recreational articles and advertisements covering the municipalities of La Paz and Los Cabos, plus additional material about the rest of Baja California. Another English-language paper is the *Gringo Gazette*, a biweekly that covers the southern Baja region. Several other publications in English are for sale at the bookstore Librería Contempo on Agustín Arreolo near Paseo Alvaro Obregón. Two Spanish dailies in La Paz—*El Sudcaliforniano* and *La Peninsular*—serve the city and the remainder of Baja California Sur.

Radio and Television Stations

La Paz has several radio stations. Estereo 96.7, has a varied selection of international music; 90.1 FM, Radio Alegría, presents traditional Mexican music. A few American radio stations come in at night. As in other parts of Baja, large hotels have satellite dishes that bring in several American TV stations in addition to the local channel and Mexico's national TV networks.

Driving in La Paz

Traffic flows smoothly on most of the long, straight streets of La Paz. Other than an abrupt terrace that rises from the bay, the city has level topography.

Jardín Yee (Cantonese), on Highway 1 about a mile southwest of the junction of Abasolo and 5 de Febrero; **Carlos 'n Charlie's** (varied menu), on the waterfront at Paseo Obregón and de León; and **Samalú** (seafood), in southwest La Paz on Rangel, between Colima and Jalisco.

Other well-known restaurants are **La Terraza** (varied menu), a sidewalk cafe in the Hotel Perla on Paseo Obregón; **Nuevo Pekín** (Chinese), on Paseo Alvaro Obregón, ¼ mile northeast of downtown La Paz; **Kiwi** (seafood), on the beach near Paseo Alvaro Obregón and 5 de Mayo; **Bermejo** (seafood, steak and Mexican dishes), in Hotel Los Arcos; **Hotel Plaza Real** (varied menu), at Esquerro and Callejón La Paz in downtown; and **El Quinto Sol** (vegetarian), at the corner of Independencia and Dominguez.

Nightclubs

By resort standards, La Paz's nightlife is on the tame side, but the number of clubs with dancing and/or live entertainment has increased with the

To avoid being disoriented, drivers should closely follow the La Paz map, which reveals that the grid pattern of streets is oriented northeast-southwest. The old business section near the *malecón* (bay-front drive) has congested irregular streets and is better covered on foot. The city has several rental car agencies.

Local Transportation

La Paz has numerous taxis, especially along the *malecón* and near the hotels. Before getting in a cab, be sure to understand the fare to be charged. The rate for two miles is about $4, and from central La Paz to the airport (about eight miles) approximately $9. Hourly rates are available as well; expect to pay about $8-9. Local city buses run frequently to all parts of La Paz. The fare is only about 30¢. Bus riders should know some Spanish and understand the layout of the city. The central depot for local buses is by the public market at Revolución de 1910 and Degollado. Service to Pichilingue and Los Cabos is provided by Transportes Aguila at 125 Paseo Alvaro Obregón.

Long-distance travel is available with Autotransportes de Baja California (ABC) to all other cities on the Baja peninsula; the terminal is at Jalisco and Héroes de Independencia (see *Appendix*, Transportation section).

Ferry Transportation

Ferryboats carrying passengers and vehicles to the mainland sail out of Pichilingue, the deep water port for La Paz. Grupo Sematur, the principal ferry company, has its ticket office on Guillermo Prieto at Cinco de Mayo (see *Appendix*, Transportation section).

growth of the city. Several well-known spots are on Paseo Alvaro Obregón, including **La Paz Lapa**, next to Carlos 'n Charlie's; **La Cabaña**, on the lobby floor of the Hotel Perla; **Bacho's**, north of Hotel Perla; **Oasis**, north of the corner of Ignacio Bañuelos Cabezu; and **Okey Laser Club**, next door to Oasis. Other popular venues include **Dynasty Dance Club**, just west of Obregón on 5 de Mayo; **Las Varitas**, at the corner of Independencia and Dominguez; and **Bahía Rock**, in the Crowne Plaza Resort.

Points of Interest

BIBLIOTECA DE HISTORIA DE LAS CALIFORNIAS *North side of Plaza Constitución. 01152 (112) 5-37-67. Open Mon.-Fri. 8 a.m.- 8 p.m. Free.* This library, occupying the old government center, has a display of vivid paintings about early Baja California Sur, and a collection of books in Spanish and English about the history of Baja California and California.

BOAT TOURS *Tourist Wharf at Paseo Alvaro Obregón and 16 de Septiembre.*

MEXICO HIGHWAY 1 – GUERRERO NEGRO TO CABO SAN LUCAS

Nuestra Señora de La Paz stands on the south side of Plaza Constitución.

01152 (114) 3-35-66 (SECTUR). Several companies offer boat trips around Bahía de la Paz. Trips to Isla Espíritu Santo are available for those who wish to dive or kayak around the island and enjoy its unspoiled natural environment. Most of the larger hotels and travel agencies also have information on boat tours.

DOVE OF PEACE MONUMENT *Junction of Hwy. 1 and Camino a las Garzas, the bypass to Los Cabos.* As a gateway to La Paz, the large contemporary sculpture bears an inscription which translates, "And if you want peace *(paz)*, I offer it to you in the sunny peace of my bay."

MUSEO DE ANTROPOLOGIA Y HISTORIA DE BAJA CALIFORNIA SUR *Ignacio Altamirano and 5 de Mayo. 01152 (112) 2-01-62, or 5-64-24. Open Mon.-Fri. 8 a.m.-6 p.m., Sat. 9 a.m.-2 p.m. Donation.* This outstanding

museum features exhibits on geology, geography, flora and fauna. Displays on anthropology explain Indian cultures with dioramas and replicas of cave paintings. History is covered through Spanish mission settlement, the Mexican-American War, and the struggle during the wars of independence. There is also a good book store.

NUESTRA SEÑORA DE LA PAZ *South side of Plaza Constitución.* This cathedral began as one of the original missions. Large bilingual plaques describe the history of the church and some of the early settlement of La Paz. Across Calle Revolución is Plaza Constitución, the city's main square and a popular gathering spot.

TEATRO DE LA CIUDAD *Miguel Legaspy and Héroes de Independencia. 01152 (112) 5-02-07, 2-91-96 (art gallery). Art gallery open Mon.-Fri. 8 a.m.-8 p.m. Donation.* The theater hosts a variety of performing arts; it also contains an art gallery showcasing the works of artists from La Paz and from throughout the country.

Museo de la Ballena *Located next to theater. No phone. Open Tue.-Sun. 9 a.m.-2 p.m. Donation.* This museum features paintings, sculptures and extensive information on whales of all species, focusing on the California gray whale.

TOURIST WHARF *Along the malecón next to the State Tourism Office.* This attractive park is at the hub of La Paz's waterfront scene. It touts a large gazebo and a plaque marking the spot where Queen Elizabeth and Prince Philip of England disembarked during their 1983 visit.

🚙 Side Route

La Paz to Pichilingue and Beaches to the North

(17 mi., 29 km.; 0:40 hr.)

The easy drive to Pichilingue and the beaches to the north makes an enjoyable half-day excursion from La Paz. The paved road to Pichilingue (Mexico Highway 11) is a northward continuation of Paseo Alvaro Obregón—La Paz's bay-front thoroughfare. The road hugs the shore of Bahía de La Paz, offering fine views of cactus-covered hills, mangrove thickets and the clear, incredibly blue waters of the bay. Playa Coromuel, an attractive beach that is popular with La Paz residents, is 2.6 miles from Avenida 5 de Mayo, the last major street of the city. About a mile farther north are La Concha Beach Resort and El Caimancito, which has a public beach, a restaurant and the official governor's mansion. At Pichilingue, nine miles from La Paz, is the government-built ferry terminal used by the La Paz-Mazatlán and La Paz-Topolobampo ferries (see Transportation section in the *Appendix*). In addition to the ferry port facilities, Pichilingue has a commercial fishing fleet, warehouses and cafes.

The road has recently been paved to the beaches beyond Pichilingue. Just after the ferry terminal is Playa Pichilingue, another popular beach. A short distance farther north the road cuts inland, then a paved spur reaches the shore of Puerto Balandra, a lovely inlet that makes a good spot for a pic-

Ferryboats to Mazatlán depart from La Paz's deep water port at Pichilingue.

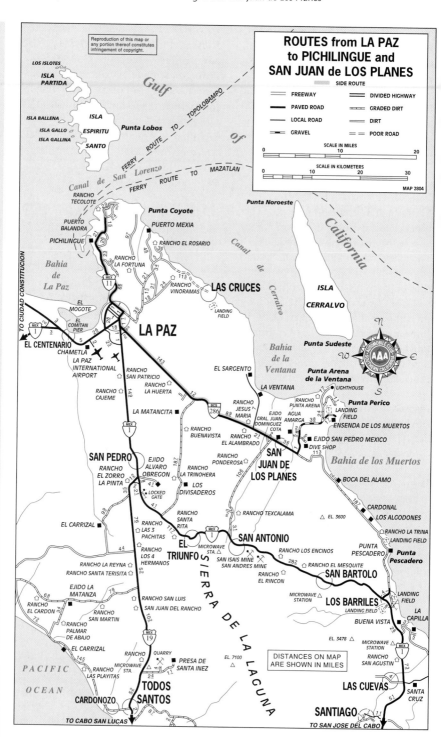

ROUTES from LA PAZ to PICHILINGUE and SAN JUAN de LOS PLANES

nic. A trail leads up a hill to a viewpoint above the inlet. Past Puerto Balandra the road runs another mile to Playa Tecolote, an attractive *playa pública*, where pavement ends. A good dirt road lined with scenic desert plants turns east and follows the shoreline to a gravel mine and Playa Cachimba, eight miles northeast of Pichilingue. Surf fishing is reportedly good here. Visible offshore is 14-mile-long Isla Espíritu Santo, a destination for divers, kayakers and wildlife observers.

🚐 Side Route

La Paz to San Juan de Los Planes
(29 mi., 45 km; 1 hr.)

An excellent all-day excursion from La Paz, the side trip to Los Planes offers travelers a chance to visit a fast-growing agricultural region and to explore a series of beautiful, isolated beaches. After leaving Highway 1 at a well-marked junction on the southern outskirts of La Paz, a paved road signed "BCS 286" runs between rolling hills for nine miles, then climbs onto the northern shoulder of the Sierra de la Laguna. At mileage 11.9 is Rancho La Huerta, a long-established cattle ranch with a brick chapel, a small cemetery and a cafe. Beyond La Huerta the road passes turnoffs to several more ranches as it winds through countryside covered with cardón, cholla, pitahaya, copalquin (a small deciduous tree) and heavy underbrush. At mileage 15.9 the road reaches a summit; visible ahead are the cultivated fields of Los Planes, the blue expanse of Bahía de la Ventana, and barren mountainous Isla Cerralvo. From the summit the road makes a long, steady descent onto a level coastal plain, where it comes to a junction at mileage 23.7. To the left a good graded road leads seven miles to El Sargento and La Ventana, fishing and ranching villages on the western shore of lovely Bahía de la Ventana. Continue straight ahead for Los Planes. At mileage 25.8 is an intersection with a new road on the right leading 14.8 miles to the village of San Antonio on Highway 1.

The route continues 3.2 miles farther to San Juan de Los Planes (or Los Planes, as it is commonly called), the center of a rapidly developing farming region. Water from deep wells irrigates fields of cotton, corn, chiles, tomatoes and beans. Los Planes is a friendly town of about 1000 with a cafe, three stores, telephone service and a health center. The pavement continues past the center of town for a few miles en route to Ensenada de los Muertos (Deadman Bay), 13.4 miles to the northeast. Here is found a beautiful, curving bay with a small fish camp. Fine primitive campsites can be found here; fishing is excellent, and swimming is good. Punta Arena, directly opposite Isla Cerralvo on the eastern shore of Bahía de la Ventana, can be reached by backtracking two miles toward Los Planes, then turning right on a signed dirt road. This road leads past a cattle ranch, an airstrip and a group of salt-evaporating ponds to the isolated Las Arenas Resort on the shore of the bay. (After several years of closure, the hotel in early 1998 was preparing to reopen.) North of the hotel is a lighthouse.

(Note: Grazing livestock, common along roads throughout Baja, are especially widespread on this side trip. Motorists should be extra alert for them along this route, and nighttime driving is strongly discouraged.)

MEXICO HIGHWAY 1 - GUERRERO NEGRO TO CABO SAN LUCAS

MEXICO HIGHWAY 1 - GUERRERO NEGRO TO CABO SAN LUCAS

A fishing panga *returns from the sea to Ensenada de los Muertos while a squadron of hungry pelicans wait for a handout.*

◤◢ Travelogue

La Paz to Los Barriles

(65 mi., 105 km.; 1:45 hrs.)

After leaving the outskirts of La Paz, Highway 1 crosses level countryside with dense growths of cardón and pitahaya (organ pipe) cacti, and various trees and shrubs. Just south of the village of San Pedro is the junction with Highway 19 to Todos Santos and Cabo San Lucas. At this point, the main highway bears left and climbs into the foothills of the Sierra de la Laguna. After passing through El Triunfo, the road descends to San Antonio in the bottom of a narrow valley. It then crosses another arm of the mountains and follows the course of a steep-walled canyon to San Bartolo. Emerging from the mountains, Highway 1 soon reaches Los Barriles on the shore

of Bahía de Palmas, famous for its superlative sportfishing.

00.0   **La Paz, at the intersection of Calzadas Abasolo and 5 de Febrero. To proceed south on Highway 1, take 5 de Febrero southeast for one mile to Carretera al Sur, then bear right.**

01.4   **Junction with the paved road (BC 286) to San Juan de los Planes (see Side Route to San Juan de los Planes).**

16.0   **San Pedro, a small community serving the surrounding farms and ranches.**

19.0   **Junction with Mexico Highway 19 to Todos Santos and Cabo San Lucas (see *Mexico Highway 19*).**

32.3   **El Triunfo, a picturesque mountain village with a cafe and a church. El Triunfo was** once a rich gold and silver mining camp, and at one time was the largest settlement in the south of Baja California. The mines closed in 1926, but with the increase in precious metal values, mining has resumed at some locations. Numerous old buildings line the highway, and on a hill just south of the village are the remains of the old smelter. Handwoven baskets are for sale on the north side of the highway.

36.8 San Antonio, an attractive farming center located in the bottom of a deep arroyo. San Antonio's history also includes a mining boom. Facilities include groceries, eating establishments and gasoline. Past the junction with the village's main street,

Highway 1 climbs sharply out of the canyon.

53.8 San Bartolo, a sleepy town strung out along a palm-lined canyon, produces guavas, oranges, avocados and other fruits. Groceries, local fruits and meals are available.

65.2 Junction with a dirt road signed "Ramal El Cardonal." This road leads 0.8 mile to another junction; the road to the left is nine miles of a rough and narrow but scenic coastal route to the resort community of Punta Pescadero. The road goes on to the village and resort of El Cardonal (see *Campgrounds & Trailer Parks*), to Boca del Alamo and farther northwest to San Juan de los Planes.

Just south of the junction is Los Barriles (see *Lodging & Restaurants* and

The coastline is scenic north of Punta Pescadero.

Of Mice and Men: Steinbeck's Sea

By Dennis Anderson
(Excerpted from *Westways*)

Millions of readers discovered John Steinbeck as a student, cutting their literary teeth on "The Red Pony," "Of Mice and Men" and "Tortilla Flat." If Hemingway wrote of solitary courage, Steinbeck celebrated the courage of people sticking together. More than a writer, he was an explorer, a sailor and a naturalist. And in 1940, after the marathon labor of finishing "The Grapes of Wrath," he sailed from Monterey, California, around the Baja California peninsula on an expedition he compared to Darwin's voyage of the HMS *Beagle*, to recharge his writerly batteries and explore the tide pools. The trip aboard the chartered *Western Flyer* provided material for Steinbeck's novel "The Pearl" and produced "Sea of Cortez: A Leisurely Journal of Travel and Research," from which "The Log From the Sea of Cortez," his best nonfiction book and a work that put Baja on the map for many travelers, was later extracted.

Making the trip with Steinbeck was his best friend, Ed Ricketts, drawn in "Cannery Row" as Doc, a marine biologist and philosopher. Ricketts coauthored the original "Sea of Cortez" and taught Steinbeck the marvels of life in the tide pools. Steinbeck's first wife, Carol, also went along, as galley mate, in an unsuccessful attempt to shore up their faltering marriage. (Nothing like sailing a couple thousand miles with a bunch of tough salts to calm the domestic squalls.) At one point she dove from the boat wearing an evening dress and a $300 watch.

Marital strain aside, the expedition held for Steinbeck the lure of a mental-health cure. The success of "The Grapes of Wrath" had given him celebrity, and this was an escape from fame into nature. During the six-week expedition, Steinbeck, Ricketts and crew collected, by Ricketts' estimation, "the greatest lot of specimens ever to have been collected in

Campgrounds & Trailer Parks), a rapidly growing tourist community on Bahía de Palmas. Visitors will find hotels, trailer parks, a Pemex station, a coin laundry, an airstrip, a marina, numerous restaurants, markets, auto parts stores and a clinic. There's also a new mini-mall with several tourism-related businesses. Sportfishing trips are available here, and sailboarding conditions are among the best on the peninsula. A large number of new California-style homes (many still under construction), real estate offices, non-Mexican license plates and the predominance of signs in English reflect the area's increasing popularity with outsiders.

Travelogue

Los Barriles to San José del Cabo
(50 mi., 81 km.; 1:30 hrs.)

The highway skirts the coastline for a few miles, then crosses a long cactus-

# of Cortez

It was a fishing trawler, like one of these resting at anchor near Mulegé, in which Steinbeck made his 1940 voyage to the Sea of Cortez.

the gulf by any single expedition." They also worked, laughed, brawled, fished, and generally had a heck of a good time.

"Sea of Cortez" combined Steinbeck's love of Mexico and marine biology in a captivating narrative about the people of the gulf. The writer saw the life of the villages as akin to life in the tide pools—complex, interesting, full of story material. Traveling in Mexico, Steinbeck chatted easily with peasants, politicians, little boys and generals. He painted a naturalist's portrait of the people he encountered.

covered plain. The towering Sierra de la Laguna looms dramatically to the west; cattle are frequently encountered on this section of highway. At San José del Cabo the road again reaches the shore of the Gulf of California (Sea of Cortez). Starting at Los Cabos Airport, the highway is a four-lane divided route all the way to Cabo San Lucas.

1.9   Junction with the entrance road of the Hotel Rancho Buena Vista.

4.4   Junction with a dirt road to the Hotel Buena Vista Beach Resort.

12.3   Junction with a paved road to La Ribera, then graded roads to Punta Colorada, Cabo Pulmo and Los Frailes (see Side Route to Cabo Pulmo). To the right is Las Cuevas, a quiet farming village with no tourist facilities.

17.4 Junction with the paved road to Santiago. This attractive agricultural community of about 4000 people sits on a pair of hills separated by a shallow palm-forested canyon. On the northern hill, 1.7 miles from Highway 1, is the town plaza, along with a Pemex station, an inn with a restaurant and several cafes and stores. Just beyond the southern hill is the Santiago Zoo, the only one in Baja California Sur, with a variety of wildlife native to Mexico.

19.4 The Tropic of Cancer, marked by a spherical concrete monument representing the 23.27 North Latitude parallel.

26.1 A Pemex station at the junction with the 1.7-mile paved road to Miraflores, a farming town known for its vegetables and cheeses. By the end of the paved road at the town entrance is a leather shop that does retail sales. Facilities in Miraflores include stores and cafes.

29.4 Junction with the graded dirt road to Caduaño, another small farming community. The town center is about a mile from the main highway.

36.3 Junction with a winding scenic road signed "Los Naranjos," which goes across the tree-covered landscape of the Sierra de la Laguna to El Pescadero and Todos Santos on Mexico Highway 19. Sturdy, high-clearance vehicles are necessary.

41.6 Santa Anita, a sleepy little town with a cafe and a small store.

43.3 Junction with the 0.9-mile paved road to Los Cabos International Airport (see *Appendix*, Transportation).

47.9 Santa Rosa, a rapidly growing community of about 3000, has a Pemex station, cafes and stores.

50.1 Junction with Calle Zaragoza, which leads to the center of San José del Cabo.

🚗 Side Routes

Highway 1 to La Ribera
(7 mi., 11 km.; 0:15 hr.),

Cabo Pulmo
(23 mi., 37 km.; 0:45 hr.)

San José del Cabo
(80 mi., 129 km.; 4:30 hrs.)

With the longest seacoast extension of any side route in Baja California, this road follows along the East Cape (Cabo del Este). From a junction 11.6 miles south of Los Barriles on Highway 1, a paved road leads eastward past fields of hay and corn for 7.2 miles to La Ribera, a farming community of about 2000 with stores, a cafe, a trailer park and a Pemex station. From La Ribera, a graded dirt road crosses rolling scrub-covered countryside for 5.5 miles to the Hotel Punta Colorada, situated atop a low bluff above a lovely beach. A little to the west a new paved road turns southeast, takes a more inland route over 11 miles of hilly terrain and reaches the gulf coast near La Abundancia, where it joins a graded dirt road.

From here to San José del Cabo, the dirt road is wide and passable for low-clearance vehicles. But motorists should be ready for a long, jarring drive on washboard surface with rough and rocky intervals—a trek that

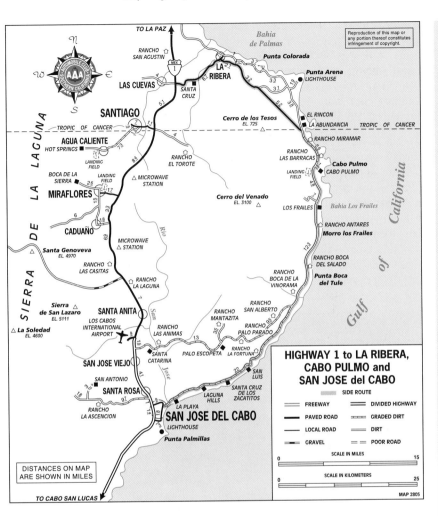

HIGHWAY 1 to LA RIBERA, CABO PULMO and SAN JOSE del CABO

	SIDE ROUTE
FREEWAY	DIVIDED HIGHWAY
PAVED ROAD	GRADED DIRT
LOCAL ROAD	DIRT
GRAVEL	POOR ROAD

SCALE IN MILES
0 — 15

SCALE IN KILOMETERS
0 — 25

MAP 2805

DISTANCES ON MAP ARE SHOWN IN MILES

MEXICO HIGHWAY 1 - GUERRERO NEGRO TO CABO SAN LUCAS

can take its toll on even sturdy vehicles and their occupants. Cautious, heads-up driving is a must, with the rusted remains of abandoned vehicles serving as ever-present reminders along the way. The payoff is miles of scenic coastline, with turquoise waters, secluded coves and white-sand beaches.

From the pavement's end, the dirt follows the shoreline to Cabo Pulmo. This village is a collection of thatched huts, small restaurants and a launch ramp

on a picturesque tropical beach. There are three dive shops as well, which rent gear and arrange offshore trips. Fishing and diving are both excellent in this area, which boasts the only coral reef on the Gulf of California.

Heading south, numerous open campsites are abundant along the coastline. Five miles past Cabo Pulmo is Los Frailes, a village named for the adjacent jagged promontory that forms the easternmost point of the Baja California peninsula. The village has vacation homes, trailers and a hotel. At mileage 55, beyond a wide sandy wash near Rancho Vinorama, is a junction with a graded road leading 24 miles southwest over the coastal foothills to Highway 1.

Ahead, the road continues to follow the coast past miles of beautiful beaches and a landscape that contains pitahaya and elephant trees. Three miles beyond the junction is a massive wild fig tree next to the road. Six miles later the rusting hulk of a large vessel may be seen by walking down to the water's edge. This coastline remains mostly open territory, but signs of

rapid growth are apparent, with tracts of new vacation homes sporting names like Playa Tortuga, Laguna Hills and EaStCAPE. The influence is distinctly foreign, with signs in English, and U.S. and Canadian license plates on most vehicles.

Several miles farther along the road swings inland, passes through densely vegetated terrain and climbs between two cone-shaped peaks to a low ridge that offers the first glimpse of San José del Cabo. After crossing many roads on the outskirts of San José del Cabo, the road enters the center of town at mileage 80.0.

Beautiful coastline vistas await travelers all along the East Cape road.

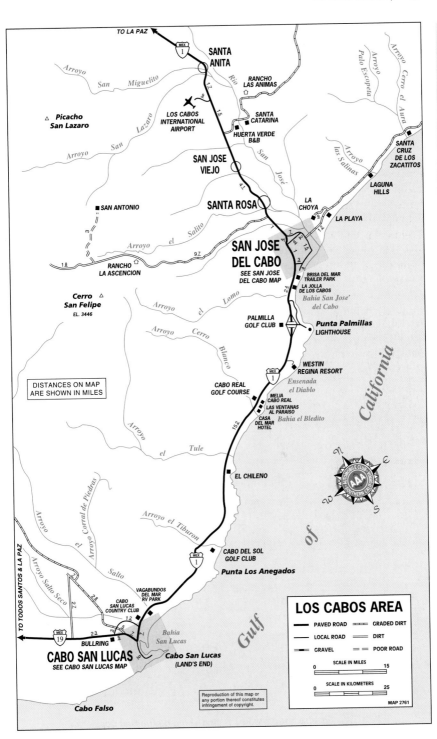

MEXICO HIGHWAY 1 - GUERRERO NEGRO TO CABO SAN LUCAS

TO LA PAZ

SANTA ANITA

MEX 1

Arroyo   San   Miguelito

RANCHO LAS ANIMAS

Rio

SANTA CATARINA

LOS CABOS INTERNATIONAL AIRPORT

△ Picacho San Lazaro

HUERTA VERDE B&B

Arroyo   San   Lazaro

SANTA CRUZ DE LOS ZACATITOS

Arroyo   Cerro el Aura

Palo Escopeta

Arroyo   San

SAN JOSE VIEJO

Arroyo   las   Salinas

San   José

■ SAN ANTONIO

SANTA ROSA

LA CHOYA

LAGUNA HILLS

Arroyo   el   Salito

SAN JOSE DEL CABO

SEE SAN JOSE DEL CABO MAP

LA PLAYA

9.7

1.8

RANCHO LA ASCENCION

Arroyo   el   Lomo

BRISA DEL MAR TRAILER PARK

SAN JOSE DEL CABO TRAILER PARK

LA JOLLA DE LOS CABOS

Bahia San José del Cabo

Cerro △ San Felipe
EL. 3446

Arroyo   Cerro   Blanco

PALMILLA GOLF CLUB

Punta Palmillas
LIGHTHOUSE

DISTANCES ON MAP ARE SHOWN IN MILES

WESTIN REGINA RESORT

MEX 1

Ensenada el Diablo

CABO REAL GOLF COURSE

MELIA CABO REAL
LAS VENTANAS AL PARAISO
CASA DEL MAR HOTEL

Bahia el Bledito

152

California

Arroyo   el   Tule

EL CHILENO

Gulf

Arroyo el Tiburon

CABO DEL SOL GOLF CLUB

Punta Los Anegados

N W E S

AAA

TO TODOS SANTOS & LA PAZ

Arroyo   el   Corral de Piedras

Salto

VAGABUNDOS DEL MAR RV PARK

CABO SAN LUCAS COUNTRY CLUB

of

Arroyo Salto Seco

MEX 19

BULLRING

CABO SAN LUCAS
SEE CABO SAN LUCAS MAP

Bahia San Lucas

Cabo San Lucas
(LAND'S END)

Gulf

LOS CABOS AREA

▬▬▬ PAVED ROAD	══ GRADED DIRT
── LOCAL ROAD	═ DIRT
▬ GRAVEL	═ ═ POOR ROAD

SCALE IN MILES
0   15

SCALE IN KILOMETERS
0   25

Cabo Falso

Reproduction of this map or any portion thereof constitutes infringement of copyright.

MAP 2761

San José del Cabo

(See also *Lodging & Restaurants* and *Campgrounds & Trailer Parks*.)

Located at the spot where Highway 1 rejoins the Gulf of California, San José del Cabo spreads over a range of low hills and a narrow, attractive coastal plain. Founded in 1730, the town serves up an eclectic mix of buildings old and new, narrow alleyways and broad boulevards, unmasking it as an old settlement in the midst of a modern-day boom. Tropical agriculture—coconuts, mangos, spices and citrus fruits—is an important part of the economy, but it is tourism that has fueled most of the recent growth, bringing the population to a present-day total of about 25,000. San José del Cabo is the seat of government of the *municipio* of Los Cabos, which encompasses the East Cape and Cabo San Lucas. (The *municipio* has about 60,000 residents.)

In spite of the population surge, San José del Cabo has retained a relaxed, dignified ambiance, one that attracts a more subdued breed of tourist than nearby Cabo San Lucas. There are two sides to San José del Cabo's tourist scene. One is the town center, which reflects the region's colonial roots, with its attractive plaza park, arched building entrances and twin-tower church. Calle Zaragoza and Boulevard Mijares are the center of the tourist trade here, offering a fine assortment of restaurants, galleries and gift shops. There is little in terms of U.S.-style restaurants or other services but the foreign influence is heavy nonetheless.

The Estero de San José is an inviting destination.

Throughout most of the year, the majority of those strolling the sidewalks are likely to be U.S. or Canadian tourists.

The other side is found south of the town center, in the new FONATUR resort development that fronts directly on the beautiful beaches of the Gulf of California. Several large, U.S.-style hotels have gone up along the sand, with a golf course and shopping center nearby. A number of condominium developments have opened as well, and more are on the way.

Along with tourist facilities, visitors to San José del Cabo will find a host of services to meet other needs they may have, including groceries, Pemex stations, auto parts, mechanical help and two hospitals.

Welcome to the farmer's market at San José del Cabo, typical of such venues all across Mexico.

Shopping

Souvenir-hunters will find a wide assortment of artisan shops, boutiques and open-air markets in San José del Cabo. While such establishments are common in tourist areas throughout Baja, San José del Cabo offers a higher proportion of handmade goods and top-quality items than most. Once more, **Zaragoza** and **Mijares** are the center of the shopping scene, particularly Mijares. This zone boasts numerous specialty shops offering paintings, pottery and handicraft items from distinct regions of the country. A number of stores sell T-shirts, beachwear and other clothing. Major hotels have gift shops of their own as well.

Dining

A fine selection of restaurants offers something for a wide range of palates in San José del Cabo. All the major hotels boast at least one restaurant,

and plenty more beckon in the town's center.

The following are some of the better-known restaurants throughout the city. Some of the restaurants listed here are AAA approved; more information about these can be found in the *Lodging & Restaurants* chapter. Non-AAA-approved restaurants are also listed here as a service to visitors.

Some of the city center spots are **Damiana** (international), on Plaza Park; **El Café Fiesta** (vegetarian), also on Plaza Park; **La Cenaduría** (Mexican), on Zaragoza near Plaza Park; **Los Gorditos** (Mexican), on Mijares across from the municipal hall; **La Bombilla** (Mexican), on Hidalgo west of Zaragoza; **Tropicana** (varied menu), at Mijares 30; **Tequila** (Mediterranean), on Mijares near the municipal hall;

and **Pietro Ristorante** (Italian), on Zaragoza near Plaza Park.

Many more restaurants scattered around the city's center and elsewhere await those who seek them out. Like other coastal cities in Baja, seafood is available almost everywhere. Those seeking U.S.-style fast food will be disappointed in San José del Cabo, however, since the town lacks any such establishments.

Nightclubs

Compared with its rowdy neighbor Cabo San Lucas, San José del Cabo has a decidedly tame nightlife scene. Still, several spots offer after-dark entertainment, though somewhat quieter and more restrained than what's available down the road. Outside the town center, there's **Bones Disco**, in the Presidente Los Cabos Forum Resort, and **La**

Quick Guide to San José del Cabo

Tourist Information
Municipal Tourism Office *In San José's plaza park. Open Mon.-Fri. 8 a.m-3 p.m. 01152 (114) 2-29-60.* Information and printed materials about the Los Cabos region are available here.

Newspapers
Several publications in English are available here, with information on tourist activities in the Los Cabos region. There's the *Baja Sun*, a monthly paper with a pullout section on Baja California Sur, the semimonthly *Gringo Gazette*, the monthly *Cabo Life* and the bilingual monthly *Los Cabos News*. All of these newspapers are aimed at visitors to the area. U.S. newspapers such as the *Los Angeles Times* and *Wall Street Journal* are available in some of the larger hotels' gift shops, as are some of the more popular U.S. magazines. In addition, there's *Tribunal*, the local Spanish-language newspaper.

Radio and Television Stations
Radio 96.3 FM, Cabo Mil, plays a variety of fine international music. All of the major hotels have satellite dishes that bring in major U.S. TV stations, along with the local channels and national stations from Mexico City.

Driving in San José del Cabo
Like most things about the town, something old and something new sums up the streets that drivers will find in San José del Cabo. U.S. and Canadian drivers will feel at home on Highway 1 (four lanes from the airport to Cabo San Lucas) and along Paseo San José, the broad boulevard that follows the coastline just south of town. In town, though, the streets are narrow, often one-way and parking is at a premium. Local police do not hesitate in issuing tickets for parking and moving violations. Luckily, the city's center is compact and lends itself to walking. Visitors would do well to park their cars elsewhere and explore these blocks on foot.

SAN JOSE DEL CABO

DIVIDED HIGHWAY
MAIN ROAD
SECONDARY ROAD

SCALE IN MILES
0   0.4

SCALE IN KILOMETERS
0   0.6

MAP 2760

Cantina, at kilometer 22.5 on the highway to Cabo San Lucas. Boulevard Mijares touts a number of spots, including **Eclipse**, **Iguana Bar** and **Tropicana del Cabo**. The center of town also boasts a number of coffee and dessert bars, along with restaurants that offer strolling musicians as part of their entertainment.

Points of Interest

ESTERO DE SAN JOSÉ *End of Paseo San José, just east of Hotel Presidente Los Cabos.* The estuary of the Río San José is bordered by dense palm groves and is replete with aquatic plants. It is a protected sanctuary, home to a variety of birds. Facilities are being developed for visitors to hike along the shores and take boat rides.

PLAZA PARK *Calle Zaragoza and Blvd. Mijares.* This small town square maintains the atmosphere of a typical Mexican colonial town. Facing the shaded plaza are the church, the tourism office and a monument to General José Antonio Mijares.

PALACIO MUNICIPAL/MUNICIPAL HALL *One block south of the plaza.* Dating from 1927, the traditional structure

The municipal hall is a prominent landmark in the city.

has offices that face on an interior patio.

SAN JOSÉ CHURCH *West side of the plaza.* Founded in 1730, this active church has been rebuilt according to the original style. It has classic twin steeples.

Travelogue

San José del Cabo to Cabo San Lucas

(21 mi., 34 km.; 0:30 hr.)

A four-lane expressway leads southwest to Cabo San Lucas, passing many hotels and restaurants, winding along the gulf through low, scrub-dotted hills, and occasionally offering tantalizing glimpses of beautiful beaches and azure waters. Signs of growth are everywhere along this stretch—hotels and condominiums under construction, earthmovers clearing the way for more new buildings, billboards in English touting new resort developments. The route remains scenic, however, and several public beaches are accessible from the highway via side roads. Finally, just before arriving in Cabo San Lucas, travelers get the first view of Land's End (Finisterra), the tip of the Baja California peninsula. At the wharf in Cabo San Lucas, 1059 miles from the U.S. border, Highway 1 comes to an end.

00.0 **Junction with Calle Zaragoza into San José del Cabo.**

01.3 **Junction with a palm-lined boulevard leading to the beach resort development marked "zona de hoteles."**

01.8 **Playa Tropical, site of Brisa del Mar Trailer Park. The highway swings to the southwest at this point.**

03.8 **Entrance road of the Hotel Palmilla resort.**

06.7 **On the north side of the highway is Cabo Real Golf Course. On the south side is Hotel Meliá Cabo Real.**

11.0 **Entrance road of the Hotel Cabo San Lucas.**

12.8 **Entrance road of the Hotel Twin Dolphin.**

15.4 **Cabo del Sol golf club.**

16.9 **Junction with the paved road leading to the Cabo Bello development, which includes the Hotel Calinda Beach Cabo San Lucas. At this point, Land's End comes into view.**

A craftsman tools leather in Miraflores.

20.4   Cabo San Lucas, at the junction with Calle Morelos, which is the beginning of Mexico Highway 19 leading north to Todos Santos, San Pedro and La Paz. Boulevard Marina, on the left, leads to the waterfront.

Cabo San Lucas

(See also *Lodging & Restaurants* and *Campgrounds & Trailer Parks*.)

The town of Cabo San Lucas fronts a small harbor on the gulf side of the rocky peninsula that forms the southernmost tip of Baja California. The bay, which in the 16th and 17th centuries was a favorite hiding place for pirates who laid in wait for Spanish treasure ships, now serves as an anchorage for fishing boats and private yachts. Because of its renowned sportfishing and the increasing popularity of its many luxury hotels, Cabo San Lucas has changed from a quiet, unassuming cannery village into an internationally known resort. From only 1500 inhabi-

tants in 1970, the town has swelled to a current total of about 28,000 and climbing.

All around is evidence of the town's transformation into a booming tourist resort. Impressive condominiums spread over hillsides to the marina, where million-dollar yachts rest in their berths. Construction cranes tower above the marina and beachfronts, as the building boom continues. Cruise ships, too, have made this a regular port of call on their way up and down Mexico's west coast. Like many Mexican resorts, most of Cabo San Lucas'

The harbor at Cabo San Lucas touts many impressive new developments.

tourists (about 80 percent) come from outside the country, hailing mainly from the United States and Canada.

Awaiting them is a full range of tourist facilities and services, including the heaviest concentration of luxury hotels in all of Baja California. Swimming, diving, parasailing and surfing are a few of the many activities available in this water sportsman's cornucopia. Kayaks, wave runners, sailboards and dive gear are all available for rent. Sportfishing is another prime attraction in the waters offshore. Landlubbers will keep busy, too, as motorcycles, all-terrain cycles, mountain bikes and horses are all available for rent. Golfing, meanwhile, has taken off here in recent years, thanks to the

construction of four championship courses.

The weather lends itself to such pursuits throughout the year, with more than 300 days of annual sunshine. Peak season is from December through April, when daytime temperatures typically run in the 70s. For many young and young-at-heart visitors, the fast times really start as the sun goes down and the town's legendary nightlife heats up. Outside of Tijuana, no town in Baja California has more clubs than Cabo San Lucas.

Those who drove this far will find a full slate of automotive services, including a car wash, Pemex stations, trailer parks, auto parts stores and mechanic shops.

Shopping

Cabo San Lucas boasts a wide selection of clothing, souvenirs and other items to meet the needs of most travelers. The downtown area has an assortment of shops catering to tourists. Near the marina, **Plaza Nautica**, **Plaza Bonita Mall**, **Plaza Del Mar** and **Plaza Real Mall** are all good hunting grounds for shoppers. Nearby is **Calle Hidalgo**, with several blocks' worth of souvenir shops. Leather goods, T-shirts, hats, blown glass, jewelry, iron, wood and ceramics are a just a few of the items to be found along this stretch. A similar assortment of keepsakes is sold in a large open-air marketplace near the south end of the marina, next to the sportfishing pier.

In addition, some nightclubs, such as **Squid Roe** and **Carlos 'N Charlies**, boast their own official stores in town. Of the arts and crafts stores, **Galería El Dorado**, on Boulevard Marina near Guerrero, is among the more attractive, having a nice selection of paintings and ceramics by local artists.

Dining

Cabo San Lucas is awash with restaurants of all descriptions, vying for their slice of the lucrative tourist market. Scores of eateries serve up a wide assortment of cuisine—seafood, Mexican, Italian, American—even Spanish and Japanese food. All the major hotels have one or more restaurants, and the tourist zone surrounding the marina has many more from which to choose. The town offers a broader

Cabo San Lucas has many upscale tourist venues, like this elaborate swimming pool at Hotel Finisterra.

Quick Guide to Cabo San Lucas

Tourist Assistance

Los Cabos Tourism Board *Edificio Posada, second floor, on Blvd. Lázaro Cárdenas, across from the Pemex station near the northeast entrance of town. Open Mon.-Fri. 9 a.m.-7 p.m. 01152 (114) 3-41-80.* This office is staffed by friendly bilingual personnel who offer tourist information on the Los Cabos region.

U.S. Consular Agency *Blvd. Marina y Pedregal No. 3. Open Mon.-Fri. 10 a.m.-1 p.m. 01152 (114) 3-35-66.* This office has tourist information and provides assistance to U.S. citizens in the Los Cabos region.

Newspapers

Several publications in English are available here, with information on tourist activities in the Los Cabos region. There's the *Baja Sun*, a monthly paper with a pullout section on Baja California Sur, the semimonthly *Gringo Gazette*, the monthly *Cabo Life* and the bilingual monthly *Los Cabos News*. All of these are aimed at the tourist market. Several U.S. newspapers are available at a steep markup, among them *USA Today*, *The Wall Street Journal* and the *Los Angeles Times*. A number of English-language magazines are sold as well, including the international editions of *Time* and *Newsweek*. Readers looking for local news in Spanish will want to pick up *Tribunal*.

Radio and Television Stations

Radio 96.3 FM, Cabo Mil, plays a variety of fine international music. All of the major hotels have satellite dishes that bring in major U.S. TV stations, along with the local channels and national stations from Mexico City.

Driving in Cabo San Lucas

Except for the main drags like boulevards Morelos and Lázaro Cárdenas, most streets in Cabo San Lucas are narrow and frequently congested. Within town, most visitors will find they can get around easier by taxi or on foot. Away from the tourist areas, many side streets remain unpaved and fraught with potholes.

Local Transportation

Taxi service is readily available downtown and at hotels. Major resorts operate their own taxi fleets, often charging hourly rates or fixed rates to the airport or other destinations in the area.

assortment of American-style establishments than any other locale on the peninsula, rivaled only by Tijuana and Ensenada. Pricing reflects that of a

tourist resort, which means dollarized menus and pricing in line with north-of-the-border restaurants. At the same time, nearly all restaurants have bilingual menus and at least some servers who speak English.

The following are some of the better-known restaurants throughout the city. Some of the restaurants listed here are AAA approved; more information about these can be found in the *Lodging & Restaurants* chapter. Non-AAA-approved restaurants are also listed here as a service to visitors.

A few of the more upscale restaurants include **Alfonso's Restaurant** (international), on the marina in Plaza Bonita; **Galeon Italiano Restaurant** (Italian), downtown on Boulevard Marina; **Casa Rafael's** (international), near the bay on El Médano; **Peacock's Restaurant** (international), two blocks southeast of Highway 1 on Paseo del Pescador; **Romeo y Julieta Ristorante** (Italian), south of downtown at the entrance to

Pedregal condominium district; and **Arrecifes** (Mexican), in the Westin Regina Resort west of town.

Other notable restaurants include **Salsitas** (Mexican), in Plaza Bonita; **Latitude 22+** (American), downtown on Lázaro Cárdenas; **Mama's Royal Café** (American), downtown on Hidalgo; **Baja Cantina** (varied menu), on the marina in Plaza Las Glorias; **Cannery Row** (steak, seafood), downtown on Lázaro Cárdenas; and **The Trailer Park Restaurant** (seafood, Mexican), one block southeast of Highway 1 on Paseo del Pescador.

In addition, many of the establishments listed under Nightclubs below, such as **Hard Rock Café, Planet Hollywood, Carlos 'n Charlie's**, etc., have full menu service during the day. There are several fast-food franchises as well,

Anchors aweigh! A schooner sets sail on a sightseeing cruise off Cabo San Lucas.

bearing such familiar names as **KFC**, **Subway**, **Dairy Queen** and **Domino's Pizza**. These and others are located on or near Boulevard Marina in the downtown tourist zone.

Along with those mentioned here, visitors will find many more good restaurants in Cabo San Lucas, their names too many to list here.

Nightclubs

When the sun goes down, Cabo San Lucas rattles and hums until long past midnight as a legion of night spots come to life. After-dark entertainment is one of the chief drawing cards in Cabo San Lucas, and the town has earned a reputation as one of Mexico's leading party spots. Revelers head for the club district centered along boulevards Lázaro Cárdenas and Marina, which vibrates with zesty rock, disco and Mexican music long into the night. The atmosphere is decidedly casual in the majority of establishments, and dress codes are all but unheard of. Many venues have offbeat monikers and themes to promote their rambunctious images.

Among the best known is **Cabo Wabo**, owned by Sammy Haggar, former lead vocalist for the rock band Van Halen. Located in Plaza del Mariachi on Boulevard Marina, Cabo Wabo is a combination dance club, bar and restaurant, replete with posters and photos of Haggar and other rock stars, who sometimes perform live on the large concert stage. It is, as well, perhaps the only club in Baja with its own in-house tattoo parlor. Nearby on Marina is **The Giggling Marlin**, another bar/dance club with loud party music and a mostly young clientele. This club is perhaps best known for its photo booth where patrons have their pictures taken while hung upside down next to a picture of a chortling marlin, fishing rod clutched in its fin. Another like spot is **Squid Roe**, on Lázaro Cárdenas near Zaragoza, a place with sawdust on the floor, irreverent maxims painted on the walls (e.g. "Beauty is in the eye of the beerholder,") and hired help who join in with the late-night carousing.

Many more clubs with varying degrees of rowdiness are in the immediate neighborhood. Among these are **Kokomo Cabo**, **Rockstone** and **Rio Grill**, all on Boulevard Marina; **Hard Rock Café**, **Planet Hollywood** and **Nowhere Bar**, all in the Plaza Bonita Mall on Lázaro Cárdenas; **Margaritavilla**, at the corner of Zaragoza and Marina; and **Pazzo's Cabo**, across from the Plaza Bonita Mall. Most of these spots double as restaurants and offer a wide range of food service by day and evening.

Nightlife is not just a terra firma activity in Cabo San Lucas, thanks to several motor and sailing craft that ply the offshore waters on evening party cruises. These drinking and dancing outings typically sail shortly before

Lover's Beach, located near Land's End, is indeed a romantic destination for tourists.

MEXICO HIGHWAY 1 - GUERRERO NEGRO TO CABO SAN LUCAS

sunset and last about two hours, with music (sometimes live) and open bars on board. Information on these cruises is available at the marina and major hotels.

Points of Interest

BOAT TOURS *Various docks along the marina.* Several boat companies offer tours of all lengths and descriptions. Prices start at about $7 for glass-bottom boat rides to Land's End and range upward depending on the type of craft and trip. Dive trips, sailing charters and sunset dinner cruises are all popular with tourists. Whale-watching trips are available from January through March, giving close-up views of the California gray whale and other species that pass through these waters.

CORTES PACÍFICO MUSEUM *On Blvd. Marina just south of Madero. No phone. Open daily 11 a.m.-10 p.m. Free.* In the heart of the tourist zone,

this small museum features handsome models of every game fish caught in Baja California's waters. Bilingual charts and pictures of different fish are also displayed.

GALERÍA EL DORADO *Blvd. Marina near Guerrero.* This arts and crafts store displays a nice collection of paintings and ceramics by local artists. Visitors are welcome to browse.

Land's End is where the Gulf of California meets the Pacific Ocean.

LAND'S END/FINISTERRA *The rocky, extreme southern end of the peninsula is situated at 22 degrees, 50 minutes north latitude.* This rugged, wave-worn series of rock formations includes The Arches/*Los Arcos*, and is one of Baja California's signature landmarks. Land's End may be viewed from Highway 1 on the approach to Cabo San Lucas or from any slightly elevated spot in town. Several glass-bottom boats make the short jaunt from the marina to Land's End on a regular schedule throughout the day, providing close-up looks of Los Arcos and the surrounding headlands. They also drop off passengers at nearby Lover's Beach. Land's End may also be reached on foot by starting on the beach by Solmar Suites Resort and climbing over a rough rocky saddle. (This climb should be made only by those in good physical shape, traveling with a partner.)

MUSEO DE LAS CALIFORNIAS *On downtown plaza south of Madero. No phone. Open Mon.-Fri. 9 a.m.-4 p.m. Free.* This small museum features historic photos, fossils and other artifacts of the Los Cabos region.

Mexico Highway 19

Mexico Highway 19 forms part of a loop with Mexico Highway 1 in the extreme southern portion of the peninsula. Travel time between La Paz and Cabo San Lucas is about one hour shorter on this route than via Mexico Highway 1. Shortcut though it may be, this two-lane paved route is a sightseer's delight as it heads south from its junction with Highway 1 and skirts the rugged western face of the Sierra de la Laguna. The only town along the road is Todos Santos, a bucolic retreat for artists and bohemian types, set amid an oasis of thousands of palm trees. South of Todos Santos, Highway 19 meets the Pacific and follows miles of unspoiled coastline before rejoining Highway 1

▶ ◢ Travelogue

Highway 1 to Todos Santos
(32 mi., 51 km.; 0:45 hr.)

This route leaves Mexico Highway 1 at a point 19 miles south of La Paz, and offers the possibility of a scenic loop trip from La Paz to Cabo San Lucas and back. Since 1986, when it became completely paved, Mexico Highway 19 has been the most direct route between La Paz and Cabo San Lucas. It is about an hour (and 30 miles) shorter than the traditional route via Mexico Highway 1. From its junction with Mexico Highway 1 the road leads southward across flat, cactus-covered countryside toward Todos Santos.

00.0 **Junction with Mexico Highway 1, just south of the village of San Pedro.**

06.0 **Club Campestre El Carrizal, a local country club with a pool and a restaurant.**

26.5 **Signed road to Presa de Santa Inéz, a dam.**

31.8 **Todos Santos, town center.**

Todos Santos

(See also *Lodging & Restaurants*.)

With its red brick buildings and wide streets, Todos Santos is still a tranquil town, despite the increasing impact of tourism. Almost directly on the Tropic of Cancer, this town of about 6000 inhabitants is set amid thousands of palm trees on a small, rolling coastal plain called the Valle del Pilar, a couple of miles from the Pacific Ocean shore.

Founded in 1733 as a mission settlement, Todos Santos remained a village until the latter 19th century. At this time ample supplies of underground water were tapped to develop agriculture, especially sugar cane. When the sugar market collapsed in recent times, farmers diversified into growing vegeta-

Forests of palm trees hug the Pacific Coast south of Todos Santos.

MEXICO HIGHWAY 19

bles, mangos, coconuts, papayas and other tropical fruits. Fishing also contributes to the economy. Ruins of sugar mills may be seen on Avenida Juárez about a block south of the ISSTE general store, and at El Molino Trailer Park.

Facing the pleasant plaza are the church, Nuestra Señora del Pilar (successor to the early mission); a theater; the town hall; and Restaurant Santa Fé (Italian dishes and seafood).

The central plaza in Todos Santos includes a theater.

Several buildings in town bear plaques honoring noted residents who fought in various struggles for Mexican independence. Todos Santos has markets, restaurants, a bank, medical clinics, a Pemex station and a park. For visitors there are six hotels and two trailer parks. A lighthouse stands at Playa Punta Lobos, an attractive beach two miles west of town.

The town today boasts a growing number of artists, many of them U.S. and Canadian nationals who have made their part-time or permanent homes in the community. There are numerous galleries and artisan shops here, along with a fine cultural center. The town also plays host to an art festival in late January or early February, at the peak of the tourist season.

Points of Interest

CENTRO CULTURAL *Avenida Juárez between calles Topete and Obregón. No telephone. Open Mon.-Fri. 8 a.m.-7 p.m. Free.* Art exhibits, photos and local artifacts are the highlights of this center,

housed in the town's original school building. Theater performances and musical recitals are also held here. The center surrounds an attractive courtyard and garden area.

HOTEL CALIFORNIA *Avenida Juárez, just west of town center. (114) 5-00-02.* Management claims this hotel, built in 1928, inspired the Eagels' 1976 album and song "Hotel California." Whether it did or not, the colonial-style inn attracts many Eagles fans and other curious onlookers, although it bears little resemblance to the hotel pictured on the front of the namesake album. The song's lyrics are painted on a wall inside the hotel bar, and a placard proclaims the inn to be "on the desert highway." A gift shop sells T-Shirts, mugs and other hotel-related souvenirs.

▰◢ Travelogue
Todos Santos to Cabo San Lucas
(45 mi., 72 km.; 1:30 hrs.)

Beyond Todos Santos, Mexico Highway 19 parallels the coastline over rolling terrain and provides access to some of Baja California's most beautiful, unspoiled Pacific beaches. Many of these are *playas públicas* (public beaches) and are notable for good surfing. Along the coast are a number of camping areas and trailer parks, ranging from primitive to highly developed, that are popular in the winter months with U.S. and Canadian visitors. To the east, the Sierra de la Laguna stands guard over the coastal plain. While still mostly empty, that is slowly changing as a number of housing developments are beginning to sprout along the shoreline.

00.0   Todos Santos, town center.

01.7   Junction with a dirt road to Playa Punta Lobos, used by fishermen and also a popular picnic spot with local residents.

03.6   El Pescadero, a farming and fishing town of 1500 located just east of the highway. Several dirt roads lead from the pavement to the center of town, where stores and cafes ring a small plaza. El Pescadero is a junction with a road leading across the Sierra de la Laguna to Mexico Highway 1, five miles north of Santa Anita.

7.5   Junction with a good dirt road to Playa Los Cerritos, a wide, beautiful beach with a private trailer park and public beach camping.

14.9   Colonia Elías Calles, a small farming community surrounded by fields and orchards. Several nice beaches lie just to the west.

26.8   Rancho Migriño, a cattle ranch.

42.2   Junction with a dirt road to Cabo San Lucas airstrip.

44.5   Cabo San Lucas, at the junction with Mexico Highway 1.

Hotel California draws many visitors to Todos Santos.

Mexico Highway 2

The most direct route from Tijuana to Mexicali roughly parallels the U.S.-Mexico border. Starting in Tijuana the hilly terrain gradually rises in elevation, culminating in the steep and rugged Rumorosa Grade. Beyond the grade the terrain levels out into barren desert as it leads into Mexicali.

Mexico Highway 2 is the more northern of the two federal highways connecting Highway 1 and Highway 5. It leads eastward from Tijuana to Tecate and Mexicali, then continues into the state of Sonora, eventually linking up with Highway 15 to Mexico City.

Crossing the Border

The Tecate border crossing, which links the village of Tecate, California, with Tecate, Baja California, gets relatively little use by tourists entering Mexico. For those returning to the United States from Ensenada and points farther south, however, it is a popular alternative to the crowded crossing at Tijuana. Delays are seldom encountered here by motorists in either direction. The border gates are open daily from 6 a.m. to midnight.

▶◢ Travelogue
Tijuana to Tecate via Highway 2
(34 mi., 54 km.; 1 hr.)

Mexico Highway 2 starts in Tijuana as Boulevard Díaz Ordaz, passes through the bustling industrial and commercial district of La Mesa, then crosses a dam and enters rural countryside that is evolving into an industrial district. Then the road climbs gradually into low rocky hills, past olive orchards, dairy farms and cattle ranches on the way to Tecate. Highway 2 is four lanes undivided to La Presa, then becomes a good two-lane road the rest of the way. Traffic is heavy in the La Mesa district, so Boulevard Insurgentes may be preferable. It is a divided road that starts in La Mesa, parallels Highway 2 for seven miles, then merges with it.

00.0   **Tijuana (San Ysidro border crossing). Proceed straight ahead and follow signs for Mexicali.**

03.9   **Caliente Racetrack. On the hills to the south is one of the city's most attractive residential neighborhoods.**

06.1   **Boulevard Lázaro Cárdenas, which goes northeast to Boulevard Insurgentes, the central bus station and Tijuana Airport.**

Fishing boats awaiting sunrise at El Golfo de Santa Clara.

11.5   **La Presa, the easternmost district in the Tijuana urbanized area.**

11.8   **Rodríguez Dam and lake, once the sole source of Tijuana's water supply. The road follows the top of the dam and is quite narrow.**

15.4   **El Florido, a large housing development; three miles farther is a dairy-farming village with the same name.**

30.1   **Rancho La Puerta, a nicely landscaped resort and spa specializing in physical fitness. It offers pleasant accommodations and strictly vegetarian meals.**

33.6   **Tecate, a friendly town clustered around a tree-shaded plaza. Mexico Highway 3 leads south from Tecate to El Sauzal and Ensenada (see description, *Mexico Highway 3*).**

◤◢ Travelogue

Tijuana to Tecate via Toll Highway 2-D

(22 mi., 35 km.; 0:30 hr.)

Opened in 1992, this toll highway—a divided, fully controlled-access expressway—provides a fast alternative to Highway 2. It begins in the Otay Mesa district of Tijuana. After crossing the border, drive 1.2 miles straight south to the first main boulevard, then turn east (left). Follow Boulevard Industrial (Eje Oriente-Poniente) through Ciudad Industrial, the *maquiladora* district, where many multinational firms have manufacturing plants. After about two miles the boulevard becomes the toll highway.

Fees are collected here for vehicles traveling in both directions.

After passing sprawling urban housing developments, the expressway heads into rural landscape. At first it follows a narrow canyon where falling rocks are a possibility. Then it goes over rolling hills, passing occasional farms and ranches. After about 18 miles it enters the Tecate Basin, where Highway 2-D presently ends at the eastern edge of Tecate. Westbound drivers should beware: upon entering the toll road in this direction, there is no exit or turnaround available before reaching the toll booths.

This route is also called Autopista Tijuana-Mexicali because it is the western section of a planned expressway that will, in the near future, extend uninterrupted from Tijuana to Mexicali. Construction of the expressway between Tecate and La Rumorosa, 41 miles to the east, is nearly complete and may open for traffic before the end of 1998.

The toll road between Tijuana and Tecate is lightly traveled because rates are quite high—about $3.90 for cars, pickup trucks and vans; $5.50 for motor homes; and $7.00 for vehicles with trailers. (These rates are peso equivalents and can vary according to the exchange rate. Fees are slightly higher for drivers paying with U.S. currency.)

00.0   **Tijuana (Otay Mesa).**
03.6   **Toll station.**
16.1   **Exit for Mexico Highway 2 and west entrance to Tecate.**
21.8   **Exit for Mexico Highway 3 and south entrance to Tecate.**

Tecate

(See *Campgrounds & Trailer Parks*.)

Lacking proximity to any large population center in the United States, Tecate has never had much of a border town atmosphere. Instead, this pleasant city of about 50,000 is a typical Mexican community, where life centers around a tranquil tree-shaded plaza. At an elevation of 1690 feet, Tecate sits in a bowl-shaped valley surrounded by rocky hills; because of its inland location, the city has hot, dry summers and cool winters with occasional frost.

Tecate came into being in the late 19th century, when farmers and ranchers, attracted by its abundant water and fertile soil, settled the area. Tecate has long been a farm market center for a productive region that yields grapes, olives and grain. Major industries include instant coffee, *maquiladoras* (assembly plants) and the manufacture of different types of clay. The town's best-known industry is beer, being

home to the namesake Tecate brand since 1940. (A microbrewery, Cervecería Mexicali, opened in 1997.)

Although Tecate lacks the feel of a border community, the town does draw its share of visitors from nearby California. Many come each weekend to tour the brewery where Tecate beer is made, the town's most prominent landmark, and enjoy the small-town feel of Old Mexico. The Tecate-Ensenada bike ride is a major magnet each May as thousands of cyclists set out from town for the trek to the seaside community. The town is also home to the famous Rancho La Puerta Spa, a health and fitness retreat that has lured rich and famous guests from around the world since 1940. Then there's Rancho Tecate, a country club five miles south of town with swimming and tennis facilities and plans for an 18-hole golf course.

Its diversified facilities and location at the junction of two major Mexican

 ## Quick Guide to Tecate

Tourist Information and Assistance

Secretaría de Turisma or SECTUR (State Tourism Office) *1305 Callejón Libertad, on the south side of the plaza. Open Mon.-Fri. 8 a.m.-7 p.m., Sat.-Sun. 10 a.m.-3 p.m. 01152 (665) 4-10-95.* Protección al Turista (Tourist Assistance) provides legal help for tourists who encounter problems while in Tecate. The staff are also helpful in providing tourist information about the town and surrounding area.

SECTUR Border Crossing Office *On Calle Cárdenas, just south of pedestrian border crossing. Open Mon.-Fri. 9 a.m.-2 p.m. and 4-8 p.m.; Sat. 9 a.m.-2 p.m. No phone.* Staff at this office also provide tourist information about Tecate and environs.

routes (Highways 2 and 3) have made Tecate a popular stopover for travelers from both sides of the border. Several accommodations can be found here, along with a variety of stores and restaurants, a hospital, Pemex stations, and auto parts and repairs. The city is the seat of government of the *municipio* of Tecate.

Shopping

Tecate lacks the plethora of gift shops or teeming open-air curio markets so common in other border towns. Still, there are plenty of venues for those in search of keepsakes; the best shopping area is just below the U.S. border crossing on **Calle Cárdenas**. A wide selection of goods can be found here; pottery is the local specialty, but leather goods, glassware, clothing and an array of handicraft items are also for sale. Several other shops selling such goods are located around the city.

Dining

Tecate has a number of good restaurants serving all manner of dishes. Non-AAA-approved restaurants are listed here as a service to visitors.

Some of the better-known venues are **La Misión** (international), west of downtown on Avenida Benito Juárez; **Jardín TKT** (Mexican), on the south side of Parque Hidalgo; **El Passetto** (Italian, Mexican), on Callejón Libertad just west of Parque Hidalgo; **El Dragón Cuchuma** (Chinese), across from the brewery on Avenida Hidalgo; and **La Escondida** (Mexican), on Callejón Libertad just east of Parque Hidalgo.

Points of Interest

CUAUHTÉMOC BREWERY *Avenida Hidalgo and Calle Carranza. 01152 (665) 4-20-11 (reservations). Beer garden open Tue.-Sat. 10 a.m.-5:30 p.m. Brewery tours Mon.-Sat. at 11 a.m. and 3 p.m. Free.*

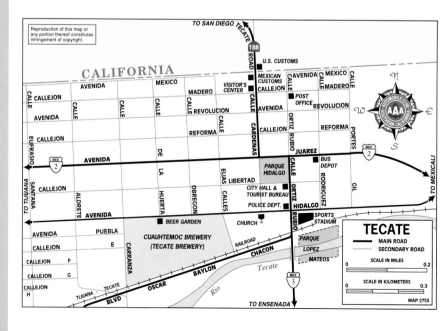

The colorful beer gardens enhance the setting of the Cuauhtémoc Brewery in Tecate.

This brewery is best known for production of the popular Tecate beer. Several other brands are produced in this huge brewing facility, by far the largest structure in the city.

PARQUE HIDALGO *On Avenida Juárez and Calle Ortiz Rubio.* This town plaza is an attractive retreat and a popular gathering point for local residents. An impressive monument to Benito Juárez is located at the northeast corner of the park.

SAN DIEGO RAILROAD MUSEUM *Tours departing from Campo, Calif. (888) 228-9246, (619) 595-3030.* Passenger train tours from the museum cross the border to Tecate, offering tours of the Cuauhtémoc Brewery, along with sightseeing and shopping in the town. Special outings to the wine-producing region south of Tecate are available from late June to early September.

◤◢ Travelogue
Tecate to Mexicali
(89 mi., 144 km.; 2:15 hrs.)

Continuing east from Tecate, Mexico Highway 2 begins a long, gradual climb onto a high plateau. It passes small farms and ranches, as well as several rustic resorts and campgrounds, which are visited mainly by Mexicans. Near La Rumorosa, at an elevation of more than 4000 feet, the highway can become impassable after heavy snows, but these rarely occur. Just east of La Rumorosa is the Rumorosa (Cantú) Grade, which is one of the most spectacular mountain highways on the continent, where the road makes a winding descent past strangely jumbled rock formations to the floor of the barren desert.

Until recently it was among the most treacherous routes on the continent as well—a twisting, two-lane, undivided

MEXICO HIGHWAY 2

road with missing guardrails, where passing was difficult and head-on collisions were a real and constant danger. That changed in 1996 when work was completed to transform the road into the eastbound lanes of the new toll highway linking La Rumorosa to Mexicali. The road has been resurfaced and some of the worst curves have been eased or eliminated. A separate two-lane route is situated across a wide arroyo and carries westbound traffic up the grade to La Rumorosa. Strong winds, numerous curves and steep drop-offs still call for careful driving along this section of road in both directions. A toll booth at the top of the grade charges fees to motorists heading east and west.

While the free road no longer exists, fees have been reduced substantially from the days when only the westbound toll road existed. Tolls are now about 70¢ for cars, pickups and vans; $3.00 for campers; and $5.70 for vehicles pulling trailers.

After reaching the base of the grade, the highway skirts the vast bed of Laguna Salada, which since 1977 has held water. The road now sweeps through low hills, then enters the Mexicali Valley—one of Mexico's richest farming areas. Although Mexico Highway 2 bypasses the center of Mexicali, well-marked paved roads lead into the city.

00.0	Tecate, at the junction of Mexico highways 2 and 3.
13.6	Loma Tova, a village with a cafe.
21.2	Colonia El Hongo, a fast-growing farming community with cafes and stores. A partially paved road winds seven miles southwest to Hacienda Santa Verónica, a cattle ranch with a hotel and trailer park.
31.6	El Cóndor, a settlement with a Pemex station and restaurant, at the junction with a graded road to Laguna Hanson in the Sierra de Juárez.
41.0	La Rumorosa, elevation 4300 feet, located on a high boulder-strewn plateau. Facilities in the town include stores, cafes, a Pemex station and mechanical assistance. Just east of La Rumorosa is the toll booth, where the highway begins its steep descent to the desert floor.

Highway 2 is now a modern, four-lane route between La Rumorosa and Mexicali.

65.8 Junction with a graded dirt road along the edge of Laguna Salada to Cañón de Guadalupe. This lovely palm canyon is 27 miles south, then seven miles west. The road is suitable for passenger cars and small RVs. The canyon features hot springs, hot tubs, a small store and a developed campground; rates start at $25 per vehicle. For information call (714) 673-2670.

79.4 Colonia Progreso, a village with a large municipal building, a motel, restaurant and a Pemex station.

83.4 Junction with Calle Guadalajara, the shortest route to downtown Mexicali and the U.S. border. The sign says "Centro, Calexico."

88.9 Mexicali, at the traffic circle intersection of Mexico highways 2 and 5 (see *Mexico Highway 5*).

▶◢ Travelogue

Mexicali to San Luis R.C., Sonora
(41 mi., 66 km.; 1 hr.)

From the traffic circle on the southern outskirts of Mexicali, Mexico Highway 2 traverses an industrial area, then strikes out across the flat Mexicali Valley, one of Mexico's most important farming areas. Irrigated farms and small communities line the highway in this section. Cotton is the main crop, with production from field to gin in evidence. Also important are sorghum, hay, wheat, vegetables and dairy farming. Although the highway has two lanes in each direction, motorists should be alert for slow-moving farm vehicles entering and leaving the roadway. After crossing a toll bridge over the Colorado River, the highway enters the state of Sonora and the booming border town of San Luis R.C.

Though just below the U.S. border, this section of Highway 2 sees comparatively few tourists, and many adventure-minded drivers may find that to be part of the appeal. The route provides a first-hand look at large-scale farming in Mexico, while passing through several typical rural communities where outside influence is minimal. What's more, it is the only major highway link between Baja California and mainland Mexico.

00.0 Mexicali, at the junction of highways 2 and 5.

06.0 Junction with a paved road to Ejido Puebla (stores, cafes, Pemex station) and the Cerro Prieto Geothermal Zone, site of a large geothermal electrical generating facility.

14.0 Double junction with BCN 1, a paved highway. To the left it goes to Mexicali International Airport. To the right it leads south past the farming towns of Nuevo León and Colonia Carranza, then intersects BCN 4, which turns eastward to Coahuila. From here, another paved road crosses into Sonora (see Side Route to El Golfo de Santa Clara, Sonora).

24.6 Bataques, which has a Pemex station.

27.4 Junction with a paved highway (BCN 2) to the agricultural center of Ciudad Morelos. Ten miles northeast on BCN 8 is the pleasant border town of Algodones. With a population of about 15,000, Algodones has gasoline, a hotel, cafes, pharmacies, dentists, optometrists, souvenir crafts, a park and a state tourism office. Near Algodones is Morelos Dam, where irrigation water for the Mexicali Valley is taken from the Colorado River. From Andrade, at the international border, California State Route 186 takes the traveler to Interstate 8 at a point seven miles west of Yuma, Arizona.

38.3   Toll bridge (about 60¢ for cars and pickups) across the Colorado River, which forms the boundary between the states of Baja California and Sonora.

40.6   San Luis Río Colorado. "Río Colorado" is used to differentiate the city from other Mexican towns named San Luis. With a population of 135,000, the city thrives from agriculture (cotton and wheat), highway transportation and the international border trade. Tourist facilities are concentrated near the international border, which is 23 miles south of Yuma, Arizona. It has an attractive plaza park which is surrounded by businesses, a classic church and government buildings, including a state tourism office. From San Luis, Mexico Highway 2 heads eastward across barren desert to Mexico Highway 15, providing the fastest, most direct link between Southern California and the interior of Mexico. For travel on the mainland, car permits are required. Car permits can be obtained in San Luis at the international border (see *Tourist Regulations and Travel Tips*, Automobile Requirements section). Those travel-

ing beyond San Luis should refer to the AAA *Mexico TravelBook.*

🚐 Side Route

Highway 2 to El Golfo de Santa Clara, Sonora

(81 mi., 129 km.; 2:30 hrs.)

Turn right at the junction with BCN 1, passing through the towns of Nuevo León and Colonia Carranza. Continue eastward along BCN 4 at the junction in Colonia Carranza (Ledón). Gasoline and a few stores are at Colonia Carranza. Crossing flat land planted in cotton, the road reaches Murguía, turns south, then eastward. Four miles past Murguía the highway reaches the Colorado River, whose flow is reduced to a shallow stream by this point, due to irrigation demands.

First-time visitors may react with bemused surprise here as the road detours to cross the river on a railroad trestle that doubles as a highway bridge. Police direct traffic across the span, which is only wide enough to handle a one-way flow. The bridge is on the main rail line from Mexicali to the interior of Mexico and officers halt traffic several times a day to make way for trains. Continuing east, the last town in Baja California on this route is Coahuila, also called Colonia Nuevas. Drive slowly on the graded dirt streets. Turn left, cross the railroad and follow the signs to Sonora.

One hundred yards beyond the railroad, travelers enter the state of Sonora; there is no checkpoint. Sonora is on Mountain Time, and the urban area of Coahuila continues under the name of Luis B. Sánchez. The two towns constitute a sizable farm market center, containing two Pemex stations, auto parts, a clinic, and several markets

The road to El Golfo de Santa Clara includes a detour across this railroad trestle spanning the Colorado River.

and restaurants. After one more mile the road runs into state highway SON 40. A left turn leads north to San Luis, Sonora; a right turn leads southeast to El Golfo. After passing a secondary school and some farmland, the road to El Golfo comes to Riíto, a small agricultural center at the end of the cultivated area. Here are gasoline and diesel, and a few stores.

Between Riíto and El Golfo de Santa Clara are 43 miles of the barren Sonoran Desert, with no services. The only real settlement is El Doctor, a railroad work station with a few buildings and a rustic cafe. The highway is very flat and in good condition most of the way. Shortly before reaching El Golfo the road curves and drops quickly to a small coastal basin. The pavement ends at the entrance to the town.

Another route to El Golfo starts in the city of San Luis R.C., Sonora. From Mexico Highway 2, turn south on Calle 2, which becomes highway SON 40 to Riíto. From Riíto follow the route previously described to El Golfo.

El Golfo de Santa Clara is a fishing town of about 3000 residents, with a fish-processing plant, Pemex station, a grocery store, general store, church and several cafes. The streets are not paved but drivers should encounter few difficulties if they stay on the main thoroughfares. Some outlying streets are sandy and the beaches are open to vehicle traffic, potential spots for vehicles to get stuck. The motorist should greatly lower tire pressure before driving in these areas. Several shops advertise "*aire*/air" for refilling the tires later.

The harbor has many fishing boats, large and small, that catch shrimp, clams and sierra. Many more small fishing launches line the sand on the beach just south of town. Arrangements can sometimes be made for sportfishing. The tidal range is great here at the head of the Gulf of California, with sandy beaches at high tide and mud flats exposed at low tide. Across the gulf the mountains of Baja California are visible.

A graded sandy road extends southeast of town, passing side roads to two RV parks and an area where signs announce a planned beach community. At 1.7 miles there is a large *playa pública* camping area (no facilities), backed by sand dunes, hills and a lighthouse. This spot is sometimes used by Americans with ATVs, with scars on the hillsides bearing evidence of their use.

Mexico Highway 3

Mexico Highway 3 is actually comprised of two distinct sections of road, connected by a six-mile stretch of Mexico Highway 1-D (Ensenada Toll Road). The northern section connects Tecate with El Sauzal, which is the shortest link between Mexicali and Ensenada. The southern section runs from Ensenada to a junction with Mexico Highway 5 at a point about 31 miles north of San Felipe. Both of these routes are two lanes and paved over their entire lengths.

The northern portion of Highway 3 will remind many motorists of nearby Southern California's backcountry, meandering through fields, orchards and ranchland, with hillsides that alternate between brown during summer and fall, and green during the winter and early spring. The southern third of this route passes through the Valle de Guadalupe, the leading wine-producing district in all of Mexico. Two of the country's largest wineries, Domecq and L.A. Cetto, are located here and offer tours to the public. After a brief brush with the Pacific at El Sauzal, Highway 3 heads southeast on its second and longer leg. The route twists and climbs through miles of coastal foothills before dropping into another large agricultural region, where Ojos Negros and Valle de Trinidad are the primary settlements. Beyond Valle de Trinidad, the highway climbs over the Sierra de Juárez before making its sharp descent into the desert and the junction with Highway 5.

Crossing the Border

The Tecate border crossing, which links the village of Tecate, California, with Tecate, Baja California, gets relatively little use by tourists entering Mexico. For those returning to the United States from Ensenada and points farther south, however, it is a popular alternative to the crowded crossing at Tijuana. Delays are seldom encountered here by motorists in either direction. The border gates are open daily from 6 a.m. to midnight.

Tecate

Described fully in the *Mexico Highway 2* chapter, Tecate is the northern gateway to Highway 3 and the surrounding countryside. A friendly community of about 50,000, Tecate sets the tone for the highway with its scenic surroundings, rural atmosphere and comparative lack of U.S. influence.

Tree-lined Laguna Hanson lies in the heart of the Sierra de Juárez.

Bienvenido To California's Other Wine

MEXICO HIGHWAY 3

By David J. Brackney

For gringos who think of Corona with lime or Cuervo Gold as Mexico's national libations, the thought of uncorking a Domecq '94 Cabernet Sauvignon or any Mexican wine might sound a bit strange. It shouldn't for those who have driven past the miles of vineyards along Highway 3 north of Ensenada.

Welcome to the Guadalupe Valley—the leading wine district not only in Baja California, but in all of Mexico. With its warm summer days, and evenings chilled by cool Pacific breezes, the valley's climate is perfect for wine grapes, rivaling that of the top growing districts in northern California or France. The region lies near the southern edge of the Northern Hemisphere's primary wine-producing belt, the mid-latitude band spanning the globe between the 30th and 50th parallels.

Located along Highway 3, Guadalupe accounts for the lion's share of northern Baja's production; along with the Santo Tomás Valley south of Maneadero, the two valleys produce 90 percent of Mexican table wines. The wide range in temperatures is ideal for growing many different wine grapes, with Cabernet, Zinfandel, Chenin Blanc and Riesling ranking among the major

varieties. Some growers send grapes to distilleries in mainland Mexico, where they're transformed into brandies.

Winemaking in northern Baja is nothing new, dating back to the founding of Mission Santo Tomás in 1791, yet outside of Mexico the region's wines have remained little known. By most accounts, though, their quality sagged until the late 1980s, when the government slashed tariffs on a wide range of goods. For the first time, Mexican producers faced the rigors of foreign competition, and they rose to the challenge; by the early 1990s Baja wines were beginning to earn international acclaim.

Production-wise, Domecq is king of Baja wineries, turning out more than 1.5 million cases per annum, followed by L.A. Cetto, whose annual sales top 400,000 cases. Then there's Santo Tomás, which ships more than 100,000 cases a year from its namesake valley farther south.

Still, Baja's wineries face an ongoing struggle to drum up business. Most of their production stays in Mexico, where the average consumer drinks less than 0.4 liters of wine (roughly a half-bottle) per annum. Nor does it help that visitors from the United States can return home with only a

Country

Vineyards in the Guadalupe Valley, like these at L.A. Cetto winery, are the leading source of Baja California wine.

single liter of any alcoholic beverage. To generate interest, the major wineries welcome visitors for tours and tasting. L.A. Cetto and Domecq, which flank opposite sides of Highway 3 in the Guadalupe Valley, are within easy driving distance of both Ensenada and Tecate. While most visitors reach the valley by car from California, some organized groups hail from cruise ships calling on the port of Ensenada.

L.A. Cetto is open daily from 10 a.m. to 4 p.m., while neighboring Domecq is open Monday through Friday from 10 a.m. to 4 p.m. and Saturday from 10 a.m. to 1:30 p.m. In Ensenada, Santo Tomás offers tours and tasting at its facility on Avenida Miramar. (See *Mexico Highway 1, Tijuana to Guerrero Negro.*) Several smaller wineries operate in the area as well and offer tours by special arrangement.

Travelogue

Tecate to El Sauzal

(66 mi., 107 km.; 1:30 hrs.)

After leaving Tecate this two-lane highway climbs into a region of boulder-strewn, scrub-covered mountains and small upland valleys, some of which are under cultivation. Several sharp curves and steep grades in this section call for extra caution. On the southern third of the route the highway runs past olive orchards and miles of vineyards, through a level valley bordered by low hills to the junction with Mexico Highway 1 at El Sauzal. Because this is the shortest route from the farms of the Mexicali Valley to Ensenada's port, large trucks are sometimes encountered along this section of Highway 3.

00.0 **Tecate, at the junction of Mexico highways 2 and 3.**

01.8 **Junction with Mexico Highway 2-D, the Tijuana-Mexicali Expressway.**

05.7 **Rancho Tecate, a resort with tennis, swimming and a golf course under development.**

17.8 **Valle de las Palmas, an agricultural community with gasoline, stores and restaurants.**

31.0 **El Testerazo, a village with a cafe. To the west are prominent rocky peaks, 3000 to 4200 feet in elevation.**

46.2 **Entrance gates to Domecq and L.A. Cetto wineries. To the left is L.A. Cetto. Across the road is Domecq. At this point the highway enters a region containing extensive, well-maintained vineyards. (See sidebar.)**

48.3 **Guadalupe. Next to the elementary school are the ruins of Mission Nuestra Señora de Guadalupe (1834), last of the Baja California missions. Russian immigrants founded an agricultural community here early in the 20th century. Museo Comunitario del Valle de Guadalupe has a collection of pictures and artifacts about these Russian-Mexican settlers. This museum is located 1½ miles west of the junction of Mexico Highway 3 and the main road into town. Hours are Wednesday through Sunday 9 a.m. to 4 p.m.; donation. Guadalupe and Francisco Zarco, an adjacent village, have two cafes, groceries, an inn and a clinic.**

59.4 **Villa Juárez, a town with a restaurant and a market. In the vicinity are new real estate developments.**

66.1 **El Sauzal, at the junction with Mexico Highway 1. Ensenada is six miles to the southeast.**

Travelogue

Ensenada to El Chinero (Crucero La Trinidad), Junction with Highway 5

(123 mi., 198 km.; 3 hrs.)

Sometimes known as the Ensenada-San Felipe Road, this section of Mexico Highway 3 usually has a good paved surface. Together with highways 1 (or 1-D), 2 and 5, this scenic route with very light traffic offers visitors an opportunity for an interesting loop trip through the northern portion of Baja California. The first 24 miles east of Ensenada are narrow and winding, as

This part of Mexico Highway 3 connects Ensenada with the eastern side of the Baja peninsula.

the highway climbs and crosses a range of chaparral-covered hills before dropping into wide, green Valle de Ojos Negros—a productive farming and ranching center. Beyond the turnoff to the village of Ojos Negros, the pavement becomes wider. Heading south, then southeast, Mexico Highway 3 climbs through semiarid foothills to a plateau known as Llano Colorado. The landscape gradually becomes drier as the highway winds through more hills and descends along the edge of Valle de Trinidad, an important agricultural development. After leaving the fields and cattle-grazing lands of the valley, the highway follows a canyon called San Matías Pass, after which it drops to the floor of arid Valle de San Felipe. To the south the rugged face of the Sierra San Pedro Mártir is clearly visible, capped by Picacho del Diablo (elevation 10,154 feet), the highest point in

Baja California. After crossing open desert bordered by low barren hills, Highway 3 meets Highway 5 at El Chinero, 31 miles north of San Felipe.

00.0   **Ensenada, at the intersection of Avenida Benito Juárez (Mexico Highway 1), Avenida Reforma and Calzada Cortez. Follow Calzada Cortez eastward from the traffic circle.**

08.1   **El Gran 13, an amusement park with rides and playground equipment, a picnic ground, swimming pool and spa.**

16.4   **Junction with a 5.2-mile dirt road to Agua Caliente, a rustic tourist resort. This road should not be attempted in wet weather.**

24.7   **Junction with the paved road leading 1.2 miles to Ojos**

Negros, a farming and cattle-raising community with two markets and a nice park. A graded road leads eastward from Ojos Negros to the Sierra de Juárez and Laguna Hanson (see Side Routes).

34.7   Junction with a signed road to Parque Nacional Constitución de 1857; the road from Ojos Negros is preferable.

57.5   Héroes de la Independencia, a scattered settlement on Llano Colorado. The town has groceries, pottery stores, cafes and auto parts. Gasoline is sold in front of a small grocery store; a sign points the way from the highway. A dirt road branches north to the ruins of Mission Santa Catarina, founded in 1797.

75.5   Junction with the short, paved road to Valle de Trinidad. This rapidly growing community is a farm market center of 3000 with stores, cafes, a bank, an ice house, schools, an unusual conical church, a mechanic, tire repair and gasoline for sale.

86.2   Junction with a good dirt road to Mike's Sky Rancho, which is 22.5 miles to the south (see Side Route to Mike's Sky Rancho).

92.5   San Matías Pass, elevation 2950 feet.

95.9   Junction with a dirt road leading first to *ejidos* Villa del Sol and Colonia San Pedro Mártir, then southeast to San Felipe. This rugged route passes close to the base of the Sierra San Pedro Mártir;

Cañón El Diablo, 20 miles south of the junction, is where many climbers begin the difficult ascent of Picacho del Diablo.

123.4   El Chinero (Crucero la Trinidad), junction with Mexico Highway 5 (see *Mexico Highway 5*). At the junction is a government-built restaurant and picnic area. About 0.7 mile south of the junction is a Pemex station and a cafe.

🚗 Side Route
Ojos Negros to Laguna Hanson
(27 mi., 43 km.; 1:45 hrs.)

This unpaved side route offers visitors a chance to explore the high plateau country of the Sierra de Juárez—a land of cool mountain air and thick forests of ponderosa pine. In the heart of this rugged region is a Mexican national park highlighted by Laguna Hanson, a small, intermittent lake surrounded by tall pines, unusual rock formations and excellent primitive campsites. Another attraction of this trip is solitude; despite its fine scenery and its proximity to the international border, the park gets very few tourists.

Laguna Hanson can be reached from El Cóndor, west of La Rumorosa on Mexico Highway 2, but the preferred route—usually accessible in dry weather by passenger cars—begins at Ojos Negros, 25 miles east of Ensenada via Mexico Highway 3 and a paved spur road. From the end of pavement in Ojos Negros, turn right onto a wide graded road running eastward toward the mountains. For the first few miles the road passes Puerta Trampa and other prosperous farms and ranches,

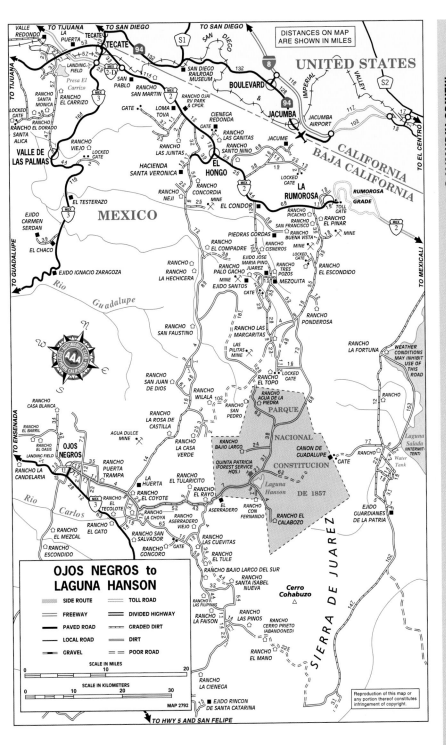

DISTANCES ON MAP
ARE SHOWN IN MILES

OJOS NEGROS to LAGUNA HANSON

SIDE ROUTE	TOLL ROAD
FREEWAY	DIVIDED HIGHWAY
PAVED ROAD	GRADED DIRT
LOCAL ROAD	DIRT
GRAVEL	POOR ROAD

SCALE IN MILES
0   10   20

SCALE IN KILOMETERS
0   10   20   30

MAP 2792

An off-road cyclist fords a shallow stream near Mike's Sky Rancho.

then enters brush-covered foothills. At mile 7.9 is a major junction; bear right here. Beyond the junction the road begins to climb steadily, but there are no steep grades. After another eight miles the road leaves the chaparral belt and traverses forests of ponderosa pine. At mileage 20.4 is another important junction; bear left. From this point the route swings north and enters Aserradero, a village of wooden buildings; the road leaves Aserradero ahead to the left. Just beyond the village the road crosses the southern boundary of Parque Nacional Constitución de 1857. Four miles beyond Aserradero is Laguna Hanson. Park regulations prohibit hunting, but camping is permitted. From Laguna Hanson, the road continues northward for another 37 miles, eventually meeting Mexico Highway 2 at a junction just west of La Rumorosa.

🚐 Side Route
Highway 3 to Mike's Sky Rancho
(23 mi., 37 km.; 1:30 hrs.)

This route to a secluded backcountry lodge begins at a signed junction at a point 10.7 miles southeast of Valle de Trinidad. Sturdy high-clearance vehicles are necessary. The first half of the trip is over a dirt road rising gradually over semiarid landscape. Cerro San Matías (elevation 7100 feet) is visible to the east. The road becomes rougher and more winding as it approaches a junction at mileage 13.8. Here is found a 6000-foot graded airstrip that belongs to Mike's. A rough road to the right goes to Ejido Los Pocitos. Bear left to continue 8.2 miles farther over rough surface to the ranch.

Mike's Sky Rancho rests on a knoll overlooking Arroyo San Rafael, a wooded valley flanked by steep, brush-covered mountains. The ranch offers motel-type accommodations for about $25, family-style meals, a swimming pool, horseback riding, sycamore-shaded campsites and information about trips into the rugged country to the east. The small stream that flows through the valley yields occasional catches of small rainbow trout. Hunters can go after deer, rabbit, quail and mountain lion.

Mexico Highway 5

From Mexicali—the bustling capital city of the state of Baja California—Mexico Highway 5 leads southward past the verdant patchwork of one of Mexico's most productive agricultural regions, then crosses open desert backed by rugged, barren mountains.

This route has a good paved surface along most of its course to San Felipe, a resort town on the shore of the Gulf of California (Sea of Cortez), and for a short distance beyond. The road is a four-lane divided highway for the first 15 miles south of Mexicali, and construction is under way to widen the route from two to four lanes as far south as El Faro. As the road approaches San Felipe, storm damage and shifting sand have narrowed the surface in spots to one lane, but motorists will encounter few delays as a result. Between Punta Estrella and Puertecitos the road is paved but in very poor condition, with many potholes and washed out sections. Sturdy passenger cars and high-clearance vehicles can make this trip, but slow, cautious driving is imperative. From Puertecitos a graded but bumpy road extends farther south to Bahía San Luis Gonzaga.

An ambitious highway construction project calls for the paving of the entire San Felipe-to-Bahía Gonzaga road sometime in the future. This would bring rapid development to a region that until very recently was inaccessible to most tourists. The highway would also provide an alternate route for those who wish to travel from the California border south to the central desert region. Ample accommodations and facilities can be found in Mexicali and San Felipe, while rustic lodging, eating and camping facilities are scattered along the gulf coast. Fishing in the Gulf of California is excellent.

Crossing the Border

California SR 111 leads through the Imperial Valley town of Calexico to the international border at Mexicali. The main border crossing at Mexicali is located at the southern terminus of SR 111 and is open 24 hours. A new border crossing known as Calexico East opened in late 1997 and is located off SR 98, seven miles east of the main gateway. The new crossing is open from 6 a.m. to 10 p.m. and usually has shorter waits for California-bound vehicles.

Wildflowers in seasonal bloom provide spectacular desert scenery near San Felipe.

MEXICO HIGHWAY 5

Mexicali

(See also *Lodging & Restaurants*.)

Mexicali is unique among Mexico's large border cities in that its size and economic well-being do not result from either its proximity to the United States or its ability to attract tourist dollars. Instead, this mushrooming metropolis of about 800,000 owes its prosperity and phenomenal growth to its position as capital of the state of Baja California, and as the seat of government of the *municipio* of Mexicali, which extends south to San Felipe. It is also a growing manufacturing center and the hub of one of Mexico's most important agricultural regions. Many tourists pass through Mexicali en route to San Felipe or to the Mexican mainland, but relatively few pause to examine this bustling, interesting city.

In the early 20th century Mexicali developed as a farm market center, and in 1915 it became the capital of the territory of Baja California Norte. For a couple of decades legalized alcohol and gambling, and land speculation attracted visitors from across the border. In the late 1930s, under the leadership of Mexican President Lázaro Cárdenas, the fertile land of the Mexicali Valley was distributed among Mexican farmers and collective agricultural colonies, called *ejidos*. Also, the flow of irrigation water from the Colorado River was guaranteed by international treaty. These factors contributed to the economic bases of farming and industry. Manufacturing is playing an increasing role in the city's economic base, fueled by *maquiladora* plants, where foreign-produced components are assembled into finished consumer goods. A growing number of sprawling industrial parks on the city's southern flank are home to many of these plants.

Water has been the key to Mexicali's growth. The Mexicali Valley is extremely arid—the pleasant winters and torrid summers bring only about three inches of rain per year, not enough to exploit the rich, silt-laden soil deposited throughout the centuries by the Colorado River. So Mexico

This imposing state government monument is located in the Centro Cívico-Comercial de Mexicali.

These proud military cadets participate in a public ceremony in Mexicali.

developed an elaborate irrigation complex tied to Morelos Dam, on the Colorado River just south of the border. The result is an agricultural empire in the midst of the desert, served by a proud city with modern commercial and industrial complexes, palm-lined boulevards, lush parks and quiet residential neighborhoods with neatly manicured shrubs and gardens. Permeating present-day Mexicali is a distinct aura of growth and vitality.

A good example of this vitality is the new Centro Cívico-Comercial de Mexicali—an innovative center for government and commerce along Calzada Independencia in the central part of the city. Included in this ambitious urban development are municipal, state and federal government offices, three hospitals, the bus terminal, a bullring, movie theaters, hotels, restaurants, private offices and shopping centers. There is increasing evidence of foreign investment in the retail sector as well, including the likes of Price Club, Wal-Mart, Holiday Inn and a legion of eating establishments.

Shopping

The largest commercial area of Mexicali is the **border business district**, located in a rough rectangle bounded by avenidas Cristóbal Colón, Alvaro Obregón, the Río Nuevo and Calle C. This typical Mexican commercial district contains shops and restaurants catering to the tourist trade, along with businesses oriented to local consumers. Articles for sale that appeal to tourists include pottery, wrought iron, leather goods, blankets, silver, jewelry and works of art. Cross-border shoppers will

MEXICO HIGHWAY 5

 Quick Guide to Mexicali

Tourist Information & Assistance

Secretaría de Turisma or SECTUR (State Tourism Office) *Located near the corner of Calle Calafia and Calzada Independencia in the Centro Cívico, Pasaje Tuxpan 1089. Open Mon.-Fri. 9 a.m.-7 p.m., Sat.-Sun. 9 a.m.-1 p.m. 01152 (65) 55-49-50 or 55-49-51.* Tourism information is available here, along with legal help for tourists who encounter problems while in Mexicali.

Mexicali Tourist and Convention Bureau *On Calzada López Mateos at Calle Camelias. Open Mon.- Fri. 9 a.m.-7 p.m.; Sat. 9 a.m.-3 p.m. 01152 (65) 57-23-76 or 57-25-61.* Friendly bilingual staff in this office provide general tourist information.

Newspapers

Mexicali has no English-language newspaper, but tourist brochures in English are available at the tourism offices. AAA-approved hotels in town often have the *Los Angeles Times* and *San Diego Union-Tribune.* Some convenience stores in town also carry these publications. Spanish-language newspapers include *La Voz de la Frontera, La Crónica de Baja California* and local editions of the Tijuana papers *Zeta* and *El Mexicano.*

Radio and Television Stations

Many California radio stations are received all through northern Baja California. Among the several Mexicali stations, Estereo 89.9 FM broadcasts a rich variety of traditional ballads and romance songs. A few American television stations are received, along with the Mexicali stations. Larger hotels have cable TV with major channels from both countries.

Driving in Mexicali

Before crossing the border into Mexicali, be sure to obtain Mexican auto insurance (see Automobile Requirements in the *Tourist Regulations and Travel Tips* chapter). Tourists driving in Mexicali find wide, flat streets, many of which are one way. Unfortunately, many streets lack signs. Mexicali has no expressway bypass like Tijuana, but three wide boulevards—calzadas López Mateos, Justo Sierra and Benito Juárez—usually allow traffic to move through the city at moderate speeds. Traffic circles, or *glorietas,* found along these boulevards pose a challenge for new visitors. When entering a traffic circle,

find it easier to leave their vehicles in Calexico and shop on foot in this zone.

Other important, newer commercial strips spread southward along **calzadas López Mateos, Justo Sierra** and **Benito Juárez**. **Plaza Cachanilla** is an impressive shopping mall touting some 250 retail outlets, 1.7 miles from the border on the northeast side of López Mateos. Neon signs on these streets present an impressive spectacle after dark. A growing business district is the **Centro Cívico-Commercial**, near the government center.

drivers should bear right, then follow the flow of traffic counter-clockwise. It is important to watch for traffic lights and street signs; lights are often small and hard to see from a distance. Stop signs are sometimes not very noticeable.

Parking is scarce in the business district near the border and around the government center, but it does not pose a problem in other parts of the city. Visitors planning to shop in the border business district should park on the Calexico, California, side and walk across. Most of the tourist-oriented stores are within a few blocks.

Local Transportation

Traveling a few miles in town by taxi costs about $6, although sometimes bargaining can lower the fare. It is wise to agree on the price before getting into the cab.

As in other large Baja California cities, Mexicali bus fare is extremely cheap—less than 50 cents to ride the length of a bus route. Riders should know a little Spanish, have an idea of the city's layout and not mind traveling in old coaches. For long-distance travel, Mexicali is an important departure point for bus and train lines to Guadalajara, Mexico City and other interior destinations.

Dining

Befitting a state capital with 800,000 people, Mexicali has a long list of fine Mexican and international eating places offering all types of cuisine. Many restaurants, especially near the border, see a steady stream of U.S. visi-

tors. Others see few if any tourists, but often exude a more authentic Mexican atmosphere. Like many Mexican cities, there has been a boom in U.S.-style fast-food restaurants in recent years, including **McDonald's**, **Burger King**, KFC and **Dunkin' Donuts**, to name but a very few. While many tourists may seek out more traditional fare, such eateries have been a big hit with the local population, especially young people.

Some of the restaurants listed here are AAA approved; more information about these can be found in the *Lodging & Restaurants* chapter. Non-AAA-approved restaurants are also listed here as a service to visitors. The restaurants mentioned here are but a starting list; many more fine eateries beckon those with the time and inclination to seek them out.

Among the sit-down restaurants, some of the better-known names are **Mexicali Rose** (steak, carne asada), in the Araiza Inn on Calzada Benito Juárez; **Old Mexicali Cafe** (steak, seafood), on Calzada Francisco L. Montejano; **Mezzosole** (Italian), in the Hotel Lucerna on Calzada Benito Juárez; **El Sarape** (Mexican food) in the border business district on Calle Mexico between Colón and Madero; **Los Arcos** (seafood), on Calle Calafia near the bullring; **El Vaquero** (steak, carne asada), in Centro Cívico-Comercial on Avenida de los Héroes near Calzada Independencia; **Sanborns** (varied menu), on Calzada Independencia across from the Centro Cívico; and **Los Buffalos** (ranch-style cooking), in the Plaza Cachanilla shopping center.

First-time visitors may be surprised at the large number of Chinese restaurants, located throughout the city. Nearly 100 of these restaurants, mostly

Ingredients For Success

By David Nelson

(Reprinted from *Westways*)

Just as gumbo symbolizes the blending of African, European and American Indian cultures in New Orleans, a bowl of the *sopa especial* served at the posh Dragón Centro Cívico restaurant could be the emblem of Mexicali. This typically mild Cantonese soup is laden with meat, shrimp, greens and vegetables; the rich flavor tastes quintessentially Chinese. But as is standard practice in Mexicali, the server places a plate of cut limes alongside the bowl. Squeeze in a trickle of the sourish juice, as many do, and effect a sorcerer's trick that transforms the soup into a Mexican *caldo* of entirely different character.

Mexicali is, without question, the most Chinese city in all of Mexico. In fact, a geographical tug-of-war conducts itself just above eye level along the main thoroughfares. The street signs honor the pantheon of Mexican heroes and bear such names as Boulevard Adolfo López Mateos, Calzada Benito Juárez, and Avenida Alvaro Obregón. But above these rise immense red-and-yellow signboards that direct drivers to Hong Kong, Canton, Hunan and other points that seem rather distantly East.

Chinese cooking has been a Mexicali staple since the city was founded in 1903. Chinese laborers, mostly from Canton, were recruited to farm the Valle de Mexicali, which had been recently irrigated when construction of the All American Canal delivered a torrent of Colorado River water. Most of the land was owned by the Colorado River Land Co., under the watchful eye of *Los Angeles Times* publisher Harrison Gray Otis. At that time, there were roughly 4000 Chinese, of whom just 60 were women, as well as some 700 Mexican nationals. Although planning to toil, save money and eventually return home prosperous, most Chinese laborers remained in Mexicali. Some married local women; others looked to Canton for wives. "Chinese, Hindus and Japanese were recruited to come plant the cotton fields because the Colorado River Land Company did not want to rent land to Mexicans for fear that they would wish to own it," says Mexicali historian Celso Aguirre Bernal. "It was the Chinese who stayed." By 1920, La Chinesca, the historic Chinatown located less than a minute's stroll from the border, had been established at the heart of the community; it expanded as other Chinese fled the periodic anti-Chinese campaigns that raged through the mid-1930s in Sinaloa and Sonora. La Chinesca includes buildings that house some of the 27 Chinese family associations as well as the headquarters of the influential Asocia-

Chinese restaurants are major players on Mexicali's culinary scene.

ción China de Mexicali. Tidy, well-stocked shops deal in Chinese foods, herbs and imports.

There was a time in Mexicali when *los chinos,* as the Chinese are known locally, outnumbered native Mexicans six-to-one. Today, within the city itself, just 2000 of the roughly 800,000 residents claim pure Chinese bloodlines, and another 4000 are of mixed heritage. But the Chinese legacy lives on in almost 100 restaurants lining the tree-shaded boulevards and weary back streets. Until the most recent wave of Chinese immigration to the United States and Canada created elegant new Asian restaurant rows in West Coast cities, cognoscenti ranked Mexicali just behind San Francisco as the center of Chinese gastronomy in this particular part of the globe.

"Restaurants are an easy business for (us) Cantonese to enter," says a for-mer president of the Asociación China de Mexicali. "In the old days, the Chinese people did not speak Spanish. They didn't need to in order to operate restaurants."

Another reason that the Chinese pursued commerce was that the Mexican government denied them citizenship, so they couldn't own land. Today, it is believed that no Mexicali Chinese work in farming. Ironically, despite the surrounding fields once farmed by Chinese immigrants, local restaurants now import Chinese vegetables from the United States.

The most important restaurants cluster along the main boulevards to the east of downtown and in the impressive, modern Centro Cívico district. Often palatial in size and possessing remarkably ornate interiors, they feature the Cantonese cuisine brought home by the city's pioneers.

Most restaurants offer commonplace fare at modest prices, but consultation with the server will sometimes turn up a notable house specialty. The multicourse prix fixe dinners, *comidas corridas,* listed on every menu and quite popular with locals, tend to be inexpensive but boring and heavy on starch and fried foods. But there are plenty of good dishes to be found, and wise diners will consult the waiter; just ask for a pair of *palillos chinos* (chopsticks) and dig in.

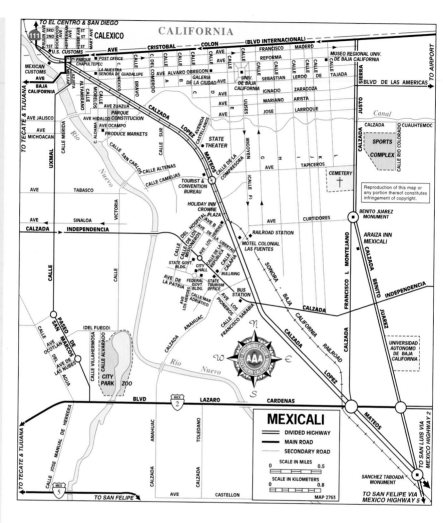

Cantonese, line the city's broad boulevards and quiet back streets. The largest concentration can be found east of downtown and in the Centro Cívico district. A few of the better-known ones are **9 Dragónes**, on Calzada Benito Juárez just south of Lázaro Cárdenas in the Plaza Mandarín; **La Misión Dragón** at Lázaro Cárdenas 555; **Nuevo Mandarín**, downtown on Avenida Reforma; **Fortune Inn**, on Calzada Benito Juárez, north of the Benito Juárez monument; and **Restau-** rant **Muralla China**, on Calzada Independencia near the Centro Cívico. (See sidebar, "Ingredients for Success.")

Nightclubs

While Mexicali lacks the raucous party atmosphere of many border towns and resort destinations, several piano bars and discotheques lie within walking distance of the international border. Live entertainment and dancing are offered at the **Salón Discotheque Ari-**

zona on Avenida Reforma between calles B and C, **Forum Discotheque** at Reforma and Calzada Justo Sierra, and in clubs at the **Hotel Lucerna** and **Araiza Inn**, both on Calzada Benito Juárez.

Points of Interest

CITY PARK/BOSQUE DE LA CIUDAD *Avenida Ocotlán (del Fuego) and Calle Alvarado, in southwest Mexicali. 01152 (65) 55-28-33. Open Tue.-Fri. 9 a.m.-5 p.m., Sat.-Sun. 9 a.m.-5 p.m. Admission $1; ages 11-16, 75¢; ages 3-10, 50¢.* The park, most easily approached from the north along calles Victoria and Alvarado, is a popular destination with local families, especially on weekends. It contains a zoo, a museum of natural history, a picnic area and a children's playground. A miniature train provides rides around the park's perimeter.

GALERÍA DE LA CIUDAD *1209 Avenida Alvaro Obregón between calles D and E. 01152 (65) 53-50-44. Open Mon.-Fri. 9 a.m.- 8 p.m. Free admission.* Housed

Decked out as a giant caterpillar, a narrow-gauge train takes visitors around City Park in Mexicali.

in what was formerly the state governor's residence, the newly expanded art gallery features works of Baja California painters, sculptors and photographers.

GLORIETA MONUMENTS The traffic circles on Mexicali's main boulevards contain impressive monuments. Crosswalks lead to the landscaped islands where the monuments stand.

LA NUESTRA SEÑORA DE GUADALUPE *Avenida Reforma and Calle Morelos.* Built in the 1920s and remodeled in 1957, this twin-tower, Spanish Colonial-style church is one of the most prominent structures in the border district of Mexicali.

MUSEO REGIONAL UNIVERSIDAD AUTÓNOMA DE BAJA CALIFORNIA *Avenida Reforma and Calle L. 01152 (65) 54-19-77. Open Tue.-Fri. 9 a.m.-6 p.m., Sat.-Sun. 9 a.m.-2 p.m. Admission 70¢.* This fine museum contains comprehensive, permanent exhibits on the history and anthropology of American Indians, and the missions and ranches of early Baja California. There also are rotating exhibits highlighting various aspects of the land and people of Baja California and the rest of Mexico.

STATE THEATER/TEATRO DEL ESTADO *Calzada López Mateos, 1½ miles south of the U.S. border. 01152 (65) 54-64-18.* Plays, musicals and dance presentations are featured here. The Mexicali Convention and Tourist Bureau also has programs and schedules.

Spectator Sports

BULLFIGHTS Plaza de Toros Calafia *Calle Calafia in the Centro Cívico-Comercial. 01152 (65) 55-43-73.* Bullfights are

Bullfights are held in the Plaza de Toros Calafia in Mexicali.

held every autumn and sometimes in spring.

CHARREADAS (Mexican Rodeo) Charro Grounds *3⁷⁄₁₀ miles east of Calzada Justo Sierra on Carretera a Compuertas (the road to the airport).* There is no set schedule for these colorful equestrian events, but *charreadas* average once a month during the winter and spring, usually on Sunday and major Mexican holidays.

▰ /ı Travelogue
Mexicali to San Felipe
(124 mi., 198 km.; 2:30 hrs.)

The most direct route to San Felipe follows Calzada López Mateos from the international border to Mexico Highway 5. Upon leaving the Mexican port of entry, turn right and follow Calzada López Mateos in a southeasterly direction to the traffic circle at the intersection with Mexico Highway 5. An alternate route, popular in previous years, follows Avenida Francisco I. Madero eastward to Calzada Justo Sierra, which leads south to Mexico Highway 5. Motorists returning to the United States from Mexicali must approach the U.S. Customs facility along Avenida Cristóbal Colón, a one-way westbound street immediately south of the international border. After leaving Mexicali, the highway skirts the western edge of one of Mexico's most productive farming regions for about 30 miles. To the southwest is the imposing mountain wall of the Sierra de los Cucapá.

Plumes of steam, visible to the east, rise from the Cerro Prieto geothermal electric plant. (Mexico is one of the world's leading producers of geothermal electricity, and some of this electricity is exported to the United States.) Mexico Highway 5 then continues southward through extremely arid desert. After about 45 miles, the road runs atop an 11-mile-long earthen levee while crossing an arm of the intermittent lake, Laguna Salada. Then it passes through the Sierra Pinta, whose dark volcanic basalt hills have an otherworldly appearance. As the highway nears San Felipe, the high Sierra San Pedro Mártir, capped by 10,154-foot Picacho del Diablo, is visible to the west. On the outskirts of San Felipe the flat, straight highway bends toward the gulf, skirting a pair of big white gateway arches as it enters the town.

00.0   Mexicali (U.S. border crossing).

03.0   Junction with Calzada Independencia.

04.1   Junction with Calzada Lázaro Cárdenas.

05.1   Traffic circle at Sánchez Taboada Monument. Bear right, then take the right fork, which heads south.

05.7   Junction with Highway 2 west to Tecate and Tijuana (see *Mexico Highway 2*).

07.7   A paved road branches west to Club Deportivo Campestre de Mexicali, which has a golf course and other sports facilities.

25.2   Junction with the paved road to the farming communities of Zakamoto and Ejido Nayarít.

26.1   La Puerta, a roadside farming center with a Pemex station, cafe and store.

29.3   Junction with highway BC 4, a paved route that crosses the Mexicali Valley to Coahuila (Colonia Nuevas) and continues to El Golfo de Santa Clara on the Sonora side of the gulf (see Side Route to El Golfo de Santa Clara).

37.0   Campo Sonora, the first of several rustic trailer camps along Río Hardy.

38.3   Río del Mayor, a village with an Indian museum. Located by the police station, it is called Museo Comunitario, Centro Cultural Cucapá.

44.2   At this point, the highway, elevated by a levee, sets out

The waters of Laguna Salada, south of Mexicali, provide a striking contrast from the surrounding desert along Highway 5.

MEXICO HIGHWAY 5

across the southern end of Laguna Salada.

71.2   **La Ventana, which has a Pemex station and cafe.**

92.7   **El Chinero (Crucero la Trinidad), junction with Mexico Highway 3, which leads westward to Valle de Trinidad and Ensenada (see *Mexico Highway 3*). At the junction is a government-built restaurant and picnic area. About 0.7 mile south of the junction is a Pemex station and a cafe.**

111.0   **A dirt road branches left to Campo Don Abel, the first of a string of rustic trailer camps on the gulf shore north of San Felipe. Facilities in these camps are usually modest.**

114.8   **A graded one-mile road to El Paraíso/Pete's Camp, a long-established popular camp with tent and RV spaces, showers, a disposal station and a restaurant-bar.**

123.6   **San Felipe, at the junction of Mexico Highway 5 and Avenida Mar de Cortez.**

◙▭ Side Route

Highway 5 to El Golfo de Santa Clara, Sonora

(69 mi., 112 km.; 2 hrs.)

This route encompasses rich agricultural land in the Mexicali Valley, the Sonoran Desert and a picturesque fishing town on the Gulf of California. Just beyond El Faro, 26 miles south of Mexicali on Mexico Highway 5, turn east on state highway BC 4 where the sign points to Colonia Nuevas. (State highways are not usually indicated on signs, but the abbreviation is printed on occasional roadside posts.) This paved highway leads across pasture

land and grain fields to Ejido Durango, a farm village with gasoline.

At mileage 10 is Colonia Carranza (Ledón), which has gasoline and a few stores. Crossing flat land planted in cotton, the road reaches Murguía, turns south, then eastward. Four miles past Murguía the highway reaches the Colorado River, whose flow is reduced to a shallow stream by this point, due to irrigation demands.

First-time visitors may react with bemused surprise here as the road detours to cross the river on a railroad trestle that doubles as a highway bridge. Police direct traffic across the span, which is only wide enough to handle a one-way flow. The bridge is on the main rail line from Mexicali to the interior of Mexico and officers halt traffic to make way for trains several times a day. Continuing east, the last town in Baja California on this route is Coahuila, also called Colonia Nuevas. Drive slowly on the graded dirt streets. Turn left, cross the railroad and follow the signs to Sonora. One hundred yards beyond the railroad, travelers enter the state of Sonora; there is no checkpoint. Sonora is on Mountain Time, and the urban area of Coahuila continues under the name of Luis B. Sánchez. The two towns constitute a sizable farm market center, containing two Pemex stations, auto parts stores, a clinic, and several markets and restaurants. After one more mile the road runs into state highway SON 40. A left turn leads north to San Luis Río Colorado, Sonora; a right turn leads southeast to El Golfo.

After passing a secondary school and some farmland, the road to El Golfo comes to Riíto, a small agricultural center at the end of the cultivated area. Here are Pemex facilities and a few

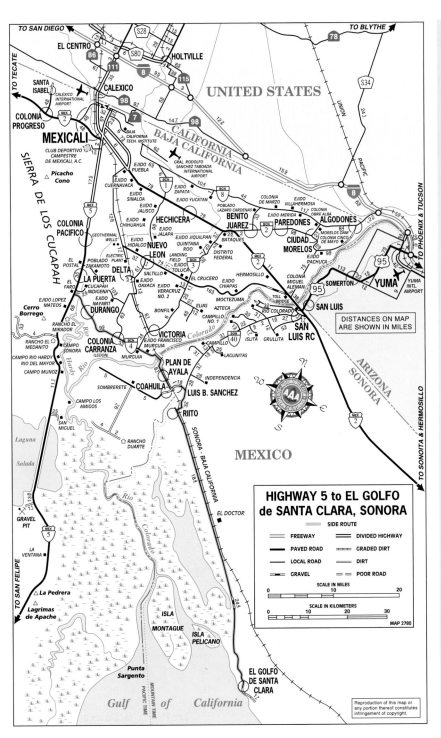

stores. Between Riíto and El Golfo de Santa Clara are 43 miles of the barren Sonoran Desert, with no services. The only real settlement is El Doctor, a railroad work station with a few buildings and a rustic cafe. The highway is very flat and in good condition most of the way. Shortly before reaching El Golfo the road curves and drops quickly to a small coastal basin. Pavement ends at the entrance to the town.

Another route to El Golfo starts in the city of San Luis R.C., Sonora. From Mexico Highway 2, turn south on Calle 2, which becomes highway SON 40 to Riíto. From Riíto follow the route previously described to El Golfo.

El Golfo de Santa Clara is a fishing town of about 3000 residents, with a fish-processing plant, Pemex station, a grocery store, a general store, a church and several cafes. The streets are not paved but drivers should encounter few difficulties if they stay on the main thoroughfares. Some outlying streets are sandy and the beaches are open to vehicle traffic, harboring the potential

for vehicles to get stuck. The motorist should greatly lower tire pressure before driving in these areas. Several shops advertise "*aire*/air" for refilling the tires later.

The harbor has many fishing boats, large and small, that catch shrimp, clams and sierra. Many more small fishing craft sit above the high-tide line along the town's beach. Arrangements can sometimes be made for sport fishing. The tidal range is great here at the head of the Gulf of California, with sandy beaches at high tide and mud flats exposed at low tide. Across the gulf the mountains of Baja California are visible.

A graded sandy road extends southeast of town, passing side roads to two RV parks and an area where signs announce a planned beach community. At 1.7 miles there is a large *playa pública* camping area (no facilities), backed by sand dunes, hills and a lighthouse. This spot is sometimes used by Americans with ATVs, with scars on the land bearing evidence of their use.

Dirt bikes sit beneath a **palapa** *between sessions on the beach at Golfo de Santa Clara.*

San Felipe

(See also *Lodging & Restaurants* and *Campgrounds & Trailer Parks*.)

This major winter resort and fishing center occupies a site where the shimmering waters of the Gulf of California lap against the shores of a forbidding desert. Clearly visible across the sandy coastal plain to the west is the steep eastern wall of the Sierra San Pedro Mártir—highest range on the peninsula. (The sight will remind many visitors of the sheer wall of the Sierra Nevada range dropping to the desert in eastern California.) The town itself is nestled beneath 940-foot-high Punta San Felipe, a rugged headland that provides a partial shelter for boats and forms the northern end of shallow Bahía San Felipe. From this point, the shore of the bay makes a crescent-shaped dent in the coastline, then swings southeastward in a line of wide, attractive beaches to Punta Estrella, 12 miles distant. An interesting natural phenomenon here is the extreme tidal range, which can reach more than 20 feet; this makes boating a tricky proposition for those without experience in these waters.

San Felipe is a friendly community of about 20,000, with modest dwellings, sandy side streets

and little vegetation. The wide variety of facilities include numerous hotels and trailer parks, markets, bakeries, restaurants, bars, launch ramps, banks, clinics, auto mechanics and three Pemex stations. Mexico Highway 5 ends at Avenida Mar de Cortez, which parallels the shore and forms the main street of town. For tourists and many locals alike, life in San Felipe centers around this street, with its many restaurants and clubs, along with the neighboring *malecón* (Paso de Cortez), one block to the east, which runs right along the beach.

Although nomadic fishermen were attracted to this area as early as the mid-19th century, San Felipe did not

These twin white arches mark the entrance to San Felipe on Highway 5.

Peaceful San Felipe is a popular destination for tourists young and old from north of the border.

become a permanent settlement until the 1920s. Large-scale fishing began in earnest during World War II, and the completion of the paved highway from Mexicali in 1951 brought a surge of American sports enthusiasts. In the years that followed, San Felipe gradually evolved from a sleepy fishing village into a popular resort. Rapid expansion during the 1980s, with the addition of many new hotels, condominiums and trailer parks, has contin-

✔ *Quick Guide to San Felipe*

Tourist Information and Assistance

Secretaría de Turisma or SECTUR (State Tourism Office) *On Avenida Mar de Cortez at Manzanillo. Open Mon.-Fri. 9 a.m.-6 p.m., Sat.-Sun. 9 a.m.-2 p.m. 01152 (657) 7-11-55 or 7-18-65.* Protección al Turista (Tourist Assistance) provides legal help for tourists who encounter problems while in San Felipe.

Newspapers

San Felipe has no newspapers in the traditional sense, but information on the town is available through the *San Felipe Newsletter*, published monthly except in the summer. This English-language newsletter contains information on points of interest and life in San Felipe, and on social events involving the local U.S./Canadian community. The English-language *Baja Sun* can also be found here.

ued throughout the 1990s. The recently modernized airport has gained international status with regularly scheduled flights to California. As a result, San Felipe has more influence from outside visitors than almost any other town on the Baja peninsula.

Off-road vehicles, such as these all-terrain cycles for rent, are popular with many younger visitors to San Felipe.

November through April is the ideal time to visit San Felipe. Days are usually warm and sunny, and nights are refreshingly cool. Summers, however, can be unbearably hot, with daytime temperatures sometimes exceeding 115 Fahrenheit. Rainfall is less than two inches per year, though it can fall hard and furiously, mainly in the late summer and early fall when the remains of hurricanes and tropical storms sometimes make their way to the north edge of the Sea of Cortez.

U.S. vacation periods (Presidents Day, Easter week, Memorial Day, Labor Day, Thanksgiving, etc.) are extremely crowded, and accommodations, trailer parks and even beach campsites are likely to be jammed. These periods draw a somewhat unruly brand of tourists, who bring annoyances wrought by motorcycles, firecrackers and loud parties. Litter is also a problem. Such tourists have brought economic benefits, however, creating a booming rental business for all-terrain cycles, personal watercraft and other mechanized vehicles. A number of off-road races and other local events also draw the mechanized vehicle crowd, including the famed Baja 1000, which passes through the town each November. The town is relatively peaceful when these tourists go home.

San Felipe is also a haven for so-called "snowbirds," mostly older visitors from the United States and Canada who arrive during the cooler months of the year, staying for weeks or months at a time. Many arrive in recreational vehicles and settle in the myriad of RV and trailer parks in and around the town, heading north when the weather turns warm. Each year in December the town puts on a "Welcome Snowbirds Fiesta," complete with mariachi music, folkloric dancing, gifts from local stores and more.

Shopping

Tourist towns throughout Baja California come replete with clothing and curio shops aimed at visitors, and San Felipe is no different. **Avenida Mar de Cortez** has many such establishments touting the usual assortment of keepsakes, including ceramics, blown glass, ironwood carvings, leather goods, blankets, etc. The inevitable beachwear shops offer items ranging from designer fashions to T-shirts of sometimes questionable taste and quality. Among the more unusual stores is **Maritza Dress Shop**, at the corner of Mar de Cortez and Zihuatanejo, which offers an extensive line of handmade, traditional Mexican clothing. Another is the **People's Gallery**, in Plaza Caliente on Mar de Cortez, which offers a wide selection of original arts and crafts made by Mexicans and locally based U.S. and Canadian artisans.

Dining

For a town of its size, San Felipe is awash with restaurants of all types, not surprising since tourism is the leading industry. There is something here for almost any taste and budget, ranging from beachside taco stands to upscale steak houses. Nearly all have menus in English and at least some hired help who speak English.

Some of the restaurants listed here are AAA approved; more information about these can be found in the *Lodging & Restaurants* chapter. Non-AAA-

approved restaurants are also listed here as a service to visitors.

Most of the best-known restaurants are in the downtown tourist strip along Avenida Mar de Cortez or one block over on the *malecón* (Paso de Cortez). Among these restaurants are **George's Cafe** (steak and seafood), on Mar de Cortez near Motel El Capitán; **Rice and Beans** (Mexican), on the *malecón;* **Cachanilla's** (steak and seafood), downtown on Mar de Cortez; **El Nido** (steak and seafood), near the south end of Mar de Cortez; **Restaurant Océano Chino** (Chinese), downtown on Mar de Cortez; **Rosita Restaurant** (seafood), at the west end of the *malecón;* and **Juan's Café** (seafood, Mexican), on Avenida Mar Baltico. Another spot popular with tourists is **Los Arcos Bar & Grill** (American-style food only), next to the arches at the west entrance to town.

Several restaurants offer casual dining along the *malecón,* with grilled seafood, shrimp cocktails and fish tacos being the main fare. Among these spots are **La Playa**, **Gaviota** and **Plaza Maristaco**, all reasonably priced and located across the street from the beach.

Nightclubs

The downtown tourist area is home to many establishments that cater mainly to U.S. and Canadian visitors. Some are dance clubs while others are sports bars or taverns with occasional live music. Several have entrances on both the *malecón* and Avenida Mar de Cortez. Such spots include **Rockodile** and **Pez Vela Discotheque**, both popular weekend dance spots, along with **Bar Miramar**, **Rice & Beans**, **Beachcomber Bar** and **The Bearded Clam**, Farther south on Mar de Cortez is **Fandango**, a pool bar adjacent to

Caliente, a club where betting on all types of professional sports is allowed. **Los Arcos Bar & Grill**, next to the arches at the west entrance of town, offers live country-western music.

Points of Interest

VALLE DE LOS GIGANTES *13½ miles south of town center, then about 3 miles southwest on a sandy road.* The title of this place translates "Valley of the Giants," and this cluster of very large cardón cacti has specimens more than 100 years old, growing amid a placid, idyllic desert setting. A cardón plant taken from here was displayed with the Mexico exhibit at the 1992 World's Faire in Seville, Spain. A sign on the highway points the way to the valley, across from another pointing to Colonia Gutierrez Polanco. The valley is open only during daylight hours, with access controlled by an attendant at a gate just off the highway. Sturdy high-clearance vehicles should be used on this road.

VIRGIN OF GUADALUPE SHRINE *Situated on a hilltop just north of San Felipe.* A panoramic view of the town and the coastline is offered from this vantage point. Adjacent is a lighthouse (not open to visitors).

◤◢ Travelogue
San Felipe to Puertecitos
(52 mi., 83 km.; 2:15 hrs.)

This route through rapidly developing and changing territory has been paved as far as Puertecitos. Plans call for additional paving south to Bahía San Luis Gonzaga sometime in the future. South of Punta Estrella, the road surface deteriorates, with numerous washed-out portions and many large potholes. Highway crews were working to repair

Huge cardón cacti and a spectacular desert setting beckon visitors at Valle de los Gigantes.

and upgrade the roadway as this book went to press, but prudent motorists will bring only sturdy vehicles and drive slowly and carefully along this portion of road.

The first eight miles run close to the bay through part of San Felipe's resort area, with a number of hotels, campgrounds and condominiums; more are under construction. The pavement is good on this first section, but drifting sand is a problem in a few spots; drive with caution to avoid skidding. The remaining 44 miles follow a route a little inland from the Gulf of California, with turnoffs leading to numerous *campos* that contain small communities of American and Canadian vacation homes and trailer camps. As yet, virtually no facilities exist for motorists on this long section. Along the route, the terrain changes very little; level to rolling countryside is interspersed with low, barren hills. Ocotillo, mesquite, cholla cactus and smoke trees are the most common forms of vegetation, although a few elephant trees and cardón cacti may be seen.

00.0	**Junction of Mexico Highway 5 and Avenida Mar Caribe (street name for the beginning of the route).**
00.5	**Junction with a graded road which also leads to Puertecitos; in the past this inland route was the preferred road for some travelers.**
00.9	**Entrance to Hotel Las Misiones and Mar del Sol RV Park.**
01.4	**Entrance to the commercial harbor.**
05.5	**Junction with the paved road to San Felipe International Airport.**

Exceptionally low tides are common at Puertecitos.

07.3 La Hacienda, a condominium development.

09.7 Turnoff to Faro Beach and Punta Estrella, at the southern end of Bahía San Felipe.

13.5 A sandy road leads southwest to Valle de los Gigantes, a group of very large cardón cacti. Across the road, a sign points in the opposite direction to Colonia Gutierrez Polanco.

19.0 A sandy spur road leads 2½ miles to Laguna (Rancho) Percebú, a growing community of American beach houses, a campground and a restaurant.

25.4 Turnoff to Campo Santa María, a large collection of trailers and vacation homes.

28.2 The village of Ejido Delicias, with a clinic and a small store. On the beach opposite are a lighthouse and Campo El Vergel, a large settlement.

40.7 Junction with the inland road leading north toward San Felipe.

51.6 Puertecitos, overlooking a small bay. At the northern entrance is a municipal delegation and a small Mexican community called Ejido Matomí. Most of Puertecitos, however, is inhabited by Americans who lease their homes and trailer sites from the owners of the land. Facilities include a motel, a cafe and bar, a small general store, a Pemex station (not always open) and an airstrip. Arrangements can be made for camping, cabaña rentals, fishing boats, trailer rentals and boat launching. Fishing is good outside the shallow bay,

Bahía San Luis Gonzaga's beauty is relatively unspoiled.

which becomes dry during extreme low tides. The short road branching to the southeast point of the bay passes a rocky footpath leading to natural hot springs; depending on the tide, three separate pools are filled with water of varying temperatures.

Travelogue

Puertecitos to Bahía San Luis Gonzaga

(45 mi., 72 km.; 4 hrs.)

Long notorious as one of Baja California's roughest routes, this graded dirt road along the Gulf of California was greatly improved in 1987. The surface is rough washboard, however, and sturdy high-clearance vehicles are recommended. Carry adequate emergency equipment, as this is a lonely stretch of road. Vegetation is sparse along this arid route, but interesting rocks can be seen in shades of orange, red and brown. Much of the road has been realigned, but motorists can see the former tortuous, rocky route alongside. Between 11 and 19 miles the road crosses several hills, with spectacular views of canyons and the gulf. The treacherous Huerfanito Grade is now bypassed. Between Nacho's Camp and Punta Bufeo are numerous signs advertising undeveloped campsites and lots for sale. The road here is level, running close to shore. For the last six miles it crosses sandy arroyos and passes among hills before reaching the shore of the bay.

Bahía San Luis Gonzaga, not to be confused with the mission of the same name in Baja California Sur, is a beautiful, pristine body of water. Although the landscape is barren, Bahía Gonzaga typifies an isolated, peaceful seaside spot in Baja California, with brilliant sunshine by day and millions of stars by night.

00.0   Puertecitos.

04.8   Campo La Costilla, a small private camp at the edge of an attractive cove, where the natural slope of the beach makes an excellent launch ramp. Refreshments can be purchased here.

11.6   The first of many good camping spots along the rocky gulf shore.

17.7   Nacho's Camp, a group of homes owned by Americans.

20.0   San Juan del Mar, a growing beach settlement with an airstrip.

35.1   Campo Salvatierra, an abandoned private campground with several good primitive camping spots.

Fishing at dawn in Gonzaga Bay.

37.8   Junction with the road to Las Encantadas.

39.4   Junction with a 1.3-mile dirt road to Campo Punta Bufeo, a collection of homes owned by Americans and an airstrip. Refreshments and simple meals are available.

42.5   Junction with the 0.9-mile road to Papa Fernandez's camp, located on Bahía San Luis Gonzaga. The resort offers meals, refreshments, boats and motors for rent, and occasionally gasoline and oil. The level grassy field to the west makes a good natural airstrip. Fishing is excellent.

◢ Travelogue
Bahía San Luis Gonzaga to Highway 1
(39 mi., 63 km.; 2 hrs.)

With careful driving, this graded dirt road can be traveled by passenger cars and small RVs. After passing the shore of Bahía San Luis Gonzaga near Punta Willard, the route comes to the junction for Punta Final, on the southern end of the bay. For the first few miles after the bay, the road ascends through gently sloping desert terrain where wildflowers form carpets of color during early spring. Then the road enters a range of hills containing numerous elephant trees. Just beyond a rocky canyon with a winding road is Rancho las Arrastras. A short distance past the ranch, the route forks to the left and then meets a road leading southwest to Mexico Highway 1.

00.0   Bahía San Luis Gonzaga, at the junction to Papa Fernandez.

Looking eastward across the Gulf of California, along the road south of Puertecitos.

02.6   Rancho Grande, a water purification/ice plant and a campground. A 1.6-mile side road leads to Alfonsina's Camp, located on a narrow sandspit facing the bay. Facilities include a small hotel, a campground, a restaurant, an airstrip and gasoline. Vacation homes line the sandspit next to the camp.

11.7   Junction with the road to Punta Final, a private beach community.

22.0   Rancho las Arrastras de Arriola, which has radiator water and cold drinks.

26.0   Junction with the road leading 13 miles southwest to Mexico Highway 1. It joins the highway just north of Laguna Chapala, 33.7 miles south of Cataviña. From the junction, turn right for Mexico Highway 1. A left turn leads east, then north to Hermenegildo Galiana and to Campo Calamajué on the gulf.

Recreation

The very soul of Baja is in enjoying the rugged outdoors. The pristine coastline lends itself very well to aquatic activities such as surfing, sailboarding, surf-fishing, snorkeling, scuba diving and swimming. Ocean waters offer prime sportfishing opportunities. For those less energetically inclined, Baja's beautiful beaches provide an opportunity for sunbathing and beachcombing. The peninsula's rugged terrain is a hunter's paradise and also offers scenic vistas for photographers.

Formalized recreational activities are less common in Baja California than the United States, but that situation is changing rapidly. Golf, kayaking, sailboarding, snorkeling and scuba diving are a few of the many pursuits available through resort hotels and independent outfitters up and down the peninsula. The availability of equipment, once severely limited, is increasing rapidly, although recreators would do well to consider the needs of their own activity before leaving home.

Information for the following listings was provided by the courses to the Automobile Club of Southern California for publication. Many courses have seasonal rates, and peak-season rates are listed here. Yardage, slope and rating are based on men's white tees. The semi-private courses may have restrictions on public play ranging from members and guests only to liberal reciprocal agreements with other courses; please contact the course directly for details. Reservations are advised at most courses.

Golfing

Baja California is developing into a major destination for golfers, drawn by a spurt of new course development in tourist areas of the peninsula. Resorts own and operate most of the courses, though several country clubs do business as well. The Los Cabos region has emerged as the number one hotbed of Baja golf, with five courses (two designed by Jack Nicklaus) now open and more in the planning stages. The Tijuana-Ensenada corridor is close behind with four courses in operation.

Bajamar

BAJAMAR OCEANFRONT GOLF RESORT Semi-private

21 miles north of Ensenada, off Hwy. 1-D at Jatay exit. Phone 01152 (61) 55-01-52. Fees include mandatory golf cart: 18 holes Mon.-Thu. $60, Fri.- Sun. $70. Hotel/golf packages available.

27 total holes. The **Lagos-Vista** course is 18 holes, par 71, 5712 yards, 118 slope, 67.2 rating. The **Vista-Oceano** course is 18 holes, par 72, 122 slope, 69.1 rating. The **Oceano-Lagos** course

A view of the golf course at Real del Mar.

is 18 holes, par 71, 117 slope, 67.4 rating. Clubhouse, locker room, golf shop, power carts, rental clubs, driving range; tennis, swimming; restaurant; cocktails.

Cabo San Lucas

CABO DEL SOL GOLF CLUB Public

5 miles northeast of Cabo San Lucas off Hwy. 1. Phone 01152 (114) 3-31-49; (800) 386-2465. Fees include mandatory golf cart: hotel guests $140-150; nonhotel guests $175-190.

The course is 18 holes. Par 72, 5843 yards, 116 slope, 66.8 rating. Professional, golf shop, power carts, rental clubs; snack bar.

CABO REAL GOLF COURSE
Semi-private

12 miles northeast of Cabo San Lucas off Hwy. 1. Phone 01152 (114) 4-00-40. Fees include mandatory golf cart: 18 holes $165.

The course is 18 holes. Par 72, 5920 yards, 115 slope, 68.7 rating. Professional, golf shop, power carts, rental clubs, driving range; coffee shop.

CABO SAN LUCAS COUNTRY CLUB
Semi-private

On east edge of Cabo San Lucas, just north of Hwy. 1. Phone 01152 (114) 3-46-53. (800) 328-8501. Fees include mandatory golf cart: 18 holes $143, guest rate $99.

The course is 18 holes. Par 72, 6135 yards, 126 slope, 69.9 rating. Profes-

At Cabo San Lucas the golf course is right on the beach.

sional, golf shop, rental clubs, driving range; restaurant,

PALMILLA GOLF CLUB Public

5 miles northeast of Cabo San Lucas off Hwy. 1. Phone 01152 (114) 4-52-50; (800) 386-2465. Fees include mandatory golf cart: hotel guests $143-154, nonhotel guests $176-192.

The course is 18 holes. Par 72, 6130 yards, 110 slope, 66.5 rating. Professional, golf shop, power carts, rental clubs; snack bar.

Ensenada

BAJA COUNTRY CLUB Semi-private

9 miles south of Ensenada via Hwy. 1, then 1 mile east. Phone 01152 (61) 77-55-23. Fee includes mandatory golf cart: Mon.-Thu. $30, Fri.- Sun. $40.

The course is 18 holes. Par 72, 6103 yards, 119 slope, 69.5 rating. Locker room, power carts, professional, golf shop, rental clubs, driving range; coffee shop; cocktails.

Loreto

CAMPO DE GOLF LORETO Public

In Nopaló, near Eden Loreto Resort. Phone 01152 (113) 3-05-54. Fee: $30.

The course is 18 holes. Par 72, 6400 yards, N/A slope, N/A rating. Power carts, professional, golf shop, rental clubs; cocktails.

Mexicali

CLUB DEPORTIVO CAMPESTRE Semi-private

5 miles south of town off Hwy. 5. Phone 01152 (65) 63-61-70. Fees include mandatory golf cart: Tue., Thu., Fri. $25; Wed., Sat., Sun. $30; closed Mon.

The course is 18 holes. Par 72, 6516 yards, 129 slope, 73.2 rating. Profes-

sional, clubhouse, golf shop, locker room, driving range; tennis; pool; restaurant; coffee shop; cocktails.

Rosarito

REAL DEL MAR Semi-private

5 miles north of town center off Hwy. 1-D (toll highway). Phone (800) 803-6038, 01152 (66) 31-34-01. Fees including mandatory golf cart: Mon.-Thu. $55, Fri.-Sun. $65. Hotel/golf packages also available.

The course is 18 holes. Par 72, 5949 yards, 122 slope, 67.8 rating. Professional, clubhouse, golf shop, locker room, driving range; tennis, pool; restaurant, snack bar; cocktails.

San José del Cabo

CAMPO DE GOLF SAN JOSÉ Public

Off Blvd. Mijares, situated among the condominiums and hotels in the resort area. Phone 01152 (114) 2-09-05. Fees: 9 holes, $25.

The course is 9 holes. Par 35, 2879 yards, N/A slope, N/A rating. Professional, clubhouse, locker room, golf shop, power carts, pull carts, rental clubs; snack bar; cocktails.

Tijuana

CLUB SOCIAL Y DEPORTIVO CAMPESTRE (TIJUANA COUNTRY CLUB) Semi-private

3 miles east of downtown Tijuana via Blvd. Agua Caliente. Phone 01152 (66) 81-78-55. Fees: Mon.-Fri. $25, Sat.-Sun. $35.

The course is 18 holes. Par 72, 6233 yards, 117.0 slope, 69.0 rating. Clubhouse, power carts, professional, golf shop, rental clubs; restaurant, coffee shop, snack bar; cocktails.

RECREATION

Hunting

Most of the hunting on the peninsula is in the north, in the state of Baja California. Several species of squirrel populate the region, as well as peccary, bobcat, fox, coyote, jack rabbit and cottontail. The Mexicali Valley is perhaps the most popular of the peninsula's hunting regions, having large quantities of mourning dove, whitewing dove, pheasant and quail. Ducks are found in the lagoons and marshes along both coasts, while quail, pheasant and dove are found in varying quantities throughout the state. San Quintín Bay is known for its large population of black brant, in addition to good shooting for quail. Throughout the peninsula, the number of birds tends to fluctuate from one year to the next, with rainy years producing optimum conditions to sustain large populations.

Although mule deer and desert bighorn sheep inhabit some areas in Baja California, they are scarce and special permits are required to hunt them. Hunting seasons vary according to species, but most open seasons occur between September and the end of February.

Hunting in Baja California requires a special-purpose visa, a consular certificate, a Military Gun Permit, a hunting permit and, during the hunt, the presence of a licensed outfitter's assistant. In addition to the above, when hunting for mule deer or desert bighorn sheep, a contract with a licensed Mexican organizer must be purchased. It is advisable to contact an American organization that specializes in hunting in Mexico to obtain the documents and to make arrangements with a Mexican contract organizer.

Weapons are forbidden in Mexico unless they are brought into the country during hunting seasons for the express purpose of hunting. Only two sporting firearms and 100 rounds of ammunition for each are permitted. Military and .22 caliber rimfire weapons and all pistols are prohibited. Bow and arrow hunting requires a special permit.

Standard Licensing Procedure

1. CONSULAR CERTIFICATE This document is issued by all Mexican Consulates. Applicants must present a letter of good conduct from their local police department or sheriff's office vouching for their moral character, plus two color, front-view passport-size photographs. The consular certificate is not a hunting permit—it is merely an authorization for the hunter to enter Mexico in this capacity, and is also required when applying for a Military Gun Permit. It will contain a description of each firearm, including kind, make, serial number, caliber or gauge and number of cartridges. The hunter needs a consular certificate for each of the peninsula's states—Baja California and Baja California Sur.

2. HUNTING PERMITS (LICENSES) Hunters must purchase permits for each Mexican state in which they intend to hunt and for each bird or animal they intend to hunt. Hunting permits are issued in the names of individual hunters and are not transferable. Each permit is only valid for the current season and in the state for which it was issued.

All the paperwork necessary for hunting in Baja California may be handled by the Mexican Hunting Association, information on which is provided below. The association also furnishes information on hunting conditions and government regulations (which are subject to change). Depending on the types of mammals or birds hunted, the total cost of all the permits ranges from about $350 to $500. For information about the specific services offered, contact the Mexican Hunting Association, 3302 Josie Ave., Long Beach, CA 90808; phone (562) 421-6215; FAX (562) 496-2412.

Note: As this book went to press, Mexican Hunting Association officials reported great difficulty in obtaining legal documents to hunt in Baja California Sur. The difficulty stemmed from the lack of a state-approved organizer, who by law must process all application papers. The situation could change, and interested parties should contact the association for current information.

Water Recreation

Boating

Anyone planning to operate a private boat in Mexican waters, regardless of size or construction, must first obtain a Mexican Boat Permit issued by the Mexico Department of Fisheries. Permits are sold on a yearly basis and are valid for 12 months from the date of issue. Fees for permits are based on the length of the craft: under 23 feet, $16.75; 23 feet to 29 feet 11 inches,

Pleasure boats from around the world find shelter in the marina at La Paz.

RECREATION

$47.60; 30 feet and over, $71.40. For small auxiliary boats carried on board vessels of 30 feet or longer, there is an additional fee of $23.80 per craft. (These fees are subject to change; the Mexico Department of Fisheries office can provide current fees.)

Obtain applications for Mexican Boat Permits and submit the completed forms to the Mexico Department of Fisheries at 2550 5th Ave., Suite 101, San Diego, CA 92103-6622; (619) 233-6956. The office is open Monday through Friday from 8 a.m. to 2 p.m.

Boat permit applications must include a copy of the boat's registration document. The boat registration document has to be shown before applying for a boat permit. Fees must be paid by cash, a cashier's check or money order for the exact amount due to Oficina Recaudadora de Pesca (personal checks are not accepted). For mail orders, include a stamped return envelope.

Fishing

The Gulf of California is widely considered to offer the world's finest fishing. Virtually every popular saltwater species—including marlin, sailfish, roosterfish, cabrilla, dorado (mahi-mahi), sierra, yellowtail, sea bass, wahoo and bonito—can be found here. Favorite gulf fishing areas are Bahía de los Angeles, Cabo San Lucas, the East Cape, La Paz, Loreto, Mulegé with nearby Bahía Concepción, and San Felipe. On the Pacific Ocean side, Ensenada and San Quintín Bay are the centers of activity, with a lineup much like that of Southern California: yellowtail, barracuda, halibut, sea bass, calico bass, rock cod, bonito and tuna, among other fish. Ensenada, for its

part, is the self-proclaimed "yellowtail capital of the world."

Licenses

Any nonresident alien must possess a valid Mexican Sportfishing License before fishing in Mexican waters. This license covers all types of fishing and is valid anywhere in Mexico. Everyone aboard private boats in Mexican waters must have a fishing license regardless of age and whether or not they are fishing. Licenses for people fishing on commercial sportfishing boats are normally provided by the boat operators. A fishing license is also officially required for underwater fishing and free diving.

Fishing licenses are issued for periods of one week, one month and one year, effective at 12:01 a.m. on the starting date specified on the license application. Fees for licenses are $15.75 for one week, $24 for one month and $31.25 for one year. (These fees are subject to change; the Department of Fisheries office can provide current fees.) Mexican fishing licenses are not transferable, and each license must include the person's full legal name, home address and telephone number.

Obtain applications for Mexican Sportfishing Licenses and submit the completed forms to the Mexico Department of Fisheries at 2550 5th Ave., Suite 101, San Diego, CA 92103-6622; (619) 233-6956. The office is open Monday through Friday 8 a.m. to 2 p.m. The Mexico Department of Fisheries also has offices in Mexico (Oficina de Pesca), but travelers are advised to obtain fishing licenses before crossing the border. Applications must be accompanied by cash, a cashier's check or money order for the exact amount due, payable to Oficina Recaudadora de Pesca (personal checks are not accepted). For mail orders, include a stamped return envelope.

Daily Bag Limits and Other Regulations

Each fisherman is permitted to catch up to 10 fish per day, with no more than five fish of the same species. In addition, anglers are subject to the following limits: no more than one billfish (marlin, sailfish or swordfish) and two tarpon, roosterfish, shad or halibut. Catching one of any of the above species counts as five of

Deep-sea fishing draws large numbers of visitors to the Gulf of California.

any other type of fish when calculating the day's limit. On inland bodies of water (rivers, lakes, etc.), the limit is five fish per day, whether of a single specie or a combination. Underwater fishing is limited to five fish per day, and only while skin diving. In all cases, once the permitted limit has been bagged, all further catches must be released.

Except when skin or scuba diving, fish must be taken by angling with a handheld line or a line attached to a rod. The use of nets (except handling nets), traps, poisons or explosives is prohibited. Skin divers may fish only with handheld spears or band-powered spear guns. For anglers of all types, it is illegal to sell, trade or exchange any of the fish they catch. Fish can be eviscerated and filleted, but a patch of skin must be left to permit identification. The taking of abalone, lobster, shrimp, Pismo clams, cabrilla, totuava, oysters and sea turtles is prohibited by

FISHING QUALITY PROFILE

Fish	Pacific				Gulf							
	Ensenada	San Quintin	Bahia Tortugas	Cabo San Lucas	San Felipe	Puertecitos	San Luis Gonzaga	Bahia de L.A.	Mulege	Loreto	La Paz	Las Cruces to Punta Palmilla
Albacore	6-10	6-10	6-10									
Barracuda	4-10	4-10									8-11	
Black marlin			6-10									6-10
Black sea bass		4-10										
Bluefin tuna			6-10								6-10	
Corvina					3-9							
Crevalle						5-8	3-9	2-6	5-10		1-10	4-10
Grouper				2-7		4-10	4-10	4-10	4-10	4-10	4-10	4-10
Marlin	6-9	6-9						6-9	5-7	5-6	5-7	4-6
Needlefish											5-9	5-8
Rockfish	10-4	10-4										
Roosterfish						6-9		11-2		10-3	4-10	7-9
Sailfish				6-9				5-6	5-7	6-7	6-11	4-11
Sea bass									5-10			
Seatrout					4-10							
Sierra					5-9	6-10	6-9			10-4	10-6	4-7
Skipjack												5-7
Snapper									4-10	4-10	4-10	4-10
Snook								5-10				
Swordfish				6-9								
Tuna				5-9								
Wahoo				6-9	11-4	11-3				1-3	4-12	6-10
White sea bass	4-10	4-10	4-10									
Yellowfin Tuna											4-12	4-5
Yellowtail	4-10	4-10	4-10	4-5		5-10	5-10	4-5		10-6	12-5	4-5

This chart indicates *best fishing months*, not legal seasons. Numbers refer to months in sequence; 6-10 is June through October. The availability of any particular kind(s) of fish varies.

Mexican law. Anyone wishing to purchase any of these species to take into the United States must first obtain a form from the Mexico Department of Fisheries; only the Oficina de Pesca located within Mexico provides this form. All purchases of these species must be made at designated public markets or fishing cooperatives.

U.S. Customs Regulations

Sportfishers may bring into the United States only fish for personal consumption. Shellfish, except for lobster and shrimp, are prohibited. The number of fish must not exceed the Mexican bag limit. Fish transported across the border can be eviscerated but must be identifiable; usually the head, tail or a patch of skin left intact will suffice. Anyone bringing fish into the United States will be asked by customs officials to present a valid Mexican fishing license or a Mexico Department of Fisheries form covering the purchase of the fish. More information can be obtained by contacting the United States Fish and Wildlife Law Enforcement Agency at (619) 661-3130.

Sites for Fishing

Sportfishing the waters off the coast of the Baja peninsula can be a rewarding and memorable experience. The following list some of the better known fishing areas. Fish listed at each locale represent only the more common or sought-after species. Most fish migrate over great distances and make only seasonal appearances at some locations. As an example, marlin and sailfish can be found at the southern cape all year but travel north only during the summer months when the water is warmer. Fishermen should check in advance to make sure a particular fish is in season.

BAHÍA DE LOS ANGELES The bay, which is protected by 45-mile-long Isla Angel de la Guarda, offers a fine sheltered anchorage for boats. Sportfishing is excellent, with corvina, dorado, grouper, roosterfish and yellowtail found in the waters around the nearby islands. Marlin and sailfish are occasionally hooked in the deeper waters farther offshore. Fishing trips can be arranged, and there are several launch ramps for private boats.

CABO SAN LUCAS AND SAN JOSÉ DEL CABO Sportfishing is the top attraction for many visitors in this region. Located at the convergence of the warm waters of the Gulf of California and the cooler Pacific waters, the southern cape offers excellent fishing throughout the year. These include dorado, grouper, marlin, sailfish, skipjack, snapper, swordfish, tuna and wahoo. Sportfishing cruisers usually cost $300 to $400 per day; skiffs (*pangas*) start about $185 per day.

ENSENADA Sportfishing for albacore, barracuda, bonito, halibut, marlin, rockfish, sea bass and yellowtail is excellent. Arrangements for sportfishing trips can be made at the sportfishing piers off Boulevard Costero and at some shops on Avenida López Mateos. Rates for charter fishing cruisers vary depending on size of craft and number of passengers; rates start at about $250 per day. Open-party boats start at $35 per person. In addition, surf fishing is good along the sandy beaches and rocky shorelines both north and south of the city.

LA PAZ Many popular saltwater species are found in the waters off La Paz, including dorado, marlin, needlefish, roosterfish, sailfish, sierra, yellowfin and yellowtail. Cruisers, which rent for

RECREATION

Fishing, Cabo San Lucas style.

about $275 to $350 per day, are available through many hotels. Skiffs *(pangas)* average $180 per day for two persons.

LORETO Famous for roosterfish, Loreto's offshore waters hold virtually every major game species that inhabits the Gulf of California, including dorado, grouper, sailfish, sierra, marlin, snapper, yellowfin and yellowtail. Because fishing is good in the hot season, Loreto attracts as many visitors in summer as the rest of the year. *Pangas* typically cost $125 to $150 per day, and trips may be arranged at any of the town's hotels. Boat trips are also available to Isla Coronado for clam digging and observing large numbers of sea lions and pelicans.

MULEGÉ Sportfishing in the Gulf of California and in nearby Bahía Concepción is excellent, and fishing trips can be arranged at any of Mulegé's hotels. The many species found in these waters include corvina, dorado, grouper, marlin, roosterfish, sailfish, sea bass, sierra, snapper, snook and yellowtail. The beach, two miles northeast of town, can be reached by following an extension of Calle Madero, a good dirt road, along the river.

SAN FELIPE The gulf waters off San Felipe yield corvina, grouper, sea trout, sierra and white sea bass. Sportfishing rates vary, with skiffs *(pangas)* ranging from $25 to $50 per hour, per person (for one to five passengers); longer open-party trips on large boats run about $60 per person, per day. Boats are available from several dealers along Paseo de Cortez, the central waterfront drive.

SAN QUINTÍN The waters of Bahía de San Quintín offer a paradise for sport-fishing. Among the fish found are corvina, barracuda, halibut, marlin, rockfish, yellowtail and yellowfin. Although the fish are comparable in size and species to those found in Southern California waters, the bay offers both an abundance of fish and a relative lack of anglers. The daily costs for fishing boats (with guide) are about $150 for skiffs *(pangas)* and $225 to $335 for cruisers. Good surf-fishing and clam digging enhance the appeal

of the beaches along the shore of the outer bay.

Kayaking

With its breathtaking scenery, turquoise waters and impressive variety of sea life, Baja California is one of North America's top destinations for sea kayaking. The world's longest peninsula, Baja boasts some 2000 miles of rugged coastline, most of it remote and inaccessible, and scores of islands along the inshore waters—a cornu-copia waiting to be explored.

The center of action is on the Gulf of California, sheltered as it is from the most pressing perils of the open sea. On this coast, the prime paddling zones lie primarily in Baja California

Kayaking is popular at Bahía de la Concepción.

Sur, including Bahía Concepción, Loreto, the East Cape region, La Paz and Cabo San Lucas. Farther north, Bahía de los Angeles is another fine and increasingly popular locale. Along with clear waters and beautiful surroundings, most of these spots provide ready access to pristine islands, sandy beaches and secluded coves. Many use their kayaks not only to explore, but as a base for fishing or diving as well.

The Pacific coast is another story, given its exposure to the waves, currents, fog and other hazards. Most of the shoreline is best left to more advanced and intrepid paddlers. A few good locations do exist, however; perhaps most notably the southwest side of Punta Banda near Ensenada. Being sheltered from the brunt of north Pacific swells and with a fine variety of sea life, it is a suitable spot for beginners and intermediates. The coastal lagoons of the southern state offer some suitable locations as well. During the winter months, however, kayaks are not allowed in the zones frequented by the California gray whale.

Many travelers bring their own kayaks to Baja—evidenced by the steady stream of such craft lashed to vehicles parading up and down Highway 1. More and more, though, hotels, resorts and independent operators are providing equipment for rent on location. In some cases, hotels loan kayaks free to their guests, while beachside services may charge an hourly or daily fee. Hourly rates vary by location with steep discounts usually available for multihour or multiday rentals. Guided tours are available as well, mainly on the lower Gulf of California coast, designed for a wide range of budgets. A 2½-hour tour might start at less than $20, while a 10-day, fully equipped expedition can cost $1000 or more.

Sailboarding

Sailboarding has enjoyed a boom in recent years along both coasts of the Baja peninsula, thanks to excellent conditions and large, still-uncrowded areas with room for riders of all skill levels. Sailboarders (also known as windsurfers) can find a wide range of conditions, from relatively calm inshore waters to big waves and heavy winds. One can usually count on steady breezes along both coastlines, with prevailing winds out of the northwest on the Pacific side from March to October and from the north from November to March along the Gulf of California.

The Pacific side, with its large ocean waves and colder water, provides the most challenging conditions and boasts several spots that draw advanced sailboarders. Punta San Carlos, a remote spot on the coast south of El Rosario, is one of these, drawing sailboarders from around the world, despite its isolation. Another remote spot with steady winds and large waves is Punta Abreojos, a coastal hamlet just north of Laguna San Ignacio. Far to the north, Kilometer 23 on the free road to Ensenada is a popular weekend spot with sailboarders from Southern California. Meanwhile, several bays on the Pacific coast have strong winds without the waves and are good spots for beginners. These include the bays of San Quintín, Magdalena, Santa Rosalillita and Almejas.

On the gulf side, Bahía de Los Angeles, Punta Chivato and Loreto all rank as popular sailboarding areas. Best known of all, though, is the East Cape region on the southern coast of the gulf, including spots like Cabo Pulmo, Los Barriles and La Ventana. Strong, steady winds are reliable along most of the southern gulf region between late November and early March, providing excellent conditions for sailboarding. The La Paz area enjoys good summer-time conditions when on-shore breezes, known as *coromueles*, kick up in late afternoon, helping cool the city as an added bonus.

Sailboarding is a popular sport in many beach resorts and equipment can be found for sale and rent there. In recent years, independent outfitters have emerged, providing rentals, instruction and transportation to sailboarding areas. In some cases, comprehensive packages are available. Those who drive with their own gear to Baja would be well advised to make sure the equipment is in top shape and bring their own spare parts along with them.

Snorkeling and Scuba Diving

An undersea world of wonders awaits those who don mask, fins, et al, and plunge into the coastal waters of Baja California. From the Coronado Islands off Tijuana to Cabo San Lucas, on around to the sheltered waters of the Gulf of California, a cornucopia beckons those who venture beneath the surface. Excellent visibility and an out-standing variety of sea life can be found at diving locales up and down the peninsula. Scuba diving is popular along both the Pacific and Gulf of California coasts; most of the snorkeling activity is on the gulf coast, due to frequently turbulent conditions along the Pacific shoreline.

Baja's far north—including the Los Coronados and Todos Santos islands, and Punta Banda—attracts more scuba divers than any other part of the peninsula, due to its proximity to the U.S. border and ready access to a variety of undersea life. Southern California divers will feel at home in this region, given the similar conditions to those across the border. Kelp beds flourish along the rocky shoreline of these locales and others like them along northern Baja's coast, chilled by waters of the southward-flowing California Current. (Surface temperatures range from the low to mid 50s during winter to the upper 60s and occasionally low 70s in summer. Full wet suits are almost always advisable.) Sea life is abundant in these waters, including bat rays, perch, giant kelpfish, cabezon, rockfish of different types, and the garibaldi—California's official state fish.

Farther south, in the Los Cabos region and on the Gulf of California, the waters are warm and harbor entirely different species of sea life. Surface temperatures near Cabo San Lucas run in the 60s during the winter months but climb as high as 90 degrees by late summer. Visibility can be outstanding, exceeding 100 feet in some locations under the right conditions.

Along the Los Cabos corridor, scuba divers will find an assortment of reefs, coves and rock formations suitable for all skill levels. Snorkeling is popular at Land's End off Cabo San Lucas and at a number of shallow-water spots between Cabo San Lucas and San José del Cabo. Up the coast on the Gulf of California, the East Cape region hosts a number of fine diving spots. The hub of activity here is Cabo Pulmo, where an offshore coral reef attracts scuba divers and snorkelers alike.

Dances With Sea Lions In the Sea off

RECREATION

By David J. Brackney

What do you say to an 800-pound sea lion bull spitting bubbles a foot in front of your face? *"¡Buenos días, amigo!"* perhaps, seeing as how we're 900 road miles south of San Diego. Then take a hint, back-paddle a few strokes and observe the overgrown brute from a more respectable distance.

Besides, there's lots to see and do besides invading a surly bull's domain—like swimming with scores of other sea lions frolicking about—diving, leaping, cutting corkscrew turns as they stage an ad-lib acrobatics show for their guests. Some venture within hand's reach, one brave cow takes a playful nip at your author's swim fin.

Truth be told, it was Stoney, my traveling companion, who had the run-in with the 800-pound behemoth. A six-foot-two, 240-pound ex-Marine, John "Stoney" Saathoff had met his match at last in this beast's territorial warning, as he backed off toward my own more secure vantage point.

There I had met up with some more benign yet still playful pinnipeds, plenty eager to enjoy my company. Like monkeys at the zoo, it's hard to say who was *really* doing the watching, we divers or our flippered friends from the depths.

So goes another tough day in the Sea of Cortez—carefree and wide-eyed at once as we donned masks, snorkels and fins to explore one of the world's great undersea playgrounds. Nearby in La Paz, TV sets brought breaking reports of yet another El Niño storm slamming the California coast.

We were on company time, mind you, after four bone-jarring days on the road and an hour-long boat ride through choppy seas to reach this teeming sea lion colony near the upper edge of La Paz Bay. My own task was to rewrite the *Baja California* guidebook, while Stoney did the driving and map-making on this, his first extended trek to Mexico.

It was a better day at the office than most, this sun-drenched morning in the winter of 1998 as we took our first dive in the lucid, 70-degree waters. In the hours ahead, we would marvel at a bounty and variety of sea life seldom observed off our own Southern California coastline.

Small wonder that we were not alone, joined by divers from half a dozen other *pangas* that bobbed in the water nearby. These small, outboard-motor boats form the backbone of the peninsula's inshore dive fleet, bearing guests from lands far removed who wish to dive with the sea lions and other creatures. Locals and lucky visitors have seen it all here, from dolphins and manta rays clear up to gentle giants like whale sharks and blue whales—four times longer than the boat in which we rode.

Sans scuba gear, we would content ourselves with the sea lions, whose court-jester antics earned grins all

La Paz

Sea lions take a break between swims off Isla Espíritu Santo.

sand-pound pinnipeds and looked ahead to the afternoon's dive.

No sea lions were to be seen as we anchored beneath a granite wall and plunged amid a menagerie of tropical sea life—angel fish, spotted boxfish, green parrot fish, Moorish idols, and school after school of sergeant majors, with their distinct vertical stripes. The sea bottom itself was a gallery to behold, with coral formations cast in strange hues of yellow, green, amber and more, offset by patches of brilliant white where new growth had occurred. Skinny, needle-like coronet fish cruised through the coral, and a scrambling octopus made a fast dash between watery lairs.

around, even from Stoney, after his early encounter with the oversized bull. "You see that? I came this close to getting kissed on the lips," he said, holding his hands about 12 inches apart.

We would head south before we could wear out our welcome, putting ashore for lunch at a crescent-shaped cove where soaring cliffs flanked a broad, quarter-mile-long beach. Cactus, sage and agave graced the arid headlands above the teal and turquoise waters; somehow the combination seemed amiss, as it does in much of Baja, where desert and sea collide in spectacular fashion. Picture the Painted Desert or Joshua Tree National Park, set amid waters from Fiji or Cozumel, and you'll begin to get the idea. Again we'd discovered no secret spot, sharing the strand with several other *pangas*, while a small flotilla of kayakers milled about the bay. Still, there was room for all as we swapped stories of thou-

Stroke by stroke Stoney and I kept the fish moving ahead as we worked our way down the reef. "We would have made good fish herders," he cracked later on, suggesting it might be time for a career change. I was inclined to agree.

Though well known to divers, this stretch of sea floor remained pristine, save a blemish or two where someone's careless anchor use had scarred the coral bed. All told, I spied a single manmade object—a slime-covered Pepsi bottle, which I dutifully retrieved from the bottom. Otherwise, we took nothing more than photos and tales from the deep—to be told, retold and continually improved upon. Heck, by day's end, Stoney had gone eyeball-to-eyeball with a teeth-bristling, 1,200-pound hulk 4 inches in front of his face...and the sea lion blinked.

A diver prepares to explore the undersea world off La Paz.

be found in Bahía Concepción, south of Mulegé.

Warmer sea temperatures bring with them an entirely different class of sea life. In shallower waters, the fish come in a riot of colors and shapes that divers are likely to encounter. They include such beauties as the Moorish idol, spotted boxfish, cabrilla, octopus, various types of angelfish, sergeant major and bumperhead parrotfish, to name but a very few. Sea lion colonies are popular destinations for inshore excursions; divers should exercise caution, however, against approaching too closely to sometimes-territorial bulls. Farther offshore, lucky divers might swim beneath a school of hammerhead sharks, take a ride on the back of a manta ray or encounter a gentle giant in a whale shark—the largest fish in the world.

Farther north along the gulf, La Paz is another magnet for scuba diving and snorkeling, particularly Isla Espíritu Santo, which offers sea lions, tropical fish and an underwater shipwreck among its attractions. Nearby, divers will find some good underwater zones for viewing schools of hammerhead sharks. Continuing north, the islands off the coast of Loreto provide excellent, unspoiled conditions, as does the so-called Midriff region off Bahía de los Angeles. Still more fine diving can

Given the popularity of diving, numerous shops do business up and down the peninsula, offering scuba and snorkeling equipment for rent and sale. Supplies are often confined to basic equipment, and not always in all types, sizes or styles. Repairs and spare parts may be hard to come by as well.

Tanks, weight belts, air fills and regulators should be available in most instances. Air compressors are a key component to a successful trip, and divers should check in advance to ensure their availability and the quality of the air they put out.

Some dive shops operate independently, while others are affiliated with hotels or resorts. Many shops have diving schools with licensed instructors who can certify new scuba divers. In addition, hotels and resorts without dive shops often have snorkeling gear for rent and can arrange dive trips for their guests.

Organized diving trips are available in many areas, starting at less than $10 for a short hop to Land's End at Cabo San Lucas and reaching hundreds of dollars for multiday trips out of San Diego or La Paz.

A meditative approach to water recreation in Cabo San Lucas.

Surfing

Baja California's Pacific coast is blessed with scores of excellent surfing spots, with waves breaking year-round and conditions suiting everyone from novices to masters of the sport. Surfing in Baja has seen a boom in popularity in recent decades, due in no small part to the opening of Mexico Highway 1 in 1973.

Most who ride Baja's waves hail from nearby California, where an ever-growing population has meant more and more competition for the same number of waves. As a result, Baja has become a last frontier for surfers looking for uncrowded conditions.

From Playas de Tijuana on the U.S. frontier to Punta Colorada near San José del Cabo, some 85 named surf spots dot the coastline, plus many more unnamed breaks. The best-known ones are in the far north between the U.S. border and San Quintín, and the far south in the Los Cabos region. Rentals are not readily available, but surf shops in Ensenada and Los Cabos offer both boards and other equipment for sale. Updated information on surf conditions is available through the Baja Safari travel club, which operates a toll-free phone number, (888) 411-2252.

Surfers in northern Baja will find conditions much like those of nearby California, with an abundance of beach breaks, reef breaks and point breaks. The most favored spots are the reef and point breaks that primarily peel "right" and work best on winter swells.

A surfer rides a small wave near Playa Punta Lobos.

Ocean temperatures are generally cold here, sometimes even more so than Southern California, making wet suits standard equipment throughout most of the year. Baja Malibu, K-38, Calafia and San Miguel—all between the border and Ensenada—are among the better-known breaks in this region. These and many other spots are more consistently "up" than those in Southern California, being less sheltered from storm swells out of the north and west Pacific.

By far the best-known spot in northern Baja is Todos Santos Island, off the coast of Ensenada and home to some of the biggest ridable surf in the world. Winter swells from north Pacific storms strike with full force here, producing waves that sometimes top 30 feet in height. These huge, pitching walls of water break mainly right and resemble those of Waimea Bay in Hawaii. One Todos Santos wave caught in early 1998 measured an estimated 52 feet from peak to trough, earning its rider a $50,000 prize for the biggest wave ridden in the world that winter.

Farther south, lying offshore from the Vizcaíno Peninsula, are Isla Cedros and Isla Natividad, which both enjoy good wintertime surf. Occasional flights from the mainland serve these two islands and are the primary access for visiting surfers.

Southern Baja generally enjoys warmer conditions than farther north, though winter water temperatures can still run surprisingly cool, dipping as low as 60 degrees. By summer, though, the water warms into the 80s. The region boasts a good variety of surf, mainly reef and point breaks, that work at varying times through the year. In the Cabo San Lucas area, Bahía Chileno, Punta Palmilla and Costa Azul are well-known breaks, while Pescadero, near the town of Todos Santos, is another popular spot. A handful of spots in the East Cape region are actually on the Gulf of California and produce waves only on southerly swells.

Along with the named breaks, countless "secret spots" exist in remote areas, ridden only by those with the time, a suitable vehicle and the spirit of adventure to seek them out.

Appendix

The information included in this chapter is provided solely as a service to our readers, and no endorsement of any service by the Automobile Club of Southern California is implied or intended.

Transportation

*B*ecause the schedules of most operators change frequently, detailed listings and fares are not given. If you plan a bus trip to Baja California, contact the bus company or companies for a list of departures; air schedules and fares can be obtained either from the individual carriers or any Auto Club Travel Agency office.

Air Service

Since flight schedules change on a frequent basis, they are not listed in this publication. Carriers listed below operate either within Baja California or between California and Baja California. Current schedules and fares can be obtained from the airlines' ticket offices or any Auto Club Travel Agency office. The Auto Club is not responsible for discontinuance of any flight or service.

Aero California *(310) 322-2644, (800) 237-6225.* Operates daily flights from Los Angeles to Loreto, La Paz and Los Cabos Airport (San José del Cabo), and from Tijuana to La Paz.

Aerolitoral *(800) 237-6639.* An affiliate of Aeromexico, flies Monday through Saturday between Guerrero Negro and Hermosillo, Son., with connecting flights from Hermosillo to destinations throughout Mexico, including Mexicali.

Aeromexico *(800) 237-6639.* Operates daily flights from Los Angeles to La Paz and from Tijuana to La Paz; it also flies Thursday through Sunday from San Diego to Los Cabos.

Alaska Airlines *(800) 426-0333.* Flies daily from Los Angeles, San Diego and San Francisco to Los Cabos.

Blue Pacific Air *(800) 600-0082.* Flies Friday and Sunday from Long Beach and San Diego (Brown Field) to San Felipe.

Mexicana Airlines *(310) 646-7321, (800) 531-7921.* Operates daily flights from Los Angeles to Los Cabos and La Paz.

Bus Service

Domestic

CENTRAL DE AUTOBUSES (CENTRAL BUS TERMINAL) *01152 (66) 21-29-82. Located in the La Mesa district on Blvd. Lázaro Cárdenas at Blvd. Alamar in eastern Tijuana.* This is the main gateway for people traveling by bus from the United States to destinations in Baja California. Information on different bus lines, fares and schedules is available by calling the station at the phone number above. The old bus ter-

Airports in Baja California range from the international jetport in Los Cabos (above) to the small facility in San Felipe.

minal located in downtown Tijuana at Calle Comercio and Avenida Madero serves some small local companies. Passengers arriving here by Greyhound bus can obtain inexpensive transportation on one of these small local buses to any business section of Tijuana.

Autotransportes de Baja California (ABC) is currently the only bus line linking Tijuana with destinations along Mexico Highway 1. The trip to La Paz lasts about 24 hours and costs about $56 one way. (Connecting service is available between La Paz and

Mexico 101: A Sociology Course on a

APPENDIX

By David J. Brackney

One sweltering morning in the summer of 1982, I boarded a second-class bus in Mexicali and rode 36 hours in stifling heat into the interior of Mexico, my first time outside the United States. Just out of college, I traveled alone and made the best of my high school Spanish, while relying on the kindness of strangers for help ordering roadside meals.

As the shantytowns and industrial parks of Mexicali gave way to endless tracts of irrigated cropland, I craned my neck and gazed about at the standing-room-only crowd—wizened old farm workers, young mothers with babies slung over their backs, wide-eyed children who shamelessly stared at the lone gringo on board.

Above the windshield in front, a crucifix shared space with a pinup of Miss August, while a tiny fan jerked back and forth in a futile attempt to cool anything aft of the second row. The driver—a sweaty, mustachioed man, 40ish with an ample gut—reached into the communal ice chest to grab another long gulp from a can of cold cola. Salsa and ranchera tunes thumped incessantly out of somebody's boom box, long

Los Cabos.) The trip to Ensenada takes about 90 minutes and costs about $6.50. ABC also operates buses from Tijuana to Mexicali and San Felipe. **Linea Elite** and **Norte de Sonora** also offer service between Tijuana and Mexicali. The trip takes about 2 hours and costs about $10 on any of these bus lines. From Mexicali there are connections for Mexico City and other interior cities.

International

Five Star Tours *(800) 553-8687 (California only), (619) 232-5049. Prices vary with number of passengers and destination. Van and bus service between San Diego and Tijuana.* San Diego pickups and drop-offs are available at San Diego International Airport and the Amtrak Depot at Broadway at Kettner Boulevard, with cross-border service to the Mexicoach Terminal at the corner of Avenida Revolución and Calle 7, and the Tijuana International Airport. Five Star Tours also provides bullfight trips.

Greyhound Lines *In Los Angeles call (800) 231-2222 or (213) 629-8402; in San Diego call (619) 239-3266. From Los Angeles, fares to Tijuana are $15 one way, $24 round trip; to Calexico, $30 one way, $49 round trip; to Mexicali, $29 one way, $55 round trip. From San Diego, fares to Tijuana are $6 one way, $9 round trip; to Calexico, $18 one way, $27 round trip; to Mexicali, $32 one way, $63 round trip.* Frequent departures leave from downtown terminals in both Los Angeles and San Diego to Tijuana. Service from both cities to Calexico and Mexicali is less frequent but still available several times a day. Some buses let off passengers in Tijuana at the old downtown terminal; others go to the Central Bus Terminal (for addresses see the preceding description under "Domestic").

Second-Class Bus

into the night as farmland ceded to barren desert and then to lush tropical lowlands.

Through it all, I struggled in fractured Spanish to field questions about where I was from, why I had come this way, how long I planned to stay, etc., etc. Whenever our bus pulled into a town, elderly women and youngsters would parade down the aisle, noisily hawking snow cones, corn on the cob, tamales and comic books.

For the price of a bus ticket, I got far more than I had bargained for—a crash course in Mexican customs, language and culture—something I never would have received traveling by automobile, cruise ship or airplane. Unwittingly too, I was sowing the seeds of a love affair with America's southern neighbor that continues to this day.

It was pressing midnight the following day when I tramped off the old coach in downtown Guadalajara— bleary eyed, stiff-legged and needing a bath. I had loved every minute of the previous day-and-a-half. On board a bus—the transit of choice for millions of Mexicans—I discovered the joys of travel are not always derived in reaching one's destination, but in the journey itself.

Mexicoach *Round-trip tickets are $2.* Many buses run daily from the trolley station in San Ysidro to the Mexicoach Terminal in Tijuana.

San Diego Trolley *(619) 233-3004. Trolleys operate from 5 a.m. to 1 a.m., with 15-minute service most of the time; maximum one-way fare is $2.* Daily rail service runs between San Diego and the international border at San Ysidro.

Car Rentals

A few American rental agencies allow customers to drive their vehicles into Mexico; others may arrange rentals with affiliated companies in Mexico. Check with individual companies for their policies. Car rental agencies are located in the larger cities and at the airports in Baja California. Auto rentals are much more expensive in Mexico than in the United States.

Ferry Service and Schedules

The ferry system, a vital transportation link between Baja California and Mexico's mainland, carries both vehicles and passengers. Formerly owned and operated by the Mexican government, the ferry system was sold in 1989 to a private Mexican company, Grupo Sematur. Rates under the new owner have increased substantially, but service has improved. In the past, motorists often had difficulty obtaining reservations.

Motorists planning to ship their vehicle to the mainland must obtain a car permit. Permits are available at border crossings. **Note: Applicants for car permits must present the original current registration or a notarized bill of sale for each vehicle; copies and temporary papers are not** accepted. (See *Tourist Regulations and Travel Tips*, Automobile Requirements.)

Ferry reservations may be made by telephone from the United States or within Mexico, but some knowledge of Spanish is necessary. Most travelers prefer to make reservations in person at the ferry offices. Reservations should be made at least a week in advance, and a month in advance during holiday periods, although some people report getting a reservation on short notice. Reservations and general information are also available via the Sematur web site, **www.ferrysematur.com**.

Pets are permitted on the ferries when accompanied by the appropriate health certificates which have been visaed by a Mexican Consul (see *Tourist Regulations and Travel Tips*).

The Cabo San Lucas to Puerto Vallarta ferry is no longer operating.

Ferry Ticket Offices

La Paz *On Guillermo Prieto at Cinco de Mayo, 2 blocks southeast of Plaza Consti-* *tución. 01152 (112) 5-38-33 or 5-46-66. Open Mon.-Fri. 7 a.m.-1 p.m. and 4-6 p.m., Sat.-Sun. 8 a.m.-1 p.m. Ferry information may also be obtained at the State Tourism Office; 01152 (112) 2-59-39.* The ferry terminal is located at Pichilingue, the deep-water port for La Paz, 10 miles north of the city.

Santa Rosalía *Located in the terminal building on Hwy. 1 just south of the main entrance into the city. 01152 (115) 2-00-13 or 2-00-14.*

Ferry Routes

Within Mexico, ferry information may be obtained by calling the toll-free number 01 (800) 696-96-00. Each ferry contains a telephone, cafeteria and medical assistance.

La Paz-Mazatlán *Ferries depart from both ports daily at 3 p.m. Salón (general seating) class only is available on Wed. sailings from La Paz and Thu. sailings from Mazatlán. Travel time is about 18 hours.*

FERRY RATES (shown in dollars)

ROUTE	PASSENGER CLASS				VEHICLE TYPE				
	Salon (Padded seats)	Tourist (Roomette with washbasin and bunks for four persons)	Cabin (Beds and bath for two persons)	Special Cabin (Beds, lounge and bath for two persons)	Car, Small Truck, and Van		Car or Truck with Trailer		Motorhome over 16.4 feet (5 meters)
					up to 16.4 feet (5 meters)	16.5 to 21.3 feet (5 to 6.5 meters)	up to 29.5 feet (9 meters)	29.5 to 55.8 feet (9 to 17 meters)	
La Paz-Mazatlán	19	38	56	75	184	239	330	624	312
La Paz-Topolobampo	13	25	38	50	112	146	202	380	191
Santa Rosalia-Guaymas	13	25	38	50	129	168	232	438	220

La Paz-Topolobampo (Los Mochis)

Ferries depart from La Paz Mon., Wed. and Fri. at 10 p.m. They leave Topolobampo Tue., Thu. and Sat. at 10 p.m. Sailing time is about 10 hours.

Santa Rosalía-Guaymas *Ferries depart from Santa Rosalía on Sun. and Wed. at 11 p.m. They leave Guaymas on Sun. and Tue. at 8 a.m. Sailing time is about seven hours.*

Tours

As a result of the increasing popularity of Baja California as a tourist destination, many tour operators offer organized tours of the peninsula. These include cruises, air tours, bus tours and even a four-wheel-drive tour. The Automobile Club of Southern California's Travel Agency can handle bookings on most tours; call or visit any Travel Agency office for details.

Speaking Spanish

This section lists some of the Spanish phrases and sentences that are most useful to visitors in Baja California. A basic knowledge of the language may be helpful. Many of the local residents who deal with tourists speak English; those who don't are glad to help you along with your attempts at their language. Spanish is not difficult to pronounce. A study of the following pronunciation rules will be sufficient to make yourself understood.

Pronunciation

The pronunciation of the Spanish language presents few difficulties. The spelling is almost phonetic; nearly every letter has one sound which it retains at all times.

Vowels

A   pronounced as in *father.*

E   pronounced as in *bed.*

I   pronounced as in *pizza.*

O   pronounced as in *hold*

U   pronounced as in *junior.*

Diphthongs

Spanish diphthongs are pronounced as very swift elisions of the component vowels equally stressed.

ue as in weh   *fuente*

au as in English ouch   *gaucho*

Consonants

Consonants do not differ materially from the English. The few differences can be summarized as follows:

C   is pronounced with a soft sound before *e* and *i*. Otherwise it has a *k* sound.

   cinco   SEEN-ko.

G   is like a strong English *h* when it precedes *e* and *i*. In all other cases it is like English *g* in go.

   gente   HEN-te.

H   always silent.

J   pronounced like a strong English *h.*

LL   pronounced like the English *y.*

   caballo   kah-BAH-yo

Ñ   combination of *n* and *y.*

niño	NEEN-yo

Qu pronounced like *k*.

Z is always pronounced like the English *s*.

Accent or Stress

1. When a word ends in a vowel, *n* or *s*, the stress falls on the next to the last syllable.

hombre	OM-bre
hablan	AH-blan
estos	ES-tos

2. When the word ends in a consonant other than *n* or *s*, the stress falls on the last syllable.

hablar	ah-BLAR

3. In some cases an accent mark will be found over a vowel. This does not change the pronunciation of that vowel, but indicates that the stress falls on that syllable.

gramática	gra-MAH-ti-ca
corazón	cor-a-SOWN

Words and Phrases

Note: Nouns in Spanish are either masculine or feminine, and there are two words meaning "the": *el* is used before masculine nouns, *la* before feminine nouns. The plural of *el* is *los*, of *la* is *las*. After words given on these pages the gender is indicated by (m.) for masculine, (f.) for feminine. For instance, say *el hotel* and *los hoteles*; *la posada* and *las posadas*. The word *"usted,"* meaning "you," is usually abbreviated *Ud.* An adjective also agrees in gender with the noun it modifies. For example, *el hombre pequeño*—the small man; *la camisa roja*—the red shirt. In most cases, the adjective follows the noun.

Language

Do you understand English?
¿Entiende Ud. el inglés?

I do not speak Spanish.
No hablo español.

Yes, sir; no, madam.
Sí, señor; no, señora.

Very little
Muy poco; (or) poquito

I do not understand.
No entiendo.

Do you understand me?
¿Me entiende Ud.?

Please speak slowly.
Por favor hable despacio.

I wish to speak with an interpreter.
Quisiera hablar con un intérprete.

What are you saying?
¿Qué dice?

Polite Phrases

Good morning.
Buenos días.

Good afternoon.
Buenas tardes.

Good night.
Buenas noches.

Goodbye.
Adiós; hasta luego.

Thank you.
Gracias.

Yes, very good.
Sí; muy bueno.

Please.
Por favor.

Excuse me.
Perdóneme.

I am very sorry.
Lo siento mucho.

A basic knowledge of Spanish can prove useful in a wide variety of situations: on a diving trip out of La Paz; stopping for coffee in Puerto Nuevo; fixing a flat on the road to San Felipe; and dealing with vendors in El Rosario.

To Explain Your Needs

I need; we need.
   Necesito; necesitamos.

I would like to telephone.
   Quisiera telefonear.

I am hungry; we are hungry.
   Tengo hambre; tenemos hambre.

I am thirsty; we are thirsty.
   Tengo sed; tenemos sed.

I am cold; we are cold.
   Tengo frío; tenemos frío.

I am warm; we are warm.
   Tengo calor; tenemos calor.

I am tired; we are tired.
Estoy cansado (a); estamos cansados.

I am sick; we are sick.
Estoy enfermo (a); estamos enfermos.

The child is sick; tired.
El niño (la niña) está enfermo (a); cansado (a).

Directions

north/**norte**

south/**sur**

east/**este**

west/**oeste**

(Note: In some addresses, east is **oriente**, abbreviated **Ote.**; west is **poniente**, abbreviated **Pte.**)

Numerals

1	**uno**
2	**dos**
3	**tres**
4	**cuatro**
5	**cinco**
6	**seis**
7	**siete**
8	**ocho**
9	**nueve**
10	**diez**
11	**once**
12	**doce**
13	**trece**
14	**catorce**
15	**quince**
16	**dieciseis**
17	**diecisiete**
18	**dieciocho**
19	**diecinueve**
20	**veinte**
21	**veinte y uno**
30	**treinta**
40	**cuarenta**
50	**cincuenta**
60	**sesenta**
70	**setenta**
80	**ochenta**
90	**noventa**
100	**cien**
200	**doscientos**

Days and Time

Sunday/**domingo**

Monday/**lunes**

Tuesday/**martes**

Wednesday/**miércoles**

Thursday/**jueves**

Friday/**viernes**

Saturday/**sábado**

today/**hoy**

tomorrow/**mañana**

yesterday/**ayer**

morning/**la mañana**

noon/**el mediodía**

afternoon/**la tarde**

tonight/**esta noche**

night/**la noche**

last night/**anoche**

midnight/**a medianoche**

What time is it?
¿Qué horas son?

It is one o'clock.
Es la una.

It is two o'clock.
Son las dos.

It is ten minutes past two.
Son las dos y diez.

It is a quarter past three.
Son las tres y cuarto.

It is a quarter of five.
Son un cuarto para las cinco.

It is 25 minutes of six.
Son veinticinco para las seis.

It is half past four.
Son las cuatro y media.

Useful Adjectives

bad/**malo**

beautiful/**hermoso**

cheap/**barato**

clean/**limpio**

cold/**frío**

difficult/**difícil**

dirty/**sucio**

early/**temprano**

easy/**fácil**

expensive/**caro**

fast/**rápido**

good/**bueno**

high/**alto**

hot/**caliente**

kind/**amable**

large/**grande**

low/**bajo**

late/**tarde**

long/**largo**

polite/**cortés**

sharp/**agudo**

short/**corto**

slow/**lento**

small/**pequeño, chico**

ugly/**feo**

unkind/**despiadado, duro**

Colors

white/**blanco**

pink/**rosa**

black/**negro**

blue; dark blue/**azul; azul obscuro**

gray/**gris**

green; light green/**verde; verde claro**

brown/**café**

purple/**morado**

red/**rojo; colorado**

yellow/**amarillo**

At the Border

passport
pasaporte

tourist card
tarjeta de turista

age
edad

marital status
estado civil

single
soltero (m.); soltera (f.)

married
casado (m.); casada (f.)

widowed
viudo (m.); viuda (f.)

divorced
divorciado (m.); divorciada (f.)

profession; occupation
profesión; ocupación

vaccination card
cartilla de vacunación

driver's license
licencia de manejar

car owner's title (registration)
título de propiedad (registro)

year of car
modelo (o año)

make (Ford, Mazda, etc.)
marca

license plate and state
placa y estado

chassis and motor number
número de chasis y motor

number of doors
número de puertas

number of cylinders
número de cilindros

number of passengers
número de pasajeros

On the Road

kilometer/**kilómetro (m.)**

highway/**carretera (f.)**

road/**camino (m.)**

street/**calle (f.)**

avenue/**avenida (f.)**

boulevard/**bulevar (m.)**

block/**cuadra (f.)**

corner/**esquina (f.)**

left side/**lado izquierdo (m.)**

right side/**lado derecho (m.)**

Show me the road to...
Enséñeme el camino a...

How far is...?
¿Qué tan lejos está...?

Can we get to ...before dark?
¿Podemos llegar a ...antes del anochecer?

Is this road dangerous?
¿Es peligroso este camino?

Is that road in good condition?
¿Está en buen estado aquel camino?

Is it paved or is it a dirt road?
¿Está pavimentado o es de terracería?

Go straight ahead.
Siga derecho.

Turn to the right; left.
Vuelta a la derecha; izquierda.

What city, town, is this?
¿Qué ciudad, pueblo, es éste?

Where does this road lead?
A dónde conduce este camino?

In Case of Car Trouble

I want to ask you a favor.
Quiero pedirle un favor.

I need a tow truck.
Necesito una grua.

My car has broken down.
Se me ha descompuesto el carro.

My lights don't work.
Mis faros no funcionan.

The starter does not work.
El arranque no funciona.

I have run out of gasoline.
Se me acabó la gasolina.

Is there a gasoline station near here?
¿Hay una estación de gasolina cerca e aquí?

Is there a garage near here?
¿Hay un garage cerca?

Please send someone to repair my car.
Por favor mande a alguien a componer mi carro.

May I go with you to get a mechanic?
¿Puedo ir con usted a conseguir un mecánico?

Have you a rope to tow my car?
¿Tiene una cuerda para remolcar mi carro?

Do you want to help me push the car to one side of the road?
¿Quiere ayudarme a empujar el carro a un lado del caiman?

Do you want to help me change a tire?
¿Quiere ayudarme a cambiar una llanta?

Do you want to be my witness?
¿Quiere ser mi testigo?

Arriving in Town

Is English spoken here?
¿Se habla inglés aquí?

Where is the center of town?
¿Dónde está el centro de la ciudad?

Where is X Street, X Square, the X Hotel?
¿Dónde está la Calle X, la Plaza X, el Hotel X?

May I park here?
¿Puedo estacionarme aquí?

Please direct me to the nearest post office.
Por favor diríjame a la oficina de correos mas cercana.

Where can I find a policeman, a hair dresser, a doctor, a drug store?
¿Dónde puedo hallar un policía, una estética, un médico, una farmacia?

Where is the police station, the chamber of commerce?
¿Dónde está la comisaría, la cámara de comercio?

Where can I find road maps, post cards, American newspapers?
¿Dónde se pueden hallar mapas de caminos, tarjetas postales, periódicos norteamericanos?

Please direct me to the railroad station, the bus station.
Por favor diríjame a la estación del ferrocarril, a la terminal del autobús.

How often does the bus go by?
¿Qué tan seguido pasa el autobús (camión)?

Does the bus stop here?
¿Para aquí el autobús?

Could you recommend a good restaurant; a good small hotel; a first class hotel?
¿Puede Ud. recomendar un buen restaurante; un buen hotel pequeño; un hotel de primera clase?

I wish to telephone, to telegraph, to cable.
Quiero telefonear, telegrafiar, cablegrafiar.

I wish to change some money.
Quiero cambiar dinero.

What is the rate of exchange?
¿Cuál es el tipo de cambio?

I want to cash a check.
Quiero cambiar un cheque.

At the Hotel

hotel/**hotel (m.)**

inn/**posada (f.)**

apartments/**departamentos (m.)**

room/**cuarto (m.)**

furnished room/**cuarto amueblado**

bedroom/**recámara (f.)**

pillow/**almohada (f.)**

blanket/**cobija (f.), manta (f.)**

air conditioning/**aire acondi-cionado**

kitchen/**cocina (f.)**

bathroom/**cuarto de baño (m.)**

towel/**toalla (f.)**

wash cloth/**toalla chica (f.)**

soap/**jabón (m.)**

dining room/**comedor (m.)**

ice water/**agua con hielo (m.)**

hot water/**agua caliente (m.)**

elevator/**elevador (m.)**

stairway/**escalera (f.)**

key/**llave (f.)**

office/**oficina (f.)**

manager/**gerente (m.)**

maid/**recamarera (f.)**

office employee/**empleado de oficina (m.)**

bellboy/**maletero (m.)**

porter/**mozo de servicios (m.)**

guest/**huésped (m.)**

I want a single room, with bath.
Deseo un cuarto sencillo, con baño.

I want a room for two; with twin beds.
Deseo un cuarto para dos; con camas gemelas.

I want two connecting rooms.
Deseo dos cuartos comunicados.

A front room; a back room.
Un cuarto al frente; al fondo.

A quiet room.
Un cuarto tranquilo.

On the lower floor; upper floor.
En el piso bajo; piso alto.

Will you have the baggage brought up? ...down?
¿Quiere Ud. hacer subir ...bajar el equipaje?

We are leaving tomorrow.
Nos vamos mañana.

We are staying several days ...just tonight.
Nos quedaremos aquí unos pocos días ...solamente esta noche.

What is the price (rate)?
¿Cuál es el precio (la tarifa)?

What is the minimum rate?
¿Cuál es el precio mínimo?

Do you accept checks in payment?
¿Acepta Ud. cheques en pago?

I want my bill, please.
Quiero la cuenta, por favor.

Have you hot running water?
¿Hay agua corriente y caliente?

The shower doesn't work.
La regadera no funciona.

Is there a garage?
¿Hay garage?

Where is the ladies' room, men's room?

¿Dónde está el baño (lavabo) de damas, de caballeros?

Where is the barber shop?

¿Dónde hay una peluquería?

Please send these clothes to the laundry.

Hágame el favor de mandar esta ropa a la lavandería.

Please clean and press this suit.

Hágame el favor de limpiar y planchar este traje.

I want it today; tomorrow.

Lo quiero hoy; mañana.

Please call me at six o'clock.

Hágame el favor de llamarme a las seis.

Please forward my correspondence to this address.

Por favor mande mi correspondencia a esta dirección.

Do you want to prepare a lunch for us to carry with us?

¿Quiere Ud. prepararnos un almuerzo para llevar?

At the Garage

How much is gasoline per liter?

¿Cuánto cuesta el litro de gasolina?

Fill up the gasoline tank; the radiator.

Llene el tanque de gasolina; el radiador.

Give me five, ten, fifteen, twenty liters.

Deme cinco, diez, quince, veinte litros.

Check the oil; change the oil.

Vea el aceite; cambie el aceite.

Please lubricate the car; wash the car.

Favor de lubricar el carro; lavar el carro.

Please tighten the brakes; adjust the brakes.

Favor de apretar los frenos; ajustar los frenos.

Please tune the engine; change the spark plugs.

Favor de poner a punto (afinar) el motor; cambiar las bujías.

My tire has a puncture. Can you repair the tube?

Mi llanta tiene un agujero. ¿Puede reparar la cámara?

The tire is flat.

La llanta está ponchada.

The horn is not working.

El claxón no funciona.

Put water in the battery.

Ponga agua en la batería.

The battery needs charging.

La batería necesita carga.

Please put another bulb in this headlamp.

Favor de reemplazar el foco de este faro.

The gasoline tank is leaking.

El tanque de gasolina está goteando.

The gasoline is clogged.

La manguera de gasolina está tapada.

The engine heats.

El motor se calienta.

The exhaust is choked.

Está obstruido el tubo de escape.

The steering gear is out of order.

La dirección está descompuesta.

The radiator leaks.
El radiador gotea.

The clutch slips.
El embrague resbala.

There is a short circuit.
Hay un cortocircuito.

The windshield wiper does not work.
El limpiavidrios del parabrisas no funciona.

The taillight does not work.
El faro trasero no funciona.

Please clean the windshield.
Favor de limpiar el parabrisas.

When will the repairs be finished?
¿Cuándo terminará la reparación?

How much do I owe you?
¿Cuánto le debo?

At the Restaurant

Please bring me the menu.
Favor de traerme el menú.

I like my meat rare (well done).
Quiero la carne tierna (bien cocida).

Please bring me the check.
Favor de traerme la cuenta.

breakfast/**desayuno (m.)**

lunch/**almuerzo (m.)**

dinner/**comida (f.)**

supper/**cena (f.)**

knife/**cuchillo (m).**

fork/**tenedor (m.)**

spoon/**cuchara (f.)**

cup/**taza (f.)**

glass/**vaso (f.)**

napkin/**servilleta (f.)**

bill/**cuenta (f.)**

tip/**propina (f.)**

Bread

bread/**pan (m.)**

crackers/**galletas saladas (f.)**

toast/**pan tostado (m.)**

Fruit

apple/**manzana (f.)**

avocado/**aguacate (m.)**

banana/**plátano (m.)**

dates/**dátiles (m.)**

figs/**higos (m.)**

fruit/**fruta (f.)**

guava/**guayaba (f.)**

lemon/**lima (m.)**

lime/**limón (f.)**

nuts/**nueces (f.)**

olives/**aceitunas (f.)**

orange/**naranja (f.)**

peach/**durazno (m.)**

pineapple/**piña (f.)**

strawberries/**fresas (f.)**

Vegetables

beans/**frijoles (m.)**

beets/**betabeles (f.)**

cabbage/**repollo (m.); col (f.)**

corn/**maíz (m.)**

lettuce/**lechuga (f.)**

onion/**cebolla (f.)**

peas/**chícharos (m.)**

potatoes/**papas (f.)**

rice/**arroz (m.)**

string beans/**ejotes (m.)**

sweet potatoes/**camotes (m.)**

tomatoes/**jitomates (m.)**

vegetables/**legumbres (f.)**

Meat, Pork, Poultry, Eggs, Fish

sausage/**chorizo (m.)**

meat/**carne (f.)**

beef/**carne de res (f.)**

beefsteak/**bistec (m.) filete (m.)**

veal/**ternera (f.)**

lamb/**carne de carnero**

lamb chops/**chuletas de carnero**

roast/**asado (m.)**

pork/**carne de puerco**

ham/**jamón (m.)**

bacon/**tocino (m.)**

chicken/**pollo (m.)**

egg/**huevo (m.)**

fried/**frito**

soft-boiled/**tibio**

hard-boiled/**cocidos duro**

scrambled/**revueltos**

duck/**pato (m.)**

turkey/**pavo (m.)**

abalone/**abulón (m.)**

clam/**almeja (f.)**

fish/**pescado (m.)**

scallops/**callos (m.)**

shrimp/**camarónes (m.)**

lobster/**langosta (f.)**

Beverages, Liquors

beer/**cerveza (f.)**

brandy/**brandy (m.)**

champagne/**champaña (m.)**

cocktail/**coctel (m.)**

coffee/**café (m.)**

with cream/**con crema**

without cream/**sin crema**

gin/**ginebra (f.)**

milk/**leche (f.)**

rum/**ron (m.)**

tea/**té (m.)**

water/**agua (m.)**

whiskey/**whiskey (m.)**

wine/**vino (m.)**

Desserts

cake/**pastel (m.)**

candies/**dulces (f.)**

custard/**flan (f.)**

ice cream/**helado (m.)**

Miscellaneous

butter/**mantequilla (f.)**

cheese/**queso (m.)**

cookies/**galletas (f.)**

flour/**harina (f.)**

honey/**miel de abejas (f.)**

pepper/**pimienta (f.)**

salad/**ensalada (f.)**

salt/**sal (f.)**

sauce/**salsa (f.)**

soup/**sopa (f.), caldo (m.)**

sugar/**azúcar (m.)**

Supply Lists

The items included in the following lists will help make a trip to Baja California safe and enjoyable. Two lists are shown: the first, for all trips, lists items that should be taken on any trip down the peninsula; the second, for backcountry travel, is more extensive and necessary only for those planning extended off-road and camping trips. Travelers should use their own discretion in deciding which items to include. It is better, however, to take along too much than too little, if there is room in the vehicle. All items on the first list should also be included in preparation for backcountry trips.

All Trips

Vehicle

Air filters

Brake fluid

Flares

Fuses (check amperage)

Motor oil

Power steering fluid

Tools

Water (5 gal. for radiator)

Window cleaner

For people

Can opener

Canteen

Dark glasses

Drinking water and cups

First aid kit

Flashlight and batteries

Insect repellent

Keys (extra, for car)

Paper towels

Salt tablets

Skin lotion

Sun block

Sunburn cream

Sun shade

Toilet tissue

Trash bags

Backcountry Trips

For vehicles

Alternator brushes

Baling wire

Battery cables

Bolts and nuts (assorted sizes)

Chamois (for straining gasoline)

Duct tape

Electric fuel pump

Electric tape

Fittings (gas lines)

Fire extinguisher

Gaskets (head, fuel pump)

Gasoline cans (two, 5-gal.)

Gasoline filter (in-line)

Grease

Hammer (heavy)

Hoses and clamps (radiator)

Hydraulic jack (small sand-support board)

Ignition coil(s)

Ignition module

Lug wrench

Radiator sealant

Spare tires (extra)

Spark plugs

Tire inflator

Tow rope

During the 1973 research trip, Auto Club personnel check out equipment and vehicles at Rancho Santa Inés.

Tube repair kit
Universal joints
Valve cores
Water cans (two, 5-gal.)
Wire (10-gauge electrical) and
Wire connectors

For people and camps

Blankets
Camp cook set
Camp knives
Chairs (folding)
Cleanser
Compass
Cots
Crowbar
Detergent (liquid)
Dishes
Eating utensils
First aid kit (large)
Flashlight (large)
Fly swatter
Fuel (stove and lantern)
Funnels (small and large)
Gloves (leather)
Grate (for cooking)

Hatchet
Lantern (extra mantles)
Matches (wooden)
Netting (mosquito)
Notebook
Pail or bucket
Pens and pencils
Portable toilet
Radio (portable, short-wave or CB)
Rags
Rope (small)
Scrub brush
Shovels (folding)
Signal mirror
Sleeping bags
Snake bite kit(s)
Soap (freshwater and saltwater)
Stove
Table (folding)
Tarpaulins
Tent
Toilet paper
Towels (bath, face)
Trash bags (large and small)
Wash cloths

Lodging & Restaurants

Accommodations in Baja California are diverse, ranging from small motels to luxurious seaside resorts. Many of the peninsula's resorts and certain hotels in major cities have all the services and facilities normally associated with first-class hotels in the United States. Tourists in Baja California should remember, however, that no matter where they are staying, they are in a foreign country, and there may be a different, more relaxed approach to service and housekeeping. If travelers keep this in mind, their visits will be more enjoyable.

Lodging & Restaurants lists hotels, motels, and resorts in Baja California operating as of December 1, 1997. Properties are listed alphabetically under the nearest town, with lodging facilities first and restaurants second. The location is given from the center of town or from the nearest major highway.

AAA-rated lodging and restaurant properties listed in these pages have been inspected at least once in the past year by a trained representative of the Automobile Club of Southern California. In surprise inspections, each property was evaluated according to AAA's extensive and detailed requirements for approval. These requirements are reflective of current industry standards and the expectations of the traveling public. Less than two-thirds of the lodging establishments open for business are listed in AAA publications.

Many listings include AAA's esteemed "diamond" rating, reflecting the overall quality of the establishment. Many factors are considered in the process of determining the diamond rating. In lodging properties, the facility is first "classified" according to its physical design—is it a motel, a hotel, a resort, an apartment, etc. Since the various types of lodging establishments offer differing amenities and facilities, rating criteria are specific for each classification. For example, a motel, which typically offers a room with convenient parking and little if any recreational or public facilities, is rated using criteria designed only for motel-type establishments—it is not compared to a hotel with its extensive public and meeting areas, or to a resort with its wide range of recreational facilities and programs. The diamonds do, however, represent standard levels of quality in all types of establishments.

This book also lists accommodations which are not AAA-rated, but nearly attain AAA standards. In these cases, the ◆ symbol will be missing from the listing. Wherever the inclusion of non-rated hotels, motels and resorts occurs, they are listed as a courtesy and convenience to readers. No endorsement is implied or intended.

The number of lodgings listed in this chapter is limited in Ciudad Constitutión, Santa Rosalía and Tecate. Information about hotels and motels in these towns may be obtained at state tourism offices throughout the peninsula and in the tourist newspaper the *Baja Sun*. These sources also mention other hotels in the larger cities of Baja California. The names of some additional hotels and motels are also mentioned in the highway route logs of this book.

There is no charge for a property to be listed in ACSC publications. Many AAA-approved lodgings and restaurants, however, choose to purchase display advertising. These display ads sometimes provide additional information about popular features of the establishment.

Nearly all lodging and restaurant facilities accept credit cards as forms of payment for services rendered. The following symbols are used to identify the specific cards accepted by each property.

AE	American Express
CB	Carte Blanche
DI	Diners Club
DS	Discover
MC	MasterCard
VI	VISA

Some lodgings and restaurants listed in Auto Club publications have symbols indicating that they are accessible to individuals with disabilities. The criteria used in qualifying these listings are consistent with, but do not represent the full scope of, the Americans with Disabilities Act of 1990. AAA does not evaluate recreational facilities, banquet rooms or convention and meeting facilities for accessibility. Individuals

with disabilities are urged to phone ahead to fully understand an establishment's facilities and accessibility. Facilities accommodating handicapped travelers are largely unavailable in Baja California. The Automobile Club recommends contacting the lodging establishment directly should a traveler have special needs.

Lodging

The following accommodations classifications may appear in this book.

Bed & Breakfast—Usually a small establishment emphasizing personal attention. Individually decorated guest rooms provide an at-home feeling and may lack some amenities such as TVs, phones, etc. Usually owner-operated with a common room or parlor where guests and owners can interact during evening and breakfast hours. May have shared bathrooms. A continental or full hot breakfast is included in the room rate.

Complex—A combination of two or more kinds of lodgings.

Cottage—Individual bungalow, cabin or villa, usually containing one rental unit equipped for housekeeping. May have a separate living room and bedroom(s). Parking is usually at each unit.

Country Inn—Similar in definition to a bed and breakfast. Offers a dining room reflecting the ambiance of the inn. At a minimum, breakfast and dinner are served.

Hotel—A multistory building usually including a coffee shop, dining room, lounge, room service, convenience shops, valet, laundry and full banquet/meeting facilities. Parking may be limited.

Lodge—Typically two or more stories with all facilities in one building. Located in vacation, ski, fishing areas, etc. Usually has food and beverage service. Adequate on-premises parking.

Motel—Usually one or two stories; food service, if any, consists of a limited facility or snack bar. Often has a pool or playground. Ample parking, usually at the guest room door.

Motor Inn—Usually two or three stories, but may be a high-rise. Generally has recreation facilities, food service and ample parking. May have limited banquet/meeting facilities.

Apartment—Usually four or more stories with at least half the units equipped for housekeeping. Often in a vacation destination area. Units typically provide a full kitchen, living room and one or more bedrooms, but may be studio-type rooms with kitchen equipment in an alcove. May require minimum stay and/or offer discounts for longer stays. This classification may also modify any of the other lodging types.

Condominium—A destination property located in a resort area. Guest units consist of a bedroom, living room and kitchen. Kitchens are separate from bedrooms and are equipped with a stove, oven or microwave, refrigerator, cooking utensils and table settings for the maximum number of people occupying the unit. Linens and maid service are provided at least twice weekly. This classification may also modify any of the other lodging types.

Historic—Accommodations in restored, pre-1930 structures, reflecting the ambiance of yesteryear and the surrounding region. Rooms may lack some modern amenities and have

shared baths. Usually owner-operated and provides food service. Parking is usually available. This classification may also modify any of the other lodging types.

Resort—May be a destination unto itself. Has a vacation atmosphere offering extensive recreational facilities for such specific interests as golf, tennis, fishing, etc. Rates may include meals under American or Modified American plans. This classification may also modify any of the other lodging types.

Suite—Units have one or more bedrooms and a living room, which may or may not be closed off from the bedrooms. This classification may also modify any of the other lodging types.

A property's diamond rating is not based on the room rate or any one specific aspect of its facilities or operations. Many factors are considered in calculating the rating, and certain minimum standards must be met in all inspection categories. If a property fails approval in just one category, it is not diamond rated. The inspection categories include housekeeping, maintenance, service, furnishings and decor. Guest comments received by ACSC may also be reviewed in a property's approval/rating process.

These criteria apply to all properties listed in this publication:

- Clean and well-maintained facilities
- Hospitable staff
- Adequate parking
- A well-kept appearance
- Good quality bedding and comfortable beds with adequate illumination

- Good locks on all doors and windows
- Comfortable furnishings and decor
- Adequate towels and supplies
- At least one comfortable easy chair with adequate illumination

Lodging ratings range from one to five diamonds and are defined below:

◆—Good but unpretentious. Establishments are functional. Clean and comfortable rooms must meet the basic needs of privacy and cleanliness.

◆◆—Shows noticeable enhancements in decor and/or quality of furnishings over those at the one-diamond level. May be recently constructed or an older property. Targets the needs of a budget-oriented traveler.

◆◆◆—Offers a degree of sophistication with additional amenities, services and facilities. There is a marked upgrade in services and comfort.

◆◆◆◆—Excellent properties displaying high levels of service and hospitality, and offering a wide variety of amenities and upscale facilities, inside the room, on the grounds and in the common areas.

◆◆◆◆◆—Renowned for an exceptionally high degree of service, striking and luxurious facilities, and many extra amenities. Guest services are executed and presented in a flawless manner. Guests are pampered by a very professional, attentive staff. The property's facilities and operations set standards in hospitality and service.

Room rates shown in the listings are provided by each establishment's management for publication by the Automobile Club of Southern California. **All rates are subject to change.** During special events or holiday periods rates may exceed those published and special discounts or savings programs may not be honored. High-season rates are always shown; off-season rates are listed if they are substantially lower than the rest of the year. Rates are for typical rooms, not special units, and do not include taxes or service charges. A 10 percent sales tax is imposed on all hotel, restaurant and nightclub bills. Some establishments, particularly in the Los Cabos region, add a service charge of 10 to 20 percent to room bills; it is typically a gratuity fee used in lieu of tipping, but this may not always be the case. Upon check in, be sure to understand what additional charges, if any, will be added to the bill.

Some hotels quote prices in pesos, others in dollars. All prices listed in this book are given in dollar equivalents. All establishments accept dollars; however, you can sometimes get a better price by paying in pesos. When making reservations, be sure to have a clear understanding of the price you will pay.

In addition to the dates for which the rates are valid, each rate line lists the prices quoted for one person (abbreviated 1P) and for two persons (2P); the two-person rate may be for either one or two beds. Figures following these abbreviations are the price(s) for the specified room and occupants. Most rates listed are European plan, which means that no meals are included in the rate. Some lodgings' rates include breakfast [BP] or continental breakfast [CP]. A few properties offer the American Plan [AP], which includes three meals, or a Modified American Plan [MAP], which offers two meals, usually

LODGING & RESTAURANTS

breakfast and dinner. Most establishments also provide a per-person rate applicable to the third or more individuals staying in the same room or unit; this rate is added to the two-person rate listed in the rate line.

Many properties welcome children in the same room with their parents at no additional charge. There may be charges for additional equipment, such as roll-aways or cribs.

All bathrooms have a combination tub and shower bath unless noted otherwise. Since nearly all establishments have telephones and color TV, only the absence of any of these items is noted in the listing. Check-in time is shown only if it is after 3 p.m.; check-out time is shown only if it is before 10 a.m. Service charges are not shown unless they are $1 or more, or at least 5 percent of the room rate. If the pet acceptance policy varies within the establishment, no mention of pets is made. A heated pool is heated when it is reasonable to expect use of a pool. Outdoor pools may not be open in winter.

Reservations are always advisable in resort areas and may be the only way to assure obtaining the type of accommodations desired. Deposits are almost always required. Should plans change and a reservation needs to be canceled, travelers should be aware of the amount of notice required to receive a refund of the deposit. The price of accommodations should be confirmed at the time the reservations are made. Always request a written confirmation from the hotel, motel or resort. Due to the slowness of Baja California mail service, all correspondence should be sent at least six weeks in advance. In the hotel mailing addresses, *BC* is the abbreviation for the state of Baja Cali-

fornia and *BCS* stands for the state of Baja California Sur. Fire warning equipment is indicated by the symbol Ⓓ (all guest rooms have smoke detectors). Some properties have reserved rooms for nonsmokers; guests should look for the ⊘ symbol in the listing and be sure to request a smoke-free room both when making a reservation and upon registration.

Restaurants

Restaurants listed in this publication have been found to be consistently good dining establishments. In metropolitan areas, where many restaurants are above average, listings include some of those known for the superiority of their food, service and atmosphere, and also those offering a selection of quality food at moderate prices (including some cafeterias and family restaurants). In smaller communities the restaurants considered to be the best in the area may be listed.

The type of cuisine featured at a restaurant is used as a means of classification for restaurants. There are listings for Steakhouses and Continental cuisine as well as a range of ethnic foods, such as Chinese, Japanese, Italian and yes, American. Special menu types, such as early bird, a la carte, children's or Sunday Brunch, are also listed. Something about each restaurant's atmosphere and appropriate attire is mentioned where possible. The availability of alcoholic beverages is shown, as well as entertainment and dancing.

Restaurant ratings are applied to two categories of operational style: full-service eating establishments, and self-service, family-dining operations such as cafeterias or buffets.

◆—Good but unpretentious dishes. Table settings are usually simple and may include paper place mats and napkins. Alcoholic beverage service, if any, may be limited to beer and wine. Usually informal with an atmosphere conducive to family dining.

◆◆—More extensive menus representing more complex food preparation and, usually, a wider variety of alcoholic beverages. The atmosphere is appealing and suitable for either family or adult dining. Service may be casual, but host or hostess seating can be expected. Table settings may include tablecloths and cloth napkins.

◆◆◆—Extensive or specialized menus and a more complex cuisine preparation requiring a professional chef contribute to either a formal dining experience or a special family meal. Cloth table linens, above-average quality table settings, a skilled service staff and an inviting decor should all be provided. Generally, the wine list includes representatives of the best domestic and foreign wine-producing regions.

◆◆◆◆—An appealing ambiance is often enhanced by fresh flowers and fine furnishings. The overall sophistication and formal atmosphere visually-create a dining experience more for adults than for families. A wine steward presents an extensive list of the best wines. Smartly attired, highly skilled servers are capable of describing how any dish is prepared. Elegant silverware, china and correct glassware are typical. The menu includes creative dishes prepared from fresh ingredients by a chef who frequently has international training. Eye-appealing desserts are offered at tableside.

◆◆◆◆◆—World-class operation with even more luxury and sophistication than four-diamond restaurants. A proportionally large staff, expert in preparing tableside delicacies, provides flawless service. Tables are set with impeccable linens, silver and crystal glassware.

Buena Vista

Lodging

HOTEL BUENA VISTA BEACH RESORT ◆◆ Resort
On shore of Bahía de Palmas, ¼ mi E of Hwy 1.
Phone 01152 (114) 1-00-33; FAX 01152 (114) 1-01-33.
US reservations: 100 W 35th St, Ste V, National City, CA 91950. (619) 425-1551, (800) 752-3555.

All year   1P $ 65   2P $ 80

XP $15. 10% service charge. 30-day refund notice. Meal plans available. Resort on hillside overlooking the sea. 60 units. Shower baths, coffeemakers; no phones, TV. 2 pools, whirlpools, beach, scuba diving, kayaking, tennis, horseback riding. Fishing trips arranged in cruisers and pangas. Pets allowed in designated rooms. MC, VI. Dining room open 6-11 am, noon-3 pm, 7-9:30 pm; cocktails, bar. Ⓓ

Cabo San Lucas

Lodging

CASA MINI FINI
◆◆ Lodge

In Casa Pedregal above town. Mail: 600 Plaza Rita, Pedregal, Cabo San Lucas, BCS, Mexico.

Phone 01152 (114) 3-10-79; FAX 01152 (114) 3-09-57.

All year   1P $125-150   2P $125-150

XP $25. 10% service charge. 7-day refund notice. Quiet residential area with spectacular view of town and harbor. Private balconies and patios. 7 units; penthouse suite, $250; 1 whirlpool. Cable TV, VCPs; some refrigerators, microwaves, coffeemakers, shower baths. Pool, barbecue. Breakfast available, $10 per person.

CLUB CABO MOTEL RESORT
Motel

2 mi E of town center on old road; turn S off Hwy 1 on rd to Club Cascadas. Mail: Apdo Postal 463, Cabo San Lucas, BCS, 23410 Mexico.

Phone & FAX 01152 (114) 3-33-48.

All year   1P $ 40- 60   2P $ 40- 60

XP $5-10. 8 units. Hotel-type rooms in RV park; short walk to beach. Cable TV, shower baths; most with cooking facilities and utensils; courtesy phone available. Pool, whirlpool.

HOTEL FINISTERRA
◆◆◆ Resort Complex

Located at southernmost tip of Baja California peninsula. Mail: Apdo Postal #1, Cabo San Lucas, BCS, Mexico.

Phone 01152 (114) 3-33-33, (714) 476-5555, (714) 450-9000; FAX 01152 (114) 3-05-90.

All year   1P $140-183   2P $140-183

XP $20; ages 12 and under stay free. 10% service charge. 7-day refund notice, 30 days for holiday periods. Spectacular location overlooking Land's End. Rooms with ocean or bay view. Large pool area surrounded by tropical gardens. 216 units. Cable TV, movies, coffeemakers, honor bars; some shower baths, private balconies; some efficiencies. 3 pools, whirlpools, health club, massage, beach, scuba diving, snorkeling, tennis, horseback riding. Fishing trips arranged. No pets. AE, MC, VI. Dining room open 6:30 am-9:30 pm; cocktails, lounge, entertainment. ⊘

MARINA FIESTA RESORT HOTEL
◆◆◆ Condominium Hotel

On E side of marina at Marina Lotes. Mail: Marina Lote 37, Cabo San Lucas, BCS, 23410 Mexico.

Phone 01152 (114) 3-26-89; FAX 01152 (114) 3-26-88.

US reservations: (800) 332-2252.

5/1-12/20   1P $195-280   2P $195-280
12/21-4/30   1P $220-305   2P $220-305

XP $40; ages 12 and under stay free. 3-day refund notice. Pueblo-style complex on the marina. 5 to 7 stories. 155 units; luxury suites, $600-650. Cable TV, movies, refrigerators, kitchens & utensils; some shower baths. 2 pools, whirlpools, exercise room, playground, boat ramp, marina, valet laundry. No pets. AE, MC, VI. Restaurant; 6 am-10 pm; cocktails.

MELIA SAN LUCAS ◆◆◆ Resort Hotel
On the shore 2 blocks E of Bl Marina (Hwy 1). Mail: El Médano s/n, Cabo San Lucas, BCS, Mexico.
Phone 01152 (114) 3-44-44, (800) 336-3542; FAX 01152 (114) 3-04-22.

4/13-12/19	1P $216-266	2P $216-266
12/20-4/12	1P $240-290	2P $240-290

XP $40; ages 12 and under stay free. 10% service charge. 15-day refund notice. Pueblo-style hotel overlooking the harbor and Land's End. 187 units. Cable TV, movies, honor bars, refrigerators, safes. 2 pools, massage, beach, boating, sailboarding, scuba diving, snorkeling. Fishing trips arranged. No pets. Gift shop. Meeting room. AE, MC, VI. Restaurant; 6 am-11 pm; cocktails, entertainment.

PLAZA LAS GLORIAS Hotel
Part of a large complex that includes condominiums and a shopping center, between Bl Marina and the harbor. Mail: Bl Marina s/n Lotes 9 y 10, Cabo San Lucas, BCS, 23410 Mexico.
Phone 01152 (114) 3-12-20.
US reservations (800) 342-2644.

1/3-1/31	1P ...	2P $157
2/1-4/19	1P ...	2P $220
4/20-6/18	1P ...	2P $180
6/19-12/24	1P ...	2P $196
12/25-1/2	1P ...	2P $231

XP $20; ages 12 and under stay free. 10% service charge. 3- to 7-day refund notice. 287 units; 65 suites. Cable TV; some refrigerators. Pool, fishing charters, snorkeling and scuba trips arranged. Gift shop, conference facilities. AE, MC, VI. 2 restaurants; open 24 hours; cocktails, bar.

PUEBLO BONITO RESORT ◆◆◆ Resort Hotel
3 blocks S of Hwy 1 on El Médano. Mail: Apdo Postal 460, Cabo San Lucas, BCS, 23410 Mexico.
Phone 01152 (114) 3-29-00, (800) 937-9567; FAX 01152 (114) 3-19-95.

4/19-12/20	1P $240-290	2P $240-290
12/21-4/18	1P $290-340	2P $290-340

XP $30. Ages 18 and under stay free. 10% service charge. 7-day refund notice. Beachfront hotel on Cabo San Lucas Bay. 144 units. Cable TV, movies, efficiencies. Heated pool, exercise room, beach, scuba diving, snorkeling, boating. Fishing trips arranged. No pets. MC, VI. 2 restaurants; 7 am-10 pm; cocktails.

PUEBLO BONITO ROSE RESORT ◆◆◆ Resort Hotel

1 kilometer S of Hwy 1 at El Médano Beach. Mail: Apdo Postal 460, Cabo San Lucas, BCS, 23410 Mexico.
Phone 01152 (114) 3-55-00, (800) 937-9567.

4/19-12/20	1P $240-290	2P $240-290
12/21-4/18	1P $290-340	2P $290-340

XP $30. Ages 18 and under stay free. 10% service charge. 7-day refund notice. Beachfront location with spacious grounds and gardens. 260 units. Cable TV, movies; some shower baths, efficiencies, safes. Heated pool, wading pool, whirlpools, saunas, steam rooms, beach, boating, sailing, scuba diving, snorkeling, health club, massage, valet laundry. Fishing trips arranged. No pets. MC, VI. 3 restaurants; 7 am-10 pm; cocktail lounge.

SIESTA SUITES HOTEL ◆ Motel

Downtown on Calle E Zapata at Hidalgo. Mail: Apdo Postal 310, Cabo San Lucas, BCS, 23410 Mexico.
Phone & FAX 01152 (114) 3-27-73.
US reservations: 8966 Citation Ct, Alta Loma, CA 91737. Phone & FAX (909) 945-5940.

All year	1P $ 50	2P $ 50

XP $10. 15-day refund notice. 20 units. Shower baths, kitchens with utensils; some air conditioning, radios, cable TV, movies; no phones. Fishing trips arranged. No pets.

SOLMAR SUITES RESORT ◆◆◆ Resort Complex

Located on the southernmost tip of the peninsula.
Phone 01152 (114) 3-35-35; FAX 01152 (114) 3-04-10.
US reservations: Box 383, Pacific Palisades, CA 90272. (310) 459-9861, (800) 344-3349.

6/1-10/31	1P $135-190	2P $135-190
11/1-5/31	1P $165-225	2P $165-225

XP $25-36; discount for ages 12 and under. 10% service charge. 7-day refund notice. All-suite hotel on the beach at Land's End. Expansive grounds and pool area. Most rooms face the Pacific Ocean. 125 units; Roca suites and condominiums available. Cable TV, movies, honor bars, coffeemakers, safes, patio or private balconies. 3 pools, whirlpool, beach, diving, snorkeling, tennis. Fishing trips on cruisers. No pets. AE, MC, VI. Restaurant open 6 am-9:45 pm; cocktails, entertainment, poolside bar.

Restaurants

ALFONSO'S RESTAURANT ◆◆◆ Continental

In the Plaza Bonita shopping center on the marina.
Phone 01152 (114) 3-20-22.

$10-24. Open 6-10 pm. Intimate dining inside or on the marina patio. Attentive service. Cocktails. MC, VI.

CASA RAFAEL'S ◆◆◆ Continental
Between Bl Lázaro Cárdenas and the bay on El Médano.
Phone 01152 (114) 3-07-39.
$22-29. Open 6-10 pm. Mexican Colonial house with quaint dining room and patio features international cuisine. Cocktails. AE, MC, VI.

DA GIORGIO ◆◆ Italian
3 mi NE of town center, then ½ mi S, adjacent to Misiónes del Cabo.
Phone 01152 (114) 3-29-88.
$6-16. Open 8:30 am-11:30 pm. Open-air *palapa* on hillside with view of Land's End. Seafood and pasta. Cocktails, bar. AE, MC, VI.

GALEÓN ITALIANO RESTAURANT ◆◆ Italian
½ mi S of town center on Bl Marina across from the wharf.
Phone 01152 (114) 3-04-43.
$8-20. Open 4-11 pm. View of the bay and the town. Pasta, veal and seafood. Cocktails, bar. MC, VI.

MARGARITAVILLA ◆ Mexican
At the marina in Plaza Bonita shopping center.
Phone 01152 (114) 3-17-40.
$5-22. Open 7 am-11 pm. Overlooking the marina. Variety of Mexican and international dishes. Cocktails, bar. AE, MC, VI.

PEACOCKS RESTAURANT ◆◆ Continental
2 blocks SE of Hwy 1 on Paseo del Pescador.
Phone 01152 (114) 3-18-58.
$12-24. Open 6-10 pm. European cuisine. Cocktails, bar.

ROMEO Y JULIETA RISTORANTE ◆◆ Italian
¼ mi S of town center at entrance to Pedregal condominium district.
Phone 01152 (114) 3-02-25.
$6-14. Open 4-11 pm. Quaint hacienda atmosphere. Pasta, pizza and seafood. Cocktails, bar. MC, VI.

SEASON'S RESTAURANT ◆◆◆ Mexican
Just E of town on Hwy 1.
Phone 01152 (114) 3-32-80.
$9-40. Open 5:30-10 pm. Pleasant *palapa* setting with Mexican and Mediterranean cuisine. Specializing in seafood and grilled entrees. Cocktails, bar.

THE TRAILER PARK RESTAURANT (LA GOLONDRINA) ◆◆ Mexican
One block SE of Hwy 1 on Paseo del Pescador.
Phone 01152 (114) 3-05-42.
$16-24. Open Tue-Sun 5-10:30 pm. Popular patio setting at a historic trading post. Mexican-style cooking with a selection of seafood, chicken and beef. Cocktails, bar. AE, MC, VI.

Cataviña

Lodging

HOTEL LA PINTA   Motor Inn
*On Hwy 1, 1 mi N of Rancho Santa Inés. Mail: Apdo Postal 179, San Quintín, BC, Mexico.
No phone.
US reservations: Mexico Condo Reservations, 5801 Soledad Mountain Rd, La Jolla, CA
92037. (619) 275-4500, (800) 262-4500.*

All year   1P $ 60   2P $ 65

XP $10; maximum 4 persons per room. 3-day refund notice. Spanish-style building in scenic rock-strewn area. 28 units; suite, $125. Shower baths; no phones. Pool, recreation room, playground. No pets. MC, VI. Dining room, 6 am-10 pm; cocktails, bar. **(See ad page 285.)**

El Rosario

Restaurant

MAMA ESPINOSA'S   ◆ Mexican
*In the center of town on Hwy 1.
Phone 01152 (616) 5-87-70.*

$4-16. Open 6 am-9 pm. Historic restaurant and home of Doña Anita. Serves lobster, fish and beef dishes in the Baja tradition.

Ensenada

Lodging

BEST WESTERN CASA DEL SOL MOTEL   ◆ Motel
*At avs López Mateos and Blancarte. Mail: Apdo Postal 557, Ensenada, BC, 22800 Mexico.
Phone 01152 (617) 8-15-70; FAX 01152 (114) 8-20-25.
US reservations: (800) 528-1234.*

All year   1P $ 53   2P $ 58

XP $8; ages 12 and under stay free. 3-day refund notice. 48 units. Cable TV, movies, shower baths; some air conditioning, kitchens. Pool. Small pets accepted. AE, MC, VI. Restaurant and bar adjacent.

BEST WESTERN EL CID MOTOR HOTEL   ◆ Motor Inn
*At Av López Mateos 993. Mail: PO Box 786, Chula Vista, CA 91910.
Phone 01152 (617) 8-24-01; FAX 01152 (617) 8-36-71.
US reservations: (800) 352-4305.*

Fri-Sat 6/1-8/31	1P $ 65	2P $ 65-86
Sun-Thu 6/1-8/31	1P $ 38	2P $ 42-65
9/1-5/31	1P $ 38	2P $ 38-52

XP $8; ages 12 and under stay free. 3-day refund notice. Attractive Spanish styling. 52 units; suites available. Cable TV; some shower baths, private balconies.

Pool. Fishing trips arranged. No pets. AE, MC, VI. Restaurant; Tue-Sun 7 am-10 pm, Mon 7 am-3 pm; cocktails. **(See ad below.)**

HOTEL CORAL & MARINA RESORT   ◆◆◆ Resort Hotel
2 mi N of Ensenada on Hwy 1-D. Mail: Carr Tijuana-Ensenada Km 103, No 3421 Zona Playitas, Ensenada, BC, 22860 Mexico.
Phone 01152 (617) 5-00-00; FAX 01152 (617) 5-00-05.
US reservations: (619) 523-0064, (800) 946-2746.

All Year	1P $135-220	2P $135-220

XP $15; ages 12 and under stay free. All-suite resort hotel overlooking the bay and marina. 147 units; Master and Presidential suites, $285 to $450 for 4-6 persons; 11 efficiencies. Cable TV, movies; some VCPs, private balconies or patios. 2 pools (1 indoor), wading pool, whirlpools, sauna, steam baths, health club, boating, sailing, marina, charter fishing, lighted tennis courts. Gift shop. Conference facilities. No pets. AE, MC, VI. Dining room; 7 am-11 pm. Wheelchair-accessible rooms available.

CORONA HOTEL   ◆ Motor Inn
At Bl Costero No 1442 (Bl Agustín Sanginés) across from Riviera del Pacifico Building. Mail: 482 W San Ysidro Bl, Ste 303, San Ysidro, CA 92173.
Phone 01152 (617) 8-24-01; FAX 01152 (617) 6-40-23.

Fri-Sat	1P $ 50	2P $ 65
Sun-Thu	1P $ 38	2P $ 46

XP $8; ages 13 and under stay free. 3-day refund notice. 4 stories. 92 units. Cable TV, movies, radios, balconies. Pool. No pets. AE, MC, VI. Restaurant; 7 am-11 pm; cocktails; bar.

DAYS INN   ◆ Motel
Just N of Av Blancarte on Av López Mateos. Mail: Av López Mateos 1050, Ensenada, BC, 22800 Mexico.
Phone & FAX 01152 (617) 8-34-34, (800) 432-9755.

5/1-8/31	1P $ 47-51	2P $ 47-51
9/1-4/30	1P $ 37-41	2P $ 37-41

XP $6; ages 12 and under stay free. 3-day refund notice. 66 units. Cable TV, movies; some shower baths. Pool, whirlpool. No pets. AE, MC, VI.

ENSENADA TRAVELODGE ◆◆ Motor Inn
At Av Blancarte 130, near Av López Mateos. Mail: 4492 Camino de la Raza, Ste ESE-118, San Ysidro, CA 92173.
Phone 01152 (617) 8-16-01, (800) 578-7878; FAX 01152 (617) 4-00-05.

All year   1P $ 58- 60   2P $ 58- 75

XP $8; ages 17 and under stay free. 3-day refund notice. 52 units; suite available. Cable TV, movies, radios, coffeemakers, shower baths, honor bar. Pool, whirlpool. Meeting rooms. No pets. AE, MC, VI. Restaurant open 7:30 am-11 pm; cocktails, bar.

ESTERO BEACH RESORT HOTEL ◆◆ Resort Complex
8 mi S of city center via Hwy 1 and graded side rd. Mail: Apdo Postal 86, Ensenada, BC, 22800 Mexico.
Phone 01152 (617) 6-62-30; FAX 01152 (617) 6-69-25.

Mon-Thu 9/11-4/30   1P ...   2P $ 28- 62
Fri-Sun 9/11-4/30   1P ...   2P $ 38- 72
5/1-9/10   1P ...   2P $ 48- 82

XP $6; ages 4 and under stay free. 3-day refund notice. Beachfront resort complex on attractive grounds. 96 units; suites, $250-285. Cable TV, movies, shower or combination baths; many private patios or balconies. Pool; beach; tennis; recreation room; playground; archaeological museum; gift shop; boat ramp; bicycle, boat and personal watercraft rentals; water-skiing; fishing; horseback riding. No pets. MC, VI. Restaurant; 7:30 am-11 pm; cocktails. ⊘

HACIENDA LAS GLORIAS ◆◆◆ Resort Complex
At Bajamar Golf Resort, 21 mi N of Ensenada off Hwy 1. Mail: 416 W San Ysidro Bl, Ste #L-732, San Ysidro, CA 92173.
Phone 01152 (615) 5-01-54; FAX 01152 (615) 5-01-50.

Fri-Sat   1P $ 85   2P $ 85
Sun-Thu   1P $ 65   2P $ 65

XP $15; ages 14 and under stay free. 2-night minimum stay on weekends. 3-day refund notice. 2 stories. 81 units; 1-bedroom suites with kitchens, $120-130. Mexican Colonial-style buildings. Color TV, movies, safes. Heated pool, whirlpool, sauna, 18- and 9-hole golf courses, pro shop, tennis. No pets. AE, MC, VI. Restaurant; 6 am-10:30 pm; cocktails; bar.

HOTEL LA PINTA Motor Inn
At Av Floresta and Bl Bucaneros. Mail: Apdo Postal 929, Ensenada, BC, 22800 Mexico.
Phone 01152 (617) 6-26-01.
US reservations: Mexico Condo Reservations, 5801 Soledad Mountain Rd, La Jolla, CA 92037. (800) 262-4500; (619) 275-4500.

Fri-Sat   1P $ 50   2P $ 65
Sun-Thu   1P $ 40   2P $ 45

XP $15. 3-day refund notice. 52 units. Cable TV, shower baths. Pool. No pets. MC, VI. Restaurant; 7:30 am-10 pm. **(See ad page 285.)**

LAS ROSAS HOTEL & SPA　　　　　　　　　　◆◆ Motor Inn
4 mi N on Hwy 1. Mail: Apdo Postal No 316, Ensenada, BC, 22800 Mexico.
Phone 01152 (617) 4-43-10; FAX 01152 (617) 4-45-95.

All Year　　　　　　　　1P $101-108　　2P $101-112

XP $22; discount for ages 12 and under. 2-night minimum stay weekends. 3-day refund notice; handling fee. Located on a bluff with spectacular oceanfront view. 2 stories. 32 units. Color TV, private balconies; shower baths, a few combination baths. Pool, whirlpool. Fee for tennis, racquetball, gym, sauna, massage. No pets. MC, VI. Restaurant 7 am-10 pm; cocktails, bar. **(See ad below.)**

HOTEL MISIÓN SANTA ISABEL　　　　　　　◆ Motor Inn
At Bl Costero (Bl Lázaro Cárdenas) and Av Castillo No 1100. Mail: Box 120-818, Chula Vista, CA 91912.
Phone 01152 (617) 8-36-16; FAX 01152 (617) 8-33-45.

Fri-Sat　　　　　　　　1P $ 55　　　2P $ 60- 70
Sun-Thu　　　　　　　　1P $ 50　　　2P $ 55- 65

XP $10; ages 11 and under stay free. 3-day refund notice. 3 stories. 58 units. Colonial-style architecture. Cable TV, movies; shower baths, a few combination baths; some air conditioning. Pool. No pets. Meeting rooms. AE, MC, VI. Restaurant; Mon-Sat 7 am-11 pm, Sun 8 am-2 pm; cocktails; bar.

HOTEL PARAÍSO LAS PALMAS   ◆ Motel
In SE part on Calle Agustín Sanginés 206. Mail: 445 W San Ysidro Bl, Ste 2507, San Ysidro, CA 92173.
Phone 01152 (617) 7-17-01; FAX 01152 (617) 7-17-01, ext 402.

All year	1P $ 50	2P $ 50

XP $5. Ages 11 and under stay free. 3 stories. 66 units; suites, $68. Cable TV, shower baths; no air conditioning. Pool, whirlpool. No pets. AE, MC, VI. Restaurant; 7 am-11 pm; cocktails; bar.

PUNTA MORRO HOTEL SUITES   ◆◆ Suite Motor Inn
On oceanfront, 3 mi N of town center off Hwy 1. Mail: Box 434263, San Diego, CA 92143.
Phone 01152 (617) 8-35-07; FAX 01152 (617) 4-44-90.
US reservations: (800) 526-6676.

Fri-Sat 3/1-9/30	1P $ 75- 95	2P $ 75- 95
Sun-Thu 3/1-9/30 &		
Fri-Sat 10/1-2/28	1P $ 68- 86	2P $ 68- 86
Sun-Thu 10/1-2/28	1P $ 58- 69	2P $ 58- 69

2-night minimum stay weekends. 7-day refund notice. 3 stories. 24 units; 2-bedroom suites for up to 4 persons, $105-145; 3-bedroom suites for up to 6 persons, $130-195; suites with kitchens and 3 studios with refrigerators. Patio or balcony, TV, movies, shower baths, fireplace. Pool, whirlpool. No pets. AE, MC, VI. Restaurant; Mon-Fri 1-10 pm, Sat from 8 am, Sun from 9:30 am; cocktails; bar.

HOTEL SANTO TOMÁS   Motel
On Bl Lázaro Cárdenas (Costero) at Av Miramar. Mail: 1181 Broadway, Ste 2 Chula Vista, CA 91911.
Phone 01152 (617) 8-15-03; FAX 01152 (617) 8-15-04.
US reservations: (800) 303-2684; FAX (619) 427-6523.

Fri-Sat	1P ...	2P $ 50
Sun-Thu	1P ...	2P $ 43

XP $8. 15-day refund notice. 3-story motel. 83 units; 2 junior suites, $57.50-$62. Cable TV, shower baths. No pets. AE, MC, VI. Restaurant, 7 am-10 pm; bar. ⊘

Restaurants

CASINO ROYAL RESTAURANT   ◆◆◆ French
SE of main hotel row at Bl Las Dunas 118, near Bl Lázaro Cárdenas.
Phone 01152 (617) 7-14-80.

$6-25. Open 10 am-10 pm. Elegantly decorated mansion-style building. Cocktails. MC, VI.

EL REY SOL RESTAURANT   ◆◆◆ French
½ mi S of town center on Av López Mateos at Av Blancarte.
Phone 01152 (617) 8-17-33.

$9-28. Open 7:30 am-10:30 pm. French and Mexican cuisine. Cocktails. AE, MC, VI.

HALIOTIS   ◆◆ Seafood
On Calle Delante (Agustín Sanginés) 179, ½ mi E of Hwy 1.
Phone 01152 (617) 6-37-20.

$5-22. Open Wed-Mon 12:30-10 pm. Closed 1/1, 5/1, 12/25. Seafood, chicken and beef. Cocktails, bar. AE, MC, VI.

LA EMBOTELLADORA VIEJA RESTAURANTE   ◆◆◆ Continental
N of the downtown area at Calle Miramar 666 at the Santo Tomás Winery.
Phone 01152 (617) 4-08-07.

$10-20. Open noon-11 pm, Sun to 5 pm. Closed Tue. Fine dining in a room once used to age wines. Extensive wine list. AE, MC, VI.

PALMIRA AT CANTAMAR RESTAURANT   ◆ American
21 mi N of town center, adjacent to Hwy 1-D at Km 46.
Phone 01152 (661) 4-12-03.

$7-17. Open Mon-Thu 11 am-9 pm; Fri to 10 pm; Sat & Sun 8 am-10 pm. Indoor and outdoor dining with a selection of Pacific Rim cuisine. Cocktails.

Guerrero Negro

Lodging

HOTEL EL MORRO   Motel
1 mi W of Hwy 1 on E edge of town. Mail: Apdo Postal 144, Guerrero Negro, BCS, 23940 Mexico.
Phone 01152 (115) 7-04-14.

All year	1P $ 22	2P $ 30

XP $4. Modest motel. 32 units. Fans, shower baths, cable TV; no air conditioning, phones.

HOTEL LA PINTA   Motor Inn
On Hwy 1 at the 28th parallel. Mail: Guerrero Negro, BCS, 23940 Mexico.
Phone 01152 (115) 7-13-01; FAX 01152 (115) 7-13-06.
US reservations: Mexico Condo Reservations, 5801 Soledad Mountain Rd, La Jolla, CA 92037. (800) 262-4500; (619) 275-4500.

All year	1P $ 60	2P $ 65

XP $10; ages 12 and under stay free. 4-person maximum per room. 3-day refund notice. Single-story hotel near Paralelo 28 monument. 29 units. Color TV, movies, shower baths, 2-bed rooms; no air conditioning, phones. No pets. Trailer park adjacent. MC, VI. Dining room; 7 am-10 pm; cocktails, bar. **(See ad page 285.)**

Restaurant

MALARRIMO RESTAURANT   ◆ Seafood
1 mi W of Hwy 1 on E edge of town.
Phone 01152 (115) 7-02-50.

$4-12. Open 7:30 am-10:30 pm. Seafood and Mexican specialties; bar; museum, tourist information. Cocktails.

La Paz

Lodging

ARAIZA INN PALMIRA ◆ Motor Inn
1½ mi N on Carr Pichilingue. Mail: Apdo Postal 442, La Paz, BCS, 23010 Mexico.
Phone 01152 (112) 1-62-00; FAX 01152 (112) 1-62-27.
US reservations: (800) 929-2402.

All year 1P $ 65 2P $ 65

XP $8. Across from bay on attractive tropical grounds. 3 stories. 120 units. Cable TV, movies, shower baths, coffeemakers. Pool, wading pool, tennis, playground, fishing/tour arrangements. No pets. Gift shop. Conference center. AE, MC, VI. Restaurant; 7 am-10:30 pm.

CABAÑAS DE LOS ARCOS ◆◆ Motel
Opposite the malecón, at Paseo Alvaro Obregón and Rosales. Mail: Apdo Postal 112, La Paz, BCS, 23000 Mexico.
Phone 01152 (112) 2-27-44; FAX 01152 (112) 5-43-13.
US reservations: 18552 MacArthur Bl, Ste 205, Irvine, CA 92715. (714) 476-5555, (800) 347-2252; FAX (714) 476-5560.

All year 1P $ 60- 75 2P $ 60- 75

XP $10; ages 12 and under stay free. 7-day refund notice. 4-story hotel wing and 16 bungalows in tropical garden setting. 52 units. Cable TV, movies, radios, coffeemakers, honor bars, shower baths. Heated pool. Fishing trips arranged. No pets. AE, MC, VI. Restaurant and bar at Hotel Los Arcos, ½ block away.

CASA LA PACEÑA BED & BREAKFAST Bed & Breakfast
On Calle Bravo, 2 blocks from La Paz Bay. Mail: Apdo Postal 158, La Paz, BCS, 23000 Mexico.
Phone 01152 (112) 5-27-48.

11/15-6/30 [CP] 1P ... 2P $ 50- 65

Open 11/15 to 6/30. 5-day refund notice. 3 units. Rooms have private patios with views of bay. Radios, VCPs, refrigerators, shower baths, bay view, no phones.

CLUB EL MORO ◆◆ Suite Motor Inn
1 mi N on Carr Pichilingue. Mail: Apdo Postal 357, La Paz, BCS, 23010 Mexico.
Phone 01152 (112) 2-40-84; FAX 01152 (112) 5-28-28.

All year 1P $ 40- 70 2P $ 40- 70

3-day refund notice. Moorish-style buildings on colorfully landscaped grounds across from bay. 2 stories. 21 units, most with kitchens. Shower baths. Pool, whirlpool, kayak rentals; tour and diving arrangements. Barbecue. Pets allowed in designated rooms. AE, MC, VI. Restaurant; 8 am-11 pm, closed Tue; cocktails, bar.

CROWNE PLAZA RESORT ◆◆◆ Suite Hotel
3½ mi W of town via Hwy 1 at Marina Fidepaz. Mail: Apdo Postal 482, La Paz, BCS, 23000 Mexico.
Phone 01152 (112) 4-08-30; FAX 01152 (112) 4-08-37.

LODGING & RESTAURANTS

US reservations: Holiday Inn (800) 465-4329.

All year   1P $120-150   2P $120-150

XP $10; ages 12 and under stay free. 3-day refund notice. On the bay. 2 stories. 54 units; 2-bedroom suites, $200 for 4 persons. Cable TV, movies, radios, safes, refrigerators, coffeemakers, wet bar. 3 pools, whirlpool, sauna, steam bath, beach, squash court, exercise room. Fishing trips, water sports and tours arranged. No pets. Gift shop, night club. AE, MC, VI. Restaurant; 7 am-11 pm; cocktails, bar.

LA CONCHA BEACH RESORT   ◆◆ Resort Complex
3 mi NE on Carr Pichilingue. Mail: Apdo Postal 607, La Paz, BCS, 23010 Mexico.
Phone 01152 (112) 1-61-61, (800) 999-2252; FAX 01152 (112) 1-62-18.

All year   1P $ 85   2P $ 85

XP $15. 3-day refund notice. On attractive shaded grounds at the bay. 3-6 stories. 119 units; condo units, $105-215; downtown suites (near *malecón*), $70. Cable TV, movies, shower baths, refrigerators, balconies. Pool, whirlpool, swimming beach, boating, windsurfing, scuba diving, snorkeling, charter fishing, kayak rental, exercise room. No pets. Conference center. AE, MC, VI. Restaurant; 7 am-10:30 pm; cocktails, bar.

HOTEL LOS ARCOS   ◆◆ Hotel
Opposite the malecón, *facing La Paz Bay, at Paseo Alvaro Obregón and Allende. Mail: Apdo Postal 112, La Paz, BCS, 23000 Mexico.*
Phone 01152 (112) 2-27-44; FAX 01152 (112) 5-43-13.
US reservations: 18552 MacArthur Bl, Ste 205, Irvine, CA 92715. (714) 476-5555, (800) 347-2252; FAX (714) 476-5560.

All year   1P $ 75   2P $ 75-80

XP $10-15. 7-day refund notice. Colonial-style hotel. 130 units; suite, $85-100. Cable TV, movies, radios, coffeemakers, shower baths. Pool, sauna (fee). Fishing trips arranged. No pets. Gift shop. AE, MC, VI. Restaurant and dining room, 7 am-11 pm; cocktails, bar.

HOTEL MARINA   ◆◆ Hotel
1½ mi N on Carr Pichilingue. Mail: Apdo Postal 34, La Paz, BCS, 23010 Mexico.
Phone 01152 (112) 1-62-54; FAX 01152 (112) 1-61-77.
US reservations: (800) 826-1138.

All year   1P $ 89   2P $ 89

XP $16. 3-day refund notice. On the bay and marina. 5 stories. 92 units; suites with efficiencies and kitchens, $142-178, XP $26. Cable TV, movies; some shower baths. Pool, whirlpool, lighted tennis court, dock, marina, fishing/diving/snorkeling trips arranged. No pets. AE, MC, VI. 2 restaurants; 7 am-11 pm; cocktails, bar.

HOTEL MEDITERRANE   Lodge
On Allende ½ block from Paseo Alvaro Obregón. Mail: Allende 36-B, La Paz, BCS, 23000 Mexico.
Phone & FAX 01152 (112) 5-11-95.

2/1-9/30	1P $ 40		2P $ 45	
10/1-1/31	1P $ 45		2P $ 50	

XP $5. 5-day refund notice. Mexican/European style villa. 6 units; 2 suites, $60. Radios, shower baths; no phones. VCR library. Whirlpool. Fishing trips arranged. Restaurant; 7 am-11 pm; cocktails, bar. AE, MC, VI.

Restaurants

EL TASTE   ◆ Mexican
½ mi SW of town center on Paseo Alvaro Obregón at Juárez.
Phone 01152 (112) 2-81-21.

$4-16. Open 8 am-midnight. Overlooks the *malecón* and the bay. Mexican cuisine including beef and seafood. Cocktails, bar. MC, VI.

LA PAZ-LAPA DE CARLOS 'N CHARLIES   ◆ Mexican
On Paseo Alvaro Obregón at 16 de Septiembre.
Phone 01152 (112) 2-60-25.

$5-13. Open noon-1 am. Casual dining across from bay. Mexican cuisine, including steaks and seafood. Cocktails, bar. MC, VI.

LA PAZTA   ◆◆ Italian
On Allende ½ block from Paseo Alvaro Obregón, near Hotel Mediterrane.
Phone 01152 (112) 5-11-95.

$3-9. Open Wed-Mon 5-10 pm; bistro open daily 7 am-4 pm. Trattoria featuring fresh, made-to-order pasta, and Swiss dishes and fondues. AE, MC, VI.

Loreto

Lodging

EDEN LORETO RESORT—ALL INCLUSIVE   ◆◆◆ Resort Hotel
At Nopoló, 8½ mi S via Hwy 1 and paved rd to beach. Mail: Bl Misión de Loreto, Loreto, BCS, 23880 Mexico.
Phone 01152 (113) 3-07-00, (800) 524-9191; FAX 01152 (113) 3-03-77.

All year [AP]	1P $160	2P $240-310

XP $80. Age restriction, 18 years & older. Rates include all meals, beverages, taxes, gratuity & most recreational services. 14-day refund notice. Modern 3-story hotel on beach with attractive landscaping. Most rooms have private patios and ocean view. 236 units. Cable TV, movies, shower baths. 2 heated pools, beach, tennis, golf, fishing, scuba diving, boating, sailboarding, bicycles. No pets. AE, MC, VI. Dining room, restaurant; 7 am-10 pm; cocktails, bar.

HOTEL LA PINTA   Motor Inn
On beach, 1 mi N of town plaza. Mail: Apdo Postal 28, Loreto, BCS, Mexico.
Phone 01152 (113) 5-00-25; FAX 01152 (113) 5-00-26.
US reservations: Mexico Condo Reservations, 5801 Soledad Mountain Rd, La Jolla, CA 92037. (800) 262-4500, (619) 275-4500.

All year	1P ...	2P $ 75- 89

XP $15; 4-person maximum per room. Spacious rooms. 49 units. Color TV, movies, shower baths, private patios; no phones. Pool, beach. Fishing trips arranged. No pets. MC, VI. Dining room; 6:30 am-10 pm; cocktails, bar. **(See ad page 285.)**

HOTEL OASIS
Motor Inn

On shore of Loreto Bay, ½ mi S of town plaza. Mail: Apdo Postal 17, Loreto, BCS, 23880 Mexico.
Phone 01152 (113) 5-01-12.

4/1-10/31 [AP]	1P $ 80	2P $115	
11/1-3/31	1P $ 52	2P $ 65	

XP $23-33. 30-day refund notice. Set in palm grove. 33 units. Modest rooms. Shower baths, 2 double or 3 single beds; some patios. Pool, beach, tennis. No phones, TVs. Fishing trips arranged. MC, VI. Dining room; 6-11 am, 12:30-3 and 6:30-8:30 pm; cocktails, bar.

VILLAS DE LORETO
Motel

On the beach, ½ mi S of town plaza. Mail: Apdo Postal 132, Loreto, BCS, 23880 Mexico.
Phone & FAX 01152 (113) 5-05-86.

All year [CP]	1P ...	2P $ 50-60

XP $14. Pleasant beachfront location; 1-story motel units and RV park. 10 units. Refrigerators, shower baths. No phones. Pool, bicycles. Kayak rentals. MC, VI. No smoking on premises. ⊗

Restaurant

EL NIDO STEAKHOUSE
◆◆ Steak & Seafood

At town entrance 1 mi E of Hwy 1 on Salvatierra 154.
Phone 01152 (113) 5-02-84.

$5-16. Open 3-10:30 pm. Closed 12/25. Ranch atmosphere, specializing in mesquite-broiled steak and seafood. Cocktails, bar.

Los Barriles

Restaurant

TÍO PABLO'S BAR & GRILL
◆ American

½ mi E of Hwy 1 in town.
Phone 01152 (114) 2-12-14.

$4-14. Open 11 am-10 pm. Casual *palapa* and patio dining with a variety of dishes prepared American and Mexican style. Bar.

Mexicali

Lodging

ARAIZA INN MEXICALI
◆◆ Motor Inn

At Bl Benito Juárez 2220, 5 mi SE of border crossing. Mail: 233 Pauline Av, #947, Calexico, CA 92231.
Phone 01152 (65) 66-13-00, (800) 537-8483; FAX 01152 (65) 66-49-01.

All year   1P $ 71   2P $ 76

XP $5; ages 18 and under stay free. 172 units; suites, $95-101 for 2 persons. Cable TV, radios, movies; some coffeemakers. Pool, exercise room, lighted tennis court. No pets. Gift shop. Facilities for meetings. AE, MC, VI. Restaurant and dining room open 7 am-11 pm; cocktails, bar, entertainment. ⊘

HOLIDAY INN CROWNE PLAZA   ♦♦♦ Hotel
5 mi SE of border crossing, at Av de los Héroes #201, Mexicali, BC, 21000 Mexico.
Phone 01152 (65) 57-36-00, (800) 465-4329; FAX 01152 (65) 57-05-55.

All year   1P $119   2P $119

XP $15. 3-day refund notice. 8 stories. 158 units; executive-level rooms, $135. Cable TV, movies, radios. Pool, exercise room. No pets. Gift shop. Meeting room, data ports. AE, MC, VI. 2 restaurants; 6:30 am-midnight; cocktails & bar. ⊘ **(See ad below.)**

MOTEL COLONIAL LAS FUENTES   ♦♦ Motel
5 mi SE of border crossing, at Bl López Mateos and Calle Calafia. Mail: PO Box 872, Suite 9, Calexico, CA 92231.
Phone 01152 (65) 56-13-12, (800) 437-2438; FAX 01152 (65) 56-11-41.

All year   1P $ 72   2P $ 72

XP $6; ages 18 and under stay free. Reservation deposit. 144 units; suites with refrigerator, microwave and coffeemaker, $115 for up to 2 persons. Cable TV, movies. Pool, wading pool. Meeting room. No pets. AE, MC, VI.

Restaurant

THE PREMIERE ◆◆◆ Continental
5 mi SE of border crossing in Holiday Inn Crowne Plaza, Av de los Héroes #201.
Phone 01152 (65) 57-36-00.

$7-14. Open 6-11 pm. Elegant dining room with formal service offering a variety of seafood, pasta and steak entrees. Cocktails. AE, MC, VI.

Mulegé

Lodging

RESORT HOTEL SAN BUENAVENTURA Resort Hotel
25 mi S of Mulegé via Hwy 1, at Km 94.5 on Bahía Concepción. Mail: Apdo Postal 56, Mulegé, BCS, 23900 Mexico.
Phone 01152 (115) 3-04-08, 3-03-08; FAX 01152 (115) 3-04-08.

All Year 1P ... 2P $ 50-60

20 units. Shower baths. Beach, kayak rentals, fishing trips arranged, charter service and concrete boat ramp. Restaurant; 7 am-8 pm; cocktails, bar.

HOTEL SERENIDAD Motor Inn
2½ mi S of town off Hwy 1 at mouth of river. Mail: Apdo Postal 9, Mulegé, BCS, 23900 Mexico.
Phone 01152 (115) 3-01-11; FAX 01152 (115) 3-03-11.

All Year 1P $ 45 2P $ 56

XP $8. Ranch-style resort. 50 units; 2-bedroom cottages, $112. Shower baths. No phones. Pool. Gift shop. Airstrip. MC, VI. Dining room 6 am-9:30 pm; cocktails, bar. Fiesta dinner with live music on Sat.

Restaurant

LAS CASITAS ◆ Mexican
In the hotel of the same name in center of town.
Phone 01152 (115) 3-00-19.

$3-12. Open 7 am-10 pm. Attractive patio setting. Mexican cuisine, specializing in beef and seafood. Features Fri evening fiesta buffet with mariachi band. Cocktails, bar.

Rosarito

Lodging

BRISAS DEL MAR MOTEL Motor Inn
In center of town on Bl Benito Juárez 22. Mail: 311 Broadway, Chula Vista, CA 91910.
Phone 01152 (661) 2-25-47, (800) 697-5223; FAX (619) 426-7873.

	1P	2P
5/1-9/30 &		
Fri-Sat 10/1-4/30	1P $ 63	2P $ 63
Sun-Thu 10/1-4/30	1P $ 53	2P $ 53

XP $10. 3-day refund notice. 2-story motel. 66 units. Cable TV. Pool, playground. No pets. AE, MC, VI. Restaurant; 7 am-8 pm; cocktails, bar.

LAS ROCAS RESORT & SPA ◆◆ Motor Inn
6 mi S of town on Hwy 1. Mail: Box 189003 HLR, Coronado, CA 92178.
Phone & FAX 01152 (661) 2-21-40, (800) 527-7622.

Sun-Thu 6/1-9/30 &		
Fri-Sat	1P $ 75-160	2P $ 75-160
Sun-Thu 10/1-5/31	1P $ 55-109	2P $ 55-109

XP $10; ages 12 and under stay free. 8-day refund notice. Hotel on a bluff overlooking the ocean. 74 units; 1- and 2-bedroom penthouses with outdoor whirlpool. Cable TV, movies, radios; some refrigerators, microwaves, coffeemakers fireplaces, ocean-view balconies. Pool, whirlpool, tennis, full-service spa. No pets. AE, MC, VI. Restaurant; 7:30 am-10:30 pm; cocktails. **(See ad page 298.)**

OASIS RESORT SUITES ◆◆ Resort Motor Inn
On Hwy 1-D, 3 mi N of town; southbound exit El Oasis, northbound exit San Antonio.
Mail: Box 158, Imperial Beach, CA 91933.
Phone 01152 (66) 31-32-53, (800), 818-8133; FAX 01152 (66) 31-32-52.

Fri-Sat 3/15-10/1	1P $109	2P $109
Sun-Thu 3/15-10/1	1P $ 99	2P $ 99
Fri-Sat 10/2-3/14	1P $ 65	2P $ 65
Sun-Thu 10/2-3/14	1P $ 55	2P $ 55

XP $15; ages 11 and under stay free. 3-day refund notice. All-suite resort and RV park on the beach. 100 units. Cable TV, movies, honor bars, refrigerators; most units air conditioned. 2 heated pools, wading pool, whirlpools, sauna, beach, putting green, exercise room, tennis. Convention facility. No pets. AE, MC, VI. Dining room, restaurants; 7 am-11 pm; cocktails; bar.

ROSARITO BEACH HOTEL & SPA ◆ Resort Complex
In S part of town on Bl Benito Juárez, facing the Pacific Ocean. Mail: Box 430145, San Diego, CA 92143.
Phone 01152 (661) 2-01-44, (800) 343-8582; FAX 01152 (661) 2-11-25.

Sun-Thu 7/23-9/5 &		
Fri-Sat	1P $ 69-129	2P $ 69-129
Sun-Thu 9/6-7/22	1P $ 49- 99	2P $ 69- 99

XP $15; ages 12 and under stay free. 3-day refund notice. 275 units; suites. Cable TV, movies, VCPs, radios, shower baths; some efficiencies, refrigerators, air conditioning; some private balconies. 2 heated pools, 3 whirlpools, sauna, beach, racquetball, basketball, tennis. No pets. Facilities for meetings. MC, VI. 2 restaurants; 7:30 am-10:30 pm; buffet with live music Fri and Sat evenings; cocktails, 2 bars; gift shop. ⊘ **(See ad page 299.)**

Restaurants

CHABERTS RESTAURANT ◆◆ French
In S part of town on Bl Benito Juárez at Rosarito Beach Hotel.
Phone 01152 (661) 2-01-44.

LODGING & RESTAURANTS

$15-30. Open 5 pm-midnight. Sep-Jun closed Mon-Fri. An elegant dining room located in a former mansion. Cocktails, bar. MC, VI.

EL NIDO STEAKHOUSE ◆◆ Steak & Seafood
At Bl Benito Juárez 67.
Phone 01152 (661) 2-14-31.

$5-20. Open 8 am-11:30 pm. Closed 9/16. Ranch atmosphere featuring mesquite-broiled steaks & seafood. Cocktails.

LOS PELÍCANOS ◆ Steak & Seafood
On the beach at Calle Ebano 113.
Phone 01152 (661) 2-17-57.

$7-20. Open 8 am-midnight. Closed 9/16. Cocktails, bar. AE, MC, VI.

San Felipe

Lodging

MOTEL EL CAPITÁN Motor Inn
On Av Mar de Cortez, corner of Manzanillo across from State Tourism Office. Mail: Box 1916, Calexico, CA 92232.
Phone 01152 (657) 7-13-03.

Fri-Sat	1P $ 45	2P $ 45
Sun-Thu	1P $ 36	2P $ 36

XP $5. 3-day refund notice. 45 units. Shower baths, color TV, radios. Pool. Fishing charters arranged. MC, VI. Restaurant open 7 am-10 pm; bar.

HOTEL LAS MISIÓNES — Resort Motor Inn
On rd to airport, 1 mi S of town. Mail: 233 Pauline Av, #7544, Calexico, CA 92231.
Phone 01152 (657) 7-12-80; FAX 01152 (657) 7-12-83.

All Year   1P $69   2P $69

XP $20; ages 12 and under stay free. 3-day refund notice. 3-story beachfront resort. 217 units; suites, $130-140 for up to 4 persons. Showers or combination baths, cable TV, movies. 3 pools, wading pools, beach, basketball, volleyball. Fee for tennis. No pets. AE, MC, VI. Restaurant open 7-11 am & 6-11 pm; snack bar, cocktails, bar. **(See ad page 300.)**

PLAYA BONITA — Condominium Motel
1 mi N of town center via Av Mar de Cortez.
Phone 01152 (657) 7-12-15.
US reservations: 475 E Badillo St, Covina, CA 91723. (626) 967-8977.

3/1-10/31 $ 80
11/1-2/28 $ 65

XP $15. 2 stories. 8 1-bedroom suites with cooking facilities, sleep up to 6 people. Swimming beach.

SAN FELIPE MARINA RESORT — ◆◆◆ Resort Motor Inn
3 mi S of town on rd to airport. Mail: 233 Pauline Av, #5574, Calexico, CA 92231.
Phone 01152 (657) 7-15-68, (800) 291-5397; FAX 01152 (657) 7-15-66.

All Year   1P $ 95-200   2P $ 95-200

XP $20; ages 11 and under stay free. 3-day refund notice. On the beach overlooking the bay. 59 units; master suite and villas, $330-500 for 6-8 persons. Cable TV, radios, balcony or patio, walk-in showers, most with full cooking facilities and utensils. 2 pools (1 indoor, heated), saunas, steam rooms, exercise equipment, beach, lighted tennis courts. No pets. Gift shop. Facilities for meetings. AE, MC, VI. Restaurant; 7 am-10 pm, cocktails, lounge.

Restaurant

EL NIDO STEAKHOUSE — ◆◆ Steakhouse
¼ mi S of town center on Av Mar de Cortez.
Phone 01152 (657) 7-16-60.

$8-16. Open Thu-Tue 2-10 pm. Closed Wed. Ranch atmosphere. Features mesquite-broiled steaks and seafood. Cocktails.

San Ignacio

Lodging

HOTEL LA PINTA — Motor Inn
1 mi W of Hwy 1, on entrance rd leading to town plaza. Mail: Apdo Postal 37, San Ignacio, BCS, 23943 Mexico.

Phone 01152 (115) 4-03-00.

US reservations agent: Mexico Condo Reservations, 5801 Soledad Mountain Rd, La Jolla, CA 92037. (619) 275-4500, (800) 262-4500.

All year   1P $ 60   2P $ 65

XP $10; 4-person maximum per room. 3-day refund notice. Spanish-style, single-story hotel set in palm grove with rooms facing interior patio. 28 units. Color TV, movies, shower baths, 2-bed rooms; no phones. Pool, recreation room. No pets. MC, VI. Dining room; 7 am-10 pm; cocktails, bar. **(See ad page 285.)**

San José del Cabo

Lodging

CASA DEL MAR   ◆◆◆ Resort Motor Inn
7 mi W of town at Cabo Real. Mail: KM 19.5 Carr Transpeninsular, San José del Cabo, BCS, 23400 Mexico.
Phone 01152 (114) 4-00-30, (800) 221-8808; FAX 01152 (114) 4-00-34.

4/16-6/30 &		
12/1-12/19	1P $275	2P $350
7/1-9/30	1P $220	2P $235
10/1-11/30 &		
12/20-4/15	1P $325	2P $375

XP $25-35. 10% service charge. 3-day refund notice. Attractive colonial-style building at the ocean. 2 stories. 56 units. Cable TV, movies, whirlpool bathtubs, refrigerators, honor bars, safes. 3 pools, wading pool, whirlpool, saunas, steam rooms, beach, lighted tennis courts, golf course, health club, full-service spa. No pets. Gift shop. Meeting room. AE, MC, VI. Restaurant, see separate listing; bar.

FIESTA INN   ◆◆ Motor Inn
On beach, 1½ mi W of town. Mail: Apdo Postal 124, San José del Cabo, BCS, 23400 Mexico.
Phone & FAX 01152 (114) 2-07-93, (800) 343-7821; FAX 01152 (114) 2-04-80.

4/14-12/21	1P $ 57	2P $ 57
12/22-4/13	1P $ 89-98	2P $ 89-98

XP $20. 3 stories. 153 units with patio or balcony. Cable TV, movies, radios. Heated pool, beach, bicycle rentals, horseback riding, scuba/snorkeling/fishing arrangements. No pets. Gift shop. Meeting rooms. AE, MC, VI. Restaurant; 7 am-10 pm.

HOWARD JOHNSON PLAZA SUITE HOTEL & RESORT   ◆◆◆ Resort Hotel
¼ mi E of town, just off Hwy 1 on Paseo Finisterra. Mail: Apdo Postal 152, San José del Cabo, BCS, 23400 Mexico.
Phone 01152 (114) 2-09-99, (800) 446-4656; FAX 01152 (114) 2-08-06.

12/1-4/15	1P $ 92-132	2P $ 92-132

7-day refund notice. Mexican Colonial and Moorish-style buildings surrounding courtyard and pool. 4 stories, no elevator. 172 units; hotel rooms and 1- to 3-bedroom suites with kitchens. Cable TV, movies. Pool, exercise room. Fee for golf, tennis; scuba/snorkeling/fishing arrangements. No pets. Gift shop. Meeting room. AE, MC, VI. Restaurant; 7 am-10:30 pm; cocktails, bar.

HUERTA VERDE   ◆◆◆ Bed & Breakfast
3 mi N of town along Hwy 1, then 1 mi E on Las Animas Atlas. Mail: Las Animas Atlas, San José del Cabo, BCS, 23400 Mexico.
Phone & FAX 01152 (114) 8-05-11.
US reservations: (303) 431-5162; FAX (303) 431-4455.

All year [BP]   1P $...   2P $115-140

14-day refund notice. 10% service charge. 7 units; 3 suites with private patio, 2 suites with kitchenette and barbecue grill. Tropical gardens in a secluded hillside setting. Shower baths, radios, refrigerators. Pool. Hiking. MC, VI. Additional meals by arrangement.

LA JOLLA DE LOS CABOS   ◆◆◆ Condominium Hotel
3 mi W of town center on Hwy 1. Mail: Apdo Postal 127, San José del Cabo, BCS, 23400 Mexico.
Phone 01152 (114) 2-30-00; FAX 01152 (114) 2-05-46.
US reservations: (800) 524-5104.

5/1-10/31	1P $135-180	2P $135-180
11/1-4/30	1P $180-240	2P $180-240

XP $15. 10% service charge. 3-day refund notice. On the beach. 3-6 stories. 55 units; studios, 1- and 2-bedrooms with kitchens. Some shower baths, cable TV, movies, refrigerators, coffeemakers. Pools, whirlpools, saunas, steam rooms, exercise room, lighted tennis courts, spa. No pets. Gift shop. Beauty salon. AE, MC, VI. Restaurant; 7 am-10:30 pm; cocktails, bar.

LAS VENTANAS AL PARAÍSO   ◆◆◆◆ Resort Complex
Hwy 1 at Kilometer 19.5, San José del Cabo, BCS, 23400 Mexico.
Phone 01152 (114) 4-06-00, (800) 525-0483; FAX 01152 (114) 4-03-01.

All Year   1P ...   2P $425-575

XP $50. 15% service charge. 7-day refund notice. Intimate oceanfront resort. 60 units; 4 1-bedroom suites with private pool, $1800. Cable TV, movies, safes, VCPs, fireplaces, patios, whirlpool tubs. Pools, whirlpool, saunas, steam rooms, health club, golf; arrangements for fishing, kayaking, sailing, horseback riding. Gift shop. Meeting room, data ports. AE, DI, DS, MC, VI. 2 restaurants; 6:30 am-10 pm; 24-hour room service; cocktails, bar.

MELIA CABO REAL BEACH & GOLF RESORT   ◆◆◆ Resort Hotel
On Hwy 1, 7 mi W of town. Mail: Carr a Cabo San Lucas, Km 19, San José del Cabo, BCS, 23400 Mexico.
Phone 01152 (114) 4-00-00, (800) 336-3542; FAX 01152 (114) 4-01-01.

4/20-10/14	1P $202	2P $202
10/15-4/19	1P $250	2P $250

XP $40. 10% service charge. 15-day refund notice. Spacious oceanfront grounds. 309 units. Cable TV, movies, VCPs. Pool, whirlpool, golf, tennis, health club, scuba diving, snorkeling, fishing trips arranged. AE, MC, VI. 2 restaurants, 2 coffee shops; 7 am-11 pm; 24-hour room service; cocktails.

HOTEL PALMITA Motel
On Paseo San José, 1½ mi W of town. Mail: Paseo San José, San José del Cabo, BCS, 23400 Mexico.
Phone & FAX 01152 (114) 2-04-34.

4/16-9/30	1P $ 50	2P $ 50
10/1-12/14	1P $ 60	2P $ 60
12/15-4/15	1P $ 70	2P $ 70

3-day refund notice. Small motel off golf course. Showers, television. Pool. MC, VI. Deli/minimart.

POSADA REAL LOS CABOS ◆◆ Motor Inn
On beach, 1½ mi W of town. Mail: Apdo Postal 51, San José del Cabo, BCS, 23400 Mexico.
Phone 01152 (114) 2-01-55, (800) 528-1234; FAX 01152 (114) 2-04-60.

3/23-11/30	1P $ 60	2P $ 60
12/1-3/22	1P $ 85-120	2P $ 85-120

XP $10. 3-day refund notice. 3 stories. 150 units; suites available, $150-200. On the beach, most rooms with ocean view. Cable TV, movies. Pool, wading pool, whirlpools, bicycle rentals, scuba/snorkeling/fishing arrangements. No pets. Gift shop. Meeting rooms. AE, MC, VI. Restaurant; 7:30 am-10:30 pm; cocktails, bar.

PRESIDENTE INTERCONTINENTAL LOS CABOS ALL ◆◆◆ Resort Hotel
INCLUSIVE EXCLUSIVE RESORT
On beach 1¼ mi W of town. Mail: Apdo Postal 2, San José del Cabo, BCS, 23400 Mexico.
Phone 01152 (114) 2-02-11, (800) 327-0200; FAX 01152 (114) 2-02-32.

4/20-12/19 [AP]	1P $290-330	2P $290-330
12/20-4/19 [AP]	1P $310-350	2P $310-350

XP $45; ages 12 and under stay free. 10% service charge. 3-day refund notice. Rates also include beverages as well as most recreational activities. 240 units; suite available. On the beach with beautifully landscaped, spacious grounds. Cable TV, movies, shower baths. 2 heated pools, wading pool, tennis, scuba diving, snorkeling, boat rentals, fishing trips arranged. No pets. Conference facilities. AE, CB, DI, MC, VI. 4 restaurants; 7 am-10 pm; 24-hour room service; cocktails, bar, disco. ⊗

TROPICANA INN ◆◆ Motor Inn
On Bl Mijares just S of town plaza. Mail: Bl Mijares 30, San José del Cabo, BCS, 23400 Mexico.
Phone 01152 (114) 2-09-07; FAX 01152 (114) 2-15-90; FAX in US (510) 939-2725.

5/1-12/20	1P $ 51	2P $ 55
12/21-4/30	1P $ 67	2P $ 67

XP $10; ages 12 and under stay free. 7-day refund notice. In-town location, attractive Mexican style with courtyard. 2-story motel. 40 units. Shower baths, cable TV, movies, coffeemakers. Pool. No pets. AE, MC, VI.

WESTIN REGINA RESORT—LOS CABOS   ◆◆◆◆ Resort Complex

On Hwy 1, 6 mi SW of San José del Cabo. Mail: Apdo Postal 145, San José del Cabo, BCS, 23400 Mexico.
Phone 01152 (114) 2-90-00; FAX 01152 (114) 2-90-11.
US reservations: (800) 228-3000.

5/27-9/30	1P $215-360	2P $215-360
10/1-5/26	1P $240-360	2P $240-360

XP $25-40. $2.50 daily service charge per room. High-rise hotel, water-themed landscape blended with dramatic architecture creating a window to the sea. 305 units; junior suites, $550. Cable TV, movies, honor bar, safes, private balconies; some whirlpool baths. 3 pools, whirlpool, saunas, steam rooms, beach, lighted tennis courts, fitness center. Fishing trips and golf arranged. Children's programs. No pets. Gift shop. Conference facilities. AE, CB, DI, MC, VI. 3 restaurants; 7 am-11 pm; 24-hour room service; cocktails, lounge. ⊗

Restaurants

ARRECIFES   ◆◆◆ Continental
In the Westin Regina Resort.
Phone 01152 (114) 2-90-00.

$15-26. Open Wed-Mon 6-11 pm. Closed Tue. Spectacular ocean-view setting. Creative dishes with an artful presentation. Cocktails, bar. AE, MC, VI.

CASA DEL MAR RESTAURANT   ◆◆◆ Mexican
7 mi W of town at Cabo Real.
Phone 01152 (114) 4-00-30.

$6-30. Open 6 am-10 pm. Regional dishes in an elegant setting. Cocktails, bar. AE, MC, VI.

DA GIORGIO RESTAURANT   ◆ Italian
5 mi W on Hwy 1 near Hotel Palmilla on a hill overlooking the gulf.
Phone 01152 (114) 2-19-88.

$8-15. Open 6-10 pm. Cocktails, bar. AE, MC, VI.

DAMIANA   ◆ Mexican
E side of town plaza at Bl Mijares No 8.
Phone 01152 (114) 2-04-99.

$5-26. Open 10:30 am-11 pm. Patio and inside dining with Mexican and seafood cuisine. Cocktails, bar. MC, VI.

LA CONCHA BEACH CLUB SEAFOOD RESTAURANT   ◆◆ Seafood
7 mi W on Hwy 1, on the beach at Cabo Real.
Phone 01152 (114) 3-25-56.

$9-22. Open 11:30 am-9 pm. Dining under *palapa* at beachside, specializing in fresh seafood with a limited selection of beef and chicken entrees. Cocktails, bar. AE, MC, VI.

LA PROVENCE GARDEN RESTAURANT ◆◆◆ Continental
Downtown, just N of Zaragoza.
Phone 01152 (114) 2-33-73.
$11-20. Open 6-10 pm. Mediterranean cuisine with upscale service in a colorful bistro and patio setting. Cocktails, bar. AE.

TROPICANA BAR & GRILL ◆ Mexican
On Bl Mijares just S of town plaza.
Phone 01152 (114) 2-09-07.
$5-20. Open 8 am-11 pm. Hacienda and patio dining featuring Mexican and European entrees. Cocktails, bar. AE, MC, VI.

San Quintín

Lodging

HOTEL LA PINTA Motor Inn
2½ mi W of Hwy 1 via paved rd to outer San Quintín Bay. Mail: Apdo Postal 168, Valle de San Quintín, BC, 22930 Mexico.
Phone 01152 (616) 5-28-78.
US reservations agent: Mexico Condo Reservations, 5801 Soledad Mountain Rd, La Jolla, CA 92037. (800) 262-4500, (619) 275-4500.

All year   1P $ 65   2P $ 65

XP $15; ages 12 and under stay free. 4-person maximum per room. 3-day refund notice. 58 units; 1-bedroom suite, $120. Attractive Spanish-style, beach-side hotel. Color TV, movies, shower baths; some 2-bed rooms, balconies; no air conditioning, phones. Beach, fishing, tennis. No pets. Restaurant; 7:30 am-10 pm; cocktails, bar. MC, VI. **(See ad page 285.)**

OLD MILL HOTEL Motor Inn
On E shore of inner San Quintín Bay, 4 mi W of Hwy 1 via unpaved rd. Mail: 11217 Adriatic Place, San Diego, CA 92126-1109.
Phone (619) 271-1304, (800) 479-7962; FAX (619) 271-0952.

All year   1P $ 30-60   2P $ 30-60

XP $8. Credit card guarantee; 2-day refund notice. Motel on site of old grist mill. 28 units; 2-bedroom suites, $85-90. Shower baths; some kitchenettes; no air conditioning, phones. Beach, hunting, swimming, hiking; guide service available. Fishing trips arranged. RV park, $15 per space. Restaurant; 6 am-9 pm; cocktails, bar.

Santa Rosalía

Lodging

HOTEL EL MORRO Motel
On Hwy 1, 1 mi S of Santa Rosalía ferry terminal. Mail: Apdo Postal 76, Santa Rosalía, BCS, Mexico.
Phone 01152 (115) 2-04-14.

All year   1P $ 23   2P $ 25

XP $5; ages 5 and under free. 10-day refund notice. 40 units; suite available, $38. Spanish-style hotel overlooking Gulf of California. Modest rooms. Shower baths, 2-bed rooms; some private patios. Cable TV, movies. Pool. No pets. MC, VI. Dining room; 8 am-10 pm; cocktails, bar.

Tijuana

Lodging

EL CONQUISTADOR HOTEL ◆ Motel
Just E of Av Rodríguez at Bl Agua Caliente 10750. Mail: Box 5355, Chula Vista, CA 91912.
Phone 01152 (66) 81-79-55; FAX 01152 (66) 86-13-40.

All Year	1P $ 50	2P $ 50

XP $5. Near Tijuana Country Club. 2 stories. 105 units. Cable TV, movies, shower baths. Pool, whirlpool, sauna, valet laundry. No pets. Meeting room, data ports. AE, MC, VI. Restaurant; 7 am-11 pm; cocktails; bar.

GRAND HOTEL TIJUANA ◆◆◆ Hotel
Al Bl Agua Caliente No 4500, ¼ mi E of Av Rodríguez adjacent to Tijuana Country Club. Mail: Box BC, Chula Vista, CA 92012.
Phone 01152 (66) 81-70-00, (800) 472-6385; FAX 01152 (66) 81-70-16.

All year	1P $ 70-115	2P $ 70-115

XP $11; ages 11 and under stay free. 23 stories. 422 units; suites. Cable TV, movies, honor bars; some radios. Heated pool, whirlpool, tennis. No pets. Gift shop, conference center, valet laundry. AE, CB, DI, MC, VI. 2 restaurants, coffee shop; 24 hrs; cocktails; bar. ⊘

HACIENDA DEL MAR HOTEL Motor Inn
At Playas de Tijuana, 5 mi W of the border crossing. Mail: Box 120578, Chula Vista, CA 91912.
Phone 01152 (66) 30-86-03, (888) 676-2927.

All Year	1P $ 34	2P $ 34

Quiet location near Oasis (Ernesto Contreras) Hospital and Bullring-By-The-Sea. 60 units; 3 junior suites, $45. Cable TV, movies; some shower baths. Heated pool, guest laundry, meeting room. No pets. AE, MC, VI. Restaurant; 7 am-11 pm. Cocktails, bar.

HOTEL LUCERNA ◆◆◆ Hotel
At Paseo de los Héroes and Av Rodríguez in the Río Tijuana development. Mail: Box 437910, San Ysidro, CA 92143.
Phone 01152 (66) 33-39-00, (800) 582-3762; FAX 01152 (66) 34-24-00.

All year	1P $ 58	2P $ 63

XP $12; ages 12 and under stay free. Modern 6-story hotel. 167 units; suites, $90. Cable TV, radios. Heated pool, tennis, valet laundry. No pets. Business center, meeting room, data ports, secretarial services. AE, DI, MC, VI. Restaurant (see listing) and coffee shop; 7 am-midnight; cocktails, entertainment. ⊘

LODGING & RESTAURANTS

HOTEL PLAZA LAS GLORIAS ◆◆ Hotel
At Tijuana Country Club, Bl Agua Caliente No 11553. Mail: Box 43-1588, San Ysidro, CA 92173.
Phone 01152 (66) 22-66-00; FAX 01152 (66) 22-66-02.
US reservations: (800) 748-8785.

All year   1P $ 54- 59   2P $ 54- 59

XP $9; ages 12 and under stay free. 3-day refund notice. 10 stories. 200 units. Cable TV, movies; some coffeemakers, refrigerators. Heated pool, sun deck, whirlpool, valet laundry. No pets. Meeting room. AE, CB, DI, MC, VI. Restaurant; 7 am-11 pm; cocktails; bar.

PUEBLO AMIGO HOTEL ◆◆◆ Hotel
At Via Oriente 9211 off Paseo de Tijuana. Mail: Via Oriente 9211, Zona Río, Tijuana, BC, 22320 Mexico.
Phone 01152 (66) 83-50-30, (800) 386-6985. FAX 01152 (66) 83-50-32.

All Year   1P $ 90-110   2P $ 90-110

XP $20; ages 12 and under stay free. New 6-story hotel. 108 units. Cable TV, movies, radios, coffeemakers. Heated pool, gift shop, exercise room, valet laundry. Valet parking only. No pets. Meeting rooms. AE, MC, VI. Restaurant; 7 am-11 pm; cocktails. ⊘

HOTEL REAL DEL RÍO ◆◆ Hotel
In Río Tijuana District, 2 blocks W of Av Rodríguez on Calle Velasco. Mail: Calle Velasco 1409, Tijuana BC, 22320 Mexico.
Phone 01152 (66) 34-31-00; FAX 01152 (66) 34-30-53.

All year   1P $ 53   2P $ 55- 60

XP $5; ages 11 and under stay free. 5-story hotel. 105 units. Cable TV. No pets. AE, MC, VI. Restaurant; 7 am-midnight; cocktails; bar. ⊘

RESIDENCE INN BY MARRIOTT/REAL DEL MAR Suite Hotel
Off Hwy 1-D (toll rd), 12 mi S by Real del Mar Golf Club at Km 19.5. Mail: 4492 Camino de la Plaza, #1246, San Ysidro, CA 92173.
Phone 01152 (66) 31-36-70; FAX 01152 (66) 31-36-77.
US reservations: (800) 803-6038.

All year [CP]   1P ...   2P $119-149

XP $10. 12% service charge. Many lodging/golf packages available. Hotel/golf resort overlooking the ocean. 75 units, including 61 suites. Cable TV, kitchens. 2 heated pools, whirlpool, exercise room. Tennis courts, basketball, volleyball, aerobics classes, golf course. AE, MC, VI. Restaurant; 8 am-11 pm; cocktails, bar. ⊘

Restaurants

BOCCACCIO'S ◆◆ Italian
Near the Tijuana Country Club at Bl Agua Caliente 11250.
Phone 01152 (66) 86-22-66.

$10-25. Open 1-10 pm. Closed major holidays. Refined atmosphere; seafood, steaks and pasta. Cocktails. MC, VI.

RESTAURANTE LA COSTA　　◆◆ Seafood
In the downtown area just W of Av Revolución at Calle 7A 150.
Phone 01152 (66) 85-84-94.

$7-22. Open 10 am-11 pm, Fri-Sat to midnight. Large selection including lobster, shrimp, oysters, whole and filleted fish. Cocktails, bar. MC, VI.

TOUR DE FRANCE　　◆◆◆ French
On Calle Gobernador Ibarra and Hwy 1, across from Hotel Palacio Azteca.
Phone 01152 (66) 81-7542.

$9-18. Open Mon-Sat 7:30 am-10:30 pm, Fri-Sat to 11:30 pm. Closed Sun & last week of Dec. Charming setting with several small dining rooms and patio. Cocktails. AE, MC, VI.

Todos Santos

Restaurant

CAFÉ SANTA FE　　◆◆ Italian
In the center of town at Calle Centenario No 4.
Phone 01152 (112) 5-03-40.

$7-12. Open noon-9 pm. Closed Tue and 10/1-31. Refined Italian dishes served in an attractively decorated dining room and lush tropical patio. Cocktails.

Campgrounds & Trailer Parks

For many visitors to Baja California, camping is the travel means of choice, as evidenced by the endless stream of trailers and recreational vehicles plying the peninsula's major highways. In response to the need for information on campgrounds and trailer parks, and because it is generally inadvisable to camp in nondesignated sites along major highways, the Auto Club has prepared these listings as a convenience to travelers.

Camping Facilities

Camping facilities in Baja California range from primitive sites with no amenities to fully developed recreational vehicle parks. Since the completion of the Transpeninsular Highway, many fully equipped private campgrounds and RV parks have been built for vacationers in popular resort areas. Their facilities generally approximate those of their U.S. counterparts; rates are somewhat lower. In addition, the Mexican government has built several trailer parks along Highway 1 as a convenience to travelers. Trailer parks and campgrounds are authorized to lease rental space for long-term parking so that repeat visitors are able to leave their trailers and motor homes in Mexico between visits.

Despite the easy accessibility brought about by the Transpeninsular Highway, camping in Baja California requires careful preparation. Supplies are readily available only in the northern and southern areas of the peninsula; they are difficult to obtain in the sparsely populated midsection of Baja California. Campers should therefore plan to be as self-sufficient as possible. Potable drinking water is scarce and should be carried, along with plenty of radiator water. Campers will also find it convenient to carry their own disposable trash bags. Travelers with recreational vehicles should bring extra fan belts, hoses and other parts, as well as tools. Tires, including spares, should be in good condition and regularly checked for air pressure. Since Highway 1 is generally narrow and without turnouts or solid shoulders, it is a good idea to carry flares in case of breakdown. For a complete list of what to take, see the Suggested Supply Lists in the *Appendix*.

Trash and waste from recreational vehicle holding tanks should be disposed of only at designated locations. This makes collection easier and protects the scenic environment. Trash and litter of all kinds constitute an increasing problem in Baja California, particularly along the roads and on the beaches.

For more adventuresome (and self-sufficient) campers, the Mexican government has designated many spots along Baja California's scenic shoreline as *playas públicas* (public beaches). These primitive camping areas supposedly charge a small fee, usually $2 to $4 per night, but the fee is not always collected. Many have no facilities, but some have *palapas* (umbrella-shaped shelters built with dried palm fronds), trash cans and pit toilets. A few are operated by concessionaires; these generally have more facilities and charge a slightly higher fee. The most popular and accessible of the *playas públicas* are listed in this publication.

About the Listings

Each of the campgrounds and trailer parks listed in this section has been inspected by a representative of the Automobile Club of Southern California. Those which meet AAA standards are listed with the symbol ✓ after the name. All listings are as complete as possible, based on information available at our publication deadline. Considering Baja California's rapid rate of growth, however, travelers should keep in mind that changes may have occurred, particularly regarding rates and facilities.

Even at well-equipped trailer parks, facilities, maintenance and services may not be up to U.S. standards. Hookups occasionally aren't usable because of generator breakdowns; when this happens, the price is sometimes lowered. Many trailer parks lack telephones. Tap water is not suitable for drinking. Bathroom facilities are sometimes rustic and crowded. In addition, some of Baja California's campgrounds and trailer parks do not have English-speaking employees. This

Pitching a tent and camping out, in this case near Todos Santos, is a good way to explore Baja California on a budget.

is especially true in small towns and outlying areas. Travelers should make use of a basic Spanish phrase book; some useful phrases and words are found in the Speaking Spanish section of the *Appendix*.

Fees indicated in these listings are for one night's camping. Some campgrounds base fees on the number of campers in each party, while others charge flat rates per vehicle or campsite. This information is included with each listing. The Automobile Club of Southern California cannot guarantee the rates, services, maintenance or facilities of any campground or trailer park described in this publication.

Campgrounds are listed alphabetically by city. The following abbreviations are used to denote hookups: **E**=electricity; **W**=water; **S**=sewer. All campgrounds and trailer parks are open all year unless otherwise noted.

In the mailing addresses of the following campgrounds, BC is the abbreviation for the state of Baja California and BCS stands for the state of Baja California Sur.

Bahía Concepción

BAHÍA EL COYOTE *(Playa pública)*
17½ mi S of Mulegé off Hwy 1; just after "Rcho El Coyote," turn at sign with beach symbol and go S ½ mi.
No phone.
$3-4 per vehicle. On shore of the bay. Pit toilets, cabañas.

EL REQUESÓN *(Playa pública)*
27 mi S via Hwy 1 and unpaved rd.
No phone.
$3 per vehicle. Attractive location on sandspit that links beach with offshore island. Pit toilets, cabañas, palapas.

PLAYA SANTISPAC *(Playa pública)*
13½ mi S of Mulegé via Hwy 1 and unpaved rd.
No phone.
$4 per vehicle. On Santispac Cove, part of Bahía Concepción. Flush toilets, showers, palapas, 2 cafes.

POSADA CONCEPCIÓN
15 mi S on Hwy 1. Mail: Apdo Postal 14, Mulegé, BCS, Mexico.
No phone.
$10 for 2 persons, $2 per each additional person. Overlooks the bay. 10 RV sites; area for tents. Hookups: EWS-10; electricity 10 am-10 pm. Flush toilets, showers, tennis, beach, skin diving, fishing.

RESORT SAN BUENAVENTURA
25 mi S of Mulegé via Hwy 1 at Km 94.5, on Bahía Concepción. Mail: Apdo Postal 56, Mulegé, BCS, Mexico.
Phone 01152 (115) 3-04-08, 3-03-08; FAX 01152 (115) 3-04-08.

$10 per vehicle. 16 RV/tent bayside sites. Flush toilet, shower, beach, fishing and dive trips, boat tours arranged, kayaks, paved boat ramp, 16 *palapas* on beach. 3 bungalows with 2 cots, $20. Restaurant, bar. Hotel adjacent.

Bahía de los Angeles

GUILLERMO'S TRAILER PARK
On the shore of the bay. Mail: Montes de Oca No 190, Fraccionamiento Buenaventura, Ensenada, BC, Mexico.
No phone.

$6 for 2 persons, $1 per each additional person. 40 RV sites. Hookups: EWS-15; electricity 7-11 am and 5-9:30 pm. Flush toilets, showers, beach, fishing trips arranged, boat ramp and boat rental, restaurant, bar, gift shop.

LA PLAYA RV PARK
On the shore of the bay. Mail: 509 Ross Dr, Escondido, CA 92029.
Phone (760) 741-9583; FAX (760) 489-5687.

$15 for 2 persons. 30 RV sites; extensive area for tents. Hookups: E-30; electricity 7 am-9:30 pm. Disposal station, flush toilets, showers, fishing trips arranged, boat launch, ice, restaurant, bar.

Cabo San Lucas

CLUB CABO MOTEL & CAMPGROUND RESORT
2 mi E of town center on the old road; turn S off Hwy 1 on rd to Club Cascadas. Mail: Apdo Postal 463, Cabo San Lucas, BCS, Mexico.
Phone & FAX 01152 (114) 3-33-48.

$7 per person. RV park and motel suites in open area; short walk to beach. 15 RV/tent sites. Hookups: EWS-10, EW-5. Flush toilets, showers, pool, whirlpool. *Palapa* with TV, barbecue, Ping-pong, trampoline, ice. Fishing trips, horseback outings arranged. Shuttle to town.

EL ARCO TRAILER PARK
2 mi E of town on Hwy 1. Mail: Km 5.5, Cabo San Lucas, BCS, Mexico.
Phone 01152 (114) 3-16-86.

$15 per site. Open area with view of Cabo San Lucas Bay. 85 RV/tent sites. EWS-65. Flush toilets, showers, laundry, pool, restaurant, bar.

EL FARO VIEJO TRAILER PARK
¾ mi NW of town center near Hwy 19, at Matamoros and Mijares. Mail: Apdo Postal 64, Cabo San Lucas, BCS, Mexico 23410.
Phone & FAX 01152 (114) 3-42-11.

$12 for 2 persons, $3 per each additional person. 12 percent surcharge. Partly shaded area surrounded by wall. 19 RV/tent sites. Hookups: EWS-19. Flush toilets, showers, restaurant, bar, curio shop. AE, MC, VI.

VAGABUNDOS DEL MAR RV PARK ✓
1½ mi NE of town center on Hwy 1. Mail: 190 Main St, Rio Vista, CA 94571.
Phone 01152 (114) 3-02-90; FAX 01152 (114) 3-05-11.
US reservations: (707) 374-5511.

$16 for 2 persons, $3 per each additional person. 10-day refund notice. 65 RV sites. Hookups: EWS-65. Flush toilets, showers, laundry, pool, restaurant.

Cataviña

CATAVIÑA RV PARK
On Hwy 1, ¼ mi N of Hotel La Pinta.
No phone.

$5 per vehicle. Open area with limited facilities. 66 RV/tent sites. Hookups: WS-66. Flush toilets.

Ciudad Constitución

CAMPESTRE LA PILA
1½ mi S of town center via Hwy 1 and ½ mi W on unpaved rd. Mail: Apdo Postal 261, Ciudad Constitución, BCS, Mexico 23600.
Phone 01152 (113) 2-05-62; FAX 01152 (113) 2-02-29.

$8.50 for 2 persons, $3 per each additional person. Open area bordered by irrigated farmland. 44 RV/tent sites. Hookups: EW-44, disposal station. Flush toilets, showers, pool, picnic area, snack bar.

MANFRED'S RV PARK ✓
½ mi N of city center on Hwy 1. Mail: Apdo Postal 120, Ciudad Constitución, BCS, Mexico 23600.
Phone & FAX 01152 (113) 2-11-03.

RVs $10-14 for 2 persons; tents $6 for 2 persons; $1.50 per each additional person. Nicely landscaped with flowering plants and trees. 80 RV sites. Hookups: EWS-80. Flush toilets, showers, pool. Restaurant, motel rooms.

Colonia Guerrero

MESÓN DE DON PEPE
1 mi S via Hwy 1. Mail: Apdo Postal 7, Colonia Guerrero, BC, Mexico 22920.
Phone 01152 (616) 6-22-16; FAX 01152 (616) 6-22-68.

RVs $8.50 for 2 persons, $1.50 per each additional person; tents $5. Partly shaded area adjacent to highway. 35 RV sites, 20 tent sites. Hookups: EWS-35. Flush toilets, showers, fishing, restaurant, bar, tourist information.

POSADA DON DIEGO
1 mi S via Hwy 1 and unpaved rd, past first RV park. Mail: Apdo Postal 126, Colonia Guerrero, BC, Mexico 22920.
Phone 01152 (616) 6-21-81; FAX 01152 (616) 6-22-48.

$10 for 3 persons, $1.25 each additional person. Pleasant area in rural setting. 80 RV/tent sites. Hookups: EW-80, S-60. Disposal station, flush toilets, showers, playground, laundry, ice, restaurant, bar.

El Cardonal

EL CARDONAL RESORT
On the beach. Mail: El Cardonal, Los Barriles, BCS, Mexico 23501.
FAX 01152 (114) 1-00-40.
Canadian reservations office: (514) 467-4700; FAX (514) 467-4668.

RVs with full hookups, $8; tents and small campers without hookups, $5. 4 RV sites, 22 campsites. Hookups: 4-EWS, 5-EW. Flush toilets, showers. Fishing and local trips arranged. Restaurant. Motel rooms with cooking facilities, $39.

El Pescadero

LOS CERRITOS RV PARK
1½ mi S on Hwy 19, then 1½ mi SW via a dirt rd.
No phone.

$4 per vehicle. Wide beach on shore of the Pacific Ocean. 50 RV/tent sites. Flush toilets.

Ensenada

CAMPO PLAYA RV PARK
1 mi SE of downtown Ensenada, near intersection of Bl Costero and Calle Agustín Sanginés (Delante). Mail: Apdo Postal 789, Ensenada, BC, Mexico 28600.
Phone & FAX 01152 (617) 6-29-18.

$13-20 for 2 persons, $2 per each additional person. Fenced area near bay. 85 RV/tent sites. Hookups: E-60, WS-85. Flush toilets, showers, recreation room. MC, VI.

ESTERO BEACH TRAILER PARK ✓
8 mi S via Hwy 1 and paved side rd (signs posted at turnoff). Mail: Apdo Postal 86, Ensenada, BC, Mexico.
Phone 01152 (617) 6-62-25.

$12-16 for 2 persons, $3 each additional person. 3-day refund notice. Large seaside resort adjacent to Estero Beach Hotel. 70 RV sites, 50 tent sites. Hookups: EWS-58. Disposal station, flush toilets, showers, beach, boat launch, canoeing, horseback riding, fishing, tennis, playground, clubhouse, restaurant, bar. MC, VI.

PLAYA SALDAMANDO
On beach 10½ mi N via Hwy 1 and steep, winding dirt rd. Mail: 3965 College Av, San Diego, CA 92115.
Phone (619) 582-8333.

$8 for 4 persons, $1 per each additional person. 30 RV/tent sites. No hookups. Trailers for rent, $25-35. Disposal station. Flush toilets, showers. No off-road vehicles.

SAN MIGUEL VILLAGE (VILLA DE SAN MIGUEL)
In El Sauzal, 8 mi N via Hwy 1-D. On Bahía de Todos Santos, just S of toll gate. Mail: Apdo Postal 55, El Sauzal, BC, Mexico 22760.
Phone & FAX 01152 (617) 4-62-25.
$8-10 per vehicle. 40 RV sites, 500 tent sites. Hookups: EWS-40. Flush toilets, showers, beach, restaurant, bar. MC, VI.

Guerrero Negro

MALARRIMO TRAILER PARK
1 mi W of Hwy 1 on E edge of town, next to Malarrimo Restaurant. Mail: Bl Zapata S/N, Col Fundo Legal, Guerrero Negro, BCS, Mexico 23940.
Phone 01152 (115) 7-02-50; FAX 01152 (115) 7-01-00.
RVs $10-14 for 2 persons, $5 per each additional person; tents $5 per person. Open area. 22 RV sites. Hookups: EWS-22. Flush toilets, showers, restaurant, bar. Whale-watching trips arranged, $40 per person.

La Paz

AQUAMARINA RV PARK ✓
1½ mi SW of city center, ½ mi off Hwy 1 on Calle Nayarit. Mail: Apdo Postal 133, La Paz, BCS, Mexico 23094.
Phone 01152 (112) 2-37-61; FAX 01152 (112) 5-62-28.
$15 for 2 persons, $2.40 per each additional person. On the bay. 19 RV sites. EWS-19. Flush toilets, showers, laundry, pool, fishing trips, marina, boat ramp and storage, fishing trips, boat trips and scuba diving arranged.

CASA BLANCA RV PARK ✓
3 mi SW of town center on Hwy 1, corner of Av Delfines. Mail: Apdo Postal 681, La Paz, BCS, Mexico 23000.
Phone & FAX 01152 (112) 4-00-09.
RVs $15 for 2 persons, tents $10 for 2 persons; $3 per each additional person. Partly shaded area surrounded by wall. 46 RV sites. Hookups: EWS-46. Fee for air conditioning & heater. Flush toilets, showers, laundry, store, pool, tennis, recreation room.

EL CARDÓN TRAILER PARK
2½ mi SW of city center on Hwy 1. Mail: Apdo Postal 104, La Paz, BCS, 23000 Mexico.
Phone 01152 (112) 4-02-61; FAX 01152 (112) 4-00-78.
$10-12 for 2 persons, $2 per each additional person. 3-day refund notice. Shaded area surrounded by wall. 80 RV sites, 10 tent sites. Hookups: EWS-80. Flush toilets, showers, laundry, ice, pool, fishing trips.

LA PAZ TRAILER PARK ✓
2 mi SW of city center off Hwy 1, on Brecha California, in residential area. Mail: Apdo Postal 482, La Paz, BCS, Mexico 23094.
Phone 01152 (112) 2-87-87; FAX 01152 (112) 2-99-38.
RVs $15 for 2 persons, tents $10 for 2 persons; $2 per each additional person. 3-day refund notice. 70 RV sites. Hookups: EWS-70. Flush toilets, showers, pool, wading pool, fishing trips arranged, boat ramp nearby, laundry. AE, MC, VI.

OASIS LOS ARÍPEZ TRAILER PARK
On La Paz Bay, 9½ mi before central La Paz when approaching from the N, in the town of El Centenario, on Hwy 1. Mail: Km 15 Transpeninsular Norte, La Paz, BCS, Mexico.
No phone.
$10 for 2 persons; $2 per each additional person. 7-day refund notice. 22 RV/tent sites. Hookups: EWS-29. Flush toilets, showers, laundry, beach, fishing, restaurant, bar.

La Salina

BAJA SEASONS RV BEACH RESORT ✓
On beach facing Pacific Ocean, 14 mi N of Ensenada off Hwy 1-D. Mail: Apdo Postal 1492, La Salina, BC, Mexico.
Phone 01152 (66) 28-61-28; FAX 01152 (66) 48-71-06.
US Reservations: (800) 754-4190.
6/15-9/15 $40-48, 9/16-6/14 $32-40 for 4 persons, $5 per each additional person. 14-day refund notice. 134 RV sites. Hookups: EWS-134. Cable TV, flush toilets, showers, heated pool, whirlpool, saunas, steam room, tennis, recreation room, horseback riding, laundry, groceries, restaurant, bar. MC, VI.

Loreto

LORETO SHORES VILLAS & RV PARK ✓
½ mi S of town plaza on beach. Mail: Box 219, Loreto, BCS, 23880 Mexico.
Phone 01152 (113) 5-06-29; FAX 01152 (113) 5-07-11.
RVs with hookups $12 for 2 persons, $3 per each additional person; sites without hookups $5 per person; villas $65-120. 36 RV sites. Hookups: EWS-36. Flush toilets, showers, beach, fishing, laundry.

PLAYA JUNCALITO *(Playa pública)*
13 mi S of Loreto via Hwy 1 and unpaved rd.
No phone.
$2 per vehicle. Attractive beach and view of mountains. No facilities.

VILLAS DE LORETO ✓
½ mi S of town plaza on the beach. Mail: Apdo Postal 132, Loreto, BCS, 2388, Mexico.
Phone 01152 (113) 5-05-86.

$12.10 for 2 persons, $5 per each additional person. 13 RV sites. Hookups: EWS-13. Flush toilets, hot showers, fishing, kayak rentals, laundry. 10 motel units, $50-60 for 2 persons; $14 for each additional person. No smoking on premises.

Los Barriles

MARTIN VERDUGO'S TRAILER PARK ✓
On beach of Bahía de Palmas, ½ mi E of Hwy 1. Mail: Apdo Postal 17, Los Barriles, BCS, 23501 Mexico.
Phone & FAX 01152 (114) 1-00-54.

$10-12 for 2 persons, $1 per each additional person. Partially shaded area. 69 RV sites, 25 tent sites. Hookups: EWS-69. Flush toilets, showers, pool, fishing trips arranged, boat launch, laundry, bar. Motel rooms $40-50. Restaurant adjacent.

JUANITO'S GARDEN RV PARK ✓
½ mi E of Hwy 1, 1 block from the bay. Mail: Apdo Postal 50, Buena Vista, BCS, 23580 Mexico.
Phone & FAX 01152 (114) 1-00-24.

$10 for 2 persons, $4 per each additional person. 10 RV sites. Hookups: EWS-10. Flush toilets, hot showers, laundry, RV storage.

Mulegé

THE ORCHARD RV PARK/HUERTA SAUCEDO ✓
½ mi S via Hwy 1. Mail: Apdo Postal 24, Mulegé, BCS, Mexico.
Phone 01152 (115) 3-03-00.

RVs $14.95 for 2 persons, tent site $6.50 for 2 persons; $2 per each additional person. Partly shaded area near river. 46 RV sites, 30 tent sites. Hookups: EWS-46. Disposal station. Flush toilets, showers, tennis, boat ramp, fishing, local tour arrangements. Cottages & villas $55-250.

VILLA MARIA ISABEL RECREATIONAL PARK ✓
1¼ mi S via Hwy 1. Mail: Apdo Postal 5, Mulegé, BCS, Mexico.
Phone 01152 (115) 3-02-46.

$13 for 2 persons, $2 per each additional person; tent site with *palapa*, $4.50 per person. Partly shaded area on river. 25 RV sites, 25 tent sites. Hookups: EWS-25. Disposal station, flush toilets, showers, pool, recreation area, fishing, boat launch, laundry, bakery.

Puerto Escondido

TRIPUI RESORT RV PARK ✓
15 mi S via Hwy 1 and paved side rd, near Puerto Escondido. Mail: Apdo Postal 100, Loreto, BCS, 23880 Mexico.
Phone 01152 (113) 3-08-18; FAX 01152 (113) 3-08-28.

RVs with hookups $14 for 2 persons, $7 per each additional person; campsite with no hookups $5 per person. 3-day refund notice. 30 RV sites, 10 tent sites. Hookups: EWS-30. Flush toilets, showers, pool, groceries, gift shop, playground, restaurant, bar.

Punta Banda

LA JOLLA BEACH CAMP
8 mi W of Maneadero on BCN 23, on shore of Bahía de Todos Santos. Mailing address: Apdo Postal 102, Punta Banda, BC, 22791 Mexico.
No phone.
$6 for 2 persons, $2 per each additional person. 120 RV sites, 80 tent sites. Hookups: E-20. Extension cords available. Disposal station, flush toilets, showers, beach, boat launch, tennis, recreation room, groceries, propane.

VILLARINO CAMP
8 mi W of Maneadero on BCN 23, on shore of Bahía de Todos Santos. Mail: PO Box 2746, Chula Vista, CA 91912.
Phone 01152 (615) 4-20-45; FAX 01152 (615) 4-20-44.
$10 for 2 persons, $5 per each additional person. 100 RV/tent sites. Hookups: E-50, W-100, S-50. Flush toilets, showers, beach, boat ramp, groceries, ice, banquets arranged, fishing trips arranged, cafe.

Punta Chivato

PUNTA CHIVATO CAMPGROUND
On Punta Chivato, 13 mi N of Mulegé via Hwy 1, then 13½ mi E on graded dirt rd. Mail: Apto Postal 18, Mulegé, BCS, 23900 Mexico.
Phone 01152 (115) 3-01-88; FAX 01152 (115) 2-03-95.
$5 per vehicle. On the beach, open sites. 40 RV/tent sites. No hookups. Disposal station, pit toilets, cold showers, fishing trips arranged in pangas, groceries, laundry, restaurant, bar. Office nearby at Hotel Punta Chivato.

Rosarito

OASIS RESORT ✓
On ocean beach 3 mi N off Hwy 1-D, toll rd (northbound, San Antonio exit; southbound, Oasis exit). Mail: Box 158, Imperial Beach, CA 91933.
Phone 01152 (66) 31-32-55; FAX 01152 (66) 31-32-52.
US Reservations (800) 818-3133 or (888) 709-9985.
Fri-Sat $53 for up to 4 persons, Sun-Thu $49 for up to 4 persons, $10 per each additional person. 3-day refund notice. Beachfront park with both concrete and grass sites, built-in barbecue. 55 RV sites. Hookups: EWS-55. Flush toilets, showers, 2 heated pools, wading pool, sauna, whirlpool, beach, tennis, putting green, playground, gym, laundry, groceries, night club, 2 restaurants, bar. AE, MC, VI.

San Bartolo

RANCHO VERDE RV PARK
8¼ mi N of town on Hwy 1 at KM 141.
Phone & FAX 01152 (112) 6-91-03.
Reservations: Box 1050, Eureka, MT 59917; (888) 516-9462, (406) 889-3030.
$11 for 4 persons, $2 each additional person. Open sites. 26 RV spaces. Hookups: WS-26. Flush toilets, showers, fishing trips arranged.

San Felipe

CAMPO SAN FELIPE TRAILER PARK
In town on the bay shore. Mail: 301 Av Mar de Cortez, San Felipe, BC, 21850 Mexico.
Phone 01152 (657) 7-10-12.
$12-17 for 2 persons, $2 per each additional person; tents $10. 34 RV/tent sites; 5 additional tent sites. Hookups: EWS-34. Flush toilets, showers, beach, billiard room, ice.

CLUB DE PESCA TRAILER PARK
1 mi S of town center at end of Av Mar de Cortez. Mail: Apdo Postal 90, San Felipe, BC, 21850 Mexico.
Phone 01152 (657) 7-11-80; FAX 01152 (657) 7-18-88.
$12-18 for 2 persons, $2 per each additional person. Large landscaped park on gulf shore. 30 RV/tent sites; additional area on beach for large number of tents. Hookups: EW-30. Disposal station, flush toilets, showers, boat launch and storage, groceries.

FARO BEACH TRAILER PARK
On Punta Estrella, 10 mi SE of town via paved rd. Mail: Apdo Postal 107, San Felipe, BC, 21850 Mexico.
No phone.
$25 per vehicle. Large, attractively landscaped park on terraced slope overlooking Gulf of California. 135 RV/tent sites. Hookups: EWS-135. Flush toilets, showers, pool, tennis, recreation room, ice, bar.

LA JOLLA TRAILER PARK
½ mi W of town center at Manzanillo and Mar Bermejo in residential area. Mail: Box 978, El Centro, CA 92244.
Phone & FAX 01152 (657) 7-12-22.
$15 for 2 persons, $2.50 per each additional person. Sites with canopies. 55 RV/tent sites. Hookups: EWS-55. Flush toilets, showers, pool, spa, laundry, ice, fishing and boating trips arranged.

MAR DEL SOL RV PARK
1½ mi S of town center on Misión de Loreto, adjacent to Hotel Las Misiones. Mailing address: 7734 Herschel Av, Ste O, La Jolla, CA 92037.
Phone 01152 (657) 7-10-88. US Reservations: (800) 336-5454, (619) 454-7166.

$11-18 for 2 persons, $5 per each additional person. 12 percent service charge. 3-day refund notice. Unshaded sites on attractive beach. 84 RV sites, 30 tent sites. Hookups: EWS-84. Flush toilets, showers, pool, laundry. MC, VI.

PLAYA BONITA TRAILER PARK
1 mi N of town center via Av Mar de Cortez.
Phone 01152 (657) 7-12-15, (626) 967-8977.
US Reservations: 475 E Badillo St, Covina, CA 91723.

3/1-10/31 $15-20, 11/1-2/28 $10-15, U.S. holiday periods $20-25 for 5 persons; $2 for each additional person. Picturesque area on beach with rocky hills behind. 27 RV/tent sites. Hookups: EWS-27. Flush toilets, showers, laundry, fishing trips arranged. Condo suites available. MC, VI.

RUBEN'S TRAILER PARK
1 mi N of town center via Av Mar de Cortez. Mail: Golfo de California 703, San Felipe, BC, 21850 Mexico.
Phone & FAX 01152 (657) 7-14-42.

$20. Picturesque area on gulf shore with rocky hills behind. 58 RV/tent sites. Hookups: EWS-58. Flush toilets, showers, beach, boat launch, fishing, groceries, restaurant, bar. MC, VI.

SAN FELIPE MARINA RESORT RV PARK ✓
3 mi S of town on rd to airport. Mail: 233 Pauline Av, Box 5574, Calexico, CA 92231.
Phone 01152 (657) 7-14-35; FAX 01152 (657) 7-15-66.
US Reservations (619) 558-0295.

10/15-4/30 $22, 5/1-10/14 $18 for 4 persons, $4 per each additional person. 3-day refund notice. Unshaded sites overlooking the marina. 143 RV sites (motor homes and trailers only). Hookups: EWS-143. Flush toilets, showers, TV hookups, pool, beach, laundry, groceries. MC, VI.

VISTA DEL MAR RV PARK
¾ mi N of town center on Av Mar de Cortez overlooking the bay. Mail: 336 Av Mar de Cortez, San Felipe ,BC, 21850 Mexico.
Phone 01152 (657) 7-12-52.

$12 for 2 persons, $3 per each additional person. 21 RV/tent sites with shaded tables. Hookups: EWS-21. Flush toilets, showers.

San Ignacio

LA CANDELARIA TRAILER PARK
1 mi S of Hwy 1 off entrance rd to San Ignacio. Turn right just beyond Hotel La Pinta, then go ½ mi SW over rough dirt rd. Mail: c/o Trailer Park El Padrino, Ctra Transpeninsular Km 0.5, San Ignacio, BCS, 23930 Mexico.
No phone.

$3 per person. Scenic area in a large grove of date palms. 30 RV/tent sites. Several *palapas*; no other facilities.

TRAILER PARK EL PADRINO
1 mi S of Hwy 1 on entrance rd to San Ignacio, just beyond Hotel La Pinta. Mail: Ctra Transpeninsular Km 0.5, San Ignacio, BCS, 23930 Mexico.
Phone & FAX 01152 (115) 4-00-89.

$8-10 per space; $2 per each additional person. 30 RV sites. Hookups: E-10, W-30. Dump station. Flush toilets, showers, restaurant, bar; whale-watching trips arranged, tourist information.

San José del Cabo

BRISA DEL MAR RV RESORT
2 mi SW of town center on Hwy 1. Mail: Apdo Postal 45, San José del Cabo, BCS, 23400 Mexico.
No phone.

$9-15 for 2 persons; $2 per each additional person. Fenced area on beautiful beach facing Gulf of California. 112 RV/tent sites. Hookups: EW-40, S-80. Flush toilets, showers, pool, laundry, restaurant, bar.

San Quintín

ENRIQUE'S/EL PABELLÓN RV PARK
9 mi S of Lázaro Cárdenas and 1 mi W of Hwy 1 via dirt rd.
No phone.

$5 per vehicle. Open area with access to beach. 15 RV/tent sites; additional tent sites on beach. Hookups: W-27. Flush toilets, showers, fishing trips arranged.

Santa Rosalía

LAS PALMAS RV PARK
2 mi S on Hwy 1. Mail: Apdo Postal 123, Santa Rosalía, BCS, Mexico.
Phone 01152 (115) 2-01-09; FAX 01152 (115) 2-22-70.

RVs $10 for 2 persons; tents $6 for 2 persons; $2 per each additional person. Grass sites. 30 RV/tent spaces. Hookups: EWS-30. Flush toilets, showers, laundry, restaurant, bar.

SAN LUCAS COVE RV PARK
9 mi S via Hwy 1 and unpaved rd. Mail: Apdo Postal 50, Santa Rosalía, BCS, Mexico.
No phone.

$6 per vehicle. Open area adjacent to beach. 75 RV/tent sites. No hookups. Disposal station, limited shower and toilet facilities, beach, fishing, boat ramp, restaurant.

Santo Tomás

EL PALOMAR TRAILER PARK
N edge of the village on Hwy 1 in olive tree-shaded area. Mail: PO Box 4492 Camino de la Plaza No 232, San Ysidro, CA 92173.

Phone & FAX 01152 (615) 3-80-02.
$12.50 for 2 persons in RVs, $2 per each additional person. 2-day refund notice. 50 RV sites and large area for tents. Hookups: EWS-25. Flush toilets, showers, pool, hunting, tennis, basketball, volleyball, groceries, restaurant, bar, curio shop, gas station; motel adjacent. MC, VI.

Tecate

RANCHO OJAI RV PARK & CAMPGROUND ✓
13 mi E of town near Kilometer 112 on Hwy 2. Mail: Box 280, Tecate, CA 91980. Phone 01152 (665) 4-47-72.

$10-15 for 2 persons, $1 per each additional person. 41 RV sites. Hookups: EWS-41. Flush toilets, hot showers, hiking trails, clubhouse, playground, horseshoes, volleyball, groceries. Log cabins available, $40-50 per night. MC, VI.

Todos Santos

EL MOLINO TRAILER PARK
At S end of town near Hwy 19, behind Pemex station. Mail: Apdo Postal 209, La Paz, BCS, 23000 Mexico. Phone 01152 (112) 5-01-40.

$10 for 4 persons. 21 RV sites. Hookups: EWS-21. Flush toilets, showers, laundry.

SAN PEDRITO RV PARK
5 mi S on Hwy 19 and 2 mi SW via dirt rd. Mail: Apdo Postal 15, Todos Santos, BCS, 2330 Mexico. Phone 01152 (112) 2-45-20; FAX 01152 (112) 3-46-43.

Rate for 2 persons: RVs $13 for 2 persons, tents $3 for 2 persons; $3 per each additional person. Open area on the shore of the Pacific. 71 RV and 25 tent sites. Hookups: EWS-71. Flush toilets, showers, pool, recreation area, playground, laundry, restaurant, bar. 10 cabañas.

Indexes

Readers will find four different indexes organized for their convenience in this section of the book. Along with the primary index starting on this page, there are separate indexes for the maps, side routes and advertisers appearing in this book.

Index to Attractions, Events, Sites and Towns

The following is a complete listing of the attractions and place names that occur within this publication. Major activities and historical figures are listed as well. A boldface page number denotes the primary reference of a particular place or activity.

Index to Maps

This portion of the index lists all maps included in this book, grouped by region, city and routes.

Regional Maps

City Maps

Route Maps

Index to Side Routes

Within the chapters devoted to describing Baja's Mexico Highway routes are side routes to interesting sites and points of interest. In copy, the 🚗 indicates a side route.

Index to Advertisers

For information about placing an advertisement in Automobile Club of Southern California publications, please contact:

Karen Clyne or Alisa Fouse

Advertising Services, A327

Automobile Club of Southern California

P.O. Box 25001

Santa Ana, CA 92799-5001

(714) 885-2375

FAX (714) 885-2335

334

Acknowledgements

Writer	David J. Brackney
Cartographer	Donald Olivares
Graphic Designer	Barbara Stanfield
Editor	Kristine Miller

Photographers

Pages 2, 3, 5, 6, 7, 8 (upper left), 9, 12, 17 (top photos, lower left), 19, 20, 21 (bottom), 36 (left), 40, 43, 44 (top), 45, 48, 52, 58, 59, 68, 70 (top), 71, 74 (top), 82, 83, 85 (bottom), 94, 99, 102, 105, 108, 113, 114, 128, 129, 130, 131, 132, 134, 135, 136, 137, 140, 141, 142, 146, 149, 152, 155 (bottom), 156, 160, 161, 165, 167, 172, 173, 176, 177, 184, 188, 190, 195, 205, 208, 212, 213, 220, 224, 226, 231, 232, 233, 234, 238, 246, 247, 253, 254, 263 (upper right, lower left), 311 — Todd Masinter

Cover photograph and pages 8 (lower left), 16, 17 (lower right), 18, 21 (top), 30, 36 (right), 41, 44 (bottom), 55, 56, 60, 69, 70 (bottom), 74 (bottom), 81, 85 (top), 89, 91, 93, 100, 107, 111, 118, 127, 144, 147, 150, 155 (top), 164, 170, 178, 179, 181, 183, 186, 189, 196, 199, 200, 203, 210, 217, 219, 221, 225, 227, 230, 236, 241, 251, 252, 257, 263 (upper left and lower right) — David J. Brackney

Pages 22, 50, 53, 54 — Automobile Club of Southern California Archives

Page 243 — Alexander W. Kirkpatrick

Page 273 — Bill Cory

A Word of Gratitude

No guidebook worth its ink is ever the work of a single person, and the latest edition of the Auto Club's *Baja California* book is in no way an exception.

More than seven decades have passed since the first Auto Club personnel blazed a path down the rugged peninsula. Those early trekkers and the colleagues who followed in ensuing years laid the foundation for the volume that you now read. Several gave advice to the current author as he commenced work on this edition. Without them, this book as we know it would not exist.

Then there are those who lent help along the road, giving directions, encouragement and their insights regarding Baja California. Their names are too many to mention here, but they include fellow motorists, tour guides, shopkeepers, police and other individuals from all walks of life. Many were Mexicans, others were Americans or Canadians who were traveling or had made Baja their part-time or permanent home.

Special thanks go to the staffs of Baja's tourism offices, from the northern border towns to Cabo San Lucas. They were generous in sharing their time and knowledge, answering countless questions, returning phone calls and doling out stacks of glossy literature. Many went far beyond the call of duty to help ensure this edition would be factual and informative.

To all those people who helped bring this book to print, and all others who met us in a spirit of cross-border friendship, we offer a warm and heartfelt *gracias*.

—Costa Mesa, California, September 1998